Hi-de-Hi! Companion

Rob Cope and Mike Fury

Published by The Dad's Army Appreciation Society

Hi-de-Hi! Companion
Rob Cope and Mike Fury

www.hi-de-hi.net

Published by the Dad's Army Appreciation Society
32 Beach Road
Dovercourt
Harwich
Essex
CO12 3RP
www.dadsarmy.co.uk

For sales etc contact the above address or
email : hi-de-hi@sky.com

Copyright © 2009 Rob Cope and Mike Fury

Cover Designs: Paul Carpenter

First Published 2009

All rights reserved. No part of this book may be reproduced or transmitted in any form by any means, electronic, mechanical, photocopying, recording or otherwise, without the prior written permission of both the copyright holder and the publisher.

Every effort has been made to trace the origin of images used in this book and no copyright infringement is intended.

A CIP catalogue record of this book is available from the British Library.

ISBN 978-0-9547702-1-1

Project Management:
Layout and Production: Paul Carpenter
Picture and Image Collators: Tony and Joanne Tarran
Additional research and material: Tony Tarran

'Crimpton-on-Sea' chapter by Tony Tarran

Printed and bound in the UK by Information Press Ltd, Oxford

Chapter		Page
	Introduction	7
	Forewords	9
1	The Real Maplin's	11
2	Jimmy Perry OBE	21
3	David Croft OBE	25
4	You Have Been Watching...	29
5	The Yellowcoats	63
6	Behind the Scenes	72
7	Episode Guide	105
8	Maplin's on TV	143
9	Happy Campers	145
10	Holiday Rock	161
11	Camp Shop	165
12	Crimpton-on-Sea - Then and Now	168
13	Maplin's on Stage	184

> Not all the photographs, locations found, or anecdotes that we were kindly given have been used due to space restrictions. However, some of these will be posted in due course on the Hi-de-Hi! website for your further enjoyment.
> **www.hi-de.hi.net**.

This book would not have been possible without the help of the following people who have provided information, photographs and assistance:
Sandra Anthony (Leslie Dwyer estate), Mick Barber, Carole Barclay, Cheryl Bargewell, Carolyn Bartholomew at BBC Worldwide, Jamie Battrick, BBC Photo Library, Sue Belbin, Amanda Bellamy, Joe Blackie, Sheila Bonello, John Branch, Rebecca Butler (Simon Cadell estate), Angela Burns, Diana Burroughes, Butlin's Memories website, Judy Buxton, Claire Carpenter, Lesley Chambers, Donna Clark, Carriad Cockcroft, Howard Cope, Shirley and Ivan Cope, Peter Cobourn, David Croft, Beverley Daniels, Bob Deex, Les Double, Aileen Farnell, Brian Fisher, Steve Foster, Andrew Foxon, Shirley and Mick Fury, Mark Goddard, Roy Gould, Matt Grindley, Paul Harrison, Trisha Hayes at the BBC Written Archive Centre, Maggie Higgins, Mary Husband, Jason James, Alan Jubb, Alain Keevil, Jean & Tony Knock, Ray Lear, Geoff Legan, Ron Lynch (John Inman estate), David Male, Dean Manders, Beverley Marsh, Ralph Montagu, Barbara Murphy, Terence Parker, Jimmy Perry, Charles Plant, Tony Pritchard, Radio Times, Vince Rayner, Andrew Ruff, Johanne, Kate & Jennifer Randall, Diana Rising, Meron Roberts, Jenny Rose, Max Samett, Don Smith, Chris Stammers, Sue Stewart, Piotr Trabszo, Anita Turnbull, Karen Turnbull, Patsy Urquhart, Alan Veale, John Wade at the Cliff Hotel, David Webb, Phil Welfare, John Willis at Orwell Photography.

Radio Times quotes and covers by kind permission of the Radio Times.
Production information and archive interviews by kind permission of the BBC Written Archive Centre, Reading

We started out with an idea to produce a book on Hi-de-Hi! and You Rang, M'Lord? several years ago but it has taken the help of many people to make the dream a reality. We haven't had a team of publishers and researchers at our disposal so what you hold in your hands it the result of many hours of time and painstaking dedication.

Our first stroke of luck was to be sitting next to Paul Carpenter of the Dad's Army Appreciation Society at the Hi-de-Hi! reunion in 2007. He listened to our tales of woe about not having a publisher for our (then) half finished manuscript, and by the end of the meal he had offered to publish the tome you now hold in your hands. He also brought his brilliant design skills to the project and the results of his hard work are impressive to say the least. Our debt to him is simply beyond words.

It was an inspired moment when we asked Tony Tarran and his wife Joanne to act as researchers for photos as well as providing additional material for the project. They have left no stone unturned in their quests to raid public and private archives for some very rare shots of the Hi-de-Hi! and You Rang, M'Lord? teams, both on screen and in off duty moments. Tony and Jo have gone beyond the call of duty on so many occasions for this book and it's as much theirs as ours really.

The cast and crew of both programmes gave their time and their memories so generously. What has come over more than anything is the great wave of love the people involved have had for the shows and their creators. I'm sure other writers of television books have not enjoyed the continued goodwill that seems to come from virtually everyone who has worked with Perry and Croft.

The final and greatest thanks must go to Jimmy Perry OBE and David Croft OBE — two of the greatest comedy writers this country has ever produced, and to whom this book is lovingly dedicated. Their talent has ensured generations have continued to laugh worldwide at their creations. We salute them and their achievements.

Rob Cope and Mike Fury

Forewords

Jimmy Perry OBE

Of all the shows that David Croft and I did together Hi-de-Hi!, from the first time it went on air, took off like a rocket. Whereas *Dad's Army* and *It Ain't Half Hot Mum* on the other hand, needed several series to catch the imagination of the viewers.

David and I had drawn from all the characters we had met whilst working at Butlin's. And they really existed. The bad tempered Punch & Judy man who hated kids. The Camp Comic up to every dodge in the book: the bingo fiddle, the holiday princess fiddle and many other scams to make a bit of money on the side. In fact, the holiday camp king Sir Fred Pontin said he recognised every one of them. Many years ago Charlie Drake revealed to me that when he was working at one of Butlin's Holiday Camps, the great man himself, Sir Billy Butlin, offered him a considerable sum of money to reveal the secret of the bingo fiddle that he did every season. Charlie Drake refused his offer and never gave in.

It was during the creation of the series that a crazy girl came to see David and me, to play the part of a chalet maid. She looked as though she had been dressed by an Oxfam shop and never stopped talking. The part only had a few lines but when we could get a word in edgeways, we booked her. And so a star was born. Her name was Su Pollard. Many other artistes joined us: Simon Cadell, Paul Shane, Ruth Madoc, Jeffrey Holland… All left their mark on the series and became stars. And Hi-de-Hi! became a legend.

All over the world if you shout "Hi-de-Hi" you will get the answer "Ho-de-Ho". Even if it is in Chinese!

David Croft OBE

At a critical time in our careers, Jimmy and I both found ourselves at Butlin's Holiday Camps. Jimmy was a 'Redcoat' while a student at RADA. I was a sort of producer, production manager, scene shifter and general factotum while 'resting' between jobs as an actor in Reporatory companies and touring musicals.

Butlin's was a great place to learn about 'Showbusiness'. The famous 'Redcoats' were in constant contact with the campers and got their instant reaction to everything that was happening day-to-day at the holiday camps. I was busily engaged in staging four one-hour concert party type entertainments in two or three holiday camps, each show consisting of a couple of comics, half a dozen chorus girls, a couple of singers and a couple of variety acts accompanied by a fourteen-piece orchestra. Each of these shows had to be devised, costumed, lit and rehearsed amid the general chaos of 5000 or so campers enjoying themselves - oh, and each show had a revolving stage which Billy Butlin decreed had to revolve at least once in every programme.

Jimmy and I never met at Butlin's – nor in the Army although we trod the same paths. All the same we had very much the same sort of grounding in the business which we both loved and in which we both prospered.

You Rang, M'Lord? was set in our early childhood which we both remembered remarkably well. It was an era of great social change. The BBC allowed us to write and stage a show in a 50 minute slot which gave us a chance to develop stories and characters for which the normal 30 minute slot was too short. The result was 26 of our very favourite shows.

1 The Real Maplin's?
The holiday camp movement

The empire of Joe Maplin has always seemed startlingly real to millions of people who have enjoyed the delights of Britain's holiday camp network. When we join the show in a train en route to the fictional south coast town of Crimpton-On-Sea in 1959, the holiday camp movement was reaching a peak. Memories of the austere war years and the subsequent rationing were now fading and a new post-war prosperity was engulfing the United Kingdom. People were flocking in millions to the 100 or so registered holiday camps that had sprung up around the country. People wanted a good time and the staff of the holiday camp circuit certainly made sure they got it.

Once inside these mighty cities of pleasure it was possible never to leave the confines of the camp, every need was catered for. Chalets back in 1959 were basic with twin or bunk beds, a basin with a chest of drawers and a wardrobe to hang your clothes. Lavatorial facilities were taken care of with large ablution blocks and the dining operations could be huge, with dining halls often having to have several sittings to accommodate all the campers with their breakfast, lunch and evening meals. By far the most important aspect of these holidays was the entertainment programme. All manner of sporting facilities were usually available ranging from tennis to football; ping pong to swimming. Competitions between the holidaymakers were fierce and usually there was a token prize on offer as the carrot dangling before participants. The live entertainment boasted nightly cabarets sometimes with big-name variety stars as top of the bill. Children were well catered for in these camps. There would often be clubs which would look after the little ones whilst Mum and Dad got a break and maybe even find their way into the bar for a quiet drink, always keeping an eye on the Baby Crying board in the ballroom. It really was an all encompassing experience booking into a holiday camp and some families would return to their favourite camp year after year. The staff would become extensions of your own family for the duration of the stay, always reliable in a medical emergency, pool side competition or simply for a good laugh.

Three names have always dominated any talk about holiday camps. Harry Warner, Fred Pontin and perhaps most famously Billy Butlin. In fact the idea of holiday camps did not arrive with these gentlemen.

As early as 1894 Cunningham Young Men's Holiday Camp had opened on the Isle Of Man. This male only environment allowed the attendees to stay in candle lit tents and boasted its own heated pool and concert hall. The first holiday camp on the UK mainland was to be found at Caister in Norfolk, opened in 1906 by former grocer John Fletcher Dodd. Dodd was a founder member of the Independent Labour Party and when he opened his camp political meetings were regularly on the agenda. First the camp housed visitors in tents which eventually gave way to wooden huts. Eventually the camp was to be served by its own railway station. Initially rules were very strict: no children, no dogs and no alcohol. Additionally all bathers were required to purchase a regulation bathing costume from the camp shop. A week at the camp would cost 21 shillings by 1924. Despite having to close for the duration of the

Second World War, when it was requisitioned for Army training, Caister Camp would be welcoming some 1,000 visitors per week by the end of the 1950s. The site of the Camp is still welcoming visitors today as part of the Haven group. These early camps were precursors to the now familiar image of holiday camps which formed the basis of Hi-de-Hi!

Jimmy Perry and David Croft have always been careful to avoid any statements saying their show was based on a particular camp or organisation. However with David producing shows for them and Jimmy serving as a Redcoat, it is hard not to think that the template for Maplin's Holiday camp was in fact the Butlin's empire. Joe Maplin was portrayed as a ruthless business man who was only concerned about his own image as he strove for a Knighthood. The reality is somewhat different. Billy Butlin was a genial entrepreneur who gained the admiration and respect of all those who worked with him.

"Billy Butlin was a very astute man. He should have got his Knighthood much earlier because her made a lot of unhappy people very happy. He staged a wonderful holiday for them. Some of the early television [comedy] shows turned Butlin's into Prisoner of War camps but it was quite the reverse. The camps had barbed wire entanglements to keep people out. Billy was very astute and didn't ask people if the food was all right, he went straight round to the dustbins to see what had been thrown away. After there had been a big flood in Skegness he knew that people coming into the camp would be checking their mattresses for damp. So Sir Billy had all the mattresses from Pwllheli transferred to Skegness and vice versa. He knew people at Pwllheli would not bother checking their mattresses. A very bright man indeed."

David Croft

Although Sir Billy Butlin was a man who defined a movement as British as fish and chips, he was in fact born in South Africa. He was born William Heygate Colbourne Butlin in Cape Town on 29th September 1899. His father had been sent to South Africa as a 'remittance man' which is more commonly known these days as the black sheep of the family! Sir Billy's grandfather had been a clergyman but the young Billy trod a path more familiar to his mother Bertha's side of the family, that of a travelling showman. When Bertha and William Senior's marriage failed she returned to the family bosom in Bristol with Billy and his brother Binkie and toured fairs with her gingerbread stall. Bertha remarried Charles Rowbotham who worked for the Bristol Gas Works. They emigrated to Canada where following outbreak of the First World War, Billy enlisted for the Canadian army.

By 1921 Billy found himself back in England with just £5 in his pocket and headed for Bristol. His mother's family made sure he was gainfully employed with a small hoopla stall. Billy made a profit from his first travelling

'Let Them Eat Cake' - The Real Maplin's?

fair and the scene was set for his entrepreneurial skills in earnest. He rented himself a prime pitch at the annual Christmas circus at Olympia and once again found himself in profit. He continued to tour the country with Hills Travelling Fair whilst his mother - whom he had sent for from Canada - ran the site at Olympia. It was during a pitch at Tiverton that Billy met a girl called Dolly with whom he fell in love and they married. Billy's most ambitious move was to lease a piece of land in Skegness from the Earl of Scarborough. It was mainly sand dunes which he knew would have to be levelled before he could stage a fair. In true business tradition Billy had the foresight to realise that sand was a useful commodity in the building trade and sold the excess to local building contractors thus again making a profit. In its place he put in a number of hoopla stalls, a tower slide, a self-built Haunted House attraction and eventually, a scenic railway! Sir Billy was also responsible for bringing the first dodgem car rides to Britain. He had seen them in Toronto and, following negotiations with the manufacturers, introduced them to Skegness in 1928. He also cannily obtained the sole agency rights for the whole of Europe. Clearly this man was going places.

Billy Butlin continued to open new fairs and rides all over the country. His mother Bertha constantly travelled supervising all his attractions but in 1933 caught a chill which developed into something far more serious and she passed away shortly before Billy's genius was to be fully realised. Billy spotted some turnip fields in Lincolnshire and knew that the location - facing the sea - would make an ideal site for his most ambitious idea yet. A holiday camp. Travelling the seaside towns of England with his fairs he had seen landladies at bed and breakfast establishments throwing out families after breakfast and not letting them back in until it was time for the evening meal. That was the norm. He would offer families a holiday experience far in excess of what was currently available. Work began and on Easter Sunday 1936 the first Butlin's Holiday Camp was officially opened. With three meals a day and entertainment thrown in, a week's full board would cost anywhere in between thirty five shillings or three pounds depending on the time of year. Adverts were placed in the *Daily Express* and within days sacks of mail were arriving, so much so that Skegness Post Office was unable to cope with the demand for the Butlin's experience. Initially the entertainment came from all sections of the admin, catering and maintenance staff (and indeed holidaymakers) who all used to display whatever skills they had on a nightly basis on makeshift stages in the dining rooms. It wasn't long before the idea of having Redcoats to organise and take part in sporting and entertainment activities came to Billy and a legend was born.

The empire began to grow quickly and to keep up with demand further camps were opened at Clacton (1938), Filey (1945), Ayr (1946), Pwllheli (1947), Mosney near Dublin (1948), Bognor (1960), Minehead (1962) and the last and smallest camp at Barry Island in 1965. The Filey camp was used as the location for the 1951 movie *Holiday Camp* starring Jack Warner and Flora Robson. Billy Butlin knew that to make a successful holiday it was necessary to take his campers away from the dull and the mundane so he set about making the Butlin's experience as magical as possible. It was a fairy land with coloured lights, costume characters, fairground style attractions, picturesque streams and bridges. All manner of decorations and theatrical effects to ensure that a visit to Butlin's was one you wouldn't forget in a long while. The rapport between the Redcoats and the campers was something special. They became an extension of the family with a smile and a laugh from the first sighting at breakfast to goodnight in the ballroom. They were even encouraged to shout 'Hi-de-Hi!' to which the campers would respond en masse 'Ho-de-Ho'. How that would come back to haunt the Butlin's management in future years. Because the camps were vast affairs covering

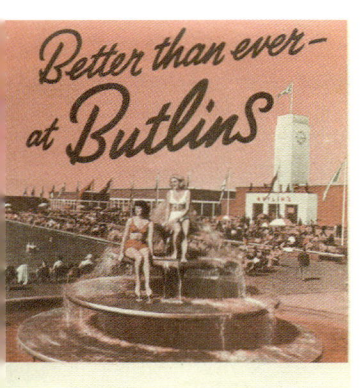

'Let Them Eat Cake' - The Real Maplin's?

a lot of acreage a Tannoy system was put in place and Radio Butlin was born. All over the camp the sound of background music, entertainment and dining information, lost children and many other announcements were made daily over Radio Butlin. Sir Billy married twice more, to Norah (his first wife Dolly's sister!) and finally to Sheila whom he had met when she was managing one of the bars at his Pwllheli camp. Billy Butlin said goodnight campers for the final time on 12th June 1980, aged 81. Just six months earlier the BBC had broadcast the pilot episode of a new comedy set in a holiday camp...

Butlin's had used the rallying call 'Hi-de-Hi' since the 1940's. The phrase had of course been in the chorus of the popular song *Minnie The Moocher* recorded by Cab Calloway and his Orchestra in 1931. The chorus went along the lines of:

Hi-de-hi-de-hi-de-hi!
Ho-de-ho-de-ho-de-ho!
He-de-he-de-he-de-he!
Ho-de-ho-de-ho!

So it was probably this source from which the phrase 'Hi-de-Hi' was purloined and started its usage in the holiday camps. Mr. Partridge has a speech in one episode of Hi-de-Hi! which refers to an American General in the army being Court Marshalled for shouting 'Hi-de-Hi' to his troops and getting them to reply 'Ho-de-Ho' back. The 1941 movie *They Died With Their Boots On* starring Errol Flynn and Olivia de Havilland features a sequence in which a general shouts 'Hi-de-Hi' and his troops roar back 'Ho-de-Ho' - another example of the phrase being used in popular culture. The great music hall entertainer and actor Stanley Holloway recorded a song he wrote himself entitled *Hi-de-Hi* on a 78 rpm record of Butlin's songs for the HMV Label. The song went along in high spirited fashion thus:

When things are looking gloomy
And skies are dull and grey
Remember that the sun will come and shine another day
So open up your faces wide
And let me hear you say
Hi-de-Hi (Hi-de-Ho)
If you're feeling grumpy
If you're feeling jumpy
And the things you plan will not come right
Don't you get down hearted
Come along get started
Sing this song with all your might
Hi-de-Hi (Hi-de-Ho)
Hi-de-Hi (Hi-de-Ho)

[The track can now be found on several CD compilations of Stanley Holloway's material].

From the moment Perry and Croft's Hi-de-Hi! made it's debut, the Butlin's Organisation distanced themselves as far away as possible from the show. It would take until 1986 though for the Organisation to officially ban any staff from using the phrase.

One of the turning points of the holiday camp movement was the 1938 'Holidays With Pay Act', where the Government under Neville Chamberlain made it compulsory for employers to provide one week's paid holiday for their workers per annum. Realising that this meant effectively many more families would have the resources to be able to afford a holiday, Butlin offered 'a week's holiday for a week's pay'. His rivals in the field were also quick to follow suit. Despite the interruption of the war, by the late 1940's the people of Britain were ready to smile again thus Butlin and his competitors were on hand to make sure that their visitors had a week to remember.

Fred Pontin had been born in London's East End during 1906. He had found himself a promising career in the Stock Exchange before buying a disused camp at Brean Sands in 1946. It had most recently been a U.S. Army base and was in a pretty bad state of repair. It was given a quick makeover and opened once more as a holiday camp, an immediate success despite the fact that it could only cater for 198 visitors. From then on Pontin began buying up sites that he could develop as additions to his rapidly expanding holiday empire. Sir Fred never set out to rival his friend Billy Butlin's huge network of holiday camps. Pontin's camps were always smaller which made them easily more manageable than the gigantic operations of Butlin. A photo once emerged of Sir Billy drinking in the bar at the Brean Sands site during a secret visit, Pontin made sure it was prominently seen in the following year's brochure with the slogan

'Let Them Eat Cake' - The Real Maplin's?

The ballroom farewell song at Butlin's camps in the '40s and '50s (to the tune of Goodnight Sweetheart):
Goodnight campers, see you in the morning
Goodnight campers, I can see you yawning
You must wake up your sleepy head
For I've heard it said, that folks die in bed
So I'll say goodnight campers,
Don't sleep in your braces
Goodnight campers,
Soak your teeth in Jayes's,
Drown your sorrows,
Bring the empties back tomorrow,
Goodnight campers, goodnight

'All the best people come to Pontin's!' As the 1960s dawned Pontin had sixteen sites and the introduction of Bluecoats was a blatant attempt at copying the Redcoat idea from Butlin. Realising he could never compete with Butlin's massive entertainment programme Pontin raised the standard of his chalets to include en-suite bathrooms, a complete overhaul of the catering operation and an increasing desire to promote self catering holidays. Sir Fred also pioneered the package holiday abroad in the '60s with his 'Pontinental Holidays'. Initially in Sardinia (later Majorca, Spain and Ibiza) you could get an all inclusive trip abroad for £50, a move that would much later spell trouble for the holiday camps around the United Kingdom. The camp at Prestatyn was to be featured prominently in the film *Holiday On The Buses* in 1973. After a £57 million merger deal with the betting company Coral in 1979, Sir Fred finally lost control of the empire he created when in 1981 his entire company was sold to brewing giant Bass.

Sir Fred was heavily involved with racehorses during his retirement from the holiday camp business and finally ascended to that great holiday camp in the sky on 30th September 2000, at the grand age of 93.

Captain Harry Warner had beaten both Butlin and Pontin in his connection with holiday camps by opening his first camp in 1931 at Hayling Island, Hampshire. Warner had taken early retirement from the Royal Artillery in 1925 and became successful in the seaside restaurant business before buying his first holiday camp. Billy Butlin and Warner were great friends, in fact Warner helped to design Butlin's Filey camp whilst Butlin served time on the board of directors at Warners Holidays in its early years. Warner's three sons Bill, John and Alan were instrumental in helping their father expand his business to that of 11 camps by 1965. Reportedly Warner senior and Butlin had reached a gentleman's agreement whereby Warner would operate in the south of England and Butlin the north. If true, Butlin obviously broke the pact when he opened the Bognor camp in 1960! The Warner camps were no rivals for the massive

FRED SAYS
This is worth looking into!

Butlin's promotional material, listing 'those that work, so you can play', from the gardener to the camp Padre!

'Let Them Eat Cake' - The Real Maplin's?

operations undertaken by Butlin, or indeed Fred Pontin for that matter, but were perfectly equipped to provide all the facilities that a camper might expect from a holiday. Warner introduced Greencoats, completing the trilogy of entertainers that have become a leisure legend. Harry Warner passed away in 1964 aged 75 although his camps continued to flourish under his sons. More recently after several take overs, the remaining camps have latterly turned into 'adults only' holiday centres. The Puckpool camp (Isle of Wight) can be seen in the cult 1973 movie *That'll Be The Day* starring David Essex and Ringo Starr whilst the 1977 romp *Confessions of a Holiday Camp* was filmed in part at Hayling Island.

"Holiday camps faded out I think in the late 1960s. Don't forget I am talking about [experiences in] 1948. We had all come back from the war, bloody glad to be alive - those that weren't nastily wounded. I was at the Royal Academy of Dramatic Art. I got a scholarship to go there. I say a scholarship but it wasn't, you got your fee paid if you passed the audition which I did. They had long summer holidays and there was a bloke in the Royal Artillery Concert Party with me, Roger Bourne. He had 'neat feet', he was a tap dancer, and he had a double act called Bourne & Barbara. In those days we had the Bernard Brothers and everybody pinched their act which was miming to gramophone records. The audiences went mad. I met up with Roger and he said 'I'm working at Butlin's as a Redcoat and entertainer, I'll talk to Wally Goodman - the General Manager - about you getting a job there'. I went up to their head office in Oxford Street which was in those days painted in the Butlin's colours of yellow and blue. As I was getting off the bus in Oxford Street, I saw Frank Muir and Denis Norden and they had wonderful suits. In those days the great thing was to own your own tailor-made suit. I had no money at all and to have a suit made in the 1940s would cost you 30 Guineas - a fortune. They would be double breasted and they lasted forever. Anyhow, there Muir and Norden were in these suits walking down the street and I thought to myself 'I wonder if I'll ever be as famous as that?' I got to the Butlin Headquarters and went to see Wally Goodman. I said to him, 'Roger Bourne told me you might interested in hiring some Redcoats'. He looked at me and told me 'I can't have someone talking posh like that for my Redcoats. What are you doing?' I told him I was studying at the Royal Academy of Dramatic Art and wanted to be an actor. 'That's no bloody good to me mate', he growled. 'I want someone to get out there and work those campers, they've got to be worked. I'll send you as a sports' organiser.' Now I don't do sports, I like to exercise, but sport I don't do. I got to Pwllheli

'Let Them Eat Cake' - The Real Maplin's?

and the first thing they did was get me to referee this disastrous football match. I had to ask somebody what 'off side' meant because I didn't know. It was a disaster. The camp Entertainments Officer said to me, 'Sorry son, it's not working.' I said 'I don't do sports'. 'Why didn't you bloody well say so!' he moaned 'I'll give you one last chance to organise the campers' concert. You mess up on this and you'll be on the next train home.' It was a tough life. If you weren't good enough they simply say 'You can bugger off for a start 'cos you're useless.' Don't forget they were paying ten pounds a week 'and cakes' which meant all your food was thrown in, plus a free chalet. So I auditioned the campers. I got some scenery and made it like a Viennese beer garden. I had them all sitting at tables. There was a famous song back then recorded by Phil Harris called the Darktown Poker Club. *Anyway, this old boy came up and said in a thick Yorkshire accent 'I'm gonna sing,* Darkt'own Poker Club' *It was terrible. But you had to be very careful not to upset them because they could turn nasty. 'Bloody hell, I went to that concert and that posh bloke told me I was crap' they'd say. The show did work though. Butlin's for 1948 had marvellous microphones and we had a clap-ometer just like in Hi-de-Hi! It was a wonderful time. David Croft and I set Hi-de-Hi! forward ten years to 1959, because it meant that it was the start of the rock and roll era."*

Jimmy Perry

By far the most important camp to this story is the Dovercourt Bay Holiday Camp and Lido built by Harry Warner on land leased from Harwich Borough Council who had purchased the land in January 1937. There is some evidence to suggest Butlin was considering this site but eventually settled on Clacton, which opened the following year. It took around 100 workers, working against the bad weather, only 4 months to build the camp at a cost of £50,000. The Dovercourt camp was opened in July 1937. Warner's purchased the site for £7,500 once the camp had been established.

When opened the camp could accommodate 1500 guests at any one time and employed 150 people. Some 4,000 rose bushes and 2,000 poplar trees were planted across the site with Harry Warner himself planting the poplar trees surrounding the swimming pool. A dining room, ballroom, bars, outdoor swimming pool, playing fields, tennis courts, boating lake and putting green were among the facilities on offer. It even had its own stretch of beach. In its first season the Dovercourt camp welcomed some 6,000 visitors to the camp but before it could become properly established as a leading holiday resort the outbreak of the Second World War saw it requisitioned by the Government as a troop station for the duration of the conflict. Prior to the 1939 season major improvements were undertaken including

Above, this page, previous page and next page; The Warner's brochure for Dovercourt Bay Holiday Camp 'On the Sunny Essex Coast'.
The chalets were the same as those used in Hi-de-Hi!

Left; Although Pontins and Butlins issued badges for each season, Warner camps did not. However an enamel badge was available.

Constructing Dovercourt Bay in 1937. Almost all the 100 workers pose next to what was to be the main building (housing the ballroom, bars and reception) with not a hard hat in sight!

'Let Them Eat Cake' - The Real Maplin's?

developing the dining hall and enlarging the ballroom. An early member of the entertainment staff at Dovercourt Bay was Bill Owen, now best known for his long running role as 'Compo' in the television comedy *Last of the Summer Wine*.

Dovercourt Bay flourished during the heyday of holiday camps in the '50s and '60s, becoming a popular destination for thousands of holidaymakers each year. By 1981, Warner's Holidays, Britain's last big independent holiday camp group with 11 camps nationally, was sold to the Grand Metropolitan Group for some £10 million and thus Dovercourt Bay camp had a new owner before missing out on major investment in 1984 by the group who then sold it again in 1985 to Bourne Leisure, who ironically also controlled the Butlin's empire.

Following extensive damage to the camp by the 1987 hurricane, the doors to Dovercourt Bay camp were finally shut in the summer of 1990. Mounting losses and under investment in the facilities had meant that Dovercourt Bay had ceased to be a viable business concern. Demolition occurred in 1992 when a proposed plan to use the site for theme park failed to obtain planning permission from the local council. Today the North of the site is a residential housing estate, the rest is overgrown waste land. At the time of writing, it is earmarked for caravans as an extension of the adjoining caravan park.

Although today there is now little to recognise the site as being one of the pioneering holiday camps of a once great movement, the camp has been immortalised in 58 episodes of Hi-de-Hi! As long as the series continues to be enjoyed the carefree fun of not only Dovercourt Bay, but the hundreds of other camps large and small during the golden age of British holidays, will be resurrected and the spirit of Redcoats, Bluecoats and Greencoats will live once more.

The Entertainments Staff at Warner's Dovercourt Bay in their smart black and yellow blazers. The play area shown was used many times for external scenes in Hi-de-Hi!

Memories of Warner's at Dovercourt Bay

"During the late Seventies and early Eighties I worked for Securicor parcel service, and my patch was covering the Dovercourt area. On several occasions I made deliveries to the Warner's Holiday Camp. During filming I had to wait outside the gate, which was my opportunity to watch proceedings through the fence. I can recall one morning delivering to the Cliff Hotel, up the road from the camp, and passing a very excited Su Pollard descending down the steps hollering "I'm late, I'm late" in typical Peggy style before running off down the road arms waving. My most vivid and memorable Hi-de-Hi! experience occurred one bright sunny morning driving through Stones Green near Wix, on my way to Tendring Hospital. I was stopped by a Policeman who informed me filming was taking place around the corner. My only option again was to watch the proceedings. I walked around the corner to be confronted by a man with two leggy girls, one on each arm, and several others milling around. It suddenly dawned on me I was in the presence of the entire Hi-de-Hi! cast. The man with the girls then turned and noticed my Securicor shirt epaulets and said in a very posh voice, "What the bloody hell are Securicor doing right out here? Are you delivering our wages?" Yes, Simon Cadell with two of the girl Yellowcoats. I watched for the next few minutes as several of the cast hid in hedges, jumping out several times before they got it right. Living in Colchester as I do, Dovercourt is within easy reach. I still visit the sea front area often during the summer. It hasn't changed much except where the camp was. It gives me great pleasure showing my children the locations."

Steve Hobrough

"Although I am not from Dovercourt and live in Hornchurch, we still have a caravan on Dovercourt Haven and have done for over 40 years. I am now a 52 year old mother of two but my teenage years were spent in Warner's bunking over the fence from the caravan and going to the Kontiki Disco, which was the in place to go in Dovercourt. At the time all the local boys and girls used to meet in there, there was always plenty of snogging and God knows what else going on in the dark corners! Although we were chased out on several occasions by the security guards and I lost my shoe running past the chalets (if you could call them that, more like prison cells.) I jumped over the ditch and hid behind the war shelter on the grass over the back which now belongs to the caravan park. This was probably the early Seventies but I also remember seeing some of the Hi-de-Hi! cast and the great big animal figures around the pool in the winter months. I don't know how they got in that water during October. It used to be freezing in the summer when we all went in there. I was also chased out of the pool on a few occasions. But every weekend we still went back for more. They were good old days with the tall trees and the Warner's sign always welcoming us on a Friday night after a depressing week in London."

Mrs Jacqueline Capper (nee Herbert)

"I was a child extra in the show, in fact I was just four years old and had just started Parkeston Primary School. The best memory of the show was an episode called 'If Wet – In The Ballroom'. I was sitting next to the older boy who spoiled all of Willy the Wizzard's magic tricks. They did a big close up of my un-happy face. I can remember seeing that very clip on Noel Edmonds' *Multi Coloured Swap Shop* when I was in a TV shop in Colchester. My face must have been seen on about fifty TVs in the shop and people started to look at me. They must have been wondering if it was me on telly or someone who looked similar."

Phil Tye

"Our family has many memories of Warner's Holiday Camp, not least the tricycles of 'happy campers' toiling up Donkey Hill on their way to the town. I was a Denney and lived in Dovercourt Hall at the bottom of Hall Lane. Our Sunday afternoons were spent with the background sounds of the merriment resulting from the Beauty Queen parade

'Let Them Eat Cake' - The Real Maplin's?

and the Knobbly Knees competition. My parents were friends of Mr and Mrs Woods who managed the camp when I was a schoolgirl, and I was friendly with their younger daughter Jean, and was allowed to use the swimming pool, and other facilities. My husband, Len Holder, remembers that his grandfather, Arthur Hatcher, was Commissionaire for a time, and his sister, Elizabeth Legge worked in the Kiosk with Sally Gower and Mrs Clark, mother of one of his friends, Tony. He also remembers stories about his friends gaining access to the Saturday night dance, and eyeing up the talent while he was away at sea! Incidentally, Mr and Mrs Williams who were Managers of Warners, bought Dovercourt Hall from my mother in the mid Seventies. Imagine our amazement when, living on the Wirral having left Dovercourt in 1963, we saw the opening credits of the new comedy Hi-de-Hi! and immediately recognised the archway and poplar lined drive which was so familiar to us! A shout went up, "It's Warners!" Of course we watched every series with great interest and amusement, trying to pick out other landmarks that were familiar to us!

Ann and Len Holder

"My parents were the general managers at Warner's until my father, Arthur Williams, retired in 1986. I also worked for a little while in the offices and remember the filming of Hi-de-Hi! Our office was next door to the Ladies toilet and Su Pollard was often in the toilets practising her tap dancing and singing. There was a wonderful echo in there and we could hear all this in our offices. We had to teach the performers the proper way to sing 'Goodnight Campers' and enjoyed quite a few parties with them."

Janey Nice

"My wife and I both worked at Warner's at Dovercourt from 1985 – 87. My wife Monique was a Dining Room Assistant and I was the first in the dining room then, glass collecting. We have very fond memories of the place as it was where we met and fell in love, later married. In 1986 we had just finished the season when the Hi-de-Hi! cast came down and held a barbeque, inviting some of the staff. We joined in and got talking to Paul Shane, The Webb Twins as well as members of the production team. The cast were very friendly towards us which was quite surprising as you would think that being famous they would not want to talk to you. But they were all very talkative and friendly and we had many laughs with them. We got a signed photo of Paul Shane which he gave us personally which we have kept. We also met Su Pollard, she was just as funny as she was in the show. Su would come into to the reception in an afternoon for a chat. Ruth Madoc was great too."

Darren Pratt

Arthur Hatcher, Commissionaire at Dovercourt Bay and grandfather of Len Holder.
Note the water feature that once stood at each end of the pool (see postcard below). These were removed long before Hi-de-Hi! commenced filming.

Bathing Pool from Cascade, Dovercourt Bay Holiday Lido.

'The Society Entertainer' - Jimmy Perry

2 Jimmy Perry OBE

Jimmy Perry is the epitome of the showman. Well spoken and out going, it is not hard to recognise that for many years he was an actor-manager. Showbusiness was in Jimmy's blood from the moment he was born. Not that he comes from a long line of actors, far from it. His father was in antiques and took a dim view of 'theatricals'. But Jimmy became entranced by his trips to the variety theatre in London where acts such as Flanagan and Allen and the rest of the Crazy Gang certainly left their mark on the young boy. The famous story goes that when his father asked Jimmy what he wanted to be when he grew up, Jimmy replied that he was going to be a great comedian. His father looked at him witheringly and said "You stupid boy."

Jimmy was born on 9th September 1923 in Barnes, London, the son of an antique dealer. When the Second World War broke out Jimmy briefly joined the Local Defence Volunteers in Watford which would shortly become The Home Guard. It was whilst on guard duty with an old soldier who insisted on recounting the battle of Omdurman against the 'fuzzie wuzzies' that seeds where planted in a young mind that were to come to fruition nearly thirty years later. Having been called up to battle in 1944, off Jimmy went to Colchester for six weeks' training and eventually would be posted to the Far East. Deolali, India was the order of the day and Jimmy's obvious talents saw him enlisted with the Royal Artillery Concert Party. Upon leaving the army Jimmy embarked upon an ill-fated stab at working as a comedian before someone suggested that he should audition for RADA which he duly did and was passed with honours by Sir Kenneth Barnes and Dame Flora Robson.

Whilst training he applied for a position as a Butlin's Redcoat during the summer holidays and became a very popular member of the entertainments staff for two seasons at Pwllheli and a further summer at Filey. So much so that Sir Billy Butlin offered Jimmy a very nice position with his company, but Jimmy declined as he wanted to follow his true love, the theatre. Jimmy's debut on the London stage as an actor was in 1952 with *The Glorious Days* at the Palace Theatre, which was followed by several more West End musicals. Jimmy became the new tenant of the Palace Theatre in Watford in 1956. During his time at Watford, Jimmy presented a different play every week. "I worked out the other day that I've played over 600 parts - 12 years of weekly repertory," says Jimmy, "I'd done every play you could think of up until 1965." Jimmy and his wife Gilda were instrumental in getting the Palace Theatre recognised as a civic venue. Two years working with John Hanson were followed by a stint with Joan Littlewood at her famous Theatre Workshop in Stratford East, giving Jimmy an insight into one of the most innovative theatrical set ups of it's day.

Jimmy as a Redcoat at Butlin's, Pwllheli. 1948.
He was a very popular member of the hard working team, which didn't go unnoticed by Billy Butlin.

21

'The Society Entertainer' - Jimmy Perry

A group photo of all the Redcoats at Butlin's, Pwllheli. Jimmy is standing in the backrow, right of centre.

Although Jimmy had secured for himself some small roles in various television series up to that point, he felt he wanted to further himself in the advancing medium. "I started off with the idea of writing a part for myself. I thought 'What shall I write about ?' Because I'd done very little writing before. I set about thinking about a situation to set my script in. I went through lots of things: Army, Navy, Airforce, Prisoner of War camp... They had either been done before or didn't feel right. Then I thought 'the Home Guard!'" Jimmy's idea utilising the sort of figures he'd encountered as a boy in the Home Guard all those years ago developed into a script he called *The Fighting Tigers*. During a break in the filming for a small part he had in a David Croft show called *Beggar My Neighbour* for the BBC Jimmy took the opportunity to give him the script in the hope that David would read it. "Come the following Monday morning I was anxious to know if David had read the script," remembers Jimmy. "I was sitting in my dressing room at the BBC Television Centre getting very worked up. At the lunch break David came crashing in gushing 'This is fantastic. I like it!'" It was the start of a writing partnership that would last twenty five years.

David and Jimmy soon sold the idea to the then Head of Comedy Michael Mills who suggested that they change the title to *Dad's Army*. A legend was born. David and Jimmy set about casting the show and David's first choice for the role of Captain Mainwaring was comedian and actor Jon Pertwee. Jimmy was very keen to get Arthur Lowe who up until that time was best known for playing Leonard Swindley in ITV's flagship soap opera *Coronation Street*. "David and I worked it out well in advance that we had a posh man playing the Sergeant and a common man - for want of a better word - as his Captain. Somebody under the man who wants the job, and knows all the answers. It came about after me telling the story to David of myself coming back from the Far East on a troop ship called the S.S. Franconia. You can't really conceive what it was like. 3,000 troops all flung together on this huge ship but it's hell. There were bunks slung across the bulkheads rather like Nelson's time, we are talking rough. We were getting a show ready having left Bombay in September 1947 and by the time we got to Suez we were all ready to go.

An officer came on board at Port Said, an Army Captain, and he said in his Cockney accent, 'You are doing the show aren't you? Well, I'm taking over because I have done a lot of amateur theatricals.' I thought to myself bloody cheek. In the war you didn't have to be anything special to be an Officer, you just had to have the tenacity and qualities to be an Officer. They didn't care about your background at all. This bloke was probably a very good Captain and had passed all the tests but of course that didn't matter to me much at the time. I was furious and about two days later I crept up on deck at 3 o'clock in the morning and I wrote in chalk all over the bulkheads: *'No Common Men as Officers'*. The next day everyone was assembled on deck and the Colonel was giving us a dressing down. 'Now look here, someone has written an abusive thing and I won't have this. There is no class distinction in the British Army. I want the man who wrote this to step forward. The man in question is not common...' He was getting himself into ever deeper water and decided to shut up. Needless to say I refused to own up. So the Colonel looked at us and told us 'Well, we are on our way home and you are all going to be demobbed so there is not much I can do. But I hope the men responsible feel thoroughly ashamed of themselves.' He went rambling on about building a

A clip from Beggar My Neighbour. Jimmy Perry stands between Pat Coombs and Reg Varney. It was during this programme that Jimmy gave David Croft the script for The Fighting Tigers.

'The Society Entertainer' - Jimmy Perry

new world with no snobbishness (and may I remind you at that time a socialist Government had taken over in Britain). I told this story to David and so that is where the idea of having the common man in charge came about." The role of the smooth talking, highly educated Sergeant went to John Le Mesurier, then a veteran of many British television broadcasts and films. "I said ' I want to play the spiv Walker' and all their faces dropped." Jimmy says. "Michael Mills said to me 'Oh no, you can't be both sides of the camera luvvie. You have got to make up your mind whether you want to be an actor or a writer, you can't do both.' David didn't want me to play it either and I had to decide whether I was going to keep up the pressure for the part but at that time I didn't feel I was on firm enough ground at the BBC. So I gave way and the rest is history."

The first series of *Dad's Army* didn't set the world of television alight. It was only after the third series that the general public latched on to the show and Captain Mainwaring and his hapless platoon became the legendary comedy team that remain icons today. Between 1968 and 1977 some 80 episodes of *Dad's Army* were produced and today the series is still shown around the world and, particularly in Britain, a screening ensures large ratings. As a result of this success Jimmy wrote a show entitled *The Gnomes of Dulwich*. "Terry Scott and Hugh Lloyd were two gnomes who would sit by a pond and commented on life, race, religion - everything. It became a little cult." The series only ran to six epsiodes in 1969 and sadly the BBC wiped the master tapes some years ago so there are no examples available of Jimmy's earliest solo television writing. Jimmy was also responsible for scripting Wilton's – *The Handsomest Hall In Town*, a 1970 BBC variety special celebrating the famous London music hall which is still going today. Among the acts on the bill were Warren Mitchell, Spike Milligan, Ronnie Barker and Peter Sellers.

Searching for a follow up show to *Dad's Army*, Jimmy's mind was cast back to the time he was running the Royal Artillery Concert Party in Deolali. It was to form the basis of *It Ain't Half Hot Mum*. This remains Jimmy's favourite series of all the shows he has written. "I liked *It Ain't Half Hot Mum* because nobody had ever done a series set in the jungle and that is more based on truth than *Dad's Army*." The central character of Sergeant Major Williams was given to Welsh teacher-turned-actor Windsor Davies. Another piece of casting for devoted Indian servant Rangi Ram seems a bold move seen from a modern day viewpoint where political correctness prevails. Having a white man made up as an Indian still raises a few eyebrows. Jimmy again: "You must understand that in 1973 there were very few Asian actors about. David and I will take responsibility for bringing on so many Asian actors - Mohammed Shamsi, Rafiq Anwar - and we taught them because they hadn't had any tradition for acting. The point was we needed somebody who could play the lead in a situation comedy. I was over at ATV Studios around 1972 writing a series for Hugh Lloyd and Peggy Mount called *Lollipop Loves Mr. Mole*. One of the parts was played by Michael Bates. I heard him drop a word of pigeon Urdu during rehearsals. We started chatting in pigeon Urdu and it turned out his father had been the District Officer in Jhansi and Michael had been born in India. I straight away phoned David and told him we could now go ahead with *It Ain't Half Hot Mum* because I'd found somebody who could be Rangi Ram." With a top notch cast including Melvyn Hayes as the drag artist Gunner 'Gloria' Beaumont, George Layton as the producer figure Bombadier 'Solly' Solomons and diminutive Don Estelle as Gunner 'Lofty' Sugden, *It Ain't Half Hot Mum* topped the ratings until 1981 having delivered 56 episodes of song and dance in the jungle. Windsor Davies and Don Estelle even developed a cabaret act around their characters resulting in a number one chart topping UK single with '*Whispering Grass*'.

Not everything has enjoyed unqualified success. Two situation comedies written for ITV, *Room Service* (1979) set in the Prince Henry, a fictitious five star London hotel and *High Street Blues* (1989) - co-written with Robin Carr - set around four shops battling to save themselves from demolition to make way for a new hypermarket, failed to excite viewers. "They were terrible," admits Jimmy. "So bad even the cameramen walked out. People are kind and they often say 'Oh they couldn't have been as bad as all that.' *Believe me, they were as bad as all that.*"

Jimmy Perry, deep in thought on location at Dovercourt. A personal moment snapped by his writing partner, David Croft.

'The Society Entertainer' - Jimmy Perry

Some ideas have never even left the drawing board. "I wanted to do a show called *True Brits* but David Croft wasn't keen. We took the *It Ain't Half Hot* situation and turned the Indians into ancient Britons and the British Officers - to be played by Donald Hewlett and Michael Knowles - would be the Roman Governors. Paul Shane dressed in fur would be the local trouble maker, a terrorist leader. 'Roman's go home' and all that. Su Pollard was going to have square wooden glasses. The whole idea I thought could have worked. I also wrote a pilot with Rosemary Ann Sisson called *Women With Wings* about the women who delivered planes during the war." Jimmy's expert knowledge of the great music hall and variety tradition resulted in him writing and presenting several series of the nostalgia show *Turns* for the BBC, in which Jimmy would delve into the archives and show clips which had not seen the light of day for decades. He also wrote several programmes under the title *The Old Boy Network*, which once again looked at the careers of eminent actors and comedians.

Despite his success in television Jimmy has always had a special fondness for the theatre and indeed was instrumental in bringing *Dad's Army*, *It Ain't Half Hot Mum* and *Hi-de-Hi!* to the stage for successful productions in the West End and seaside summer seasons. His most ambitious theatrical venture was a stage musical about the cut-throat world of comedy and the variety theatre which he called *That's Showbiz*, 'The Lights, The Music & The Knife In The Back'. With music by Roy Moore, the show premiered at Wimbledon in 1997. It featured an all star cast which included Ted Rogers, Su Pollard, Carmen Silvera and Peter Baldwin. The desire to produce the show had gestated over twenty years. "The show became an obsession." Jimmy now reveals. "I got carried away totally with my own conceit and ego. But it was nearly there. It was originally called *Dirty Old Comics*. If I could have cut about half an hour off it and re-cast some of it, the show could have worked. Unfortunately I lost about £80,000."

Jimmy achieved a long held ambition in publishing his autobiography in 2002, *A Stupid Boy* dealt with his early life in the army, right up to the time he worked at Butlin's in the late 1940s.

Jimmy Perry and Mary Husband (Costume Designer) on location filming You Rang, M'Lord?

One of Jimmy's own favourite projects over the years has been his radio comedy *London Calling*, which ran for four episodes in 1994 as part of BBC Radio 2's *Comedy Week*. It was a fictional account of the birth of BBC Radio set in 1923. A stickler for period detail, Jimmy did a great amount of research into conditions at the Savoy Hill headquarters of the British Broadcasting Company prior to writing the scripts. Jimmy has some regrets about the idea being short lived as a programme. "That was the one that got away. *London Calling* could have been great if I had had some support. The BBC were going to do it [on television] but then in came Alan Yentob as Controller of BBC 1 and everything stopped. All the other misses in my career are the way of the world but London Calling could have worked." In the series Lord Reith who had masterminded those early pioneering days as the first Director-General of the BBC was replaced by a puritanical Scotsman named John Brown. Played with typical fierce gusto by Graham Crowden, his resistance to anything vaguely entertaining is the bane of the lives of his staff. The cast were hand picked by Jimmy for the roles he had created. He didn't have to look far for the role of General Manager Colonel Beecham for Jimmy himself played the part in his own inimitable style. Also on hand were Jeffrey Holland as Sound Technician Roger Eccles, Peter Cellier as Controller Admiral Carpenter, Amanda Bellamy and Logan Murray as 'Aunty Phyllis' and 'Uncle Rex' (with Jeff Holland below) - the presenters of '*Children's Hour*' who are engaged in a torrid secret affair - and Bill Pertwee as Sergeant Lucas. Into the fray arrives a new Announcer Jeffrey Stainton played by Christopher Luscombe. The grubby Comedian Ted Hicks who incurs the wrath of John Brown with his mucky jokes and songs is wonderfully portrayed by that other great authority on variety theatre, Roy Hudd. Jimmy describes the scenario as "The best idea I've had since *Dad's Army*." Sadly the 14 strong cast was too expensive for a regular radio series, Jimmy is adamant though that "recording *London Calling* was the happiest week of my life."

3 David Croft OBE

David Croft could almost be described as the Godfather of British Sitcom. He remains one of the most acclaimed writers and producers in the field. He can boast at least six classic sit-coms in a field where it is considered extremely lucky to gain a single entry. He has so dominated this field that the term 'Croftcom' was coined to describe his particular take on the genre.

Born in Poole on 7th September 1922, to popular variety stars Reginald Sharland and Anne Croft, it was perhaps inevitable that the young David Sharland would find a niche in showbusiness. His parents were West End stars between the wars and when aged nine David went on tour with them to Australia. Sadly it was around this time that the marriage failed, and whilst Anne and David headed back to Britain, Richard headed for America where he became a star of radio when he wrote and appeared in the successful series The Honorable Archie Chiselbury. David continued his theatrical education and by the age of sixteen he was negotiating percentages on behalf of his mother with theatre managers up and down the country! This young boy full of theatrical promise even found himself appearing as the butcher's boy in the classic 1938 film Goodbye Mr. Chips opposite Robert Donat.

The Second World War saw David acquire duties as an Air Raid Warden (an experience that was to come in very handy when penning a rather famous programme a few years later...) and subsequently in the Royal Artillery where he was posted to India and Malaya. David's obvious leadership qualities were recognised by the army and he at one point found himself accepting the surrender of a Japanese officer in Singapore. "There was this fellow called General Kinoshito" remembers David, "He claimed he hadn't surrendered his sword so we arranged he should come and surrender it to us. I think he wanted a big ceremony in point of fact, but I saw no reason why he should have one. The Japanese had behaved atrociously during the war. So we had him hand the sword over in our office. Through the translator who came with him, General Kinoshito told us all about how the sword was made. It was very valuable, about 800 years old. I was asked to stay on in the army and was offered two posts, one of which was on the War Crimes Commission. I was young though and wanted to do other things." The theatre beckoned back in Blighty.

As an actor David did several repertory seasons and a tour of The Belle Of New York in which David met his future wife Ann who was understudying the Leading Lady. Around this time he met the musician and composer Cyril Ornadel and together they wrote music and musicals which graced many theatres in the West End and further afield. Their biggest hit being the production of Ann Veronica which is still revived to this day. Under the watchful eye of his agent Richard Stone, David also found himself writing and producing the in-house shows for the Butlin's holiday empire. With one eye still on the fledgling ITV network, David found a position at Rediffusion Television (which became Thames TV) which in turn led him to Tyne-Tees Television which George and Alfred Black had been setting up running out of offices in Newcastle.

The first assignment for David in the north was Ned's Shed, a magazine programme extolling the virtues of the latest gardening and Do-It-Yourself apparatus. On more familar ground David produced a comedy series entitled Under New Management, set in a derelict northern pub with storylines provided by Johnny Speight. A move to the BBC (on a salary of £1,200 per annum) brought a relative failure to the Croft C.V. with the 1961 offering The Eggheads, a series based on students sharing a London flat. Not well received by the public, Croft was then assigned to look after Benny Hill who was working on a series for the BBC. David and Benny did not however hit it off and the partnership was short lived.

Following a brief time producing This Is Your Life, a major hit surfaced when David paired Terry Scott and Hugh Lloyd in the sit-com Hugh & I which ran for six years and some 70 episodes. With The Dick Emery Show under his belt, David went on to produce another successful

'The New Broom' - David Croft

comedy in the shape of *Beggar My Neighbour*, centered around two sisters who live next door to each other and enjoy a domestic rivalry. The show reunited Peter Jones and Reg Varney, from ITV's successful *The Rag Trade*, plus June Whitfield and Pat Coombs as the sibling rivals. The role of Reg Varney's common brother was played in one episode by an actor named Jimmy Perry, who brought with him the idea for a show based on the Home Guard which of course developed into *Dad's Army*. As a BBC staff producer David was assigned to look after episodes of two very familiar BBC comedies. "I wasn't long on *Steptoe & Son*, but it was fascinating." David remembers. "*Up Pompeii* I enjoyed doing enormously. It was quite a tedious thing to do because Frankie Howerd was a difficult person to work with. He was very slow and took a long time to get his performance together. Mind you, when the audience came in he was magic. Long before that I did a dozen shows with the great northern comedian Jimmy James at the BBC called *Don't Spare The Horses*. Rehearsal was a miraculous time, Jimmy was terribly funny. Unfortunately they tried to make him conform to television, and his comedy was so spontaneous. Also Jimmy wasn't particularly interested in which camera he was on. A comedian shouldn't be bothered with the technical stuff because it inhibits them. I think Jimmy Jewell and Ben Warriss were the same but they got a bit wiser. I wrote songs for Jewell & Warriss, they were wonderful workers and terribly funny in their heyday."

Whilst enjoying enormous success with *Dad's Army*, David also struck up a writing partnership with Jeremy Lloyd. Jeremy had recently returned from America where he had been one of a team of writers responsible for the long running *Rowan & Martin's Laugh In* show for the NBC network. Lloyd had an idea for a comedy set in a department store based on his own experiences working at Simpson's of Piccadilly. A pilot was commissioned and *Are You Being Served?* was born. The Lloyd-Croft

ARE YOU BEING SERVED? was devised as a vehicle for Trevor Bannister, who had at that time scored a huge success in the ITV sit-com *The Dustbinmen*. The original cast comprised of Mollie Sugden as the battleaxe of ladies' apparell Mrs. Slocombe, Wendy Richard - whom David had discovered as the cockney girl who interrupts Mike Sarne's hit single *Come Outside* - as her assistant Miss Brahms. Over in the Menswear Department Arthur Brough played Mr. Grainger, the long standing head of Gent's Outfitting. John Inman camped it up as Wilberforce Clayborne Humphries with Bannister as the cheeky Junior Mr. Lucas. The cast was completed by Frank Thornton as Floor Walker Captain Peacock, Nicholas Smith as Head of the department Mr. Rumbold, Larry Martyn as Mr. Mash, the sarcastic union rep from packing and Harold Bennett as 'Young' Mr. Grace. The first slice of life at Grace Brothers went out suddenly during a break in transmission from the Munich Olympics. It was the beginning of a run of 69 episodes that would give David Croft one of his biggest hits. Inman coined a catchphrase in "I'm Free" which would haunt his career to the very end, and Mrs. Slocombe's references to her pussy walked the tightrope of double entendre to maximum effect. In Australia, the Channel 10 network commissioned its own version in 1980 and flew out Inman to recreate Mr. Humphries with Australian actors being barely disguised tributes to the originals in 15 slices of life from Bones' Brothers of Sydney utilising scripts from the BBC series. Beanes Of Boston was an illfated attempt in 1979 to make the show for the American market with respected Amercian producer Garry Marshall overseeing production of a pilot. It isn't something that either David or Jeremy are particularly proud. After the original show ended in 1985 (with several cast changes following the death of Arthur Brough and the decision by Trevor Bannister not to carry on beyond the seventh season), it would be another seven years before viewers were to see them again. This time in *Grace & Favour* (or *Are You Being Served, Again?* as it is known in America). The premise being that following the death of Young Mr. Grace, the most loyal staff members find their company pension fund has been used to buy a country manor house, now in disrepair. They all decamp to the country in a bid to restore the property and run it as an hotel. With Mollie Sugden, John Inman, Wendy Richard, Frank Thornton and Nicholas Smith all recreating their roles it was indeed a chance to find out what had become of the telly favourites. Twelve episodes were produced in 1992 and 1993 but it is fair to say that despite some wonderful performances the magic of the Department Store was sadly lacking. *Are You Being Served?* continues to attract a new and eager audience through repeats and DVD releases and looks set to continue its popularity several decades after it first hit our screens.

'The New Broom' - David Croft

David Croft (right) with Jimmy Perry, Jeffrey Holland and Paul Shane filming the pilot show's opening sequence of their last collaboration You Rang, M'Lord?

partnership was just as prolific as that of Perry-Croft, and later turned out *Come Back Mrs. Noah* which saw Mollie Sugden launched into space set in the year 2050 and featuring a collection of Croft favourites: Ian Lavender, Donald Hewlett, Michael Knowles and Gorden Kaye. It was for Gorden Kaye that Jeremy and David penned *Oh Happy Band!* The premise of the programme was that a Brass Band in the small hamlet of Nettlebridge should lead the protests against the building of a new airport nearby. Sadly Kaye was not available to take on the role of the band leader so it was instead given to veteran comedian Harry Worth. *Like Come Back Mrs. Noah* before it, the programme lasted only six episodes. With two relative failures under their belt, amid the massive success of *Are You Being Served?*, Jeremy then came up with an idea set in occupied France during the Second World War, focusing on the Resistance Movement.

'Allo 'Allo went on to become one of the most popular British comedies ever worldwide. With outrageous plot lines and near-the-knuckle dialogue, audiences lapped up the zany antics of café proprietor René Artois. With David and both his major collaborators having come from the theatre, it was natural to take his successes to the stage. Three with Jimmy Perry and two with Jeremy

'ALLO 'ALLO - It seemed an unlikely prospect for a television comedy to tackle the often dangerous and horrific scenario of war torn France during the occupation by the Nazis. It would either be a soaring success or a disaster of epic proportions. Thankfully with the genius of David Croft and Jeremy Lloyd at the helm *'Allo 'Allo* proved to be the biggest international hit of their careers. Apeing the BBC's hard hitting drama serial *Secret Army*, we find ourselves in Café René where the owners - one René Artois and his wife Edith - unexpectedly find they are required to smuggle stranded British Airmen out of France. Gorden Kaye provides a masterful performance as René, not only having to cope with the attentions of the Germans and the resistance but also trying to keep his affairs with his waitresses Yvette Carte-Blanche (Vicki Michelle) and Maria (Francesca Gonshaw) from his faithful, but tone deaf wife Edith (Carmen Silvera). Into the fray come some extremely incompetent German Officers Colonel Von Strohm (Richard Marner) and Captain Hans Geering (Sam Kelly), the Gestapo in the form of Herr Flick (Richard Gibson) with his assistant Helga (Kim Hartman) whilst ageing forger Leclerc (Jack Haig) and Edith's senile mother (Rose Hill) add to the confusion as Michelle of the Resistance (Kirsten Cooke) appears unexpectedly to deliver the latest instructions to René. Later episodes see the love struck undertaker Monsieur Alfonse (Kenneth Connor), Crabtree a British Secret Agent who thinks he can speak French (Arthur Bostrom) and diminutive waitress Mimi La Bonque (Sue Hodge) added to the rosta of outrageous citizens. With 85 episodes produced it is indeed the longest running David Croft comedy of them all, although the writing honours would see the creators penning only 61 of the total tally. Without a doubt the most farcical of all Croft's successes it never the less provided the cast with a springboard of memorable moments which have endeared themselves to viewers around the globe. It's incredible ten year marathon from 1982 until 1992 yielded such nationally mimicked catchphrases as "You stupid woman!", "Good moaning", "Ohhhh Reennneeé" and perhaps most famously that of Michelle of the Resistance, "Listen very carefullee, I weeel say zis only wernce." The stage version enjoyed unparalleled popularity and is regularly revived by amateur societies wanting to inject a large dose of good old British sauce to their farce.

'The New Broom' - David Croft

Lloyd: *Are You Being Served?* was staged only once in the Winter Gardens, Blackpool featuring five of the television cast in the summer of 1976. "I tried desperately to put it on after that, but billing disagreements between the two major stars [John Inman and Mollie Sugden] meant that I was never able to get them together for another season." *'Allo 'Allo* proved much more enduring and profitable, with two sold out seasons at the Palladium, one at the Prince of Wales plus several national tours of the United Kingdom, Australia and New Zealand. "Every date it played was always capacity business by the Monday night. It seemed to happen at the right time and the public came in their droves. *Dad's Army* they thought would run forever at the Shaftesbury Theatre but when the kids went back to school the business fell away and we couldn't wait for three months for the next school holidays." Despite not being able to present a second season of the *Are You Being Served?* stage show, David and Jeremy did find a use for it using the same basic plot for the movie version which hit the cinema screens in 1977.

David rates his own favourite comics as Les Dawson, Tommy Cooper, Robb Wilton and Jimmy James. He has often been scathing of the BBC and the direction it has taken towards producing television comedy. In 1997 he told the fan magazine *Hello Campers* "I think it [television comedy] has been misdirected now for a number of years. There was a mad rush to do 'alternative comedy' but on the whole people don't want to be besieged by it. There should be a platform of regular comedy to which there can be an alternative. There is a wish to attract the younger element who frankly don't watch television. There is no reason for the BBC to want to attract that generation. They are an important market from a commercial point of view but the BBC is not in that race. So, by pursuing that route they are misguided. There is too a terrible lack of entrepreneurial skill. I don't think they could recognise a good proposition when they see it at the moment. I do see the situation improving at the BBC, it's getting better now and there are some fresh faces which give me a bit of hope."

When asked about the highlights of his working life, the answer might surprise some people. "I suppose with Jimmy, it would have to be when we put our shows into the theatre really. Jimmy, Jeremy and I all started in the theatre so it's very much our background. I used to write musicals and pantomimes so that background is very useful really. There are certain routines that are basic to comedy and they keep cropping up in different forms."

A big surprise to David was being caught by Michael Aspel for *This Is Your Life* in 1995. "I had no idea at all. I should have done thinking back. There were indicators. They fooled me completely. It's a shame you don't know it's coming because you could be more prepared for it. They did marvellously though, especially finding the old footage of Mum and Dad [performing their act in the theatre] which I didn't know existed. I would have bet a thousand pounds it didn't actually exist."

Above: David on location with Melvyn Hayes during *It Ain't Half Hot Mum*, but judging by their attire, it wasn't!

Left: David and Jimmy at the Cliff Hotel, Dovercourt for the 2007 Hi-de-Hi! reunion. The cast used to stay at the hotel during location filming and a plaque was unveiled in the hotel's lobby by the writers commemorating the connection.

'Only the Brave' - The Cast

4 You Have Been Watching...
The Cast

One of the great talents of Jimmy Perry and David Croft is to match the character they create on the written page with the perfect performer, to such an extent that it is very hard to think of any other actor playing the role. Imagine *Dad's Army* without Arthur Lowe, or *It Ain't Half Hot Mum* minus Windsor Davies. When Jimmy and David create a series they spend an unusual amount of time searching for the right actor, the right look, the right face. When they have got their actor, they start to tailor their scripts to the strength of the performer. So bit by bit the character and the actor merge to generate a unique comic creation. Sometimes the casting can be a piece of total serendipity: the original choice for Jeffrey Fairbrother couldn't be released from his theatre contract, hence the brilliance of Simon Cadell by default. Sometimes a sheer willingness to give a sure fire talent a big chance is the key. Su Pollard so amazed Jimmy and David during an informal chat that they knew they had a dynamo on their hands and set about creating the Chalet Maid we all know and love to tap into the energy and sparkle that emanates from Su.

Jimmy and David had worked the camps and based most of their Maplin's staff on real people. In casting Hi-de-Hi! they not only created a sit-com ensemble that worked together on screen brilliantly, they also created a new generation of their comedy repertory company. Most of the Maplin's gang were virtually unknown to the wider television audience when recording commenced on the show. Within twelve months they would all be topping bills in plays and pantomimes, an instant ascent into the realm of celebrity. It is a term that has now come to stand for the mediocre and self obsessed. Back then being a celebrity was something. To ascend to that level you had to prove yourself with talent. During 58 episodes the cast of Hi-de-Hi! whipped up a comedic storm interpreting Perry and Croft's brilliant scripts, carefully nurtured and guided by their gurus with the pen, to establish themselves as comic actors of the very finest pedigree.

David coined the term 'You Have Been Watching' to mark the television equivalent of the final walk down to the footlights in the theatre, a bow before the great British public. And watch they did in their many millions. So now we present the diverse and very special talents from those in front of the camera that bought the staff of Maplin's Holiday Camp to life. Each one from major character to supporting player left their indelible stamp on the programme and helped bring gales of laughter to homes throughout the land. Let's turn the spotlight in the Hawaiian Ballroom on the actors who brightened up our lives for eight glorious years. So if you got the blues, I got some news, join in the fun in your blue suede shoes....

'Only the Brave' - The Cast

Simon Cadell b1950 - d1996
Jeffrey Fairbrother

Jeffrey Fairbrother arrives at Maplin's having resigned from his position as Professor of Archaeology at Cambridge. His mother and the Dean of the University are aghast at his decision. With a failed marriage behind him, Fairbrother is looking at expanding his horizons in an attempt to rid himself of the stuffy academic environment and learn something of life in the outside world. The down market atmosphere of Maplin's initially comes as a great shock to him but Fairbrother is made of sterner stuff and despite being a fish-out-of-water for much of the time, strives always to do the job to the best of his ability and occasionally hopes to raise the cultural expectations of the campers in his charge. He relies heavily on Ted Bovis for guidance, and when Gladys Pugh sets her sights on him he can do no wrong as far as she is concerned.

Even in the over populated world of showbusiness, Simon Cadell was considered very special. A superb actor of theatre classics but more than that: a comedy performer with immaculate timing. He brought many of these qualities to Jeffrey Fairbrother, the hapless Entertainments Manager for the 1959 season at Maplin's Holiday Camp. 33 episodes were all it took to establish Simon Cadell as one of the most recognisable, and popular, faces on television. His Fairbrother was a master-class of timing and invention, and his character was by far the most important to the structure of the programme in the early days. Without a fully convincing portrayal of the ex-University Professor none of the inhabitants at Maplin's would work. They needed a solid wall from which to bounce their comic volleys and Simon not only rose to the occasion magnificently but also managed to bring such subtlety and depth to Fairbrother that it is difficult to imagine how the show survived without him at the helm.

Simon was born into a theatrical dynasty on 19th July 1950. His father John Cadell was a leading actors' agent and his mother Gillian, the Principal of the famous Guildhall School of Speech and Drama. Selina, Simon's sister, is a successful actress too following in the footsteps of their paternal grand-mother, Jean Cadell, the star of many West End plays and films. With such a rich heritage in his blood it probably didn't surprise Simon's parents that by the age of seventeen he had joined the National Youth Theatre and was appearing in the original production of Peter Terson's *Zigger Zagger*. Shortly afterwards he headed for one of Britain's most prestigious drama schools, the Bristol Old Vic where fellow students included Jeremy Irons, Tim Pigott-Smith and the director John Caird. His first tentative steps into a precarious profession were made with seasons in repertory. It wasn't long before Simon's obvious talent had found a place on the West End stage and by 1971 he was appearing opposite Sir Ralph Richardson and Dame Peggy Ashcroft in *Lloyd George Knew My Father*. In 1992 Simon was interviewed for the fan magazine 'Hello Campers!' during which he remembered his entry into Maplin's. "I am certainly classically trained," he offered. "I'd done bits on rather good and prestigious dramas on television - *The Glittering Prizes, Edward & Mrs. Simpson*, Simon Gray plays and things like that. I got my first bigger break in a series called *Enemy At The Door* about the German occupation of the Channel Islands in which I played SS Officer Reinicke, a really nasty piece of work. That ran for two years at London Weekend Television. They wanted to do a third series which would have prevented me being in Hi-de-Hi! but fortunately for me Michael Grade (who was running London Weekend Television) made a snap decision and said 'No, I don't want anymore.' I don't know why he said it and we were all rather upset at the time. However a week or two later I was called in to audition for Hi-de-Hi! and got it."

The cast of Hi-de-Hi! were an eclectic mix of performers with many of them coming from backgrounds that encompassed the variety theatre. "It was a side of the business that I'd never really come across before," Simon admitted. "I was the 'lardy' and they were all 'turns' as Paul Shane put it. People like Felix Bowness, who is a stand-up comic and a warm up man; Paul Shane, who is a genius stand-up comic; Barry Howard, who did summer shows and pantomimes and Su Pollard who is almost a law unto herself. So we were an odd

'Only the Brave' - The Cast

As SS Officer Reinicke from the LWT series *Enemy at the Door*. His next role would be as Jeffrey Fairbrother, the two characters were poles apart!

mixture of people but we very quickly worked very well together. The person who was perhaps most similar to me was the dear departed and much missed Leslie Dwyer. Leslie had spent his entire working life in every aspect of the business. Such a fascinating man to watch, he possessed an almost genius expertise because of his vast experience." The enormous recognition in the street was something that Simon embraced wholeheartedly. "It made a change from being hit when I was an SS Officer! I didn't mind it at all. In fact I get rather angry with actors who get poncey about being recognised. It's when you are not recognised in the street you want to start worrying because you are only useful to this profession when you are a sellable commodity." Simon stayed with the show for the first five series but was acutely aware of the typecasting trap that successful actors can fall into. Having completed two seasons in the Hi-de-Hi! stage show Simon headed for Birmingham where the role of Hamlet awaited him. He never returned to Maplin's Holiday Camp. The chance of playing the Dane Prince was an opportunity that Cadell seized and in the event the reviews were glowing. His stage career continued to blossom and his name went above the lights for a variety of work in the theatre as audiences flocked to see him in such productions as *The Musical Comedy Murders Of 1940*, Tom Stoppard's *Jumpers*, *Blithe Spirit* and a season at the actors' Mecca, the Royal National Theatre. He was reunited in 1990 with Su Pollard for the first time since he had left the confines of Maplin's in the hit stage farce *Don't Dress For Dinner*. Although he was never again able to find another television character to match the meteoric success of Jeffrey Fairbrother the medium had not deserted him. Simon's portrayal of the blundering Civil Servant Dundridge in Tom Sharpe's celebrated *Blott On The Landscape* brought many of the qualities of his Fairbrother back to the fore as he proved yet again he was the master of the introvert. Other high profile television roles included three series as Estate Agent Larry Wade in *Life Without George* and as flamboyant failed actor Dennis Duvall in *Singles*. A chance to play his hero, Noel Coward, led Simon to star in the West End production of *Noël & Gertie* opposite Patricia Hodge as Gertrude Lawrence. It was undoubtedly a highlight in his career. The young Cadell had encountered Coward in his early years through his father's connections and remained in awe of 'the master' all his life.

When asked whether he would appear in another high profile, Perry and Croft comedy if asked, Simon had this to say: "Yes, if the part was different enough from Jeffrey Fairbrother. I certainly would, without a doubt. I always choose work because of the quality of script not for the particular branch of acting it happens to be in. I hate to be put in a box as an actor so the quality is always the prime motive for doing a job." As for returning to the role of Jeffrey Fairbrother if the opportunity arose, Simon paused for a moment before saying, "No. I think that would be a backward step and not a forward move."

'Only the Brave' - The Cast

The Cadbury's Wispa campaign featured several Croft & Perry partnerships.

Simon's greatest achievement on the stage could be said to have been his final stage role, that of both Aunt Augusta and Henry Pulling in the West End adaptation of Graeme Greene's *Travels With My Aunt*. During the run he suffered a heart-attack and had to miss several months of performances following a triple coronary by-pass operation. His exquisite performance was eventually rewarded by an Olivier Award for Best Comedy Performance. Just as it looked as if the corner had been turned for Cadell there came the knockout blow. It was discovered that he was suffering from non-Hodgkin's lymphoma, a form of cancer the Doctors diagnosed was 'inoperable and terminal'. He immediately cancelled plans to star in a new ITV series *Downwardly Mobile* as Doctors gave him only a matter of months to live. Despite the odds and with the help of painful chemotherapy Simon continued to cheat the disease and lived as active a life as his condition allowed. Always a heavy smoker, he refused to be parted from his big cigars that had almost become his trademark to members of the profession.

In 1994 Simon Cadell returned to television as a corrupt property dealer opposite Dennis Waterman in the television movie *Circles of Deceit*. It was to be Simon's final acting appearance. In truth his final public appearance came in early December 1995 when the BBC chose to make his father-in-law, David Croft, the subject of a television *This Is Your Life* special. Simon Cadell passed away on 6th March 1996 aged just 45. Tributes immediately poured in from colleagues and friends as the nation mourned the loss of one of its most cherished entertainers. Perhaps Su Pollard summed up the mood when she said "The saddest thing is that he had 30 years of brilliant acting left in him and we've been cheated out of that." At a Memorial service held at St. James' Church, Piccadilly some months later Donald Sinden gave a sparkling reading of T.S. Eliot's *Gus, the Theatre Cat*, just one of many tributes offered by the cream of the profession. A strong contingent from Maplin's were on hand to offer their respects and Su Pollard sang *Look For The Silver Lining* from the Hi-de-Hi! stage show. Perhaps the most fitting tribute came in the form of a song by Simon's beloved Noël Coward performed by Patricia Hodge. "But I believe that since my life began / The most I've had is a talent to amuse / Hey ho, if love were all." For many admirers, Simon's talent and courage stretched way beyond a 'talent to amuse'.

Simon with co-author Rob Cope, being interviewed for the Croft & Perry Fanzine 'Hello Campers!'.

'Only the Brave' - The Cast

> We had decided to cast a National Theatre player in the part of Jeffrey Fairbrother in Hi-de-Hi! When it transpired that the National could not be sure that they were in a position to release the actor we had selected for the dates of the production we were therefore compelled to tell agents we were having to recast. Simon walked into the large, empty and unfriendly BBC rehearsal room to read for the part. We chose the first scene of the first episode of the first series for him to read. This was a dualogue between Jeffrey, who was a Professor of Archaeology, and his mother. She was berating him for making such a stupid change of career. Simon was a little bewildered when he realised that Jimmy Perry was reading the part of his mother. Simon later told me that, having met Jimmy for the first time, he felt sure that he was wearing two toned shoes. He looked at Jimmy's feet and assuredly he was. After about thirty seconds it was quite evident that Simon had the very essence of the part. He was the discontented if misguided academic who was determined to broaden his surroundings. From day one Simon set a new standard in character comedy playing. The level of everybody's performance in the series was lifted to new heights and everyone enjoyed the challenge. Personally, Simon and I struck up a firm friendship. Simon was a great companion and superb conversationalist. He loved good food. He loved fine wine. He loved good acting and he loved good writing. On location in the evening after the filming we explored every local restaurant together and I never tired of his company. He became a great friend of my family and in due course married my daughter Rebecca. They produced two fine sons - Patrick and Alec. Simon's career went from strength to strength until his heart attack, his by-pass operation and the later tragic discovery that he was suffering from an inoperable cancer. The fight he put up delayed the inevitable outcome but we will never forget the dignity and courage with which he faced his fate. When he died the country lost one of its great drama players. I and my family lost a great friend.

David Croft

33

'Only the Brave' - The Cast

Paul Shane b1940
Ted Bovis

Once one of the *Mississippi Minstrels*, Ted Bovis has been with Maplin's for 16 years when we first meet him (13 of them at the Crimpton-On-Sea camp) and he is more a part of the fittings than the Olympic sized pool itself. Ted has worked his way up to the position of Camp Host and prides himself that he has knows every aspect of what makes a successful comic. "The first rule of comedy is..." becomes Ted's catchphrase whenever he tries to pass on his knowledge to Spike or one of the other Yellowcoats. The thorn in Ted's side are Jeffrey Fairbrother and Gladys Pugh. They know of Ted's fiddles but frequently have trouble proving the scams, somehow Ted manages to stay one step ahead when it comes to fleecing the campers of their hard earned cash.

Actor Paul Shane once commented that 70% of him is Ted Bovis. The comparisons are easy to see. He was initially a miner when in 1967 an accident in the baths of Silverwood Colliery at the age of 27, caused him a back injury resulting in Paul having to rethink his future. As a part time Singer and Comedian on the tough northern club circuit he took a gamble and tried to make it a full time occupation. He never looked back. Born on 19th June 1940 in his native Rotherham, Paul (real name George Frederick Speight) started out singing for beer and cigarettes on a Saturday night at his local club. He counts himself as a Singer first and foremost, his act only started using elements of comedy further down the line. A love of performing led Paul to his first acting appearance in Alan Bennett's play *A Day Out* (muttering his immortal first lines, "My bum's numb!") This in turn led to roles in several BBC Play For Today productions directed by Stephen Frears. Having won a role in Brian Glover's play *Keep an Eye on Albert*, the author went to see Paul performing his cabaret act and was so impressed he persuaded the BBC to cast him as comedian Ricky Avon in *Summer Season*, a play he had been working on. Other work quickly followed including Alan Bennett's acclaimed *The Old Crowd* and several roles in the Godfather of British soaps, *Coronation Street*. It was a small appearance as a Grocer in an episode of 'The Street' that was spotted by Jimmy Perry when he and David were having major problems finding the right actor to play Ted Bovis. "I went to his [Jimmy's] flat and read for him, then he had me back a fortnight later because David Croft was away counting his money in Barbados," laughs Paul. "So, I went to the North Acton rehearsal rooms and had a go with Jeff Holland. I was one of the last to be cast. I actually turned the show down at first. The money was poor and I had a club act's brain. They were paying me per night in the clubs what I was going to get for the entire pilot so I turned it down. David Croft doubled the money. For years after that I was waking up in a cold sweat. I thought 'you fool' - what could have NOT been."

Such was the initial reaction to Paul's contribution to the series that within twelve months of the first batch of episodes going out he was the surprise subject of *This Is Your Life*. The sudden national interest in Paul Shane left him reeling. "They'd only known me in the north of England, I wasn't nationwide you see. I'd won 'Comic Of The North' for ten years on the trot. The reason I became known as a comedy actor is because of the all-powerful box, all of a sudden I'm known nationally. There's a hell of a difference I can tell you. Thank God I was 39 at the time. It made me realise how young kids who get to number one straight away can become big-headed. I could never understand it before but I can now. I couldn't go out of my front door in my own village. I didn't dare go down the market..." As well as taking the Hi-de-Hi! theme song to number 34 in the charts Paul was soon in demand for appearances in other major television shows. Paul was given his own series as Harry James, the boss of a talent agency, in *Very Big, Very Soon* for ITV and appeared as recurring characters in the medical soap *Holby City* as Stan Ashleigh and *Emmerdale* as Solomon Dingle. Paul also guested in *Frost* with David Jason. He was also cast as Mr. Bumble in the London Palladium production of *Oliver!* It is though, a string of appearances in David Croft productions, that have been his biggest successes. Aside from Ted there is the devious Butler, Alf Stokes in *You Rang, M'Lord?* and paranoid railway

'Only the Brave' - The Cast

Although the fictional Ted Bovis failed an audition for *Coronation Street*, Paul played Jeff Robert's boss from the Post Office, Frank Roper, in 1979.

Paul as Harry James, a theatrical agent in ITVs *Very Big Very Soon*. Unfortunately the series only ran for six episodes in 1991.

porter Jack Skinner in *Oh Doctor Beeching!* "David Croft always calls us his engine room - me, Su Pollard and Jeff Holland. He knows I won't let it go downhill. I'm the same with any show I appear in. I'm capable of that." Paul's favourite scenes would often be when Ted collided with Jeffrey Fairbrother in the Entertainments' Managers Office. "It was the West End versus the West Riding of Yorkshire. There was this comic there who was not an actor and there was a public school boy who was a wonderful actor and it worked. Simon was brilliant as Fairbrother. Ted would always talk his way out of the fiddles. Fairbrother could never catch him. Ted always wanted to run the camp but he never could. He'd have closed it within three weeks. There would have been thousands of pounds missing if Ted had got hold of it. He was capable of doing the job but not the administration. Ted would have had his hand in the tills. I loved Leslie Dwyer's character, a kid's entertainer who hates kids. Wonderful stuff. Jimmy and David both worked at Butlin's and there was a man at one of the camps exactly like that which is where the character comes from. Leslie had wonderful lines like 'My day is over when them little brats are in bed.'" When David suggested to Paul that they wanted him to play the butler in *You Rang, M'Lord?* Paul was very unsure. "I remember saying to them at rehearsals 'Are you sure you've got the right guy for this? Me? A Butler?' David said 'Paul I know what I'm doing. Get on the set' I didn't feel comfortable at all with that role whilst we were rehearsing but when we got into it I loved it. A great role. He wasn't a very nice man Alf Stokes."

At heart Paul is a family man. You won't find him at showbusiness parties or attending theatre first nights. When he is not working he can be found back in the South Yorkshire village where he has lived for many years. He can be found appearing in pantomimes and performing his stand up comedy routine around the country.

'Only the Brave' - The Cast

Ruth Madoc b1943
Gladys Pugh

Gladys Pugh is affectionately known as the 'Vamp from the Valleys'. She has been with Maplin's for many years and worked herself up from the bottom rung to the exalted position of Chief Yellowcoat. She takes her job very seriously and takes great pride in her position, keeping the Yellowcoats in her charge on their toes. She also has an eye for a good looking man and when Jeffrey Fairbrother arrives at the camp she immediately falls in love with him - a devotion that is not returned by Fairbrother. She falls for Squadron Leader Clive Dempster and by the end of the series has married him. When her authority is questioned Gladys has been known to reveal a bitchy streak which she usually reserves for Sylvia, who bates Gladys whenever she can.

Hi-de-Hi! turned jobbing actress Ruth Madoc into a star overnight. The commonly held conception is that Ruth is about as Welsh as it is possible to be, but in fact the reality is somewhat different. Ruth explains: "I was born in Norwich [16th April 1943], my mother was a Matron at the General Hospital there. It was during the war and my mum couldn't get home [to Wales]. My mother was very much a career woman which was unusual really for somebody in the 1940s. I was brought up very much in a matriachal family, full of strong women. It was just natural to assume that every woman had a career, a vocation or whatever. This again was unusual because mums usually stayed at home. If you wanted to go into a profession you had to be very academic. I wasn't like that. My mum especially guided me into acting. I can't say that she forced me because she didn't. When I was 11 years old we were living in East Yorkshire where I went to a Youth Club. Here, a youth leader and I sent a Grundig tape to [Sir] Harry Secombe which I wanted him to pass on to a man called Huw Wheldon who used to front a programme called All Your Own.

Harry didn't send it to Huw Wheldon, instead Harry's agent got hold of it and the next thing I know I was being summoned down to his agent's office. Frank Barnard, who was Harry's agent for 30 years or so until he passed away, guided me and by the age of sixteen I'd won a scholarship to the Royal Academy of Dramatic Art." Before attending Drama School Ruth had gained valuable experience working as an Assistant Stage Manager at Nottingham Rep which would be good theatrical experience for a career that beckoned. At RADA Ruth was surrounded by other students who would go on to become household names such as Roy Marsden, Ian McShane, John Alderton and Lynda La Plante. Whilst still studying Ruth was snapped up for a role in the West End production of Playboy Of The Western World opposite Siobhan McKenna. Upon graduating, Ruth found herself appearing twice daily in the famous Black & White Minstrel Show at the Victoria Palace and shortly thereafter was engaged to play Principal Boy in pantomime at the Palace Theatre in Watford by Jimmy and Gilda Perry. She appeared in four pantomimes at Watford for the Perrys. Little did Ruth realise at the time but Jimmy was going to be a major player in her career a few years later. Ruth married the actor Philip Madoc and although the marriage didn't last they have two children together Lowri and Rhys.

Despite having a young family to support Ruth continued to get prestigious roles such as Frumah Sarah in the film version of Fiddler on the Roof opposite Topol and in the West End productions of Man of La Mancha and Robert & Elizabeth. "I remember David Croft coming down to see the last pantomime I did at Watford." Ruth recalls. "My 'Gladys Pugh' persona used to manifest itself itself at 3.30 in the morning when, during a technical run that invariably was dragging on and on, I was trying to keep the very tired cast amused. Jimmy left [Watford] and almost straight away he got Dad's Army off the ground. Whilst they were doing that show they were thinking of other things and decided that they wanted to do a show with a jungle theme which was of course It Ain't Half Hot Mum. They thought originally of Philip for the role of BSM Williams. Jimmy rang up asking Philip to go and read for this part. During the conversation Philip asked Jimmy if he really thought he was a Sergeant-Major type and Jimmy just said "Well,

'Only the Brave' - The Cast

Above: Ruth with Philip Madoc.
Right: As Miss Hannigan in the stage version of *Annie*.
Below: 'The Vamp of the Valleys' in action.

you are the only Welsh man we know who can act it." Philip and I had worked with Windsor Davies a lot on *Under Milk Wood* so he suggested him and funnily enough Jimmy already had him down among his list of possibles for the part. The rest is history of course because Windsor got it and went on to become a big star." Due to the success of the Welsh Sergeant-Major Perry and Croft immediately thought of having another Welsh character in Hi-de-Hi! Gladys Pugh was born.

Ruth became a much imitated person as the success of the show spread throughout the nation. It was through an appearance in Leicester during the broadcast of the first series that brought home to Ruth just what an impact the series was having. "I was to give a cheque that the *Elvis Presley Fan Club* of Great Britain had collected for the Blind Association. It was a substantial amount, £12,000 or thereabouts. I went along and met this bloke who had worked with Elvis and he looked at me and said 'Who are you?' I'm an actress I told him and informed him what I was there for. 'Are you nationally known?' he asked and I told him I didn't think so and I really didn't know why they had picked me to go and do it. The organisers wanted to know how to announce me and I suggested they said to the audience 'We've got somebody here who I think you might know, listen to this voice' and I would do a 'Hi-de-Hi!' as Gladys over the microphone to

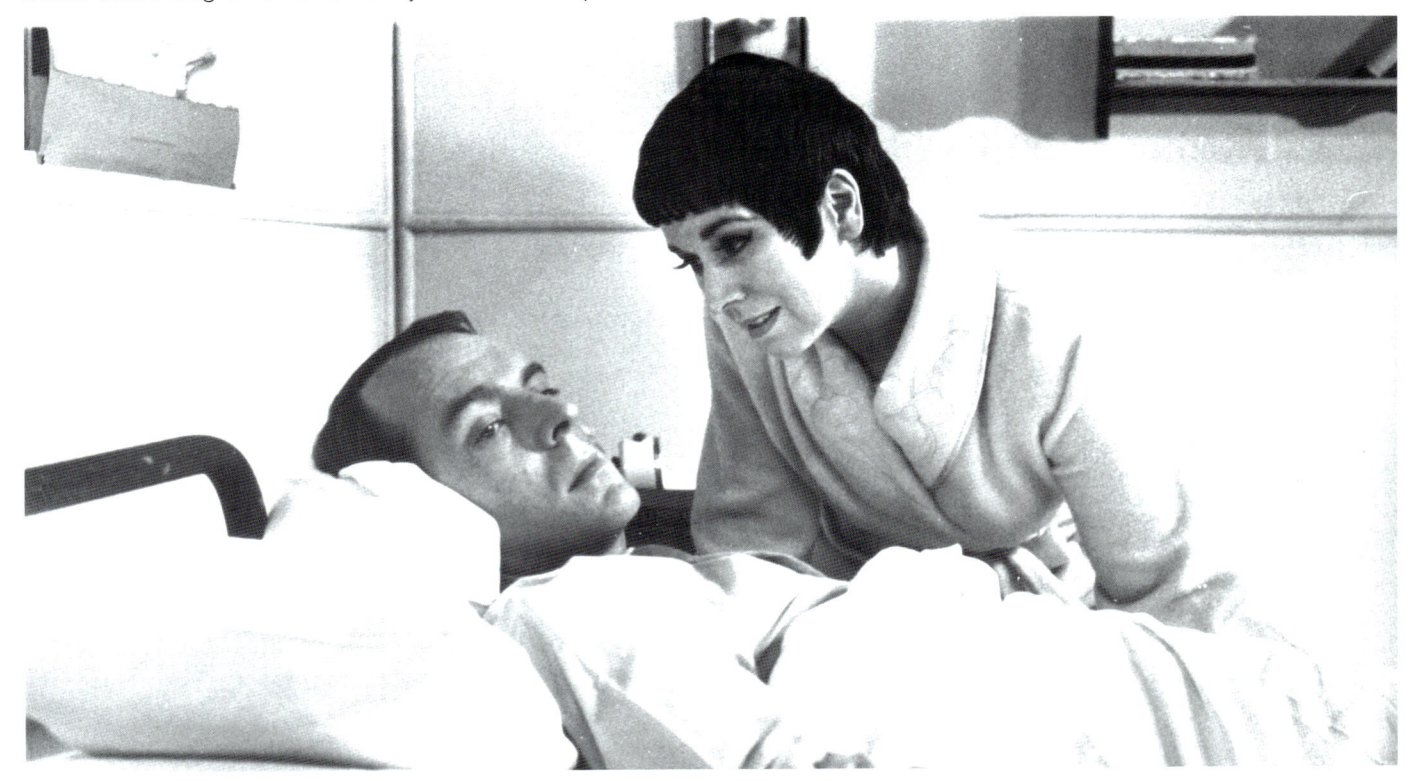

'Only the Brave' - The Cast

see what sort of response we get. So we did this and the place just ERUPTED. It was the very first time I realised what sort of impact the show was having. They all stood up and this packed hall of about 2,000 people gave me such an ovation. They asked all sorts of questions wanting to know about the show. We did a question and answer session for about half an hour." Through her success as Gladys, Ruth was chosen as the subject of a *This Is Your Life* television tribute and was constantly in demand for television and theatre appearances.

In the early 1980's Ruth married former soldier John Jackson, who is now her manager. Since then she has continued to wow theatre audiences in productions such as *Gypsy, 42nd Street*, Mrs. Bardell in the musical *Pickwick*, Miss Hannigan in *Annie* and Meg in a theatre tour of *Last of the Summer Wine*. Despite all manner of successes following Hi-de-Hi! - including the television series *Jack of Hearts, Mine All Mine, Big Top* and as Dyffed's all knowing mother in *Little Britain* - Ruth looks back with affection at the role which made her a household name. "I get very sentimental about things and I suppose that if they had said in 1987 that we could carry on doing it then we'd all still be there now. I miss the cast very much. I still keep in touch with Su a lot and my husband and I see Paul Shane because he was Best Man at our wedding. It's getting back together at the start of each series that I miss terribly."

Ruth Madoc's official website: www.ruthmadoc.co.uk

Ruth and her husband/Manager John Jackson with Barbara Windsor.

In the stage version of *Last of the Summer Wine* 2009 as Meg. Seen here with John Pennington as Foggy.

Ruth as Dorothy Brook in the musical, *42nd Street*, based on the 1933 film of the same name..

'Only the Brave' - The Cast

Jeffrey Holland b1946
Spike Dixon

Spike Dixon arrives at Maplin's having given up his job in the Tax Office to pursue his dream of becoming a star. Inspired by the meteoric success of young Tommy Steele, Spike has similar aspirations and turns to his mentor Ted Bovis in an attempt at learning comedy from the bottom rung upwards. At the same time, he is highly disapproving of Ted's attempts to fiddle the campers with outrageous schemes and whilst openly obstructive in these plans he always backs Ted up when the going gets tough. When Yellowcoat April Wingate arrives Spike falls in love with her - although he makes it clear that showbusiness comes first and plans to marry and settle down a firm second. Spike's many and varied costume characters are a mainstay of events around the pool and when Ted shouts to the campers "What shall we do with him?" He knows the inevitable response "Chuck him in the pool" will result in yet another dunking.

By the time Perry and Croft were casting Hi-de-Hi!, Jeffrey Holland was already a stalwart of many of their shows. Jeff was born Jeffrey Michael Parkes in Walsall on 17th July 1946. "I came from a Catholic background, so my upbringing was quite strict," he recalled some years ago. His father died when he was fourteen. "It was a terrible time. He had a heart attack. I still remember being taken out of class by the Headmaster and being told my father had died." To help his mother he took a job in a wine shop, "I would still be in the business if a mate hadn't introduced me to amateur dramatics. It was then that I learned I could make people laugh and what a great feeling it was."

Sometime later Jeff found himself enrolled in a Birmingham drama school, and his talent for mimicry has led to voice work on Spitting Image among many other shows. Jeff had already got extensive theatrical experience under his belt with repertory seasons at the Belgrade Theatre, Coventry to his credit. In fact it was due to his desire to stay on for further plays during a season at Chichester that he nearly didn't encounter Perry and Croft at all. Jeff explains: "It was almost like a stroke of luck that changed my life. An audition I didn't want to go to. It was in 1975 and I was doing the Chichester Festival season and my then agent rang me up and asked if I'd do an audition for the Dad's Army stage show for director Roger Redfarn. I was particularly brassed off at the time because I was having to leave the season at Chichester having only been booked for the first two plays of the season. I was in a foul mood on the day of the audition. I didn't want to go up to town to do it. So I didn't prepare anything because I knew that Roger Redfarn and the Choreographer knew me and that would get me through the first part. All I had to do was meet David and Jimmy and get their seal of approval. It was at the Mermaid Theatre. I had a look through the script and found a version of the old song Yes, We Have No Bananas which was done by Private Walker in the show. Sure enough I was asked to sing a song and also read a couple of scenes with the Company Manager and me playing the parts of Pike, Walker and a mad German scientist who was part of the show. So, I asked the pianist if he knew the song and he did. So I sang this version of Yes, We Have No Bananas with the script in my hand. Everyone just fell about laughing which was partly at my performance, I like to think, and also the fact that they hadn't actually heard their words being performed before. As a consequence I was booked for the show." It was the start of a long and prosperous association with Jimmy Perry and David Croft.

Following the West End season - when he had been part of the ensemble playing various characters in the show - Jeff was in for a pleasant shock before the nationwide tour began. "I was at home one morning when the phone rang. It was Jimmy Perry to ask if I would be prepared to take the part of Walker on the tour. I was flabbergasted but none the less delighted. As it turned out John Bardon who had been playing the role (James Beck having died a couple of years before) didn't want to commit to a six month tour as he had other fish to fry, so as I was the understudy anyway, it would make sense for me to do it. I felt I was too young really (only 29 at the

'Only the Brave' - The Cast

time) but no-one thought that would matter so I agreed. I'll never forget that first night as Walker as long as I live. The wonderful moment, when after the patriotic opening montage, the scene parted to reveal Captain Mainwaring and his men in a triumphant tableau which always got a round of applause - and this night I was part of it. I nearly cried with pride."

As a consequence Jeff was asked to appear in a small part during the *Wake Up Walmington* episode of the *Dad's Army* television series. The connection with Perry and Croft didn't stop there. Holland was drafted into *It Ain't Half Hot Mum* for a couple of memorable appearances. In *Flight To Jawani* he was a Solider stationed in a far corner of India who had not seen civilisation for some time, and had eventually gone a bit doolally. When he spies 'Gloria' Beaumont, who has dragged up for a number in the show, there is a riot. The following year, in *The Superstar*, Aircraftsman Ormanroyd arrives at the camp to audition and it turns out he is a far better performer than most of the Royal Artillery Concert Party's current line up. A couple of roles as a customer in Grace Brothers for David Croft's other popular sit-com of the 1970s, *Are You Being Served?*, gives him quite a pedigree of appearances in Croftcoms.

The role of Spike Dixon turned Jeff into a star overnight. For many years Jeff was a stooge to Russ Abbot in his television series, the most notable being *Russ Abbot's Madhouse* on ITV. As a complete contrast to his comedic work there have been a trilogy of appearances for BBC 2s Shakespeare season (*Richard III, As You Like It, Henry V*) giving some idea of the immense versatility of the actor. Jeff is now happily married to his second wife, actress Judy Buxton. Of course Jeff went on to appear in two more David Croft productions following the end of *Hi-de-Hi!*'s phenomenal television run, namely *You Rang, M'Lord?* and *Oh Doctor Beeching!* where he played station master Cecil Parkin. He also found himself providing the voice of Technician Roger Eccles in Jimmy Perry's radio series *London Calling*. Jeff was invited by Spike Milligan to play the part of Peter Sellers in a 50th anniversary *Goon Show* recording, *Goon Again*, which Jeff - a major Goon fan - cites as being the best night he has ever had in a theatre and one of the highlights of his career. Jeff has continued to use his talent mainly in theatre since working on all the projects for Perry and Croft, his roles have included *Travels with my Aunt*, the Alan Ayckbourn / Andrew Lloyd Webber musical *By Jeeves*, *It Runs in the Family* with Su Pollard. In a bold move Jeff took on the role of René Artois in a stage tour

Russ Abbot's Madhouse. Jeffrey (right) was a regular on this very popular Saturday evening show.

Jeff Holland and Paul Shane as the immortal Laurel and Hardy. Jeff is proud to be a member of the pairs' active appreciation society *Sons Of the Desert*.

In Panto with a nervous looking Windsor Davies

'Only the Brave' - The Cast

With James Bolam in As You Like It.

Jeff in one of the many amazing costumes created for the programme. This one is, of course, Bertie Bassett..

of another of David Croft's hits *'Allo 'Allo* to rave reviews, with his wife Judy playing opposite him as Michelle of the Resistance. "It was the one hit David Croft show I had never appeared in." Jeff says. " When the television series was in production I was busy with Hi-de-Hi! and then *You Rang, M'Lord?* So the time never seemed quite right. I feel as though I have completed the set now." Jeff has been a regular in pantomime for nearly forty years, and his Dame is considered one of the best in the business. For all this activity in various branches of showbusiness, it is as Spike Dixon that he will forever be associated.

Jeffrey Holland's official website: www.jeffreyholland.co.uk

Jeff as René with his wife Judy Buxton as Yvette during the popular 2009 touring version of 'Allo 'Allo

Jeff played Teddy Deakin in a National touring version of Arnold Ridley's classic thriller Ghost Train in 2007.

41

'Only the Brave' - The Cast

Su Pollard b1949
Peggy Ollerenshaw

Peggy Ollerenshaw is one of Maplin's army of Chalet Maids. Being assigned to work the staff chalet lines is an ideal position for Peggy as her one ambition in life is to reach the dizzy heights of becoming a Maplin's Yellowcoat. With an innocent outlook on the world Peggy will do almost anything to be given her big chance. She is the first to volunteer if the Entertainments Manager needs anybody to be one of a myriad of costume characters on display around the camp. The bell and make shift bicycle horn that adorn her trolley can be heard around the camp from the early hours until it's time for Peggy to go and watch the fun in the Hawaiian Ballroom. Although Gladys frequently berates her for getting involved in the entertainments, there is really a strong bond between the two of them.

She's been called 'dotty', 'potty', 'zany', 'over the top', 'eccentric' and a million other descriptive words which try to pin down Su Pollard's unique personality. The truth is she is a total original. Often dressed in bright flamboyant clothes, with large multi-coloured glasses and a voice that can be heard from miles hence, Su Pollard has rightly become a British institution. Her continuing success is mostly down to Su's big break, her portrayal of the loveable Chalet Maid Peggy Ollerenshaw.

Nottingham born Susan Georgina Pollard arrived on 7th November 1949 and she has barely drawn breath since according to her friends and colleagues. A taste for amateur dramatics quickly manifested itself with Su joining the Co-Operative Arts Theatre in the city, proving herself a fine actress in everything from *Lorca* to Shakespeare. Whilst working as a Secretary in the day Su developed a cabaret act as a Singer and Comedienne on the working men's club circuit around the county. Her powerful voice became a firm favourite and her repertoire was diverse ("I'll now sing the *Nun's Chorus* - if I'm not too knackered!" became a familiar cry from Su). Having gambled on a move to London, Su secured a role opposite John Hanson in tours of *The Desert Song* and *Rose Marie*. There were a few lean times too. "Once in a café I only had enough money for baked beans on toast. The bloke opposite me was having a pork chop, chips and peas. He looked at his watch and went out leaving his pork chop. I couldn't resist it. Without anyone seeing I leaned over and forked it off the plate and ate it. To my horror I saw him coming back - he'd only gone out to check if his car was all right!" It was clear that this lady had a big future on stage and wasted little time in continuing to delight theatre audiences in *Grease* (co-starring with a young Tracey Ullman) and Sir Cameron Mackintosh's West End production of *Godspell*. Su had made her television debut sometime before on Hughie Green's highly rated talent show *Opportunity Knocks* but was beaten into second place by a singing Jack Russell dog appearing with his owner who sang along. Su was of course dignified in defeat. "The Cameraman said the dog was only howling because the man had his finger up the dog's bum," she was heard to tell interviewers many years later.

A more earnest entry into television came with a 1979 BBC sit-com alongside Paul Nicholas. The premise of *Two Up, Two Down* was that Jimmy and Flo - Nicholas and Pollard - are two hippies squatting in the house of a staid, middle class couple. It wasn't a big hit lasting only six episodes but it provided some solid television grounding before the soon to be heard Maplin's tannoy would echo over Su's illustrious career. Su's agent at the time, Richard Stone, also represented Perry and Croft and was able to persuade the authors to see the startling actress with a view to using her in their upcoming comedy about a holiday camp. "I duly took myself up the 369 steps to Jimmy's penthouse. When I got there he opened the door and said 'No, we don't want any pegs thank you!' because I had a long hippy coat on, I must have looked like a Yak. I thought it wasn't a very salubrious start, but we started chatting about the usual stuff. Things I'd done etc. At the end Jimmy and David thanked me and said they'd be letting me know one way or the other. I didn't hear anything for about a year by which time I reckoned they'd got somebody else for the

'Only the Brave' - The Cast

1974 Television debut - *Opportunity Knocks!* But the viewers voted for a singing dog instead.

With Paul Nicholas in the 1979 BBC sitcom *Two Up, Two Down*.

job. But as I have since come to learn about them they take a lot of time casting. During that year that's what they were doing, seeing the world and his wife for the various roles.

The next thing was Richard Stone 'phoned me saying that they'd like to offer me the role of the Chalet Maid. It was only a small part but if I wanted a go at it they promised that Jimmy and David would look after me and make sure I got a decent ride if it went to a series. Of course I decided to give it a whirl and the rest is history." The first read through was quite nerve racking for Su and all the other cast members. "On the first day of rehearsal I got there really early because the Central Line is notorious for getting stuck in the tunnel at White City. I was there at 9.30 and about 10.25 I wandered off to find the rehearsal room. As I walked in David took one look at me and said 'Good God, you haven't walked off the street dressed like that have you?' Simon Cadell was marvellous. He said, 'Darling, I can tell we are going to be great mates' and had a big fat cigar in his mouth. I was a nervous wreck at the read through. I slow down a lot now but then I read it like a bat out of hell. Afterwards you get talking and you realise that you are all in the same boat."

Su has gone on to become a much loved entertainer, starring in *You Rang, M'Lord?* and *Oh Doctor Beeching!* for David Croft in addition to appearing as a guest star in inumerable television shows. In the mid 1980s Su had a hit single *Starting Together* which climbed to number 2 in the pop charts and a big selling album. Theatre audiences have been treated to her talent starring in a wide array of musicals including Miss Hannigan in *Annie*, Audrey in *Little Shop of Horrors*, the pirate maid Ruth in *The Pirates of Penzance*, the international hit *Menopause The Musical* and to rave reviews in the West End for the

As Ivy Teasdale in *You Rang M'Lord?* With Paul Shane as Alf Stokes.

'Only the Brave' - The Cast

1960s nostalgia musical *Shout!* She also created the role of Suzette in the original West End production of *Don't Dress For Dinner*, a crazy psychic in the comedy *A Happy Medium* and made her Shakespearian debut as the Nurse in *Romeo & Juliet*.

Su's appearance in the cult comedy *Gimme Gimme Gimme* as singing teacher Heidi Honeycomb ("Heidi - hi!" says Kathy Burke in the show) ensured that the trendy young generation also paid homage to her legend. Su's marriage to Australian Peter Keogh ended in divorce and she's now happily single, indulging in what she calls "a varied social life." Does she have a favourite episode as Peggy? "I was very proud of the scene where I didn't get my Yellowcoat. [*Peggy's Big Chance*]. If it elicits a response like 'ah, poor thing' at least you've hopefully brought across the reality to people. There was another one in a Christmas special where I had to 'Obligon' the campers and put them to sleep [*The Great Cat Robbery*] and I was running around with my balaclava on my head stuck up like a peanut. I love doing slapstick comedy. I really really enjoyed *Tell It To The Marines* as well where I had to pretend to be a man and go over an army assault course. There were other memorable times too. Scenes with Ruth Madoc where she was sewing her wedding dress and Gladys would have a heart-to-heart with Peggy. There have been some wonderful moments."

Su Pollard's official website: www.supollard.co.uk

Su has played a variety of roles since her time on *Hi-de-Hi!*
Above: Ruth in *The Pirates of Penzance*
Middle left: In the 2009 stage play *Shout!*
Bottom: As Ethel Schumann in *Oh Doctor Beeching!*

'Only the Brave' - The Cast

David Griffin b1943
Squadron Leader Clive Dempster DFC

Squadron Leader Clive Dempster DFC arrives as the 1960 season at Maplin's is about to commence. Clive comes from a privileged background - his full title is the Honourable Clive Dempster - but at heart he is a playboy who shirks responsibility and is not above conning those around him if he sees it as a way of having a good time. Upon his arrival at Maplin's he asks to be shown to his office "I'm in charge of something or other" he tells Peggy. Gladys despairs at his lack of interest in running the entertainments programme yet feels attracted to the man who she openly realises is something of a cad. Clive has the taste for champagne and a pretty girl but when he is railroaded into an engagement with Gladys he schemes to get out of it. Eventually though he does genuinely fall for the charms of the Chief Yellowcoat and they marry in the penultimate episode of the series.

David Griffin was very much a jobbing actor when he was picked by Perry and Croft to replace Simon Cadell as the Entertainments Manager at Maplin's. Born on 19th July 1943 in Richmond, Surrey, David hailed from a family of musicians. Rather than following in the footsteps of his family David decided at the age of 14 that he wanted to become an actor. His entry into the profession was as an assistant to an ice-skating chimpanzee act! Training in earnest took place at the Italia Conti Stage School and at the tender age of 16 made his first television appearance in a live episode of the Police drama *Dixon of Dock Green*. A career followed in repertory as well as appearances in many television programmes including Michael Palin's *Ripping Yarns, Maybury, Emmerdale Farm, Nicholas Nickelby* and *Stalag Luft 211B* in addition to appearing with screen legend Joan Crawford in the movie *Trog*, opposite Peter Cushing in *The Blood Beast Terror* and as a Captain in the cult musical *Privates on Parade* to name but a few of the big screen appearances he has to his credit.

As an often struggling actor David was grateful for the opportunity of playing Clive Dempster as he explains: "I was working on a building site, being out of work at the time. When I got home that evening my wife said I had a call from my agent. I didn't want to go at first to see David and Jimmy because a) it meant taking a day off work and the train fare from Sussex to London, neither of which we could afford, b) I had nothing to wear and c) I never believed I would get a job as big as that. Of course I ended up going. My wife dusted off my one and only suit and off I went. Oddly enough I was the last person they saw and although I didn't know it at the time they had already made up their mind until I walked in. How lucky was that? Reluctant as I was to wear a suit to the interview, David and Jimmy told me later that they were impressed that I made the effort when so many actors think jeans will do. A lesson learned. As David Croft succinctly put it 'The difference between the Drama Department and the Light Entertainment Department is that we in Light Entertainment dress better!'" Overnight David became a celebrity as Clive strove to come to terms with the staff of Maplin's and indeed two years later David along with Paul Shane and Ruth Madoc, appeared in the stage farce *Hi-De-Hi Spirits*

He was though very careful to avoid being typecast as an upper crust cad in the wake of the massive exposure he was getting in the show. "[*Hi-De-Hi Spirits*] was a 'romp' more than a play. Good fun at the time but I wouldn't have wanted to repeat it. I was grateful after that to be offered many stage roles that were in complete contrast to Clive and that gave me the opportunity to stretch myself as an actor and not rely on Clive for the rest of my career. I was aware - and Jimmy impressed this on me - that Hi-de-Hi! wouldn't last forever and I must progress in other areas if I was to survive in this business. Too many actors rely on the 'gravy train' (as Jimmy put it) and forget that one day the train will come to a halt. So to be able to do plays by the likes of J.B. Priestley, Willy Russell etc. could only do me good." The desire not to be typecast paid off when in 1991 David was offered the role of Emmet for the second series of Roy Clarke's *Keeping Up Appearances*, a series he stayed with for several years

'Only the Brave' - The Cast

With Josephine Tewson in Keeping Up Appearances.

and one with which he is universally identified. "How lucky I have been," David declares "To be associated with two of the most successful series in television history. *Keeping Up Appearances* was a wonderful break. And what a difference between the two roles. Emmet could not have been a bigger contrast to Clive. A complete opposite. So, that helped me break away and create someone new. I loved every moment of *Keeping Up Appearances* (as I did with Hi-de-Hi!) and as a cast we got on so well. It was hugely successful and is still repeated on the BBC and sold to over 45 countries world wide. Patricia Routledge was just wonderful to work with and has a great sense of humour. Referring to how I started in the profession, Pat said to me recently 'Well, David, nothing has changed - you are still skating on thin ice with a load of monkeys!' Not so far from the truth."

David continues to appear in stage productions all over the UK ranging from farce, thrillers, pantomime and comedies. But he will be forever remembered to millions all over the globe as Clive or Emmet. "I have been very lucky in my career and I am aware of it," David reflects "I have worked with some wonderful people on both series and am fortunate to count them as friends as well as fellow actors. We still meet up occasionally and some I have had the pleasure to work with since then. Su Pollard remains one of my closest friends as does Josephine Tewson and Judy Cornwall. But, if I think back? It all started 25 years ago with the amazing David Croft and Jimmy Perry. Love and thanks to them both."

Playing Attenborough in Ripping Yarns.

David revelling in the role of the evil Captain Hook in pantomime 2008.

46

'Only the Brave' - The Cast

Leslie Dwyer b1906 - d1986
Mr Partridge

Mr. Partridge is Maplin's Punch and Judy children's entertainer. After topping the bills in variety theatre as "Wizard Willy, the Juggling Joker" and entertaining the troops during the war with ENSA, the old man's career is on the decline. With a heavy drink problem and intolerance of people - children especially - he is not the ideal employee at the camp. Mr. Partridge sums up his feelings about the camp when he is asked to give a speech during the unveiling of a statue of the Maplin's founder. There can be no mistaking the venom when he says "...and in conclusion I just want to say - Joe Maplin, you're a right one!"

There was a world of difference between the on and off screen personae of Leslie Dwyer. As Partridge he was a pain in the backside to everyone around him but in real life Leslie was a kind and genial man who liked nothing more than making people laugh. A genuine Cockney, he arrived to theatrical parentage in Catford on 28th August 1906. His mother was a straight actress and his father the singing Comedian Johnny Dwyer. As a small child his parents would have him appear in skits on the variety stage and his proud claim was that he appeared with such legendary figures as Marie Lloyd (a friend of his mother's) and Harry Champion. He was sent to the stage school run by star maker Italia Conti.

An early boost to the young Dwyer career came when J.M. Barrie personally chose him to play a wolf in the London production of Barrie's now classic tale of pirates and lost boys, *Peter Pan*. By the age of 20 he was to be found stage managing pantomimes and a mere two years later found chance to prove his dramatic skills in earnest for the first time in Somerset Maughan's *The Letter* playing an oriental with the unlikely sounding name of Ong Chi Seng! It was the beginning of a career which would eventually encompass countless stage productions. In 1937 Leslie was touring in a show called *The Amazing Dr. Clitterhouse* when the author sent for him and said to Leslie that he was creating a part especially for him in his new West End play *The Man in Half Moon Street*. Leslie was seldom out of work thereafter. Having started in silent movies as a child, Leslie can be seen in over 100 films including such cinematic classics as *In Which We Serve* (he was cast by Noël Coward personally) and *The Way Ahead* opposite David Niven. Television beckoned strongly for the Dwyer talent too where he turned up in *Coronation Street* as the father of the girl who was marrying Elsie Tanner's son. He could be also be seen in *Steptoe & Son* playing, rather unsurprisingly, a rag and bone man and opposite Jon Pertwee in a *Doctor Who* adventure as an intergalatic showman. Just three of a wealth of small screen appearances that would also see his face gracing such well remembered shows as *Z Cars, Dixon Of Dock Green, Terry And June, George And Mildred* and *Angels*. For three years he voiced a character in the popular radio drama *Waggoner's Walk*. Although Leslie never appeared in the Hi-de-Hi! stage musical, he did join his Maplin's colleagues - Paul Shane, Jeffrey Holland, Ruth Madoc and Barry Howard – as Friar Tuck in *Babes in the Wood* at Birmingham for the 1981/82 pantomime season.

For all his vast experience in many media it will be for his role as Mr. Partridge that he is most fondly remembered. Leslie and his actress wife Thelma lived in Truro, Cornwall. They met when they appeared on stage together. "I was 33 and had been a dreadful philanderer," Leslie told the press. "I can't tell you the number of women I had affairs with. Then I met Thelma and proposed to her within a week. We started living together almost immediately - quite a thing in 1939 - and were married six weeks later. We only had one rule - faithfulness. We both knew that if either of us strayed that would be it. And neither of us ever has. We have a very alive marriage. We're always cuddling and telling each other we love each other. But don't imagine we don't have rows. Sometimes the whole house shakes. We both believe that a happy marriage is the result of a lot of hard work on both sides. Thelma and I believe we were just lucky to meet each other. Bloody lucky."

In January 1984 a local paper in Cornwall ran an

'Only the Brave' - The Cast

interview with him. Of course the main topic of conversation was Hi-de-Hi! "We did the pilot first," Leslie recalled, "During which everything went wrong and I thought I wouldn't do the series. But it sort of took off and we've never looked back. None of us ever thought the series would catch on but it's now in it's fourth year. I suppose it's popular because it's such a good laugh. And the characters are well drawn."

On the subject of his continuing association with the show Leslie told reporter Jenny Burnett: "Hi-de-Hi! will be at the Winter Gardens, Blackpool - Thelma and I played there with Jack Buchanan in the 40s - this Summer, but I'm not going to be in it. There will be a new series in September, which they want me to do. But I'm not sure whether I want to carry on, there has to be a time when you call it a day." Giving a hint that he might be on the verge of quitting the role that had finally made him a star, Leslie did indeed appear in the location filming for the fifth series the following September. Sadly, his declining health meant that he was not well enough to take part in the arduous studio recordings that followed. Leslie passed away on 29th December 1986, aged 80. Colleagues and fans alike mourned the passing of the veteran entertainer. Ironically it was children themselves who took to Mr. Partridge so readily. "Mr. Partridge is supposed to hate kids, but in fact I love them. Thelma and I have never had children of our own but I get lots of fan mail from young viewers. They seem to warm to me."

A small selection of Leslie's work. Top: *The Hour of 13* (1952).
Middle: Wartime drama in *The Way Ahead* (1944)
Above: R F Delderfield's *Peace Comes to Peckham* (1948)
Left: With Jon Pertwee and Cheryl Hall in *Doctor Who* (1973).

'Only the Brave' - The Cast

> In the early Sixties I did a farce, on tour, called Off The Rails. The play was written by John Waterhouse for the famous comedian Jimmy James. At the last minute Jimmy James bowed out and Leslie Dwyer, at very short notice, took over. The play was very topical at the time - it was all about Doctor Beeching closing his railway stations. Leslie played the Station Master of a little rural station. I played his only Porter. We struggled around the country not doing particularly good business but always with the carrot of a West End run spurring us on. Alas, like so many before, the play bit the dust at the Golders Green Hippodrome. My one very strange story about Leslie happened when we were sharing digs at Stockton (Incidentally during that week we had a matinee performance planned but come the time the audience consisted of one lady. Our Director, Frank Dunlop, went on stage and asked the lady if she would like to see the play or prefer a cup of tea with the cast. She settled for a cup of tea. Leslie said 'She's not a bad judge!'). One night in the digs Leslie said, 'Would you like me to tell your fortune?' Of course I said 'Please' and whether he used cards, tea leaves or what I can't remember now. The one thing I do remember him saying was 'Write these letters down.' I did and kept the scrap of paper for years. The letters were: N.S.M.P.M.W.O.L. He said 'These letters will come to mean something in your career.' I tried all sorts of ways of deciphering the word - song titles, play titles. No good until I got my television break with the satirical revue Not So Much a Programme More a Way Of Life. As I said the play folded and I never met Leslie again but I did have a nice letter from him when I congratulated him on his perfect Mr. Partridge.

Roy Hudd OBE

> Leslie once stayed with me for eight weeks when we were filming because he wasn't too well. I used to go straight from rehearsals to do a television warm-up so my wife Mavis would pick Leslie up from the station. They'd have their evening meal after which Leslie would have a nap until I arrived home at about 11 o'clock and then we'd sit up until 1am joking and laughing. The next morning we'd get the train to the studios and Leslie would get on and shout loudly "Hi-de-Hi!" and all the people in the carriage would yell back "Ho-de-Ho!" We would laugh all day long. He was lovely man. David Croft would say to everyone, "We're going to rehearse Leslie and Felix's scene now, would everyone not directly involved please leave because you know what they are both like. They'll start blasted laughing and we'll never get the scene done !" Once everyone was out of the way we'd do it fine. We'd then go and have a couple of glasses of wine with our lunch and sit in my Volvo having a kip. Roy Gould - the Production Manager - once came tapping on the door saying we'd have to do our scene again as something technical had gone wrong. We did it three parts to the wind thanks to the wine. I used to think we'd get the sack for laughing so much.

Felix Bowness

In Panto as Fryer Tuck, showing an old billing for the Grand Theatre, Leeds, with Leslie as top billing.

'Only the Brave' - The Cast

Felix Bowness b1922 d2009
Fred Quilly

Fred Quilly is Maplin's Riding Instructor, put in charge of the ageing horses and donkeys by Joe Maplin. In truth Quilly is a former jockey who had his licence revoked in a scandal over pulling a horse during a race. Fred is convinced that one day he will be granted his licence back and looks after the Maplin's horses and donkeys like children. His particular favourite is Flight with whom he has a special relationship. Fred shares a chalet with Mr. Partridge who complains that he "stinks of horses". It is revealed in one episode that Fred was once an instrument mechanic in the RAF and his skills are called upon to alter the mechanism of one of the displays in the ballroom. Always willing to help, Fred remains a backbone of the entertainments staff throughout the series.

It is a dream role for actor and comedian Felix Bowness who had a long had a major interest in the racing game, and in fact the role was written especially for him. He was also known as the king of the audience warm-up (or studio host as the more modern term has it). Felix has 'warmed up' over 5,000 studio audiences including all of the Perry-Croft shows at the BBC.

Felix was born in a six centuries old thatched cottage in the Oxfordshire village of Harwell on 30th March 1922. His uncle kept riding stables which cemented Felix's lifelong love of horses. For a time he was an apprentice Shop-Fitter for Elliots of Caversham. In 1941 Felix was called up to serve in the Royal Berkshire Regiment during the Second World War and became involved in the D-Day landings. Following demob, Felix found a flair for boxing which he took up at amateur level and which resulted in him becoming the ABA Flyweight Boxing Champion for London and the Southern Counties. A talent for comedy and singing emerged as Felix took his first small steps into show business. Having won a talent competition he was asked to do an early spot on the weekly variety bills at his local theatre, the Palace in Reading. "One week Vera Lynn was topping the bill," he recalls, "I used to finish my act of jokes and impersonations with a song in my own voice so to speak. She used to come to the side of the stage and whisper 'Felix darling, you've got a lovely voice why don't you make a record?' I said to her 'I like to make people laugh really' but she was insistent that I concentrate on singing and said that if I went up to her house in Finchley she'd give me some lessons." Sure enough Felix made regular trips to see the Forces Sweetheart in order to improve his vocal technique. As a result of being spotted doing his cabaret the Producer of Gert & Daisy's Working Party booked him to appear on his top-rated radio show starring the legendary Elsie and Doris Waters and their brother Jack Warner, later of Dixon of Dock Green fame. It wouldn't be long though before Felix would progress to television where he played some supporting roles to popular comedians. It was one such show with Benny Hill which was responsible for his career as television's most brilliant warm-up man. "I was booked to do a bit of acting on a show and Benny Hill said, 'I'm in costume now, could you go out and have a bit of a chat with the studio audience?' Then the following week he told me he wanted me to do it for the rest of the run for an additional fee. Then Eric Sykes' Producer and David Croft started asking me to do their warm-ups.

Gradually I was doing so many that they were taking over from the acting roles. One week I did fourteen, flitting between Family Fortunes and Porridge." In addition to his studio warm-ups Felix has appeared in many comedies including the role of Wally Threadgold in The Growing Pains Of PC Penrose, Gay Gordon in Porridge, two episodes of Are You Being Served? and as Sir Jimmy Saville's butler in Jim'll Fix It. It was whilst appearing in cameos during Dad's Army that Felix got himself a reputation as being obsessed with horse racing. "I'm always talking about racing. When we were on location for Dad's Army I'd say 'I've got a good horse today' and Clive Dunn or whoever would say 'Put a pound on for me Felix.' So about four years before it actually happened David Croft said he was working on a pilot about a holiday camp in which they were thinking of having a riding instructor who was also a jockey. He told

'Only the Brave' - The Cast

Felix often appeared in front of audiences he 'warmed up'. Here he confronts Captian Peacock (Frank Thornton) in Are You Being Served?

me 'You are always on about blasted racing so we're going to give you the part!' So I took up my riding again to prepare myself but it turned out they had stunt men to do the riding in case I fell off. It was all to do with money. If I'd have come off and hurt myself it would have cost a packet to re-write the scripts and change the filming schedule. I didn't believe the pilot would ever happen but of course it did. There was a good chemistry between us all, they all helped me learn my lines and I used to keep everyone amused between takes." When Felix was caught by ITV for a *This is Your Life* tribute it came as a big surprise. "I was booked to do four warm-ups for them [*This is Your Life*] and on the fourth one it turned out to be me. The BBC had given me permission before hand because we were rehearsing Hi-de-Hi! at the time, and it meant I had to go early. Everyone on the programme knew except me.

On the night rehearsals were running late and I was panicking. When I got there the producer at Thames TV said 'Where have you been... You should be on.' So I

Doing what he did best, talking to the audience before a television recording.

Resting between scenes as Mr Pearson, the Grocer on the set of You Rang, M'Lord?, with his newspaper turned to the sporting section.

51

'Only the Brave' - The Cast

dashed straight on and I was told to introduce Eamonn Andrews from the side of the stage which I thought was bit odd because usually he wandered through the audience at the start of the show. We both wandered down into the audience doing a bit of banter and a lady sat with the red book on her lap with the name covered by sticky tape. Eamonn asked me to pull it off and it said 'This Is Your Life - Felix Bowness'. I thought it was a joke but the next thing I knew I saw a mass of colour coming towards me. Paul Shane with all the Yellowcoats. That's when I realised it was me." A bogus cabaret booking was the decoy for the late night party plans after the recording. "My agent had told me I would be doing a late night cabaret that evening, setting me up. What he didn't know was that on the previous night I'd gone down to the hotel at Heathrow on a dummy run to see the venue. When I got there all the waitresses recognised me and were saying "Hi-de-hi!" I told them I would be doing cabaret the following night and they said 'Are you?' Not seeming to know anything about it. It was the Entertainment Manager's night off, if he had been there that night he would have told me there was no booking and I would have become suspicious. It could so easily have gone wrong." Among the stars paying tribute to Felix on that glittering night included Elsie Waters, Ken Dodd, Ernie Wise, Mollie Sugden and Wendy Richard.

Following his appearances as Fred Quilly, Felix went on to appear as Mr. Pearson the Grocer in several episodes of *You Rang, M'Lord?* and relief guard Bernie Bleasdale in *Oh Doctor Beeching!* in addition to being Bert the Buglar for most of the television run of Noel's House Party. In the years before his death in September 2009, Felix made the occasional appearance on television and was in much demand as an after-dinner speaker.

As Fred Quily in the 'Drown your Granny' Competition.

A very early publicity shot of a very young Felix

'Only the Brave' - The Cast

Diane Holland b1930 - d2009
Yvonne Stuart-Hargreaves

As her husband is keen to point out during the Best Yellowcoat Competition 1959, Yvonne Stuart-Hargreaves was born in 1914 and hails from Southport. Yvonne frequently despairs at the coarse nature of both her fellow Maplin's staff, Ted in particular, and the campers with whom she is forced to mix. We learn that she had a fling with an Hungarian acrobat from the Magyar Trio which left her pregnant. It was then that Barry proposed to her and they became a husband and wife dance partnership. Yvonne's relationship with Barry is prickly to say the least, referring to him on one occasion as "prune face" whilst he during one heated exchange calls her a "frosty faced old cow". However, in public they are a united force. Their supercilious manner, and acid asides, making them a very stand-offish couple. During the course of the series we meet Julian Dalrymple-Sykes, a former amour whom Yvonne met when she was an Auxiliary Nurse during the war. When Barry leaves her, it is Julian who races to be at Yvonne's side and steps in to trip the light fantastic nightly in the Hawaiian Ballroom.

Diane Holland was born June Diane Neeltje on 28th February 1930 in Melbourne, Australia. Partly Dutch (from which her stage name originated) her father had been gassed in the Battle of the Somme during the Second World War and consequently was hampered by ill health throughout the rest of his life. Finding a talent for dance as a young girl, Diane trained for the professional stage at the Cone-Ripman, later to become the Arts Educational, School. "I was primarily a dance student focussing on ballet, modern and tap." Diane recalled in 2004. "However I disliked the tap dancing and replaced it in my curriculum with the drama class. It was frowned upon by the Principal of the school and when I wanted to appear in the drama showcase at the end of the year I was forbidden to do so. I was a dancer and that was that." It was though a grounding in two disciplines that would prove advantageous throughout Diane's career. She worked her way to becoming Principal Dancer in many shows including Palladium seasons with the likes of Evelyn Laye, Arthur Askey, Beryl Reid, Max Bygraves, Danny La Rue and Tommy Trinder. "I once made the dreadful mistake of ad-libbing to Tommy Trinder. I thought I was being funny but he ran rings around me in front of everyone with his fantastic wit and one liners. A lesson learned." As a member of the 'Page Hatton Trio' accompanied by two male dancers, Diane performed for three seasons in Monte Carlo and other prestigious cabaret centres. Theatre has included repertory all over the country and plays such as a Blackpool season of *My Perfect Husband* with Thora Hird and Freddie Frinton, *Her Excellency* with Cicely Courtnidge, the European premiere of *Ballad Of The Sad Café* and Edna O'Brien's *A Pagan Place* at the Royal Court Theatre. One of her most memorable stage roles was with Eric Sykes and Jimmy Edwards in their legendary production of *Big Bad Mouse*. "I walked into the audition and Jimmy said to me 'You're tall aren't you?' as the actress leaving was quite a small, rotund woman. I took this to mean that I wasn't suitable, apologised for wasting their time and went to leave. They decided to audition me anyway and I read it for them and began miming a few of the stage directions. Suddenly Eric Sykes started directing me saying 'When you do it on stage you will have to do so-and-so'. I got the part and it was an amazing experience working with them. They were so generous to me as an actress." Diane was among performers who appeared in early BBC live broadcasts from Alexandra Palace. "If you were in two scenes in a show, you would be expected to run down the corridor after the first sometimes changing costumes en route and into the next studio in time for the following scene. If you didn't make it they would just carry on without you because it was all live." She appeared in Morecambe and Wise's 1954 ill fated debut television series *Running Wild*. "The critics really lambasted them. We were supposed to do six but they cancelled the show after the first three. Morecambe and Wise really had the stuffing knocked out of them and they lost a lot of confidence. A bit ahead of its time really." Film work has included *Lilacs in The Spring* with Anna Neagle, *The Sands of the Desert* with Charlie Drake and *Tommy*

'Only the Brave' - The Cast

A selection of Diane's other television work illustrated on this page. Above: ITV's Tales of the Unexpected (with Joss Ackland). Middle: Some Mothers Do 'Ave 'Em. Bottom: Crossroads.

The Toreador with Tommy Steele. In 1966 Diane won the role of Sarah Maynard in ITV's cult soap *Crossroads*, then at a peak in popularity, which she played "on and off" for 3 years. Other pre-Hi-de-Hi! television work encompasses *Emergency Ward 10, Sykes, Clochemerle, Tales of The Unexpected* and *Some Mothers Do 'Ave 'Em*. It was through her brother-in-law, Jimmy Perry, that she came to audition as Yvonne Stuart-Hargreaves for David Croft. "At the audition I read through the script for the lines and rather cheekily asked if it was worth reading having seen how few lines Yvonne had been given. Then I said 'I've discovered another line!' which David Croft found quite funny and it got me the part of Yvonne." Diane had in fact worked with Barry Howard before in a theatre tour of *Salad Days* in the 1960s and the pair were reunited on screen many years later as Yvonne and Barry, Maplin's champion ballroom dancers. "There was a great chemistry between Barry Howard and myself which made our scenes work so well. We were a haven of respectability in the middle of all the chaos going on around the camp. Yvonne and Barry were always being very nasty to each other but the minute anybody else in the camp was disrespectful to them they would leap to the other's defence." One episode that sticks in Diane's mind is *Carnival Time*. "That was the episode where the burning wagon had to be pushed into the swimming pool. I was wearing a leotard on that day and the water was absolutely freezing. One of the Yellowcoats was hit by the shaft as the wagon plunged into the pool and Simon Cadell dived in to save him. The filming was stopped whilst they got him out but we had to stay in the water until they were ready to carry on. My teeth were chattering I was so cold and my wig had started to slip from my head. I always dread seeing that episode as the memories of the discomfort come flooding back." The newspapers reported that she had in fact become a pin-up of the British forces serving at that time in the Falklands but Diane dismissed this image of a 'forces sweetheart' as fiction. "I did get a handful of requests from serving Soldiers but I think the BBC press office made it into far more than it was. They were always looking for a good story." Yvonne was later to be pared with Ben Aris as Julian Dalrymple-Sykes, "A delightful actor and very generous" she summed up. There were however slight reservations about her character development. "Yvonne's character seemed to change. In my mind I had her background and how she would behave in given situations. But you are in the writers' hands and they made her completely different to what I had decided she must be. I started to think 'Hang on, this is not what Yvonne started out like.' But they are not really interested in an actor's opinion so you just have to play what is written." Following Hi-de-Hi! Diane Holland continued to act in series such as *Grace & Favour, The Upper Hand, Lace II, Bergerac* and *Casualty* where she played Wendy Atkinson, a Surgeon's Wife who finds out she is terminally ill. Diane's dancing career was revived at Covent Garden as the maiden aunt in Peter Wright's successful production of *The Nutcracker* which was also televised. Diane lived in Godstone, Surrey and continued to work occasionally up until her death of bronchial pneumonia on 24th January 2009, aged 78.

'Only the Brave' - The Cast

One of Diane's last appearances was as Surgeon's wife Wendy Atkinson in *Casualty*.

Diane worked for David Croft again, appearing as Celia Littlewood in the *Are You Being Served?* spin off, *Grace and Favour*.

55

'Only the Brave' - The Cast

Barry Howard b1937
Barry Stuart-Hargreaves

Barry Stuart-Hargreaves' real name is Bert Pratt, so he is forced to use his wife's family surname for professional purposes. A fact Yvonne never stops reminding him of. She criticises his looks, the way he walks, how he holds his cutlery and mocks the fact that his father was a Bus Inspector. He bares this with good grace, mostly. Like Yvonne, Barry detests being forced to take part in the low brow entertainments laid on by Joe Maplin. His nadir comes when he is forced to be Percy The Pixie in the playlet *Tuffet Tantrums* when the camp finds itself without a Children's Entertainer. Barry's cutting one liners are a constant around the staff room and in the Stuart-Hargreaves' chintzy chalet. When he hurts his back and Yvonne's old flame Julian Dalrymple-Sykes arrives to temporarily replace him, he knows that he will only ever be a poor substitute as both a husband and dancer for Yvonne. Mid-way through the 1960 season, Barry ups and leaves Yvonne, presumably exhausted at her constant snipes and criticisms.

Barry Howard was born in Nottingham on 9th July 1937. Having served in the Navy during his National Service, Barry found himself wanting to train for the theatre at the renowned Birmingham Theatre School based at the Old Rep in the city. He couldn't get a grant from his local council so took a backstage job at the Alexandra Theatre for 21 months to fund himself through drama school. Upon leaving he quickly became known as an expert in the field of pantomime, and together with his stage partner John Inman were referred to as 'the best dressed Ugly Sisters in showbusiness.'

Barry also specialised in character comedy and among his Summer season credits are playing Arthur Askey's son in *What A Racket* in Bournemouth, Hylda Baker's boyfriend in the stage version of *Nearest & Dearest* in Blackpool, three seasons as Freddie Frinton's next door neighbour in *His Favourite Family* and several stage comedies with *Carry On* legends Kenneth Connor, Bernard Bresslaw, Charles Hawtrey and Terry Scott. Add to that appearances as Sir Andrew Aguecheek in *Twelfth Night* in the West End, Mr. Sowerberry in *Oliver!* and Herr Schultz in the musical *Cabaret* to name just a few more stage productions he has graced and you begin to get the idea of just what a vastly experienced stage performer Barry had become before Maplin's entered the equation. He had in fact started out working for Butlins at the beginning of his career. "My first job after leaving drama school was at a Butlins camp. When I arrived I saw men putting plastic blossom on the trees. I told Jimmy and David about it but they said the viewers wouldn't believe it." It was a theatre role that had secured Barry the role of Stuart-Hargreaves. "I'd been led to believe that I had been seen 17 years before Hi-de-Hi! started. I was on tour with a musical called *Salad Days* for a year and one of the tour dates was at the Golders Green Hippodrome, a wonderful building where they sadly don't do touring shows anymore. Unbeknown to me and John Inman, who was also in the show, David Croft came to see it. He liked what we did playing two Policemen and apparently promised himself that he would one day give us both something to do in his television series. John beat me to it with *Are You Being Served?* and a few years later it was my turn in Hi-de-Hi! It was just that it took 17 years."

Following the recording of the pilot Barry, and the entire cast, waited with bated breath to see how it would be received. Barry was donning his traditional Dame's frock in Swansea during pantomime when the pilot was broadcast for the first time.. "I got a phone call from Ruth Madoc telling me they [the BBC] were going to show the pilot on New Year's Day [1980] and to watch it to see what the reaction was. So on the night in question I started to watch the programme as I thought and because I was in Wales it wasn't Hi-de-Hi! at all on BBC Cymru it was a poetry reading in Welsh! So I missed my opening night. I wasn't best pleased. Luckily a friend had videotaped it and I got to see it sometime later. I HATED what I did in it because I don't like seeing myself on screen." It was though Barry's wonderful outraged facial expressions which were the mainstay of many a

'Only the Brave' - The Cast

Top left: Barry with Mitchell Ray in the 2006 production of *Open Casket*.
Bottom left: A scene from *Terry & June* with Terry Scott.

belly laugh during his stint in the show. His rapport with Diane Holland on camera was instantly recognisable. "She [Diane] was wonderful. So good that she made it easy for me. She's a splendid actress and a lovely woman. Diane acted Yvonne so well that is became instinctive to give her one of those looks. It also saved, Jimmy and David admitted, thinking of endings for our scenes because they would write in the script *'Barry gives Yvonne a look. Fade Out'* It saved having to think of a punch line for our scenes." Barry has his own theory on the success of the characters. "The whole programme is about a bunch of losers. If Ted had been a good comic he wouldn't have been at Maplin's and likewise with Yvonne and Barry. If they had been good dancers they would have been working in a better place. That was the secret of the show. We were all third rate people pretending to be at the London Palladium."

Barry left the show after 46 episodes but he looks back fondly on his time with the programme and has a couple of favourite episodes. "One featured a canoe race. I had a grass skirt on and a bone through my nose. It was freezing. It was filmed at 8 o'clock in the morning on the East Coast and it was not warm I can tell you. Getting drenched, having to re-take for close-ups...

We spent days in and on the water for that one [*The Great Cat Robbery*]. We were wrapped in sheepskin coats and heaters blowing our legs warm. So that is a favourite and also the other special where Yvonne and I have to try and lift a ladder [*Eruptions*] with lines like 'If I had the strength of a labourer I'd dance like one.' And the exchange about the wife looking her best in black in the most ridiculous circumstances." In 2007 Barry hit the headlines when it was discovered that an unexploded incendiary device from the Second World War had been found when workers at his home in Poole, Dorset, had removed a chimney breast. Post Maplin's, Barry's career has continued to blossom landing the lead in an ITV situation comedy *The House of Windsor* and regular stints playing the narrator in *The Rocky Horror Show*, appearing as Jacob Marley opposite Anthony Newley and Tommy Steele in tours of *Scrooge The Musical*, with Russ Abbot in *Lord Arthur Savile's Crime* and reuniting with Paul Shane in Ray Cooney's *Out Of Order*. Although retired from the gruelling twice daily pantomime circuit, Barry continues to appear in plays and musicals. Barry made a high profile return to television in David Tennant's swansong as Doctor Who and in Jonathan Harvey's cult series *Beautiful People*.

57

'Only the Brave' - The Cast

Right: As Count Zarkoff in the *You Rang M'Lord?* episode *Royal Flush*
Middle Right: As Jacob Marley in the 2005 production of *Scrooge* with Tommy Steele in the title role.
Below: In the 2008 tour of the popular farce *Run for your Wife*, with Mark Wingett, Melvyn Hayes, David Callister, Paul Henry, Michelle Morris and Tiffany Graves.
Bottom: Barry and John Inman were two of the most successful ugly sister acts in the business. This rare photograph shows them in all their finery.

Nikki Kelly b1951
Sylvia Garnsey

Sylvia Garnsey is the only Yellowcoat to appear in all 58 episodes. Good looking with flowing blonde hair and impossibly long legs, she is a very popular figure among the campers. She is not so popular with Gladys Pugh who sees Sylvia as a threat to her authority. Unlike the chief Yellowcoat, Sylvia personifies cool and is a frequent visitor to London's trendy nightspots. She walks around the camp with her hands in her pockets and heads turn - particularly the young men holidaying at Maplin's. Gladys sabotages Sylvia's attempt at taking over as the voice of Radio Maplin but she still manages to pip Gladys to the post to be voted Most Popular Girl Yellowcoat 1959. Sylvia is not above flirting with Jeffrey Fairbrother and later his successor Clive Dempster - this brings out a war of bitchy words between Sylvia and the lovelorn Welsh maneater.

Nikki Kelly comes from a family steeped in theatrical heritage. Nikki's great uncle, Sir Johnston Forbes-Robertson, opened the Royal Academy of Dramatic Art with Sir George Bernard Shaw and Sir Herbert Beerbohm Tree in 1904. Born on 23rd November 1951 in Leamington Spa, it was as a teenager that Nikki got the theatrical bug. "When I was sixteen I started working as an Usherette at the Chichester Festival Theatre. During that season there were productions of *Peer Gynt* starring Roy Dotrice and *The Cherry Orchard* starring Dorothy Tutin. Being able to watch the shows every night was rivetting: the power, the fear, the fun. There was simply nothing else I wanted to do except ride horses and I couldn't make money from that." Attending the Rose Bruford drama school wasn't all that Nikki was expecting. "It took me a while to get into it. Everyone else seemed to be so completely dedicated and driven. I found it slightly embarrassing. My parents really tried to talk me out of it. I tended to stand back when people were being an orange and un-peeling in the drama lessons. I questioned the validity of it a bit." Regarding herself as something of a rebel - "I was expelled from three boarding schools" - all her life,

Nikki's first television role found her in trouble with the actor's union, Equity. "In those days it was really hard to get an Equity card. I got this role in an episode of *Dixon of Dock Green*, directed by Vere Lorrimer. It was back then a rule that before you were allowed into the West End or on television you had to have forty weeks paid work to your credit. However, I went straight in and did this part for television. I sent my contract to Equity expecting to be granted my union card but they sent it back saying I shouldn't have been given the part and they were refusing me my card despite me being seen nationally in the episode when it was shown on the BBC. I was absolutely furious. In the end Equity explained the way around it was to get myself work as a variety artist so I accepted roles in pantomimes and did a six month season in a Paul Raymond revue to get my full Equity card." Nikki's first meeting with David Croft and Jimmy Perry was an audition for the role of a Chinese girl in an episode of *It Ain't Half Hot Mum*. "Well, I mean. Can you imagine it?" says Nikki incredulously. Despite not getting the role, the authors remembered the charismatic lady and asked her back to audition for Sylvia. "I had to go to the Acton Hilton rehearsal block. David and Jimmy were standing at one end of the long rehearsal room and you had to walk the length of this room when you went in. I had a black pencil skirt on, split to the upper buttock. I remember it was like walking the plank, but I made sure I was swinging my hips all the way. When I got to them at the other end of the room I felt I had already done my audition judging from the grins on David and Jimmy's faces."

Nikki was offered a role in the big movie version of *Flash Gordon* at the same time as the pilot of Hi-de-Hi! was due to be filmed. "They were offering me £5000 to do the film and just £150 to do the pilot episode of Hi-de-Hi! In the end you have to go with your heart and against all financial sense I chose to do Hi-de-Hi!" When the script fell onto the mat Nikki had some misgivings about the decision. "I felt it just wasn't funny. Then at the read through when I met all the extraordinary people

'Only the Brave' - The Cast

As Lady Honoria Delock in Dickens' *Bleak House*.

they had gathered together - Simon, Felix, Paul, Su, Barry - every single character was so dramatically different. I was screaming my tits off by the end of it. I knew then it was going to be a stonker of a show." The filming at Dovercourt was always the highlight of any series for Nikki. "We'd party until 4am and then be up again to be in make-up for 6am. John Kilby, the Director, used to stand behind me of a morning and say openly to the make-up team "Go on, trowel it on her!" In 1982 thirteen episodes of the show were commissioned and Nikki found herself in South Africa appearing in a production of *Who Goes Bare?* "It was me that went bare actually," she says candidly. "I flew back to do six episodes then off to Johannesburg to continue with the play then flew back again to make another seven then back again to finish the tour. It was worth it though because I met the love of my life out there. Actually you can put that in the book to annoy all the others!"

Was Hi-de-Hi! a blessing or a curse for Nikki's career? "A blessing in that everyone knew my face but Casting Directors only ever saw me as a leggy blonde which was frustrating." In addition to appearing in such television shows as *The Sweeney*, *The Life Of Shakespeare*, *The Ken Dodd Show* and *The Upper Hand*, Nikki has found greater versatility in the theatre. "*Medea* at the Liverpool Playhouse was probably the best thing I have ever done" she acknowledges. Other theatre work includes *Bleak House*, *Lord Arthur Savile's Crime*, *The Happiest Days Of Your Life*, *Bedside Manners* with John Inman and several seasons as the evil Queen Natasha in *Snow White*.

In panto as **The Wicked Queen**.

Nikki as she appeared at the 2007 Reunion in Dovercourt.

'Only the Brave' - The Cast

David & Tony Webb b1941
Stanley & Bruce Matthews

Stanley and Bruce Matthews cause much confusion at Maplin's. Being identical twins they are prone to play tricks on the campers who confuse their identity. Joe Maplin insists that one of them grow a moustache but this is short lived. When Ted decides to challenge the Army over an assault course the twins are instrumental in being doppelgängers when Ted fixes it so that the Maplin's team win.

Born on Valentine's Day 1941 in Harwich, identical twins David and Tony Webb became the backbone of Hi-de-Hi! appearing in all but one episode as Stanley and Bruce Matthews respectively. The twins spent their childhood in Mistley near Manningtree and soon discovered a talent for using their respective voices and harmonising to the popular songs of the era. The resort Entertainments Manager at Clacton discovered them in a talent competition and introduced them to impressario Bunny Baron and subsequently the duo left their full time employment and performed their first Summer season as a fully fledged cabaret act in Hastings. From there David and Tony gained valuable experience performing throughout Britain including the tough northern club circuit.

The Webb Twins have been seen on television specials all over Europe a highlight of which was singing with the Dutch Metropole Orchestra. Having worked as extras on several British television series, it perhaps wasn't surprising that the BBC team working on the pilot of Hi-de-Hi! came to hear about the talented twins who lived locally. Tony explains: "We had a call from Evan King, the Production Manager on the pilot episode, asking how tall we were. They were after a couple of blokes to throw Spike into the swimming pool. It would be a running gag if the pilot went to a series we were told. When he mentioned David Croft and Jimmy Perry we hadn't got a clue who he was talking about. Being a variety act doing the clubs, Summer seasons and pantomimes we had no reason to know television writers. In fact the tip-off came from Cliff Castle who was in the Casting Department of the BBC. He used to give us work as 'stand ins' on Top of The Pops. That meant you had to be in the studio all day standing in for pop groups while the Director lined up his shots. Cliff suggested to my brother David that he got in touch with Evan which of course he did." As it turned out David and Tony would be perfect as the Yellowcoats. "David and I were booked as extras, but we were extras in Yellowcoats, that was a big difference. We had no idea who was in the cast. It was a pleasant surprise meeting Barry Howard who we had been in pantomime with a short time previously in Birmingham. And our dear friend Felix Bowness, whom we had been with in concerts on the Isle of Wight." Tony - who used to live in the very shadow of Maplin's overlooking the site where Warner's Holiday Centre once stood - has studied classical guitar at the Trinity College of Music and teaches this specialised musical field in schools as well as continuing a cabaret career as a vocalist. "I usually tell the audience that I studied with the great opera singer Guiseppi Maplioni, who when he retired came to this country and changed his name to Joe Maplin, opened up a string of holiday camps and called them Maplin's Holiday Camps. Every Saturday night in the ballroom when Joe Maplin wanted to get rid of the drunks, he'd put me on. Maplin's very own Mario Lanza still lives."

As well as appearing in several seasons of the successful Hi-de-Hi! stage musical, David and Tony found themselves in Cromer working as 'The Jolly Follies' in the last episode of You Rang, M'Lord? David's career has taken him away from the stage and into broadcasting. "I worked for many years at BBC Suffolk" David says, "Whilst I was there I won a Gold Award for a radio documentary I made in America on an Elizabethan Suffolk explorer. I have since moved into video work, making corporate films and working for Ipswich Town Football Club where I film and produce material for the club's website. The last show Tony and I did together was at a holiday camp in Norfolk when they had a Mapin's night. It was a night of nostalgia for us both but those days of cabaret are over for me. I am much happier away from the spotlight."

61

'Only the Brave' - The Cast

With Joanna Lumley for an advertising 'shoot'.

David Webb as a pilot for *Only the Brave*.

At Weybourne Station with Chris Andrews (*Opening Day* and *Together Again*).

Some of the most imaginative costumes created in the stage musical were used for the Ugly Bug Ball.

5 The Yellowcoats
In alphabetical order

CHRIS ANDREWS b1946
Gary Bolton No2

Gary, a fit and good looking Yellowcoat, is the backbone of the sporting programme at Maplin's. He is a dab hand at posing for the young girls and the staff notice a certain vanity in his demeanour when tries to duck out of any activity which will mess up his carefully streaked blonde hair.

Chris Andrews took over the role of Gary from the second series. Chris was born in Carlshalton, Surrey, and as a schoolboy developed a flair for boxing. After turning professional as a boxer Chris also started to do some television extra work whenever producers needed a boxing or a similar sporting element in their shows. "I went in to audition for the BBC comedy *Seconds Out* starring Robert Lindsay and my agent suggested that whilst I was there I pop in and have a chat with David Croft who was looking for someone to replace one of the male Yellowcoats in the programme. Luck must have been on my side because I took over the role of Gary and stayed with the show for seven fantastic years." In between filming Hi-de-Hi! Chris also started to carve out a name for himself in concert and artist security, beginning with a world tour with 80s' pop group *Aha*. He became a much sought after bodyguard to a wide range of 'A' list celebrities including Prince, Kylie Minogue and Frank Sinatra. One memory that Chris remembers well is the night that he accompanied Kylie Minogue and Jason Donovan to the premiere of the film *Batman* in Leicester Square. "I continued to do bits in acting and I hadn't told Kylie or Jason that I had a very small part in the film as a Waiter. When I appeared on screen Kylie sat up excitedly and starting saying very loudly 'Look it's Chris, it's Chris!' Nobody had a clue who she was referring to but it certainly earned me a few points with Kylie." Chris also appeared in *Henry V* with Kenneth Branagh as well as roles in such programmes as *The Two Ronnies*, *Doctor Who* and as a German Officer in *'Allo 'Allo*. Chris has for many years been Personal Assistant to singer Chris De Burgh, a far cry from chucking Spike Dixon in the Olympic sized pool. "My days as a Yellowcoat will always be very special to me. We had such a wonderful time doing the show. A particularly vivid memory is appearing at the Royal Command Performance with the Hi-de-Hi! gang on the same bill as Twiggy and Gene Kelly. When it was broadcast on television I was first in the list of people in the show alphabetically in the credits so Su Pollard was always ribbing me about being the star of the show. Wonderful times."

BEN ARIS b1937 - d2003
Julian Dalrymple-Sykes

As pig farmer-come-ballroom dancer Julian Dalrymple-Sykes, Ben Aris was called upon to provide another dimension to the love interest of Yvonne Stuart-Hargreaves. It was intimated they had been secret lovers in years gone by ("Never mention Southport" Yvonne pleaded when Julian had to stand in for her husband Barry in an earlier episode). When Julian arrived at the camp full time to partner Yvonne his romantic intentions were kept at arms' length. "Give me time Julian, give me time..." became Yvonne's oft repeated catch phrase.

Benjamin Patrick Aris was born in World's End, Chelsea, the son of an insurance Clerk. A keen amateur actor he attended the Arts Educational School and trained in dancing at the Buddy Bradley School. An early television appearance was as a Flower Fairy in *Muffin The Mule*. "I was 10 years old and Annette Mills and Muffin were the stars." Ben recalled many years later. "Most of them were girls. As I was a pretty big lad I got to play the ugly flower - Deadly Nightshade, in fact." Ben made his film debut, aged 13, as the schoolboy Tadpole in *Tom Brown's Schooldays*. His subsequent career would be spent portraying upper crust charmers in a variety of productions on stage plus the big and small screen. In theatre he would specialise in musicals during his early years touring nationally in *Zip Goes a Million*, *Finian's Rainbow*, *A Funny Thing Happened on the Way to the Forum* (with a cast which would also include Frankie Howerd, Kenneth Connor and Jon Pertwee) and the ill-fated Lionel Bart attempt at staging the Robin Hood legend, *Twang!* Dramatic theatre came later with the male lead Geoffrey in the Richard Harris' award winning comedy *Stepping Out*, the Royal National Theatre production of *The Second Mrs. Tanqueray* and Rosencrantz in *Hamlet* at The Roundhouse. Film appearances include

'God Bless Our Family' - The Yellowcoats

> *I was delighted when Ben Aris joined the team. He certainly had a hard act to follow after the departure of Barry Howard but he took the bull by the horns and did it his way. I remember he arrived for the first day of rehearsal full of beans but very nervous. He had, of course, already given us Julian Dalrymple-Sykes in the series five. He played a past amour of Yvonne's as a guest in just one episode but he was now in at the deep end permanently! He was well known for his passion for bird-watching (the feathered variety, that is!) and he always brought his telescope along to Dovercourt when we went filming. He got very excited on one occasion, I remember, when the "twitching" world put it about that there was a very rare lesser-spotted something-or-other somewhere near where we were filming but I don't think he had time to go and find it! He would love to quote the names of his favourite rare breeds as often as conversation would allow and blind us with science, but I do remember asking him if I could borrow his telescope myself one evening. I have always been a keen amateur astronomer and as it was a particularly clear night, he brought the 'scope to my room as there was an excellent view of Jupiter and its four main moons. I then proceeded to name them for him to which he replied, "Ah, there you have the advantage of me - but I deserve it!" His performance as Julian was always an absolute delight, as was Ben himself. It was wonderful to watch him dance, particularly his great skill at tap dancing which he relished, and the relationship he had with Yvonne, which was full of frustration! - was a joy to behold! After Hi-de-Hi! finished, I was involved with Ben through the Royal Theatrical Fund for several years before his death and right up to the end, no-one at all (apart from his family) knew that he had been suffering with Leukaemia for six years. It is a fitting mark of the bravery and integrity of the man that he kept any upset well away from his many friends. He is sadly missed by his family and, not least, by the profession.* **Jeffrey Holland**

Hammer's *The Plague of The Zombies* and Captain Maxse in *The Charge Of The Light Brigade* in which he starred opposite Trevor Howard and John Gielgud. The role of Julian Dalrymple-Sykes was just a one-off performance in 1983, or so Ben thought. "I never dreamed that I would be asked back into the show as a regular," Ben told a national newspaper in 1986. "After a lifetime of obscurity I want my role to be a success for myself and for the sake of the show. There are some programmes that are notorious for not welcoming newcomers but Hi-de-Hi! is the reverse. I have never worked in such a friendly atmosphere in 41 years in the business." But there was one aspect of becoming one of the Maplin's gangshow that Ben had reservations about. "I don't relish the loss of my privacy that this role will bring me," he said. "The thought of people shouting "hi-de-hi" at me across the street fills me with horror." Ben was philosophical about replacing Barry Howard in the show. "I met Barry several times and liked him. But actors spend so much time out of work they can't afford to agonise about why they have been offered roles." As well as his best known role as Julian, Ben would be a regular in many popular television programmes notably as Simon Anderson in *September Song* and Spalding in *To The Manor Born*. He was reunited with Frankie Howerd in ancient Rome for the comedy special *Further Up Pompeii* and even found himself alongside his former colleagues when he appeared as a Special Branch Policeman in an episode of *You Rang, M'Lord?* Ben's final appearance on the West End stage would be opposite Dame Maggie Smith in Alan Bennett's autobiographical play *The Lady In The Van* in 1999. Ben married ballet dancer Yemaiel Oved in 1966 and together they have a daughter Rachel and son Jonathan. Ben had battled the effects of Leukaemia for several years before passing away on 4th September 2003, aged 66.

SUSAN BEAGLEY b1956
Tracey Bentwood

Tracey Bentwood was the last of the Yellowcoat arrivals for the 1959 season, with Mary and Val we assume having moved on to other camps in the Maplin's empire. Tracey is keen to impress Mr. Fairbrother and indeed any management personnel. When Joan Wainwright arrives at Maplin's and demotes Gladys, she makes Tracey the new Chief Yellowcoat which causes Gladys to nickname her "The little shrimp."

Susan Beagley was born in Northfleet, Kent. Although her family had no connection with the theatre Susan's younger brother Stephen became a Principal Soloist with the Royal Ballet in Covent Garden. Aged 17 Susan headed for the Corona Stage School in West London but the education wasn't all it could have been. "I found it pretty unruly." Susan maintains, "I felt I wasn't learning enough. We were always being sent out on auditions for commercials and films instead of studying. I answered an audition in *The Stage* newspaper for a dancer in an Old Time Music Hall with Hugh Lloyd in Newquay, Cornwall for 26 weeks through the summer and I got it! That was my first professional appearance and I got paid £18 a week when we opened." Susan's agent sent her to an audition for the part of Tracey "I'd never done any real television before only bits of 'extra' work. I'd spent all my time touring around the country in repertory, learning my trade I suppose. I was playing Principal Boy in pantomime in Guildford with Bernard Cribbins when the call came through that I'd got the part. I don't think I remember doing that matinee!" Susan was no stranger to the leading ladies of the show either. "I got on particularly well with Ruth and Su as I'd worked with them both before. I think that went a long way in me getting the part, as David and Jimmy didn't want a new person coming in and 'rocking the boat' as it were and the fact I knew the girls was a bonus. I'd shared a dressing room with Ruth at Salisbury Rep and had toured with Su in the musical *Godspell* sharing dressing rooms and digs. That was long before Hi-de-Hi! started. *Godspell* was one of Cameron Mackintosh's first shows. We became good friends and I did two more of his early shows 'signing on' together after the run had finished and I do remember him saying 'One day I am going to put on a fabulous show.'" A favourite episode for Susan was the first of the Christmas specials, 'Eruptions'. "We were all dressed in our gorgeous grass skirts and long black wigs waiting for the volcano to explode." Susan was lured away from Maplin's by the theatre. "I did three series of Hi-de-Hi! which I really enjoyed but then I was offered the part of Sybil in *Daisy Pulls It Off* at the Globe Theatre for Andrew Lloyd Webber in the West End. The contract was for a year so I couldn't do Hi-de-Hi! as well and decided to be in the West End and be available to do commercials and other television as I was based in London. It turned out to be a good move as I landed the part of Jane in Yorkshire Television's production of the musical *Salad Days*". Continuing to appear in theatre, Susan has encompassed the role of Hava in a national tour of *Fiddler On The Roof*, Miss Scarlet in *Cluedo*, the wife in *Eastwood Ho!* for the Royal Shakespeare Company and the leading lady in Chaucer's *Canterbury Tales* at the Shaftesbury Theatre. "Being in Hi-de-Hi! was very special to me because I learnt a great deal about working in television especially in front of a live audience. Also they were lovely people and it will always be a special part of my life." Susan now lives in East Sussex and although she no longer acts professionally she has recently started a drama group in her village.

KENNETH CONNOR M.B.E. b1918 - d1993
Sammy Morris

Uncle Sammy Morris was first spotted on the beach trying to amuse the kids for a few coppers. With an old pram serving as his "theatre" the tramp was whisked away to Maplin's and given a wash in order to replace the absent Mr. Partridge as the resident children's entertainer. Sammy finds it hard to adjust to clean lodgings having lived as a tramp for many years. He carries scraps of food around in an old shoe box as a reminder that he never knows where his next meal is coming from. Little is known of Sammy's past but it later turns out that he knows Joe Maplin of old.

Showbusiness legend Kenneth Connor is chiefly remembered for his starring roles in 17 Carry On films which span the original *Carry On Sergeant* in 1958 through to the final entry of the original series *Carry On Emmanuelle* in 1978. His gift of strong visual comedy and creating frustrated little men continue to endear him to new generations continually discovering the *Carry On* phenomenon. He made his stage debut aged two in Portsmouth where father was Petty Officer on the Royal Yacht *Victoria and Albert*. Much later Kenneth attended the Central School of Speech and Drama. Serving with the Middlesex Regiment during the war, he went straight to the Bristol Old Vic upon finishing with the armed forces playing all manner of roles from classical to comedy. He became a household name through radio particularly with Ted Ray in *Ray's A Laugh* where among his most popular creations was the character of Sidney Mincing. "Sidney Mincing personified petty authority and was based on an erstwhile landlord and an itinerant librarian. He was humourless and when he laughed it was a stricken hellish effort to laugh and something for which he had to apologise afterwards." Connor told one magazine in the late 1980s. Kenneth Connor's stage career is as impressive as his screen credits, ranging from the original production of *A Funny Thing Happened on the way to the Forum* (he later directed the national tour of this

> ❝I'm a great admirer of Kenneth Connor. The character he played in 'Allo 'Allo worked much better than Uncle Sammy I felt. We had to clean him up in the later episodes as he was very dirty and a bit pathetic. It was difficult to get sympathy for him. Kenny held the fort in Hi-de-Hi! and was brilliant in 'Allo 'Allo. One of the very first shows I did, a puppet show which Ian Carmichael had created, featured Kenneth Connor as one of the voices. It was called 'It's a Small World.❞ **David Croft**

'God Bless Our Family' - The Yellowcoats

musical with fellow Carry On-er Charles Hawtrey taking over Connor's role) and opposite Harry Secombe in the *The Three Musketeers* at Drury Lane to the amazingly successful review *Carry On London* at the Victoria Palace with the rest of the gang. Not every role has been an unqualified success however, "I set out to enjoy myself and have been doing it ever since. I just wanted to be on stage. I've perpetrated some horrific things in my time but I don't blame myself. There are a number of fellow boys in our profession who find it expedient to put on the tattiest plays and pantomimes or summer seasons. Unless one is blessed with a private income, there comes a time when one has to keep the tradesmen happy. I'm sweating with embarrasment at some of the things some of us [the Carry On team] have been forced to be in, but I hope people will take that with a great laugh." David Croft cast Kenneth in 1984 as Monsieur Alfonse in *'Allo 'Allo*, the Undertaker who has designs on Madam Edith (Carmen Silvera). Two years later he was seen as Uncle Sammy for the first time. His final appearance in a Croft-com was an episode of *You Rang, M'Lord?* Kenneth Connor passed away on 28th November 1993, aged 75, just two days after appearing as a guest artist on the popular BBC show *Noel's House Party*.

RICHARD COTTAN b1955
Marty Storm

Marty Storm alias Wilf Green is the winner of the Elvis Presley look-a-like competition and is the face of rock and roll in the Crimpton-on-Sea camp. His versions of Presley classics - such as 'Love Me Tender' - in the ballroom attract the Teddy Boys of the 50s. In 1959 Marty is the face of new youth. Marty Storm appeared in the first two episodes and mysteriously disappeared from the staff.

Richard Cottan has also made appearances in *'Allo 'Allo* as well as playing guitar in various bands including Ten Pole Tudor and The Sadista Sisters. His talent as a writer first came to public attention with a BBC 1 sit-com *Wilderness Road* (1986) co-written with Bob Goody starring Leslie Sands and Gary Olsen. This was followed by *Tygo Road* (1989) co-written with Christopher Douglas and starring Kevin McNally. Both of these shows "sank without trace" in the author's own words. It was though his solo writing projects that were to establish Richard as a writer of real merit most notably the BAFTA nominated *Men Only* and *Love Again*, a BBC 2 film about Philip Larkin starring Hugh Bonneville, Tara Fitzgerald and Eileen Atkins. More recently he has scripted the big budget mini series of *Colditz* for ITV and the docu-drama *Hancock and Joan* for the BBC, about the doomed love affair between Tony Hancock and Joan Le Mesurier. "I have dined out on the fact that I was the only regular Croft / Perry character to get the boot quite so sharply!" says Richard. He continues to develop scripts in both television and the cinema, proving that Marty Storm has indeed emerged from the shadow of Joe Maplin to reach greater heights than anyone at Maplin's could ever have forseen.

TERENCE CREASEY b1955
Gary Bolton No1

Gary, the good looking yet vain Yellowcoat, was played in the first seven episodes by Terence Creasey.

Terry was born in South Benfleet, Essex, but his parents emigrated to Australia when Terry was just five years old. His good looks resulted in some modelling assignments during his teens which led to a series of commercials. When Terry reached 21 he decided he would like to see a bit of the world. "I went with my mate on a round the world cruise," Terry now recalls. "I stopped off in London. I had met a singer on the ship named Jenny who would later become my wife. She was appearing in the theatre for a while and I signed up with some agencies for modelling and walk-on work. It was through the Alandar Agency that I was called up to be in Hi-de-Hi!" It was to lead to an association with the show which is remembered fondly. "I have great memories of Maplin's and all the crew. Everyone made me so welcome and I formed a special relationship with the Webb twins as the male Yellowcoat team. I actually loved the role as it suited my personality really well, mixing with people is what I do best. Filming was a real laugh. Su Pollard was my favourite as she is such a genuine person. However I was always a bit of a one for the girls so Penny Irving was good on the eye and I loved Ruth's voice." After the filming of the first series Terry returned to Australia and waited for the call to start the second batch

Terry Creasey carries the Olympic Torch in Australia 2000

of episodes. Whilst back in Australia Terry's father had a heart-attack which resulted in open heart surgery. Unable to leave his mother at such a crucial time, Terry made the decision not to take part in the upcoming episodes resulting in the role of Gary being re-cast. Happily Terry's father survived and Terry and his family decided to stay in Australia for good. "I did a few more commercials but nothing matched my time back in the UK. So I started my own business." Terry is now a successful franchise owner of three McDonald's restaurants in Western Australia and is instrumental in raising many thousands of dollars for charity.

GAIL HARRISON
Val

Val joined the entertainments staff when Mary (Penny Irving) left at the end of the first series.

Among Gail's stage appearances are *A Close Shave* at Nottingham Playhouse playing opposite Simon Cadell, *Poor Horace* at the Lyric Theatre and as Wendy in *Peter Pan* opposite Maggie Smith and Dave Allen at the London Coliseum. Gail was seen as Marian Wilkes between 1972 and 1975 in *Emmerdale Farm* and has appeared in numerous television productions over the years including yuppy Joanne in *Only Fools And Horses: The Jolly Boys' Outing* but is perhaps best known as Isobel Hardacre in the successful ITV sitcom *Brass*, a role she played for three series. Other credits are *North And South, The Return of the Antelope, The Les Dennis Show* and *Game, Set and Match*. Gail's brother Jeremy is married to Jimmy Perry's niece Sally.

Rikki Howard relaxes with her newspaper during a read through at BBC's Acton rehearsal rooms.

RIKKI HOWARD b1953
Betty Whistler

Betty Whistler is a hugely popular Yellowcoat. A tall buxom blonde who is the mainstay of the sports and entertainments programme at Maplin's. The sight of her in a bikini always attracts a loyal band of followers around the Olympic sized pool. According to Peggy, Betty wears dark shades in the morning so that Gladys can't look her in the eyes to see if she has "been naughty" the night before!

Rikki was born in Walton on Thames. Having trained at Elmhurst Ballet School, Rikki's professional debut was at the Stardust Theatre, Blackpool in the chorus of a summer season. Her many screen credits include the role of the Countess in Ken Russell's *Lisztomania* and *A Funny Thing Happened on the Way to the Forum* with Phil Silvers. As a singer/dancer she also backed the late Ian Dury and the Blockheads on tour. Television roles have included *Minder, The Kelly Monteith Show, Going Straight* and three episodes as Elaine, a radio operator for the French Resistance in *'Allo 'Allo*. Rikki enjoyed a particularly successful working relationship with *The Two Ronnies* (Barker and Corbett) appearing opposite them in seven series of their successful BBC show, a six month stage run at the London Palladium and a particularly memorable cameo as a red head in their silent classic *By The Sea*. "I will always adore both of the Ronnies," says Rikki. "Every time I worked with them was just an extraordinary insight into the minds of two fantastic comedians. I have to admit I did have a huge crush on Ronnie Barker! Doing the stage show at the London Palladium was probably the best and most fun theatre job I ever had." Rikki auditioned for the role of Betty Whistler in Hi-de-Hi! and ended up staying with the show for the whole of the Simon Cadell era. Being very much part of the eye candy did mean some very testing times filming around the pool in autumn conditions. "It was freezing cold. Nikki Kelly and I used to joke that our sticking out bits were so cold they were going to drop off. Diving in the pool was purgatory and I have never swam so fast. I reckon I beat the Olympic 200 yards free-style! I have never ever been so cold in my life. When we filmed the pilot we actually stayed in the chalets on the holiday camp. It was so wet and so cold that one day Simon Cadell came to breakfast and announced he had shared his bed with a fish because it was so damp. Nikki and I stayed only one season at the Cliff Hotel, our unit base, we then rented accommodation just down the road. We had lots of post working yummy dinners as there are some great restaurants within a 20 miles radius of

'God Bless Our Family' - The Yellowcoats

Rikki and Ronnie Barker in *By The Sea*.

Dovercourt." Rikki married French businessman Oliver in April 1984 and soon after found herself pregnant with her eldest daughter and had to be written out of Hi-de-Hi! After spending several years raising her family (she is the proud mother of four daughters), Rikki's next career move went in a very different direction. "I decided to train as a counsellor and spent four years counselling survivors of childhood and adult sexual abuse. Most recently I have been training to become an accredited Journey Therapist. I help clients to confront cellular memories, clear them out and this helps the healing process of either physical or emotional problems. It is the most extraordinary tool for healing your life, and the results are so rewarding for both myself and my clients." Rikki currently lives in Dorset and still makes the occasional acting appearance.

PENNY IRVING b1955
Mary

Mary is one of the original Yellowcoats when we arrive at Maplin's for the first time. She comes from Scotland and we know that she wears a bra with a clasp at the front!

Penny (real name Ann Marie Tricki) began her career as a model before drifting into acting. Her best known role is as Miss Bakewell, secretary to Young Mr. Grace, in several series of *Are You Being Served?* She has also been seen in *The Professionals* and *Dad's Army* on the small screen and *Carry On Dick*, *The Bawdy Adventures of Tom Jones* and *The Likely Lads* in the cinema. Penny has also appeared on stage as Bessie in *The Corn in Green* at the Yvonne Arnaud Theatre, Guildford with Annette Crosbie Penny retired from acting to write children's poetry.

Penny relaxing between takes by the Olympic sized swimming pool

LAURA JACKSON b1960
Dawn Freshwater

Dawn was one of the intake of Yellowcoats for the year that quite coincidentally the actress who played her was born. Nothing is ever proved but it is suspected that at one point Dawn gets very friendly with Gary. "He's definitely all man!" she admits in one episode before realising she has said too much. When Dawn develops appendicitis and has to go into hospital, it gives Peggy her chance to be a Yellowcoat at last.

Multi-lingual Laura was born in London and had a French education at the French Lycée in South Kensington. She graduated from the Central School of Speech and Drama and gained a Degree in Spanish from the London University. Among Laura's stage work are appearances at the Thorndike Theatre, Leatherhead in productions of Peter Nichols' *Privates on Parade* and Sheridan's *The Rivals* and several seasons of *The News Revue* at The Gate, Notting Hill and later the Canal Cafe Theatre. Hi-de-Hi! was Laura's very first television job. "I had in fact auditioned for *'Allo 'Allo*. David liked my audition but thought I sounded too authentic. Because I could speak fluent French it wasn't comedic enough, he was looking for a 'cod French' approach. He couldn't decide on casting me and wrote the word 'USE' on the back of my curriculum vitae. Sometime later I went to see him with a view to being in Hi-de-Hi! My agent told me they were looking for a Yellowcoat and I remember thinking 'What's that?' I never watched television much and had no idea about the characters at that point. I had to read one of Ruth Madoc's speeches for Radio Maplin. David Croft really liked what I did. He said to me 'I've written USE on the back of this paper so I think I'd better use you.' I didn't know if he was being sarcastic or not. Anyhow when I got home there were several messages on my answer machine saying I'd got the role of Dawn. I was thrilled." It was the start of a long and happy association with the show. "I was always mindful of not being given enough to do though. When it came to signing contracts for future seasons of Hi-de-Hi! I was always the last to sign as there was often so little for Dawn and indeed the rest of the Yellowcoats to do. Just the odd line here and there. David always promised me he had given me as much as he could. With such a large cast it was understandably difficult to spread the dialogue around." Laura's favourite episode is the 1985 Christmas special 'The Great Cat Robbery'. "I was always freezing in those scenes around the pool and I think the reason I like that episode so much is that all the scenes involved wearing black woolly jumpers, trousers and balaclava hats as we raided the campers' chalets. Being warm was a luxury." Laura's career in television blossomed with roles in *The Legacy of Reginald Perrin, EastEnders, Roger Roger*, as a stroppy shop assistant in *French Fields*, Pilar's sister in *Eldorado* and on the big screen *U.F.O.* with Roy 'Chubby' Brown. As trendy wine bar sophisticate Marsha she also witnessed the now legendary scene of Del Boy Trotter falling through the open bar in *Only Fools and Horses: Yuppy Love*. Laura's voice has also been heard reading French poetry on BBC Radio 4. Laura has a more lasting connection with Hi-de-Hi!, she married the series sound recordist Michael Spencer in 1986 and together they have a son. "My son now watches the videos and is amazed to see his Mum dressed as a lion or taking part in some bizarre situation. I get a little embarrassed by it sometimes but never the less look back on it all with real affection. It is wonderful to have been involved with something that is now recognised as a comedy classic."

JEAN LEAR b1923 – d2004
Ramona

The fun around the Olympic sized pool was always accompanied by the jaunty sounds of an organ. Hilda (played by Marianne Tollast) was the original organist but was soon replaced by Ramona. Ted's familiar cry of "Hit it Ramona" was the cue for an fanfare on the keys which added much of the fun atmosphere as some of Maplin's more outrageous competitions were in full swing.

Originally from East Ham, Jean learned the piano from the age of seven and went on to achieve high grades studying with Edward Parker in Barking. "One day a man who presented amateur talent shows persuaded me to play for one of the shows and it took off from there," says Jean. "I did some playing in pubs too. We had no money at all and the only way I could think of getting some money was to play in a pub, but I didn't like them at all and so I only agreed if the money I earned would go towards us going away for a holiday." With husband Rex on the drums they ended up becoming a double act playing for summer seasons and shows all over the country. (In 1973 they were part of the orchestra in Coventry for the musical *Salad Days* featuring a young actor named Jeffrey Holland!) "There was an ad in The Stage newspaper for an organist to be in Hi-de-Hi! When the original girl couldn't do it anymore I got a 'phone call from the production office asking me to take over. I said I would only want to do it if I could really play - Marianne Tollast only mimed - and they said that is what they wanted so they gave me the name of Ramona. Ted's theme tune was '*Happy Days are Here Again.*' I used to sit with a bag full of music beside me just in case David Croft should want something playing at the drop of a hat." Ramona was to remain the mainstay of activities around the poolside for the duration of the series. Rex Lear, Jean's husband, would also have some minor roles in the show. (Look out for him as the Gate

Keeper in 'The Graven Image'.) "The cast were always very friendly towards me. Ruth Madoc made sure that I had a Yellowcoat. Someone once tried to take the coat away from me and it was Ruth who stood up for me and said ' Of course she's a Yellowcoat'. They didn't think the organist should wear one but Ruth was insistent." Jean even joined all the major cast members on the front cover of the Radio Times in November 1981. "That was Barry Howard's doing. He told me to sit at the front and show my legs." In 'Tell It To The Marines' Peggy has to play the organ for the Royal Marines and this involved Jean playing out of shot. "It was taking place in a muddy field and I had to sit and play whilst Su Pollard mimed to my music. It was all rather funny." Jean was familiar with the holiday camp environment because for fourteen years on the trot her family had holidayed at Butlin's. "We had a badge for each year we went. We couldn't wait to get our badges out each summer. I loved it." Following the end of the series, Jean continued to teach piano in Norwich. She sadly passed away in 2004 after bravely battling cancer for some years.

LINDA REGAN b1959
April Wingate

April Wingate was a Hairdresser before coming to Maplin's at the start of the 1960 season. April has an innocence and shy quality about her that soon attracts the attention of Spike Dixon. Before long they are an item. On one occasion the staff arrange to take April to see the film *Bambi* for her birthday but Ted's schemes backfire and she is upset to find a war film being shown in its place. April tries to railroad Spike into marriage but at the end of the series Spike makes it clear that showbusiness comes first.

Linda Regan comes from a showbusiness background. Almost born in a suitcase, Linda has acted since she was a child. Learning her craft in many repertory theatres around the country, early television appearances have included *Z Cars, Dixon of Dock Green, On The Buses, General Hospital* and Dennis Waterman's girlfriend in the very first episode of *Minder*. She could also be seen on the big screen in *Quadrophenia* and *Carry On England*. Linda reveals that her career was going somewhat differently before Maplin's came along. "I had done some comedy but principally I was really a dramatic actress, certainly as far as television was concerned. When I went to see David Croft about the role of April in Hi-de-Hi! he told me 'I think you are a bit overqualified for the part' but I was so desperate to work with him. Hi-de-Hi! totally changed my career. I remember the first time I was recognised, it knocked me for six. Any actor on television gets that a bit no matter what the job is but with Hi-de-Hi! it just grew and grew. I remember being mobbed when I left the studio and it was quite frightening." Did Linda find that she warmed to April? "April was really sweet. Jimmy wrote a version of myself. I collect Teddy Bear's and he used that in the show. The other Yellowcoats would all answer back to Gladys but April never would. She was very much a Goody Two Shoes." The episode 'Man Trap' is very memorable for Linda in that it called on April to suddenly slap Spike. "In the rehearsals I kept tapping Jeff Holland on the face and David Croft got a bit concerned saying 'You will hit him won't you?' I was working up to it as I saw no reason to keep slapping Jeff for real when we were just rehearsing. By Wednesday David was getting very worried and at the technical rehearsal I still hadn't hit Jeff for real. After the dress rehearsal David Croft was very annoyed but I promised him faithfully I would go for it on the actual take. When the cameras were rolling before the studio audience on the Firday night I knocked Jeff for six. David said they all started clapping in the gallery above the studio. Jeff said he saw stars. Looking back I should have done the slap properly at least once in rehearsal to let him know what to expect." April was also one of the characters in the spin-off stage play *Hi-De-Hi Spirits!* "It was a specially written piece for the four television characters. My main memory of that season is looking after Ruth Madoc's daughter Lowri. I particularly remember taking Lowri shopping and when we came back her hair had been cut short, her ears had been pierced and I had brought her a pair of G-string knickers. Ruth nearly killed me." Following the show Linda has continued as a dramatic actress with roles in *Men Only, London's Burning, The Detectives, The Bill* and in the BAFTA award-winning children's drama *Harry and Cosh*. Her theatre work has included a season with the Royal Shakespeare Company, *You're Only Young Twice* (appearing with her husband, actor Brian Murphy), Tom Stoppard's *Dirty Linen* in the West End also Marilyn Monroe in *The Legend* and the role of Irene in Jimmy Perry's musical *That's Showbiz*. What does Linda think would have happened to April and Spike when the series ended? "They would never have got married. Spike would still be trying to make it as a comedian and April would be mooning after him, nothing would have changed.." Linda is now a successful Writer of crime novels, and her debut novel *Behind You* has attracted rave reviews and has been followed by *Passion Killers*. More novels are in the pipeline.

Linda's official website: www.lindareganonline.co.uk

JULIE-CHRISTIAN YOUNG
Babs Weaver

Babs was a new Yellowcoat at the beginning of the 1960 season at Maplin's. Young and pretty, she naturally caught the eye of Clive Dempster.

Julie-Christian Young was born in Bath but lived for a while in Pakistan due to her father who designed nuclear submarines for a living. Having trained at the Webber Douglas Academy, Julie's first professional job was in a stage tour of the play *Darling Mister London* playing a Swedish Telephonist opposite David Jason. "I had been up for parts in *Are You Being Served?* and shows of that ilk but ended up turning them down because at that time I was very much into theatre and more serious drama" says Julie. "I knew the director Robin Carr and he put me up for the role of Babs. In reality I had just bought a new house and needed a new kitchen so that was a prime motive for me wanting to do the show." It was a series that Julie was quite familiar with however. "A few years before my then boyfriend Richard Cottan had got the part of Marty Storm in the pilot and I remember having to help him learn the Elvis song in the show."

It was the start of two very happy seasons with the Maplin's gang. "I loved the location filming. We would go out for some fabulous meals with the crew after the day's work, I seem to remember we ate an awful lot of wild fowl for some reason. We used to stay at the Cliff Hotel and one night the fire alarm went off. I slept right through it, but apparently there were twice as many people coming out of the rooms than were booked into the hotel!" Julie's favourite episode remains *The Great Cat Robbery*. "I decided to leave the show, not because I had completed my new kitchen, but to pursue other work. Babs really didn't have enough to do to warrant turning down other work for. It was though a great time in my life and I made some good friends through it." Following Hi-de-Hi! Julie did a couple of voice overs for *'Allo 'Allo*. "I once got a repeat fee of 1p for that from a showing in Tasmania. I also got repeat fees when the programme had been dubbed into another language which I never quite understood." Among Julie's appearances on television are roles in *Casualty, The Bill,* Sue Jackson (Carol's sister) in *EastEnders* and *Party Time* with Harold Pinter for Channel 4. Julie's stage work has encompassed *Abigail's Party* at Worcester, *Habeas Corpus* at the Sheffield Crucible and *Absent Friends* at the Theatre of Hamburg. "A short while ago I made the decision to leave acting behind and left London where I was living to move back to Bath. It was a fairly painful decision at the time, but the right one I think."

Julie-Christian Young, Linda Regan and Laura Jackson on location at Weybourne Station between takes, with Jimmy Perry in the foreground.

'Carnival Time' - Behind the Scenes

6 Behind the Scenes
Including Costumes, Sets and a day's filming at 'Moulton Junction'

The subject of doing a series set in a holiday camp had been bubbling under ever since Jimmy Perry and David Croft had got together to write *Dad's Army*. Their backgrounds were remarkably similar and both had first hand experience of working the Butlin's camps of the 1940s and '50s. Writing a comedy set in a holiday camp had briefly been mooted when Perry and Croft were looking to follow *Dad's Army*, but the idea of a programme set in India with the Royal Artillery Concert Party drew their interest more, and thus *It Ain't Half Hot Mum* was born in 1973. However, with *...Hot Mum* riding high in the ratings, in 1978 David and Jimmy seriously turned their thoughts to a holiday camp comedy.

"We were working on Dad's Army *for a number of years, and during that time we must have discussed the idea for a year or so. When we first met, Jimmy and I realised how much we had in common because he was a Redcoat during his holidays from RADA, so very much the same background. We knew how the camps worked. We knew the staff were completely engaged in entertaining the campers and also gently fiddling them. Butlin's was a very magic place. They had windmills, bridges over the streams. All the ballrooms had a theme. It was another world to most people. They had a sensational time."* **David Croft**

With creative juices flowing, David and Jimmy set about writing the pilot. Both writers recalled their experiences in the camps and the sort of people who used to frequent the entertainments staff.

"All of our characters are based on real people. We had Uncle Jimmy, the children's entertainer. You won't believe this but his name was Jimmy Perry. No relation to me. He was a miserable old sod in his late '60s. He would say 'Bloody kids, I hate the sods.' The kids would shout out things to him, like 'I can see the flags sticking out of your sleeve!' It was all based on fact, that's why Mr. Partridge is a sad old drunk. Programmes had been done about holiday camps before but they'd all failed because they relied on old jokes about people wanting to get out, digging tunnels, armed guards, patrol dogs and the like. We just made our programme about the staff. It is no good focussing on the campers because they would change every week. Most of Maplin's staff really did exist. Certainly Yvonne and Barry Stuart-Hargreaves. I enjoyed writing their relationship, they live in a fantasy world. The reason that it works is because it is all based on truth. The camp comic was a man named Gordon Mitchell and he came from Halifax. He was awful, his catchphrase was 'Do you mind?' which I didn't think made sense. It wasn't funny. I knew Billy Butlin personally, he offered me a full time job. I was in love with a girl called Pamela Moore. She was beautiful. The sister of Eileen Moore who was in the film An Inspector Calls. *I was besotted with Pamela and her father said 'I can't have my daughter marrying an actor'. He was a wholesale Butcher. I had to make my decision and say goodbye to her. This was the basis for the episode 'Sausages or Limelight'. Jeffrey Fairbrother is based on a University Professor we had who was an alcoholic. He was drunk most of the time. That character was too deep and too sad so I had to change it, but there was a University Professor. Gladys Pugh came from a Chief Redcoat I knew at Pwlhelli who was the voice of Radio Butlin. The only character I fully invented was Fred Quilly because the riding instructors I knew were called Blodwyn and Olwyn, two Welsh girls. Fred is a bit one dimensional, a bit cardboard, and I think that is because I made him up. Nothing to do with Felix though who played him wonderfully."* **Jimmy Perry**

Casting got underway for the new project, now called Hi-de-Hi!, and Jeffrey Holland was among the first to be cast.

"Jeff came into our orbit because he knew the Director of the Dad's Army *stage show. He was Spike actually. If we wanted someone for a small part, dash off, get changed and come on as someone else he was the one to do it. He was terribly useful for the stage show. We wrote Spike especially for him."* **David Croft**

Man hungry Gladys Pugh went to Ruth Madoc whom Jimmy had worked with several times during his days running the Palace Theatre in Watford. Felix Bowness had done warm-ups for David for many years and was well aware that Felix had always been interested in horse racing, so it seemed natural to cast him as the failed Jockey Fred Quilly. Another actor David wanted in the show was veteran film and stage actor Leslie Dwyer.

'Carnival Time' - Behind the Scenes

Jimmy Perry and David Croft, looking very pleased with themselves on location at Dovercourt. The paraphernalia of filming can be seen in the background. The large animals for the pilot were brought in from Skegness.

"Leslie I have known forever. He was in a musical with my mother called The Belle Of New York *playing Blinky Bill. I was about 17 at the time. He had a distinguished career as a character actor in films. He had stomach problems which meant he couldn't go into the war and we had never worked together until Hi-de-Hi! It was written for him. There was no question of asking Leslie to come in and read for us as he was such a bloody good actor. Whatever you asked him to play he could play. In fact he met his wife Thelma in* The Belle Of New York *in which she played little sister Kissy."* **David Croft**

The snooty ballroom dancers were found through both Jimmy and David. Diane Holland and Barry Howard were brought together on screen to create a dynamic pairing.

"Barry Howard I had a great conscience about because he had partnered John Inman for years in pantomime. Wonderful entertainers although they were not very well known. I took John away to do Are You Being Served? *But was always conscious that I had never used Barry. Although Barry wasn't a Dancer he fitted our idea of the part. Diane Holland was related to Jimmy, his sister-in-law, and was a very fine Dancer. She had been part of the famous variety act The Ganjou Brothers. They used to throw Diane around in the air. What was called an 'adagio act'. In a strange way Yvonne was very much a part of her personality too."* **David Croft**

Rookie production assistant Robin Carr saw first hand how the characters were developed as the series progressed.

"Very early on in the first series, Barry had a line. Me, the new boy on the block and all that, plucked up the courage to say to David Croft, "That line is too long, it spoils the rhythm of the scene." How could I say that to the bloke who'd written so many TV shows? "You are quite right," he said, "Well done for spotting it. The thing is, we need the line because the viewers don't know his character yet. In the next series he'll get a laugh just by raising an eyebrow." And of course, that's what happened. Barry had one of the best comedy faces ever on TV." **Robin Carr**

The part of Ted Bovis was one of the last roles to be cast as the writers just couldn't find the right actor to play the part. Harry Secombe was among the names put in the hat for the central role of the loveable rogue who commanded the Hawaiian Ballroom.

"I had several ideas for Ted Bovis. Frank Windsor from Z Cars *was an original choice. Singer Ronnie Hilton was another. I directed him in a Summer show and he did*

'Carnival Time' - Behind the Scenes

Robin Carr's first job was on the stage management team at the Belgrade Theatre, Coventry – where both Jeff Holland and Simon Cadell were fledgling actors. He was a successful stage director before moving into television by joining the BBC. He started as an Assistant Floor Manager (AFM) and went onto being a Production Manager (PM) and finally a director. He was either AFM or PM on Hi-de-Hi! from 1980 to 1986 – missing only one series in order to production manage *Carrott's Lib*. He cut his teeth directing TV on such shows as *Are You Being Served?*, *Hi-de-Hi!*, *'Allo, 'Allo*, and *Alas Smith & Jones* amongst others. Robin was then headhunted by London Weekend Television where he spent eight years as Executive Producer for Comedy. There he produced and / or directed over 200 shows including the comedy series *The Two of Us* and *The Piglet Files* (both of which starred Nicholas Lyndhurst) and *Second Thoughts* (which starred James Bolam and Lynda Bellingham). There followed a successful time working in children's TV, including being co-creator, producer, director and writer of *The Tweenies*.

Robin currently has many diverse productions in development for both his own indie, Rolling Globe Productions and also for Reg Osterley Productions. Robin is a fully qualified cricket umpire and a Wolverhampton Wanderers fan.

sketches very well indeed. He came in and read it but he just wasn't experienced enough and I didn't dare risk it. Paul Shane had won 'Comic of the Year' in the tough Northern working men's clubs, several years running. Jimmy saw him in *Coronation Street* and he came in to read for us. He's a natural. Not a trained actor. He has terrific command, he takes no prisoners when he is a comic. Paul possesses a fine singing voice too."

David Croft

Su Pollard shared the same agent as Jimmy and David, and they were persuaded to see her one morning at Jimmy Perry's Westminster flat. It was after this meeting - with both writers shell shocked at the bundle of energy who had talked none stop throughout - that they wrote the part of Peggy to showcase Su's energy and comedic talents.

The pivotal role of Jeffrey Fairbrother was originally given to actor John Quayle. But problems occurred, Quayle was at the time contracted to appear with the National Theatre in its repertoire of plays. There was no problem letting Quayle off to record the pilot, but if he was wanted for a series there was no way permission was going to be granted. Despite lengthy negotiations a deal could not be reached and auditions continued. Fortune then smiled on Simon Cadell.

"Simon came up to the rehearsal rooms where we were rehearsing something else, and Jimmy read the the part of his mother in the script. Simon was absolutely right. The whole series was based on the impact of this ordinary man in the world of the holiday camp. The only thing we didn't exploit was the womanising side of it. Holiday camps used to attract men because of this factor but that wasn't Simon's forte so we elbowed the idea. We used the fact that he was unhappily married and his wife wanted to divorce him. Simon set the standard for the whole cast really, the rest of them played up to his standard. A lynchpin of the entire cast." **David Croft**

With the pilot commissioned the search began to find a holiday camp suitable to use. One of the major players in this search was Evan King.

Evan King (born 1930, Lanarkshire) became a professional Ice Skater and Comedian in 1951 appearing in ice shows in Glasgow, Kirkcaldy, Paisley and five Summer seasons in Blackpool. Upon joining the Tom Arnold Organisation, he played Dame in pantomime many times as well as appearing on the Moss Empire variety circuit. In 1961 Evan joined the celebrated Holiday on Ice as a solo comedian in the Far East. Eventually, joining BBC Glasgow in the scene dock and the stores. "I made myself indispensable to the visiting crews at BBC Scotland", remembers Evan. "My background in the theatre gave me a good understanding of how things should be organised so I kept applying for better positions. In 1965 I moved to the BBC in London as an Assistant Floor Manager. I met David Croft in 1966 and worked for him on *Beggar My Neighbour* which starred Reg Varney and Peter Jones. I stayed with David until 1968 having worked with him on *Hugh And I* and a version of *The Mikado* entitled *Titti Poo*. I got to work on the first series of *Dad's Army*. It was a great challenge because we wanted to get it right." In 1969 Evan became a Production Assistant - now known as a Production Manager - this involved assessing the script, finding film locations, negotiating the availability of locations and sorting out finances, arranging the catering, scheduling the film, booking the extras. "Masses of responsibility" Evan says. Evan's career at the BBC saw him mostly setting up new shows. He also worked on *The Likely Lads, Last Of The Summer Wine* and *Rosie*. Evan retired from the BBC following his work on *Just Good Friends* in 1986 and now lives with his wife in Suffolk.

"Originally we approached Butlin's about using their Clacton-on-Sea camp. But they said no. Warner's turned out to be ideal though, it just had the right look about it with its 1950s chalets. It was also close to London which

'Carnival Time' - Behind the Scenes

Filming by the pool. Summer has passed, as is evident by most of the crew wearing overcoats.

is an important consideration when half the production will be recorded there. The fairground animals I found in Skegness and had them brought down to the camp for the pilot. I also found a laughing clown in Clacton, like the one they use on the sea front in Blackpool. They added a nice touch and made it look as it might have done in the holiday camp heyday. Su Pollard was originally only down to appear in the studio scenes. During the pre-filming rehearsal Su was so impressive and I saw David look at me and instinctively knew what he was thinking. I arranged for Mary Husband to create a Chalet Maid's uniform for her almost overnight and we had Su come up to Dovercourt so that she could be seen in the location filming." **Evan King**

The script called for the camp to be seen at the beginning of the season in the Spring, arriving at Warner's in the Autumn meant the leaves from the big Poplar trees that surrounded the camp were all over the floor. Evan led a team sweeping up the foliage in a desperate attempt to recreate the summer of 1959. Another of Evan's duties on that all important pilot episode was to find the film footage that would make up the opening and closing titles.

"David was particularly keen to include Elvis and also Soviet leader Nikita Khrushchev banging his shoe on the table at the United Nations. I tried everywhere to get the Khrushchev footage and eventually went to the United Nations themselves who denied the incident ever happened. I found the clips in studios at Borehamwood and from archive libraries all over London. I also found lots of holiday camp footage from the era and thankfully Butlin's did not hold the copyright on it. I then assembled them with an Editor into the four screens and showed them to David on the Quantel video editing system.

Originally the circle featuring the artistes was much smaller. In later episodes they enlarged it." **Evan King**

The recording of the pilot was to take just two weeks. Filming started at the Warner's Holiday Centre at Dovercourt on Monday 15th October 1979 for three days, the cast and crew staying in the chalets on site in order to keep the overall budget for the production down. Mary Husband had been given the responsibility of creating the look of the camp, mirroring the outfits worn at Butlin's and Pontin's during the era. Designer Garry Freeman also studied the look of the camps and tried to give a flavour of the old style chalets and the facilities of the time, matching what Warner's had naturally with plausible, slightly run down, interiors. The original plan had been to use the Marine Suite function room of the Cliff Hotel on the seafront at Dovercourt as the Hawaiian Ballroom. The Cliff is a 27 room hotel, built during 1858 in a prime seafront location marking it out as a fine base for the BBC cast and crew. Whilst other hotels in the area were often used, The Cliff established itself as the BBC's centre of operations whilst in Dovercourt. The Marine Suite was in fact built on the site of the Victoria Concert Hall. It was shortly before the recording of the pilot that a wedding function had been booked into the Marine Suite ensuring that the room would not be available for the full week, so the production team went to Plan B and used the actual ballroom of the camp itself and dressed it up in Hawaiian theme. Although the hotel missed out on housing the famous Hawaiian Ballroom, it would be seen in later episodes as a backdrop for scenes on Dovercourt beach and more specifically in the episode 'Spaghetti Galore' where it became the 'Fisherman's Rest.'

Su Pollard with Terry Creasey during a break in filming. The broom has been inscribed 'BBC Props'.

'Carnival Time' - Behind the Scenes

Costumes : Mary Husband

Mary Husband was educated at the Queen's School in Chester and gained a National Diploma in Dress Design from the Liverpool Colleague of Art. At the age of 23 Mary became a Costume Designer for BBC Wales when they first opened a Costume Department. From 1962 Mary transferred to Television Centre in London, working on many different shows: period, modern and musical. Ultimately Mary came to specialise in comedy series and Light Entertainment. Among her vast array of credits for the BBC are *Open All Hours, Sorry!, Porridge, Nice Day At The Office, The Stanley Baxter Show* and she enjoyed a very happy and successful time with *The Two Ronnies*, Barker and Corbett, in their legendary BBC series. For the stage Mary has designed for *Dad's Army* at the Shaftesbury Theatre, *The Two Ronnies* at the London Palladium, *Bedful of Foreigners* at the Victoria Palace, *It Ain't Half Hot Mum* at the Pavilion Bournemouth and *That's Showbiz* at Wimbledon. Mary still designs on a freelance basis and lives in London with her partner Jimmy Perry.

> *I had designed the costumes on a series of* Dad's Army *and* It Ain't Half Hot Mum *with Jimmy Perry and David Croft. When we came to the end of a series of …*Hot Mum *Jimmy said to me, "Which do you prefer working with Mary, the old men or the young boys?" I thought for a moment and said, "Isn't there something in between?" It was shortly after that that they came up with the idea of Hi-de-Hi! Funny older men, charming young boys and lots of lovely, beautiful, entertaining young girls. It was 1979!*

They asked me to design this series from the very beginning – I hadn't done this for their previous shows, so it was a very exciting and demanding project. I knew nothing about holiday camps, I had never even been to one. But as Jimmy had been a Redcoat for Billy Butlin, he was my source of information. He had many photographs from his time at Butlin's and they set the date of the first episode in 1959. Rock and roll, then 'The Twist' all featured at parties I went to in 1959 when I was a Costume Designer for BBC Wales – their first – and I was of course familiar with the appropriate clothes of the period.

As Jimmy and David had both worked at Butlin's at the very start of their careers, they knew we couldn't have Redcoats on the staff and Pontin's had Bluecoats. After

The Maplin's Entertainment Staff in all their glory.

much discussion they settled for Yellowcoats for the Hi-de-Hi! *staff! I started work sourcing the materials. All the staff wore blazers and I found in John Lewis in London, a wonderful yellow blazer fabric which I thought would be perfect. Without asking anyone on the production team I trimmed these blazers with Royal Blue braid to outline them, on colour television yellow could spread in those days. I designed a blazer badge for the pocket and the rest of the costumes were white – pleated skirts and shorts for the girls and white cotton trousers for the boys. I added white shirts with a blue insert because white on its own would have flared on screen.*

I was at a bit of a loss for a costume for Ted Bovis (Paul Shane). I felt a straight comedy checked suit might have been wrong for some scenes. So I chose a checked tweed of beige, yellow and blue, which worked very well. Su Pollard as the Chalet Maid was a joy to dress, in an overall of straight forward yellow and white checked

'Carnival Time' - Behind the Scenes

Peggy's outfit had to be sourced at short notice and has become as much a part of HI-de-Hi! as the Yellowcoats. Note the torn pocket.

DID YOU KNOW?

That for Series Five of Hi-de-Hi! Ruth Madoc's Maplin's badge on her Yellowcoat is sewn on the wrong way. No one spotted the mistake during the recording of scenes on location so they had to keep it the same throughout the series for the sake of continuity. Ruth kept the same coat until Series Seven when a new one was made with the badge sewn on correctly. Ruth Madoc now owns the Yellowcoat with the upside down badge.

cotton – from John Lewis again – trimmed with Royal Blue. I gave her a little Maid's cap to push her hair under (as they did) but she wanted to have some hair showing so we compromised.

When costumes for the pilot were ready for fittings I gathered my preferred team. The makers I used for Hi-de-Hi! were Pat Harrap, who had worked in the BBC workroom but left to form her own business with a friend, Sue. My tailors were 'Paul the Tailor' with whom I worked on The Two Ronnies and the drag costumes for It Ain't Half Hot Mum. I called upon the services of another brilliant costume maker, Roger Oldhampstead. He also worked with me on The Two Ronnies and when we did the stage show of Hi-de-Hi! at the Victoria Palace he turned Felix Bowness into a caterpillar and Barry Howard into a Stick Insect for a big musical number, 'The Ugly Bug Ball'.

The make-up designer on Hi-de-Hi! was Jill Haggar, so when Jimmy and David cast the show we joined forces to look at the hair and to create the 'look' of the characters. Our first victim was Ruth Madoc – what a lovely face, and voice - but we felt we should do something 'in period' with her hair. I mentioned a film actress Renee Jeanmarie, famous in 1959, and that is what we decided on. Jill darkened her hair and cut it short to frame her face. She looked wonderful and I think Ruth loved it too.

For the other girls in the show we followed their own hair styles, but adapted them for the late '50s. The boy Yellowcoats were very straight forward. Hair of the period and nice straight make-up.

Jeff Holland was a great pleasure to work with as he adapted so well to the comedy clothes he had to wear for events with the holidaymakers. Paul Shane was happy in his suit and dinner jacket for the ballroom and Felix Bowness as Fred Quilly looked great in his satin yellow and blue jockey's outfit with cap. I made Leslie Dwyer more colourful with a velvet blouson as he was the Punch and Judy man. The ballroom dance duo – Yvonne and Barry Stuart-Hargreaves – were a joy to dress. Diane Holland had a perfect balletic figure and Pat Harrap had made costumes for dance routines for years and the 1950s was her favourite period. Barry Howard had a perfect dancer's physique and wore his standard white tie and tails with great elegance.

There were other girls in the team. One, Penny Irving who left the show after the first series. Nikki Kelly was a lovely character, very direct and strong and Jimmy had met Rikki Howard with me when I was doing The Two Ronnies in which she had quite a 'feature' part. He thought she was most attractive and cast her in Hi-de-Hi!- she and Nikki were truly a glamorous duo. There was a young guitarist who appeared only in the early episodes and did a 'turn' a la Elvis Presley. The character was called Marty Storm, that was very reflective of the 'hot rock' of the 1950s. Simon Cadell played Jeffrey Fairbrother, who was going to be the new Manager of the holiday camp. He was a brilliant actor and very charming. Sadly Simon was seduced by the classical theatre and

'Carnival Time' - Behind the Scenes

left after the fifth series. He used to read John Betjeman poems to me in the wardrobe department when I was not on set. A pity he didn't record them! There were three other young men in the cast, The Webb Twins and Terence Creasey who made up the Yellowcoats.

Some amusing incidents occurred during the run of the first series. I worked only on the pilot at first as I had commitments to the Ronnies and another designer, Jan Wright, took over from me. It was quite funny when the girls asked her to have their shorts shortened as that was more fashionable in 1979. However when this was done and the girls were filmed from the rear they looked as though they were wearing no knickers at all!

As the series progressed it became very popular indeed with the public. At the time, the advertisers of Heineken Beer were doing a series of posters displayed all over London on huge billboards. I was contracted and asked for photographs of Su Pollard for an advert for the firm. She was always talking about wanting to be a Yellowcoat and in the advert she gets her wish.

Altogether Hi-de-Hi! was a marvellous series to work on as the atmosphere was so friendly and everyone so co-operative. A real joy to be involved with. ”

The striped jacket created for Ted Bovis in the episode *Stripes*.

Production continued at the BBC's famous rehearsal rooms in Victoria Road, Acton, south London - 'The Acton Hilton' as it became affectionately known to all who used it. The cast performed before an audience in studio TC 4 at the BBC Television Centre on Friday 26th October 1979. With a running time of 40 minutes, the episode over-ran the normal half hour slots but it was considered necessary to establish all the new characters needed in the pilot. The recording went very smoothly. Felix Bowness was on hand to offer his brilliant warm-up patter between scenes, and the studio audience laughed heartily in all the right places.
Everyone was optimistic but nobody could really be sure how it would be received when the programme went to air. The verdict would come on 1st January 1980 when BBC 1 screened the much anticipated new comedy from Jimmy Perry and David Croft.

The general audience reaction was very favourable, although holiday camps had already started their fall from grace the nostalgia factor was high for the heyday of the Butlin's and Pontin's empires. A finally timed exercise in British social history. The full series was commissioned and the following Autumn the cameras were turning in Dovercourt once more on six further episodes which reunited the cast of the pilot.

Thursday 25th September 1980 saw recording commence on the location block for the first series with the opening scenes for *Desire in the Mickey Mouse Grotto*.

One casualty of the series though was Richard Cottan's Elvis impersonator Marty Storm.

"We just had too many people. It's a pity really as he was a good character but we had too many people sitting in the staff room. Any singing to be done we wanted Ted to do, so it would have taken away from the Ted

The cast and writers attend a read-through at the BBC Acton rehearsal rooms. David Croft sits at the head of the table.

'Carnival Time' - Behind the Scenes

Film Cameraman Max Samett poses in front of the cast (who appear a bit fed up!).

Bovis character somewhat. This unfortunately happens at the start of a new series. You find that you have two characters that are very similar. It happened to me with Dad's Army. *One of the characters we wrote was treading on Godfrey's toes too much. Similarly we didn't need a Fireman AND an Air Raid Warden. It was difficult supplying everyone with dialogue. John Laurie once said 'I could 'phone in my performance this week!' The* Dad's Army *cast used to count how many lines they'd got each week."* **David Croft**

The show got off to an incredible start with some masterful scripts involving inspired moments. Perhaps the classic moment of the first series was the scene in *Day of Reckoning* where the pantomime horse rides a real horse over the sand dunes to the astonishment of a drunken Mr. Partridge. The stunt scene was supervised by Derek Ware, whose prowess as a stunt man earned him work on countless television shows over the years. The scene featuring the panto horse holding the real horse was recorded on Sunday 5th October 1980, whilst the scene on the sand dunes would be filmed the following day.

"Myself and fellow stunt man Stuart Fell were employed to double Su Pollard and Jeffrey Holland acting as a pantomime horse. Apart from running around the sand dunes at Dovercourt we had to ride horseback in the fake horse costume. This was hardly a death-defying stunt but as I know from bitter experience a horse can be an unpredictable animal so Stuart and I were extremely careful in mounting the 16-hand Hunter the BBC had hired for the day. As I recall we took the precaution of blind-folding him until we were mounted and fully dressed with the fake horse's head in place. I must say the belly laugh from the audience when the scene was transmitted made it all worthwhile." **Derek Ware**

"When the real horse first saw the panto horse during the sequence where they were leading it off to go to the sand dunes, it took - shall we say - a real shine to it and started to sniff around. Su at the back said to Jeff Holland who was playing the front half of the horse, "I think it likes me, what shall I do?" Quick as a flash Jeff replied "You brace yourself, I'm going to eat some grass!" Just as the horse was going to mount the panto horse David Croft stepped forward and grabbed the reigns, pulling it away. It could have been very dangerous, it was such a mighty beast it would have broken Su's back. Thank goodness David took the initiative when he did. Sometimes situations can turn quite nasty." **Paul Shane**

One major character who was never seen throughout the entire run of the show was Joe Maplin, the all powerful founder of the holiday camp empire. Many people assumed he had been based on Billy Butlin or Fred Pontin. The truth is a little more complicated.

"Joe is in fact an amalgam of various people. He was largely based on a bloke my daughter was working for at that time in that he used to dictate wonderful un-grammatical letters. I borrowed that feature from him. If Joe had ever appeared I think he would have been played by Charlie Drake. A little man, very down to earth, not well educated but a dynamo. Charlie Drake never knew this." **David Croft**

As ever David Croft assembled a trusted team behind the cameras which would include his long serving film cameraman Max Samett, Production Manager Susan Belbin (who would go on to produce many programmes including *One Foot in the Grave*), sound recordist Michael McCarthy and Jan Wright on costumes. Robin Carr found television training ground at Maplin's.

"I'd met David Croft before I'd even thought of going into television. Prior to joining the BBC, I was a Production Manager for the theatre company that produced the

Former Red Coat, Charlie Drake - the real Joe Maplin?

'Carnival Time' - Behind the Scenes

Dad's Army stage show. I was vaguely involved with the pre-production and rehearsals and stood in for the Stage Manager twice - once in Richmond, Surrey, and then again at the Shaftesbury Theatre in the West End. At the time I was starting to carve out a career as a Theatre Director and chatted to David about this a couple of times. Two or three years later I'd moved to the BBC as an Assistant Floor Manager and one day I literally walked into David. I told him I was AFM-ing. He said "You can't do that, you are a Director. Better come and work for me." Within a couple of weeks I was assigned to David's office as Assistant Floor Manager on series 2 of Hi-de-Hi! I grew up in television terms with Hi-de-Hi! I started as the Assistant Floor Manager (AFM) became the Production Manager (PM) and ended up as a Director. I would have made the final leap and been Producer of the series but was headhunted by London Weekend Television and so left the BBC. David never forgave me. The AFM is the Stage Manager. The responsibilities are much as they are in the theatre: organising props and prop lists, calling actors, prompting during rehearsals etc. Additionally the AFM books the extras, liaises with design, lighting, sound, make-up, costume, special effects and anyone else who 'needs to know' something. The Production Manager organises much of the above, delegating most of it, and also watched over the budget. Although the budget is the responsibility of the Producer, the every day costs are kept in check by the PM. At the BBC - though not anywhere else - the PM also acts as Floor Manager (FM) during recordings, both on film and in the studio. In the studio the FM is the one that runs the studio floor - cues the actors to start a scene, explain what re-takes are needed and why, having been told by the Director who talks into the FM's headset and tells everyone all is okay, move onto the next scene... The

The production crew, including Jimmy Perry and David Croft watch, the cast go through their paces on the monitors in the autumn sunshine.

The ballroom musicians were known as 'Bert Swanley and the Debonairs' and were played by a changing roster of actors. The music itself was recorded and supervised by Roy Cloughton. This would involve booking the musicians, arranging the songs and both conducting and playing the piano through the recording of the 'wild tracks' (sound recordings that are synchronised into a scene later) of the tunes. Roy was a Doctor of Music and played on over 600 broadcasts of *Women's Hour* for BBC Radio and also on television for The 60 70 80 Show starring Roy Hudd. He was resident Musical Director for the famous *Cascade Revue* in Clacton for 29 years and became Musical Director for West End singer Andrew Robley and Keep Fit legend Eileen Fowler. Sadly Roy passed away in 2008, however his contribution to the legacy of Maplin's was immense.

Left to Right: Albert Welch, Michael Leader, Jason James, Bruce Guest and Tommy Winward.

Director works with the actors, working out how they perform, where they need to stand or sit. The same as in theatre. Then additionally, in television and film he or she will then work out how to shoot a scene; write a camera script and be in charge of what ends up on the final videotape. He / she will then oversee the editing and dubbing that leads to the finished product. The Producer is overall in charge. Often in television, the Producer will also be the Director. In movies the Producer is the one who raises, maybe even provides, the finance. In television the Producer is in control of the finance but will not usually have raised or provided it." **Robin Carr**

Following a repeat of the pilot (trimmed to 35 minutes) the first series went to air on 26th February 1981 in the 8pm slot following *Top of the Pops* and before the start of another brand new comedy show, the Ronnie Corbett vehicle *Sorry!* Jimmy told the Radio Times for the opening week: "In Hi-de-Hi! we have tried to use as many new faces as possible. I like working with new people. They are exciting. The prestige of theatre doesn't really matter much to me. I'm not interested in that. All I want to be able to do is to be in an atmosphere where I

Charlie the Parrot

> *The Cliff was a very useful hotel, rather old fashioned and draughty. One of the great features was Charlie The Parrot in the lounge. Su Pollard used to try like mad to get him to say 'f***'. Finally the Manager put up a notice which said: 'WILL THE LADIES AND GENTLEMEN OF THE CAST PLEASE NOT TEACH THE PARROT FOUL LANGUAGE'. I gather that when we left the hotel after the shoot, the parrot would continue uttering the obscenities in front of guests that followed us into the hotel. It must have been a very funny sight.* **David Croft**

The Hotel Manager of The Cliff back then, as now, was John Wade. He too remembers the annual invasions of the Maplin's entourage to Dovercourt.

> *Su's teaching the parrot to swear is something that has now passed into legend. Her task one year was to try and get Charlie to say 'bollocks' by the last day of filming. It took her three weeks of filming but she did do it. On the day that the Cliff was used in the programme, the whole road was completely closed off to enable filming to take place. One of the locals got very annoyed by this and demanded his right to drive along the road at all times. I remember we had to throw the cast out one night because they kept setting off the fire alarm. They were very happy days though. When my wife and I went to see the Hi-de-Hi! musical in London, we were spotted in the audience and invited backstage. I was really glad when Tony and Joanne Tarran decided to use the Cliff for the 2007 reunion. It was great to see cast members again, they all remembered me. A fabulous weekend.* **John Wade**

Above; Su and Charlie during their stay at The Cliff Hotel. The annotation on the photo reads 'I'll see u next year Charlie for some more rude words, luv Su'. Below; Su and Charlie reunited in 2007.

can produce good work, and where I can enjoy working. If you have that you have an awful lot to be grateful for." The gamble on new faces paid off better than anyone could have predicted. An incredible 15.45 million people tuned in to see what life had in store for the staff of Maplin's Holiday Camp. Within days the streets of Britain were echoing with the catchphrase "Hi-de-Hi!" and people were mimicking Gladys' sultry tones.

The BBC Viewing Panel report on *Desire In The Mickey Mouse Grotto* was a bit more muted than the general audience reaction. The report noted: "it had provided an amusing nostalgic entertainment. They [the viewing panel] considered the theme original, the characters and storyline true to life and generally felt the series has potential." Praise was also singled out for the performers, "Ruth Madoc as Gladys Pugh was considered to have given a most convincing performance," the report went on to say, "as was Simon Cadell as Jeffrey Fairbrother. Su Pollard as Peggy was also commended for her entertaining contribution." Asked if they would watch further programmes the report noted that 20% of the respondents would, whilst 37% were probable and another 24% voted as possible. 14% voted probably not whilst only 5% were a definitely not. All in all though the BBC's internal analysis was very positive.

A further report undertaken at the end of Series One was equally enthusiastic, but it did note "…the series is not without its critics and 10% of its sample audience decided to stop watching. The most frequent complaint was that Hi-de-Hi! was 'silly rather than funny', with poor stories and weak characters. These viewers considered the series boring and contrived." Proving that you

'Carnival Time' - Behind the Scenes

can't win 'em in all even in the wake of an enormous ratings hit.

Such was the demand for more that when the first run ended on the 2nd April, the BBC took the unprecedented step of repeating the entire series again in a peak time slot on a Saturday just six weeks later. It seemed the entire country had gone Hi-de-Hi! crazy and both the audience and the BBC wanted more. EMI released the single version of the theme tune in the Summer of 1981 which had made the Top 40 followed by a full LP by the team for the Christmas market. Series Two was quickly commissioned and again the cameras headed for Dovercourt. The cast was as before with the exception that Gail Harrison came in as new Yellowcoat Val replacing Penny Irving, and Gary was now played by Chris Andrews after Terence Creasey decided he couldn't make the second series filming. Now that the writers had seen their cast in action during series one they began to write much more sharply for them. No better place was this evident than when they showed Su Pollard's potential in the episode *Peggy's Big Chance*. Perhaps one of the most memorable scenes of the entire series saw Peggy finally get her interview for a Yellowcoat position only to be knocked back. The climatic scene in the office with Peggy choking back the tears as she relays her fate to Jeffrey and the others marked a turning point for Su Pollard. It showed everyone that not only was she a fine slapstick player but an actress capable of real depth to. A facet the writers capitalised on in many future scripts. That same episode featured a set piece in the pool with Peggy playing a shark and Spike dressed as a bathing-belle having to be rescued by the girl Yellowcoats from 'her' peril. It was a sequence that haunts Jeffrey Holland to this day.

"David and Jimmy insisted I had a pool episode in every series. I think it was the sadistic streak in them that used to come out. Spike parades out in a funny costume and Ted gets him thrown in the pool. Normally they used to write me into a costume that I could get a wet suit underneath, because it was flippin' cold in that water. When we got into the camp to film the location stuff it was usually late September or early October when the camp had shut. I was dressed on this occasion as Miss Maplin, with long blonde hair, high heels and fishnet tights. I was supposed to be menaced in the water by Peggy dressed as a rubber shark. We were delayed in filming that sequence for a fortnight due to technical reasons and by the time we came to do it the water was about 43 degrees Fahrenheit, really icy. They spent all night pumping steam into the water to get it warmer but it only rose by one degree. I was dreading this scene, but I did it and was in the pool treading water whilst all the action was going on. We only ever had one go at doing those pool scenes because when you are wet, you are wet. There were no reserve costumes to do it again. I suddenly became aware that I was losing the sense in my legs. I was becoming a serious victim of hypothermia. I tried not to panic but suddenly thought 'If I don't get out now they are going to have to pull me out.' I yelled to David 'I've got to get out' because I was on the edge of panic by then. David carried on shooting even though I was supposed to be in the pool as part of the action too. When the editing was done you would never had known that there was a problem. It was brilliant. Spike just disappeared from the scene, but everything else carried on as per the script. After that one of the newspapers printed the story under the title The Day I Nearly Hi-de-Died!" **Jeffrey Holland**

DID YOU KNOW?
Make Up Assistant for Series Six, Sunetra Sastry, went on to marry Rowan Atkinson.

Jeffrey Holland's Nemesis, the 'Olympic sized' swimming pool. The extras in the foreground cling to their overcoats.

Barry Howard and David Webb during the filming of Carnival Time. Both clearly se to enjoying themselves as one half of 'F' troop.

'Carnival Time' - Behind the Scenes

Professor Guy Higgins (1932 - 2007)

Professor Guy Higgins was a legendary Punch and Judy performer, an expert in an increasingly rare field. His knowledge on the subject was sought by both media and scholars. He sadly passed away on 19th June 2007, prior to this he had shared his memories of being the expertise behind Mr. Partridge's Punch and Judy booth at Maplin's

> *Believe it or not it all started when I made a glove puppet of J.R. Ewing, the infamous villain in the very popular television series* Dallas. *An invitation came for me to attend the BBC Television Centre, bringing with me my Punch and Judy show, and in particular the J.R. Puppet to appear on* What's on Wogan.

A few weeks later I was invited to BBC Television Centre again but this time to read a script using the unique squeaky voice of Mr. Punch. It was required that whatever was said by Mr. Punch could be clearly understood. The audition proceeded and I was invited to sign the contract to be the Advisor and Puppeteer for the new BBC comedy series Hi-de-Hi!

Every year I do my Summer Season with the Punch and Judy show on the soft golden sands at Weymouth in Dorset, then back home to Worcestershire for whatever the Autumn, Winter and Spring have to offer. However this year, I was off to Warner's Holiday Centre at Dovercourt to add my support to the production of Hi-de-Hi!

In the series set in a holiday camp, the children's entertainer, one Mr. Partridge (played by the great veteran Leslie Dwyer) hated kids and would sooner or later partake of thoracic lubrication. In other words 'he got drunk'. Whenever he did Punch and Judy, or you heard the voice of Mr. Punch, that was done by yours truly. The first scene we did was set in Mr. Partridges chalet (The Partridge Season). Leslie did not have much to say to me, he was concentrating on his part, for that matter so was I. The sound team fixed up the microphones, the camera crew were outside, we did some tests for sound level... Then it was "Action!" A voice outside called "Cut" and was then heard to say "That was all right." Leslie turned to me and beamed, "That's what I like, a take in one." He shook hands with me and said "I couldn't have done better myself." Later in the day Jimmy Perry and David Croft approached us and David said to Leslie, "How are you two getting on?" Leslie put his arm across my shoulder, gave me a reassuring squeeze, and replied "I will work with this boy anytime, he's a real pro." David nodded, Jimmy smiled and Leslie said to me "Come on Guy, let's go and have a well-earned cup of tea."

I soon discovered that Leslie Dwyer, by this time pretty much a veteran performer, had done pretty well everything in the course of a very long career. Music hall, variety, stage, films and television. I was particularly interested in the first two, and very soon Leslie was happily filling in time between shots by telling me about his earlier experiences and the stars with whom he had met and worked. He was a good impressionist which added to these hilarious pro stories. He asked me about my career and who was my favourite performer? I replied "G.H. Elliott" (A very famous and popular song and dance man who appeared as a Minstrel wearing chocolate coloured make-up doing a superb soft-shoe dance, this is similar to tap-dancing without the 'taps'.) I thought I would be told more about G.H. Elliott, but to my surprise Leslie commented rather sharply "I've no time for G.H. Elliott. My father was a great pal of Eugene Stratton (another Minstrel performer) and he reckoned that G.H. Elliott had pinched his act!" I knew that this could not be true, but decided to steer the conversation in another direction. I was also keen on the sand dancers Wilson, Keppel and Betty. "Ah," said Leslie "Did you ever hear about them being in trouble for smuggling a dangerous and unknown substance

83

'Carnival Time' - Behind the Scenes

into America?" I breathed a sigh of relief. I was off the hook. Leslie was happily telling me another pro story again.

The second day on location Leslie and I were walking along by the chalets when a girl appeared dressed as a Chalet Maid. Leslie spoke to her. "I want to introduce you to the real Punch and Judy man. This is Professor Guy Higgins, and (to me) this is Su Pollard. We exchanged hellos. Leslie continued, "She is the present day Nellie Wallace." Su raised her eyebrows, pursed her lips and asked "Who is Nellie Wallace?" Leslie laughed, winked at me and said, "He knows who Nellie Wallace is." I couldn't help but smile. Leslie grabbed my arm muttering "Time for a quick exit" which we did.

Paul Shane with his 'dummy' head created by Professor Higgins..

A rare picture of Professor Guy Higgins flanked by Leslie and Felix.

Over the Christmas of 1981 he was Friar Tuck in the pantomime at the Alexandra Theatre in Birmingham along with several other stars of the show. Paul Shane had commissioned me to make a ventriloquial head in the likeness of his famous character Ted Bovis. I took this along to the theatre and was looking forward to meeting up with friends who had made up the cast of Hi-de-Hi! Paul was very pleased with his other head, and told me Leslie was out of the panto due to ill health. The first hint I had that Leslie was being plagued with health problems.

Episodes came and went. Leslie always knew his lines and the bits of business that went with them. Unlike Fred Quilly, the Jockey, alias Felix Bowness. The scene was a railway station, with the camp entertainers waiting to meet the holidaymakers for the next week. Really this was a glorious send-up of a scene in the film High Noon. Everyone was waiting for the train that was very late. The command "Action" came, then after a pause "Cut." Jimmy Perry spoke to Fred Quilly. "Fred". "Yes Mister Perry?" Answered Felix. He used the title Mister for comical effect. Jimmy continued. "Fred, you have not studied your script have you?" "Oh Mister Perry, how could you say such a dreadful thing? Of course I have studied my script." Very patiently the smiling Jimmy Perry replied "Well why aren't you picking your nose with your riding crop?" The expression on Fred's face had to be seen to be believed. "I think that's disgusting Mr. Perry. I've never picked my nose with my riding crop. If you want me to do it, you show me how!" By now the rest of the cast were in near hysterics. Even more so when the very gentlemanly Jimmy Perry sat down beside Felix and proceeded to demonstrate what was required in the script. To me this was far funnier than what went out on TV.

I have had many years in entertainment in a variety of ways and always enjoyed whatever I was doing at the time. Although some experiences sound better in retrospect. Over a period of time my experiences include that of being professionally a Magician; Illusionist; Children's Entertainer; a Song and Dance man in Old Time Music Hall; and Punch and Judy showman (30 summer seasons at Weymouth). These gradually led me to membership of The Inner Magic Circle - with Gold star - and that most prestigious theatrical lodge, the Grand Order of Water Rats.

While on location for Hi-de-Hi!, the battery on my car died. There was only one other car about and David Croft was getting into it preparing to drive off. He very kindly allowed me to jump start my car from his, but to my embarrassment it did not work. Then the camera crew appeared and decided a push start would be better. David wished me luck and drove off. The camera crew joined forces, gave me a push which did the trick. I am very grateful to all of them for their help. For their part they found the episode very amusing, but I shall never forget their kindness. "

'Carnival Time' - Behind the Scenes

One of the behind the scenes arrivals on the second series was Assistant Floor Manager Robin Carr who would rise to the position of Director later in the run. One of his tasks was the booking of the many extras needed for the pool scenes.

Inside the Hawiian Ballroom. The cast, including Diane Holland, Paul Shane, David Webb, and Jeffrey Holland discuss the next scene. Felix Bowness remains seated.

"Stories of the days of Hi-de-Hi! having 100 extras are now legendary. This number of extras for a sit-com is unheard of and probably remains to this day the largest cast ever for a sit-com. I think the most we ever had on any one day was 153. We wanted the extras in swimsuits when they were around the pool. Quite often temperatures in October would be somewhere near freezing and so the extras had to wrap themselves in blankets and overcoats to keep warm in between takes. When we were ready to roll there would be loud shouts of "Overcoats off" before the word "Action!" When we'd cut and the extras heard the cry "Overcoats on!" the cheers could be heard in Southend. Most of the extras remained with us and came back year after year. They were all local bookings (so we didn't have to pay their hotel bills) and many became part of the family." **Robin Carr**

The hundreds of extras used would include future *That's Life* presenter Adrian Mills, George Formby's sister Mary, comedian Charlie Drake's son Chris and Yvonne Marsh, who would later be more prominent as Madge Cartwright in *You Rang, M'Lord?*

Once again the series was an enormous hit. The team got their first Radio Times cover to emphasise the importance of the programme in the schedules and it was promoted to a peak time slot on a Sunday evening. The Christmas episode featuring Jeffrey getting drunk and waking up naked in his chalet, with Gladys keeping tight lipped on what had actually happened, was a typical example of the show at its very finest. This episode saw an ad-lib moment that neither writers or cast were expecting. In the scene Ruth Madoc had to open a bottle of champagne in Jeffrey's office.

"I had to quietly open a bottle of champers for Simon's character and as the stuff has never been in my line Simon gave me a lesson on how to do it. But before we shot the scene a joker shook up the bottle. The cork flew out and the bubbly spurted all over Simon's deadpan face and my clothes. Now I pride myself on being a 'one take' actress. So instead of dissolving in laughter like everyone else I ad-libbed in my sexiest voice 'Oooh we are feeling frisky tonight, aren't we?' Everyone thought it was so funny so we left the line in." **Ruth Madoc**

Even the reading of Joe Maplin's letters were no escape from the japes of the crew for Simon Cadell.

"We used to kid Simon Cadell he was a real actor whereas the rest of the cast were 'Turns' (comedians or singers) which wasn't strictly true as Jeff or Su will tell you. Certainly Simon was a great one for motivation - the reason an actor does or says something. Often the script would call for Jeffrey Fairbrother to read a letter from Joe Maplin to his entertainment staff. As Assistant Floor Manager I would have to provide this. Simon originally requested the actual words of the script were NOT in the letter. As an actor he had learned his lines and wanted to act them, not read them. This was OK but the letter had to have some writing on it because the lights in the studio shone through the notepaper. Rather than type gibberish, I'd write a real, often quite rude, letter. The first time Simon would see it, during camera rehearsals, he'd laugh and after that ignore it. Unfortunately one letter really tickled him and each time he read it he laughed - including the actual take in front of the audience. From

Su joined by Paul Shane and Ruth Madoc as guest presenters on the game show It's a Knockout with Stuart Hall.

'Carnival Time' - Behind the Scenes

Setting up for a scene in The Graven Image. The houses in the background are still there, the main site entrance is indicated by the line of trees.

then on we agreed it would be absolute gibberish - but always the same amount of letters per word as the original script." **Robin Carr**

The rising profile of the cast meant additional promotion work on *The Generation Game, It's A Knockout, Russell Harty* and *Cheggar's Plays Pop* where Paul Shane gave a spirited performance of 'Holiday Rock'. Paul also became the first of the series stars to become the surprise victim for *This Is Your Life* in December 1981. Several members of the Maplin's staff were also contracted to perform pantomime together - so Paul Shane, Ruth Madoc, Jeffrey Holland, Leslie Dwyer and Barry Howard packed their bags and headed to Birmingham for the pantomime season, appearing with Lena Zavaroni in *Babes in the Wood*. Leslie Dwyer's continuing health problems meant that he missed much of the run but thankfully he was able to rejoin his colleagues by the time Maplin's called once more.

One again the internal BBC Viewing Panel Report commissioned to find out the reaction from a sample audience, gave a very definite thumbs up to the second outing of the series. "The appeal of Hi-de-Hi! seemed to be two fold," it went on to say. "Reportedly viewers warmed to it because the situations seemed true to life and the characters were all well-rounded… the scripts were felt to be particularly well written and because they did not stretch the limits of credibility too far but created the comedy from within the characters, extremely successfully, it was said." The regular doses of the Maplin's staff caused favourites to emerge. The report further summarised: "Su Pollard as Peggy was marginally the most popular and she was thought to have given an extremely funny and very natural performance. Very close behind her was Ruth Madoc as Gladys, and the relationship between these two was often regarded as one of the funniest elements. Of the men, Simon Cadell was praised and he was often felt to have the most difficult role, which he carried off very well, according to the sample audience. Paul Shane as Ted was also very well liked."

A sure sign of the programme's importance in the schedules was that it started to be imitated in other shows. Notably the comedy sketch series *Three Of A Kind* had a go at lampooning the show with David Copperfield as Ted, Lenny Henry as Gladys and Tracey Ullman as Peggy. This unlikely trio used the catchphrase "Why De Why?" as they poked fun at the Maplin's crowd. Similarly Les Dennis and Dustin Gee became Gladys and Peggy on their primetime BBC Saturday evening *Laughter Show* with a sketch that also included an appearance from Su Pollard as herself.

The filming schedule for 1982 saw two blocks of recording. Series Three (5 episodes) would begin recording in April whilst a further block of 8 episodes for Series Four would include the first 45 minute Christmas special, *Eruptions*, and commence recording

'Carnival Time' - Behind the Scenes

in September. Although commissioned as two separate series all 13 episodes would be shown as one long run on BBC 1 beginning at the end of October 1982. Once again the scripts were of the highest quality, and the calibre of guest artistes was also impressive. John Le Mesurier from *Dad's Army* played Jeffrey's Dean from the University. Paul Shane's old pal from his club land days, Rikki Lee, arrived to play Ted's estranged wife Hilary and sadly another *Dad's Army* stalwart Talfryn Thomas wouldn't live to see the broadcast of his touching role as Gladys' misunderstood brother Gareth. One sequence that proved very memorable was the recording of the burning carnival float in the episode 'Carnival Time'.

"Once again Stuart Fell and myself were hired to double for two of the regular cast, Stuart for Su Pollard and me for Felix Bowness. There was a sequence were the horses bolted off and pulled them both after it. In addition we were asked to assist jointly on staging a stunt which required a runaway wagon to crash into the Maplin's swimming pool. This would require the three Yellowcoat boys and Simon Cadell (possibly doubled by a stuntman) to fall into the pool fully clothed in cowboy costumes as the theme of the carnival was 'cowboys and Indians'. However when it came to filming the scene Stuart and I were a little surprised to learn that Simon Cadell's character was going to be in the wagon as it plunged into the pool and Simon was going to attempt the stunt himself! Although the risks to a seasoned stunt performer would be minimal there is always an 'X' factor in every stunt attempted and an experienced eye will quickly estimate and eliminate these risks. But when an actor undertakes his own stunting and if the shot is set up so that the audience can see it is actually him it adds a new dimension to the action which offers added production value. If time and costs permit, a stuntman will perform a 'dummy run' of the gag for the benefit of the camera but Hi-de-Hi! was always filmed on a tight schedule and in this instance we did not have the luxury of pre-staging the stunt then dragging the coach out and drying it off ready for a second take with the cameras running. So the shot seen in the show was a one-off and it went very smoothly and Simon performed exactly to order."

Derek Ware

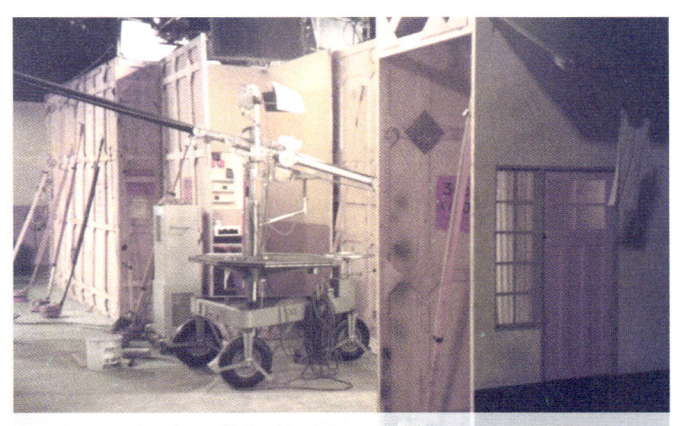

A picture taken literally 'behind the scenes'. To the right there is a chalet door with a washing line hanging outside.

The stunt that nearly went very wrong for Chris Andrews.

However, an unplanned moment occurred when Chris Andrews and Tony Webb were pulled under the cart as it went into the water. Seeing the predicament Simon Cadell quickly and expertly dived under the water and released Chris, who was in more trouble, from being caught up in the gig of the wagon thereby avoiding what could have been a very nasty moment. It was decided not to do another take and, upon examination, even though it still held, the safety wire was down to one strand.

1983 finally saw Hi-de-Hi! triumph at the BAFTA awards. After being nominated in the 'Best Comedy Series' category in 1981 and 1982, the coveted trophy featuring the masks of comedy and tragedy was awarded to the series beating off competition from *A Fine Romance, Last Of The Summer Wine* and *Only Fools and Horses*. The award was accepted by director John Kilby on behalf of himself and David Croft who was recuperating after a heart by-pass operation. It was finally proof from industry peers that Hi-de-Hi! had firmly made the grade at the very top of the television comedy tree. Both the series and Ruth Madoc (for 'Best Light Entertainment Performance') would be nominated the following year too, only to be runners up. But the very fact that the show was continually recognised by the BAFTA panel pointed to the sheer quality of production in all areas on the series. The end of the year also saw the accolade of the cast making a surprise appearance in the *Royal Variety Performance* held in the presence of HM The Queen and hosted by Gene Kelly.

Perry and Croft announced that most of the television names were to re-create their roles live on stage in Hi-de-Hi! *The Holiday Musical*, twice daily for the 1983 summer season in Bournemouth. The box office was booming

'Carnival Time' - Behind the Scenes

within days and a try-out week at the Alexandra Theatre, Birmingham was booked. On the whole the show worked very well from the off.

"I remember one thing that wouldn't work and I improvised something else on the first night which worked better than the original. Ruth Madoc was being a damsel in distress in a jungle and there was a big 'Tarzan cry' on tape so the audiences were expecting me to swing in on a rope and save her. I was supposed to jump on a trampolene then back onto the rope and swing onto stage. But I thought 'I can't do this, I'll break my back.' So on the first night the Tarzan call went out and I just walked on, looked at the audience as if to say 'Do you really think I was going to swing in on a rope?' It worked like a gem and got a huge round of applause."

Simon Cadell

Series Five found it had particular need of a thatched cottage for the episode *Save Our Heritage*. Production manager Susan Belbin (who had started working with David Croft on *Dad's Army*) was despatched to find the correct location.

"I had to go further afield than usual, into Suffolk, because I wanted a cottage with authentic thatch for the period because all the others I had looked at had been re-thatched. When we found our cottage it was on the edge of an Air Base and there was a lot of noise interrupting filming. I made enquiries at the Base and was told there was nothing that could be done. I then decided to call a contact I had at the Ministry of Defence who couldn't admit to anything but gave me an idea when it might be possible to film without any noise. It transpired that the noise was from the testing of the new Stealth Bomber." **Susan Belbin**

"One day unannounced a lady from the BBC (Susie Belbin) knocked on the door and asked if she could use our cottage for some location filming for an episode of Hi-de-Hi! Apparently we were second choice as another cottage had been found nearby but the owner had declined permission for its use. We jumped at the chance and were very excited at the prospect. Confirmation was given by the BBC and a date set, it was all to be done in one day. On the day very early in the morning Paul Shane was the first to turn up and had a desperate need to use the toilet which in those days was a chemical toilet out in the garden but he didn't mind.

Gradually everybody else turned up; we had never seen so much activity outside the cottage and in the lane. It was raining most of the day which changed the first scene because an umbrella was now suddenly required and the prop man had to shoot off to Stowmarket for a period umbrella. Alterations had to be carried out to the cottage, the door was false and again the prop man had to go looking for period hinges and a letter box, this time in Hadleigh. The first floor window had to have the glass removed and be reglazed in sugar glass to enable it to be broken in one of the scenes. The crew had to all struggle up the very narrow staircase to get to the bedroom window for one shot. It was a long day with filming carrying on to early evening. At the time we kept ducks which were a bit of a problem as every time one of the actors spoke they would quack! We had to keep feeding them to keep them quiet. For the final scene (in the episode not as filmed) we made the jam sandwiches in our little kitchen and Ruth Madoc came and helped. Everybody was so nice during the day and every thing was put back as it was found. For the privilege we were paid £100." **The Knock Family**.

Save Our Heritage - Cast and crew gather in the front garden.

The rain resulted in some improvisation with an umbrella.

'Carnival Time' - Behind the Scenes

In the Studio

After the fun and hard work on location it was back to the studio to record the show in front of a live audience. Episodes would normally be recorded on a Sunday evening and Felix Bowness would be on hand to do the warm up in his usual style, explaining to the audience what to expect and pointing out that any location footage would be screened on monitors above their heads.

The designers would have constructed any additional sets that the episode dictated, ensuring a seemless transition from studio to location and vice-versa.

Photographs of actual recordings taking place are rare (the audience are not permitted to bring cameras), but the BBC did use professional photographers to record the dress rehearsal. The BBC also made a photographic record of the sets used for their archives.

Recording a show would normally take between 60 and 90 minutes depending on the complexity of the sets. Some were built out of sight of the audience due to space constraints, the action being relayed via the monitors. Canned laughter was never used. Three episodes were recorded over two days, 'Eruptions', 'The Great Cat Robbery' and 'Only the Brave'. This was necessary to pre-record some scenes (or in the case of 'Only the Brave', add extra sets) so the audience recording sessions were kept to a maximum of two hours. The same policy was used for *You Rang M'Lord?*

Below : Su Pollard during rehearsals for *Sausages or Limelight*, while a camera creeps into view.

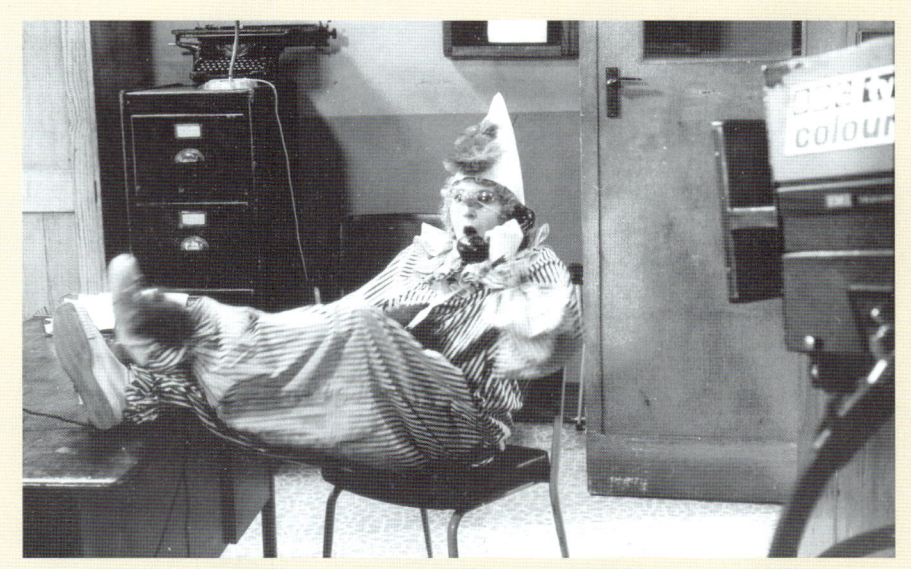

Left : The Entertainments Manager's office.
The Crittal windows are very much in keeping with the era, with the backdrop clearly seen.
The set is dressed with Clive Dempster's mac' hanging on the coat stand.
Also note the different door to the one in the picture above.

89

'Carnival Time' - Behind the Scenes

Rare images of the audience eye view of the recording studio and sets.

Top left : The episode being rehearsed appears to be 'Raffles' from series six.

Sets seem to be scattered around the studio. Filming a scene in Ted and Spike's chalet, the large monitor on the left can be seen clearly. At the rear are the stables, (above with Jeffrey Holland in his Christmas pudding costume).

Left : Setting up in the main office, the monitors are showing action from another part of the set. The staff room can just be seen to the right, and to the left is a line of chalets which are glimpsed outside when filming inside a chalet. They are also in evidence to the right in the picture above.

Left : The familiar staff room. There are some lovely touches, including the small sink with Ascot wall heater, the single ring gas stove, the water jug in the foreground with cups on the tray, including two china cups, one presumes for Yvonne and Barry. Oversized comedy props are placed above the cupboards.

'Carnival Time' - Behind the Scenes

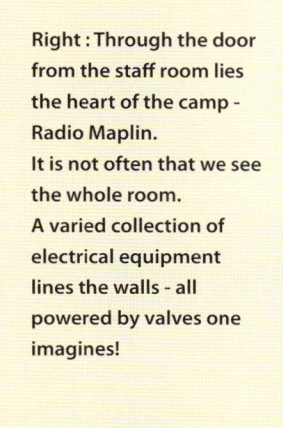

Right: Through the door from the staff room lies the heart of the camp - Radio Maplin.
It is not often that we see the whole room.
A varied collection of electrical equipment lines the walls - all powered by valves one imagines!

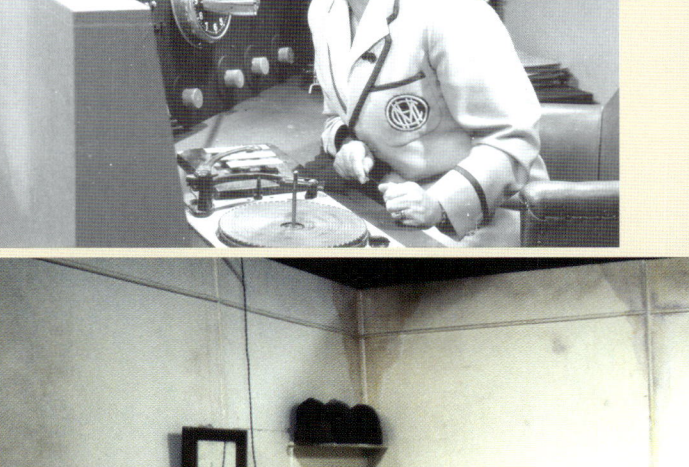

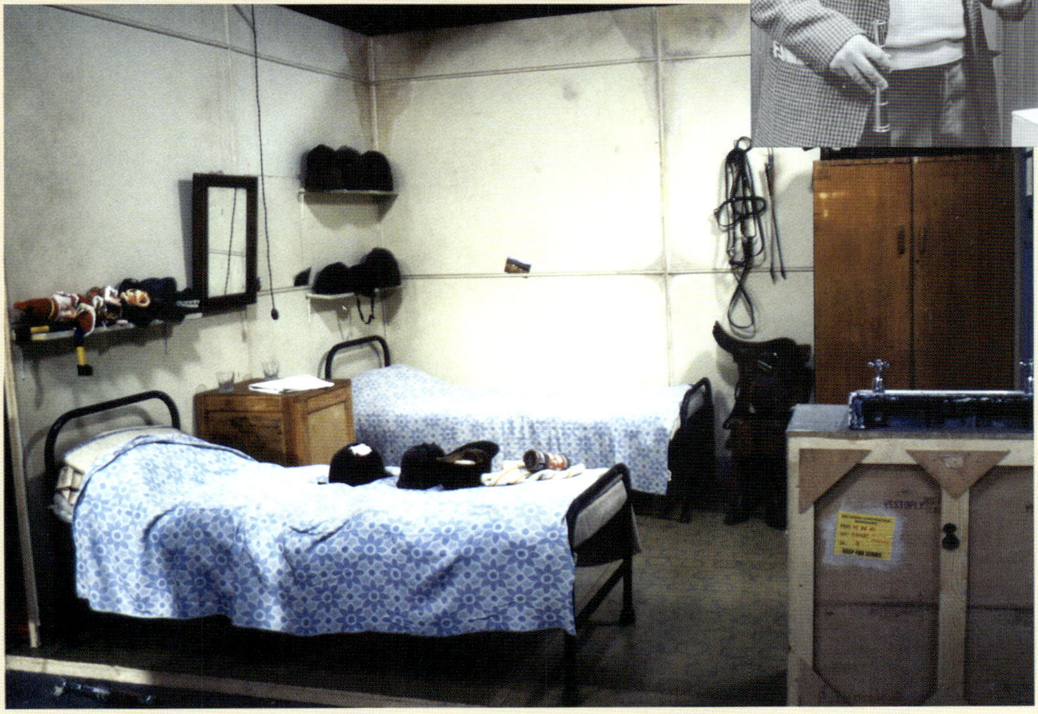

Left: Mr. Partridge and Fred Quilly's chalet.
The designers have recreated an authentic chalet, with the thin panel walls complete with staining. Fred's riding gear can be seen on the walls and shelves by his bed, and Mr Partridge has placed Mr Punch on the shelf above his.

91

'Carnival Time' - Behind the Scenes

Save Our Heritage - the early rain cleared enabling filming to commence.

The programme was riding the crest of a wave, one of the biggest ratings pullers for the BBC. But then came the news that everyone feared. Simon Cadell had been getting restless in the role of Jeffrey Fairbrother. He wanted to move on, and had been offered the role of Hamlet in Birmingham. He was intending to leave at the end of Series Four but the production of the Shakespeare play got put back by twelve months so he found himself unexpectedly free and able to record another six episodes in the autumn of 1983. But with his commitments to the Hi-de-Hi! stage musical, which by then had moved to the Victoria Palace in the West End, completed in March 1984, Simon finally bade farewell to the character that had established him as a major star. Simon told Sheridan Morley in *The Times* exactly why he was leaving. "Fairbrother begins to bore me, and when a character does that then you must stop playing him as soon as you can. Not that I would have wanted to miss the chance, these last four years of my life have been extremely happy, and there's not doubt that a hit comedy series on television moves you further forward in the theatre than a hit drama series." As he headed to the Midlands to take up the challenge of playing Hamlet, Simon bemoaned: "I live in dread of the night in Birmingham that I go out to do the first soliloquy and somebody calls out 'hi-de-hi' from the gallery. It's already happened to me before on a tour of *Private Lives* and it's the kind of thing you lie awake worrying about." In the Hi-de-Hi! musical Simon was replaced by *It Ain't Half Hot Mum* star Michael Knowles, who would also stay with the cast when the entire production moved to Blackpool for the summer of 1984.

"It wasn't really a brave decision, my daughters needed to be educated. It was daunting taking over from someone but on the other hand I figured it was maybe a part that I could have played originally. Duncan Weldon, the Producer of the stage show, came up to me afterwards and his only comment was 'Very good, but you're too good looking for the part.' It seemed a very odd reaction to me taking over." **Michael Knowles**

With planning firmly underway for series six, the question was how could the absence of such a pivotal television performance be replaced? Never wishing to offer audiences a pale imitation of an outgoing character, Jimmy and David invented The Right Honourable Squadron Leader Clive Dempster DFC. A titled playboy who had somehow got himself decorated in the war and now offers his services to Joe Maplin.

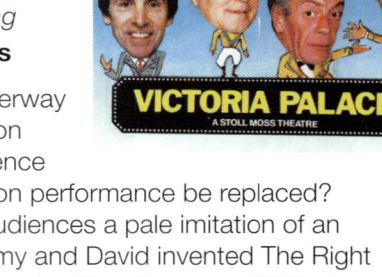

"Generally speaking ex-Army people - usually Majors - used to be in charge of holiday camps because they were good organisers, had authority and integrity to do the job. After the war Butlin's was run by Colonel Brown who been in the Army with my agent Richard Stone. So that's why a Squadron Leader found his way into the Maplin's hierarchy." **David Croft**

The search was then on to find an actor to play the part. Casting is always done very carefully by Croft and Perry, ensuring they get exactly the right actor for the character they have written. Quite a few actors were seen for the role but none of them quite matched the character on the written page.

"Clive Dempster was based on the Kenneth More part in the 1955 movie *The Deep Blue Sea*. The Squadron Leader who can't settle down. He's gigolo-ing and he hates himself for it. A wonderfully flawed character. We saw a photo in *Spotlight* [the actors' directory] of David Griffin in a uniform from a part he had played previously and that gave us the idea to see him. He played the part in a slightly raffish way. I liked David Griffin's performance very much." **Jimmy Perry**

David was familiar with the holiday camps before joining the fictional staff at Crimpton-on-Sea. "Strangely enough my first theatrical job was in Butlin's holiday camp at Clacton." he told the press when his appointment was announced. "We used to put on six one-

DID YOU KNOW? Clive and Gladys were not the only couple to hear wedding bells chime at Maplin's? Production Manager Roy Gould met his wife Sarah on the show, Yellowcoat Laura Jackson married Sound Recordist Michael Spencer and Production Manager Susan Belbin also met her husband Props Assistant Johnie Shier on set.

'Carnival Time' - Behind the Scenes

Leslie Dwyer and veteran comic Jan Harding as the Station Master who appeared in *Together Again* and *Opening Day*.

hour plays every two weeks. Two farces, two thrillers and two comedies. We got eight quid a week and I seemed to have a good time on it. I've had my ups and downs over the years. I've done just about everything to keep a roof over my head. I've been a car delivery driver, a painter and decorator, a gardener - I have developed a lot of skills to support my career as an actor."

The arrival of Clive Dempster proved to be a new start for Hi-de-Hi! It was a particular challenge to Ruth Madoc who had to play less of the vamp. She had been used to flirting outrageously with Jeffrey Fairbrother but was now in the position of spurning Clive Dempster's none too subtle invitations to his bed. So forcibly a new dynamic was created. And the series veered off into a different direction. It became clear during the recording of the location work at Dovercourt that Leslie Dwyer's health was failing rapidly.

"It was during the filming at Weybourne Station that I realised that Leslie was having further health problems. He looked and behaved well enough, and seemed superficially to be his usual self. We, Leslie and I, were in the Punch and Judy booth on the railway station. Playing the part of Mr. Partridge, Leslie was to have an argument with the ticket collector, played by the droll comedian Jan Harding, whilst leaning through the proscenium arch of the Punch booth. To do this comfortably he was stood on a stool that I had made for him. I was out of sight at the time and holding Mr. Punch. Leslie looked down and me and asked "What are we doing now?" Without realising that Leslie had a problem I said "What do you mean?" He replied, "Give me the cue. What's next?" "We are on the railway station, you are going to have a row with the ticket collector and your cue is...." "OK, I've got it." He interrupted. Somewhat puzzled I breathed a sigh of relief and reflected that it is very easy to confuse one scene with another. Within a couple of minutes Leslie repeated the question and received the same answer. Fortunately the command "Action" came as I gave him the cue. Leslie delivered his lines, the scene was finished and all seemed well.

That concluded my work for that episode. The following day as I drove home I heard on the car radio that the veteran actor Leslie Dwyer had been taken to hospital by ambulance with suspected heart problems. That explained his confusion. I was glad to have been able to help him conclude the scene without his being embarrassed." **Professor Guy Higgins**

Finally he accepted he could not be involved in the following studio recording blocks. This caused some headache for the writers as the scripts had been written with Mr. Partridge taking full part. However, a compromise was reached with a new character – the camp plumber - played by Ronnie Brody filling in some dialogue in the gaps left by Leslie's absence.

"During the next few months he was fitted with a pacemaker which most certainly gave him a new lease of life. When we next met on location he grabbed my hand, pushed it under his shirt at chest level and grinning said "Feel that, I am bionic now." Sure enough, the pacemaker could be felt through his skin. He was back to his old self, telling jokes and pro-stories and acting the part of that infamous alcoholic child-hating children's entertainer Mr. Partridge. Apparently he was more active than the pace-maker could manage, and sadly died a few months later. A sad loss to family and friends and to Hi-de-Hi!" **Professor Guy Higgins**

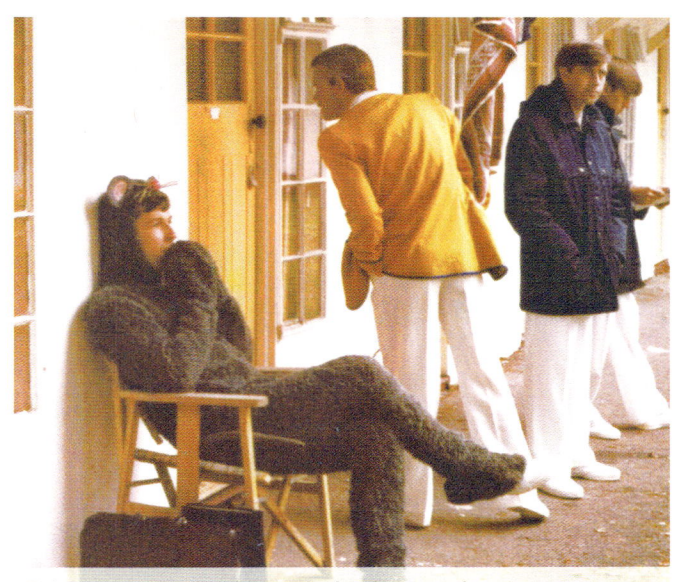

Relaxing between takes outside the chalets on location. Jeff Holland, Terry Creasey and the Webb Twins.

'Carnival Time' - Behind the Scenes

Filming at 'Moulton Junction'

Recording for series six commenced on Wednesday 26th September 1984, but this time not at Warner's Holiday Centre, but Weybourne Station in Norfolk which was to be seen twice in the forthcoming episodes as Moulton Junction.

The day would be taken up with musicians recording a 'wild track' for episode 3, namely tuning up and 'Jolly Good Company'. Then the shots were taken for the Maplin's staff arrival at Moulton Junction in episode 1, *Together Again*. To give an idea of the massive operation that a location shoot like this can be, the 'call sheet' for Saturday 29th September 1984 at Weybourne to record the scene in *Opening Day*, where the campers arrive by train and are greeted by the Maplin's entourage, was as follows:

A copy of the 1984 series six Filming Schedule.

Paul Shane	Ted
Su Pollard	Peggy
Jeffrey Holland	Spike
Felix Bowness	Fred
Diane Holland	Yvonne
Barry Howard	Barry
Ruth Madoc	Gladys
Jan Harding	Station Master
David Webb	Bruce
Tony Webb	Stanley
Chris Andrews	Gary
Linda Regan	April
Laura Jackson	Dawn
Julie-Christian Young	Babs
Nikki Kelly	Sylvia
David Griffin	Clive
Albert Welch	Bert Swanley
Jason James	Trumpeter
Tommy Winward	Saxophone
Michael Leader	Big drum
Colin Bower	Porter
Mervyn Eden	Porter
Martin Townsend	Guard
Professor Guy Higgins	Punch and Judy

Joining them were the many supporting artists employed as extras. All were named on the call sheet, alphabetically; Mitchell Armstrong, Adrian Kirk Ash, John Gordon Ash, Roy Bradley, Richard Briddock, David Caddick, Tim Cooper, Nigel Descombes, Maxmillian Fox, Norman Fisher, Chris Holland, Steve James, Mark Kelly, Rex Lear, Lloyd Mahoney, Dennis Marriot, Billy Maxwell, Mervyn Miller, Johnny Pat, Andy Pearson, Vince Rayner. Jenny Richards, David Thompsen, Terry Treloar, John D. Vincent, Nigel Wren, Jimmy Jermain, Tony Dennis, Adrian Hutson, Cyril Crook, Tony Fabian, Michael Taylor, David Corner, Anthony Noel, Theresa Ash, Marjorie Butters, Phyllis Coleman, Yvonne Collier, Kelly Condell, Laura Foster, Mary Formby, Sue Franklin, Liza Gray, Kristin Helga, Alison Howard, Sarah Jones Parry, Jean Lear, Glen MacKeith, Christine Marriott, Ros Murray, Stephanie Miller, Jill Oliver, Barbara Ray, Diane Raynor, Amanda Jane Rickett, Honra Sims, Dorothy Smith, Janet Sparham, Gloria Stewart, Mary Tovey, Julie Reynolds, Lorraine Turner, Patsy Urqhart, Sue Whitemarsh, Jean Wren, Loretta Jeanette Wren, Alison Lesley, Karen Wragg, Jackie Howe, Jana Garcia, Suzanne Rayner, Patricia Hughes, Jean Kitson

All told 96 artists were booked for the scene plus 30 children from Kelling Country Primary School, Holt, Norfolk were hired to be junior campers. The props requested for the day were:

Accordion / trumpet / saxophone / big drum / long trestle table / 200 paper cups / 8 large jugs of water / catering

'Carnival Time' - Behind the Scenes

trays / 100 full sized rock cakes / 2 large seven pound tins of lemonade crystals / Gladys' watch / pint mug beer / ½ pint shandy / 2nd pint beer / letter on yellow note paper with dialogue / large spoon / staff gratuity box / crinkled brown paper parcel / Porter's ticket punch / red clown's nose / £5 note / 5 x £1 notes / gent's wallet / 2nd gent's wallet / Guard's flags / whistle / station bell / chewing gum / whip / tickler / megaphone / luggage for 100 campers / Porters' trolleys / Punch and Judy puppets / large gin and tonic / money for campers.

The graphics department were asked to provide a banner to go on front of the steam engine, 'Maplin's Holiday Express'. Whilst the steam train would be the main feature of the scene, also required for the day were 3 coaches and Clive's M.G. sports car.

There is a note against the graphics section which reads '2 off large notice, red on a white background (to go across the top of the tunnel) "Welcome to Maplins" (2nd notice to have great black mark up the middle').

The caterers were kept very busy providing coffee for 82 at 8.00am, breakfast for 22 at 8.30am, rolls (10.30am), lunch (1pm) and afternoon tea (4pm) for all 210! Two dining coaches were required to accomodate them in a couple of sittings.

The shoot would last from 9am until wrap at 6pm, although on some days they were only allowed to film before 11am and after 4pm to allow for the train service to run. During the time at Weybourne a photo shoot was arranged which would provide Hi-de-Hi! with its second Radio Times cover to launch the new series. The unit would spend a full week at Weybourne Station before returning to the more familiar environment of Warner's at Dovercourt on Tuesday 2nd October 1984. The recording continued until Monday 15th October when the sequences raffling Clive's car would be recorded in the Hawaiian Ballroom from episode 6. It was back to London for all the cast and production team for rehearsals and studio recordings at TV Centre for the next six weeks.

'Carnival Time' - Behind the Scenes

There was also a change among the girl Yellowcoats. Although Nikki Kelly was a constant it was now time for a change in the personnel although this wasn't always by choice of the producer.

"Penny Irving decided she didn't want to do a second series, for whatever reason. Gail Harrison arrived but then got more important work. Susan Beagley got a big break in a television version of Julian Slade's Salad Days playing the lead. We didn't get rid of them, they got rid of themselves by getting alternative employment."

David Croft

Rikki Howard had earlier decided to leave the series due to her pregnancy, it was a chance for Perry and Croft to introduce three new girls. Linda Regan would play April Wingate, a girlfriend for Spike. Laura Jackson became Dawn Freshwater and Julie-Christian Young made up the new trio as Babs Weaver. The Radio Times arranged a photoshoot involving all three newcomers in a variety of poses and outfits, these pictures were uncovered during research for this book.

As if to re-launch the series with the change of line up, Jimmy and David chose to echo the original pilot by having Ted, Spike and Peggy on a train headed for Crimpton-on-Sea and the start of the 1960 season. The staff do not know that Jeffrey Fairbrother has taken a post in archaeology based in Wisconsin, and the opening episode *Together Again* deals with his departure and in particular how the loss of her beloved Jeffrey has affected Gladys. But by the following episode Squadron Leader Clive Dempster ups the ante with his arrival at Maplin's to give the series the kick start it needs to stop it dwelling on missing faces. The staff are taken off the camp and down to Moulton Junction. Incorporating Clive Dempster into Maplin's was a difficult task for the writers.

Filming on location in the basement bar of the Cliff Hotel, Dovercourt. The main actors and production staff stayed at the hotel.

Their original premise for the show, of a fish-out-of-water Entertainments Manager, had been cut short by force of necessity. It would take the whole of series six before the programme fully accepted the Squadron Leader into its bosom. Initially his qualities of being a cad threatened to make him a little un-likeable, but finally the writers settled on a characterisation that would settle well into the niche of Maplins. From the following season, David Griffin would firmly establish himself as a major force in the hierarchy of the camp.

A cracking Christmas special *The Great Cat Robbery* heralded the start of the seventh series. A full one hour slot was allocated to the show, and it was put to full use as Ted discovers a valuable necklace has been hidden on the camp by a burglar. Of all the specials the show produced, this perhaps is the finest. The staff ransacking the chalets and doping the campers creates comic gold. Perry and Croft devised a way to write out Mr. Partridge

Creating the Summer sunshine outside the chalets.

Preparing a scene outside the staff chalets. Were the roses props?

'Carnival Time' - Behind the Scenes

with some dramatic happenings around the pool as the full series got underway. The body of Mr. Partridge is apparently discovered floating in the pool. 'Who Killed Mr. Partridge?' was a spirited attempt at lampooning detective dramas and Agatha Christie, where everyone present is under suspicion.

Carry On veteran Kenneth Connor was signed up to be a guest star, portraying entertainer Uncle Sammy Morris whom Ted and Spike discover entertaining kids for a few shillings on the beach. Ted had suffered the indignities of being Humpty Dumpty and Spike Wee Willie Winkie in the episode *A Lack Of Punch* (not to mention the hysterical sight of Yvonne and Barry being forced into playing Little Miss Muffet and Percy The Pixie). Ted therefore decides that he will get Sammy, who has fallen on hard times and become a tramp, to be the new kids entertainer on the camp. Connor's performance is masterful as you would expect, and this episode remains among the best the series had to offer. Connor was at the time also appearing as Monsieur Alfonse in another David Croft classic, 'Allo 'Allo. A regular face on the set was choreographer Kenn Oldfield. Kenn had trained with the Ballet Rambert and had gone into directing and choreography. He found himself on the set from the fifth series and would help provide all aspects of staging the ballroom numbers.

> **DID YOU KNOW?**
> The interior coach scene in 'Only The Brave' supposedly outside the Electric Palace Cinema at night, was in fact recorded outside the Cliff Hotel using 'day-for-night' photography.

"I'm not quite sure how I got the job with David Croft. It might have been on the recommendation of Su Pollard. Anyhow, my agent got the call and I went down to Dovercourt. My main concern I suppose was making the routines of Barry and Yvonne look as good as it could be. Mind you part of my job was to make sure the routines were 'in character'. That is to say, making sure they didn't look too good as the characters were not supposed to be at the top of their professions. David would only let the band or the organist record their tracks once, because he didn't want it to sound too good. The first run through was all he wanted. Working with Diane Holland was a joy. She had a very painful hip and would walk with a limp into rehearsals. But when she played the scenes as Yvonne you would never know. She hid it very well. Barry Howard wasn't a dancer per se, but he had had a lot of experience in musicals and could act the role of a dancer very well. Sometimes the scenes were so well organised anyway I used to think 'What am I doing here?' I remember one routine where Barry was dressed as a Monk and Diane was a Nun I think. We went away

Flming 'The Perils of Peggy' in the sand dunes at West End Beach, Dovercourt.

'Carnival Time' - Behind the Scenes

The final line up, although Kenneth Connor was to join from series eight as 'Uncle Sammy'.

and did some rehearsal away from the main recording and then I asked David to come and look what we had done. He nearly wet himself laughing! Diane had hitched up her habit and was doing some very suggestive bump and grind moves and Barry was being all Dirty Dancing. Suffice to say there was no way he would allow it in the programme but we all laughed ourselves silly at the time. I just remember the fun really. It led to work on 'Allo 'Allo and later You Rang, M'Lord? for David. One year it was decided that several of us would stay in caravans nearby to the camp and there were parties galore. I don't think I have ever had hangovers quite so bad since. Very happy times." **Kenn Oldfield**

The recording block for the eighth series at the end of September 1986 saw a major cast change. It was announced by The Sun newspaper that Barry Howard was being replaced in the series. He had been suffering from an addiction illness for some time and eventually David Croft took the difficult decision to drop the character of Barry Stuart-Hargreaves from the series.

"Barry Howard became very ill which affected the whole company and he became very bad tempered. His performances were suffering but when he left the series it also created a huge gap. Barry is a great performer. A few years later he gave a wonderful performance for me in You Rang, M'Lord? *It was a natural step to ask Ben Aris back to re-create his role as Julian Dalrymple-Sykes, Yvonne's former amour, to try and plug the gap. From a comedy point of view it wasn't as funny because the relationship wasn't so subtle."* **David Croft**

"I think I saw a couple [of Ben Aris' episodes]. I felt a bit sorry for Ben Aris because the scriptwriters were governed by the situation: Yvonne had to have a partner. He couldn't play Barry Stuart-Hargreaves but had to find similar qualities. So he wasn't as free to find his own characterisation." **Barry Howard**

Another returning face in series eight was Kenneth Connor. Paul Shane and Jeffrey Holland had enjoyed working with Connor so much on *A Lack Of Punch* that they harangued Jimmy and David for a long time before the two writers gave into pressure and brought Sammy back to Maplin's to join the regulars. Whilst the character proved popular, David conceded they found it hard to get sympathy for

> **DID YOU KNOW?**
> The MG sports car that Jeffrey Fairbrother's wife Daphne drives in 'The Marriage Settlement' is the same car driven by Clive Dempster in several of the later episodes.

'Carnival Time' - Behind the Scenes

what is basically a dirty, smelly old man. For the following series, they had him cleaned up and outfitted in order that he was not the pariah among the rest of the staff that he had been.

Series seven and eight also saw Robin Carr taking the Director's mantle. David Croft was always keen that his staff should advance themselves if he saw their potential.

"The reason everyone returned year after year to Hi-de-Hi! - and all other David Croft productions - was the man himself. As a Producer and a man, David engendered loyalty like no one else I have ever met. Once you worked with David - and the feeling was you worked with him and not for him - you wanted more. The conditions at Warner's were far from perfect, and sometimes the weather made it downright miserable, and yet every year the same faces were there - and wouldn't have been anywhere else. Although the cameramen were BBC staff, most of the other's - the gaffers, best boys and so on - were freelance and spent much of their year at Pinewood or Shepperton Studios making movies. One year the making of a Superman movie was brought to a standstill because the crew were already booked on Hi-de-Hi! The director realised his best people were going to be missing, cancelled the shoot and gave everyone a three week holiday. Fantastic but true." **Robin Carr**

The eighth series had a slightly darker edge, and moved towards a more episodic format, with the arrival of Camp Controller Alec Foster (played magnificently by Ewan Hooper) who would be a real Mr. Nasty. The cosy atmosphere of Maplin's was shattered as he threatened to sack staff and even sought to lure Peggy back to his chalet for immoral purposes. It takes Uncle Sammy's intervention to stop all the camp regulars from becoming a victim of Foster's wrath.

Perry and Croft took a decision in the Christmas special for 1986, *September Song*, to allow Paul Shane a storyline involving much pathos when Ted falls for a talented young pianist, Betty Barlow, whom he plans to marry. However Betty's mother turns up putting a spoke in the works, leaving Ted for once totally bereft. Shane's performance in this is one of his finest in all the programmes he has made for David Croft, showing just what an instinctive actor he can be. There was still time for merriment though as the cameras rolled in Dovercourt.

"Whenever David allowed one of his juniors to direct a series he'd always keep one episode to himself. In the studio this would mean he would be taking rehearsals each day and also run the studio. On location though, this meant David would direct a scene and once it was in the can, he'd leave the rest of the day to the Director. David's episode in this series involved a long, complicated Ballroom scene and for the whole day I had nothing to do. The make-up girl and the costume girls took pity on me and decided I had to appear as an extra. As a female extra, that is. They spent hours costuming me, finding a wig and making me up. Finally I was smuggled onto the set. There I sat, unnoticed until I eventually stood up at the beginning of a scene, took the clapperboard and said "Scene 114. Take 1." It was then David realised I'd been in his scene all day. And yes, I can be seen in drag in Hi-de-Hi!" **Robin Carr**

Just three days after the broadcast of *September Song*, one of Maplin's original inhabitants Leslie Dwyer died peacefully in hospital. With a case of extreme bad timing a repeat of the Hi-de-Hi! episode *Who Killed Mr. Partridge?* had been scheduled just days later. David Griffin, who worked with Leslie on just one series of the show, was sure he wouldn't have been offended. "I don't

DID YOU KNOW?

In the episode 'Lack of Punch', the scene with Kenneth Connor in the bath was actually mocked up with 'flats' in the ballroom.

Paul and Ruth happily sign fans' autograph books while on location.

'Carnival Time' - Behind the Scenes

think Leslie would have minded in the slightest." Griffin told Today newspaper. "He would have seen the funny side." Memories of working with the veteran of so many films and stage productions, were vivid in David's mind. "Leslie was terribly absent minded and while we were staying at a hotel in Norfolk during filming I walked over to Leslie and Felix Bowness, who were having breakfast. Now don't forget we had been working together for something like ten days. But when I got to the table I opened my mouth to say hello but he greeted me with 'Ah waiter… we'd like some more toast.' I stood there absolutely stunned for a moment until I collected my wits and replied, 'Yes sir… can I get you some more coffee as well?' Everyone ribbed him mercilessly and after that he used to deliberately pretend he didn't know who I was." It was during the making of series eight that Croft and Perry finally revealed to the cast that the following year would be the last at Maplin's.

"I think there is always a time to stop. It is a big mistake to make another series when you feel it is time to go. I remember making speeches to the cast before they went on saying 'You are all big stars but remember your characters are failures, otherwise you are defeating the object.' Actors can turn into caricatures of what was originally intended." **David Croft**

"We were all doing it. The only one who wasn't guilty was Diane Holland. She never altered her character from day one to the last minute. Never. She was brilliant."

Paul Shane

And so in the Autumn of 1987 as the BBC rolled into the sleepy bay of Dovercourt for the final time, a certain sadness descended over the cast. Sure they were all having fun producing the latest batch of episodes but the end was drawing near. Perry and Croft however had something very special up their sleeves for the end of Maplin's on our screens.
The filming at Dovercourt went smoothly. The final sequence with Peggy walking down the camp, before

Dress rehearsal for Let Them Eat Cake. *The characters go through their scripts with Ted.*

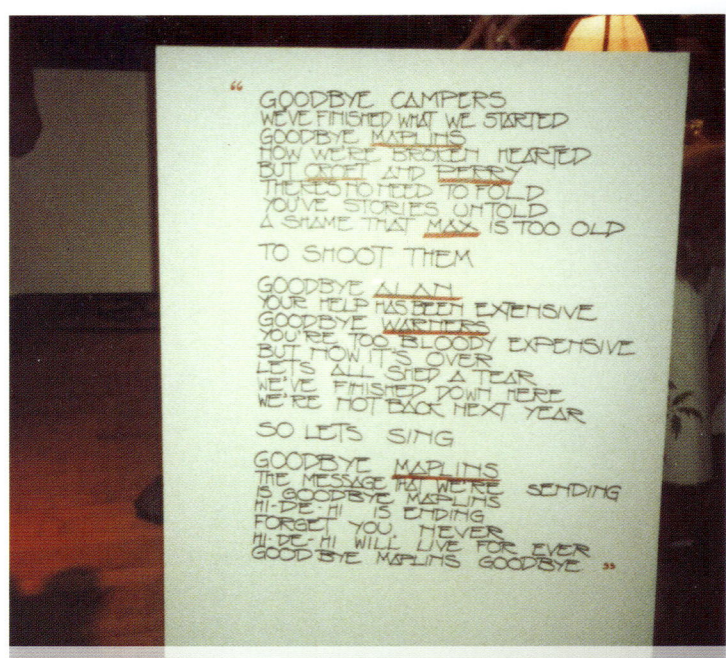

Goodbye Campers - the lyrics to a special rendition the cast and crew sang to Jimmy Perry and David Croft on the last day of location filming.

shouting one final triumphant "Hi de Hi" to camera, took 28 takes to achieve. Very cleverly David Croft inserted this moving final piece into the middle of the filming schedule, so that it didn't feel too much like an end as they still had plenty of recording to do for other episodes. Just as the unit reached the end of their three week stay with most of the location footage in the bag, fate had one final surprise in store for them. On 16th October 1987, a mighty storm hit the south coast of England which would have a devastating effect on the country. Winds in excess of 100 miles per hour were recorded, the destruction was huge and resulted nationwide in a death toll of 16 people.

"During the night Ruth Madoc came down to The Cliff Hotel reception and told the Night Porter her room was moving. The floor was apparently lifting due to the joists which ran through the wall to from the balcony, which of course was incurring the full force of the sea front winds. Ruth took up residence in the kitchen answering telephone calls whilst the Night Porter braved the weather to fetch me from home, as the storm worsened."

John Wade

The little camp at Dovercourt was caught in it's fury as roofs were ripped from buildings. One of the production team decided to brave the storm and headed to the toilet block for a call of nature. When he returned one of the poplar trees had crashed right through his chalet! A lucky escape indeed. It was a scene of carnage that greeted the cast and crew as they emerged from their chalets and hotels the following morning. They were due to record the final sequence that day, with the Yellowcoats and a crowd of extras playing the campers singing "Goodnight Campers" for one final time. The wind of

'Carnival Time' - Behind the Scenes

'The Wind of Change' certainly came to Dovercourt with devastating effect. Some of the chalets were also destroyed.

change had indeed made it's presence felt, and looking at the battered camp it was now evident that Maplin's was closing for good. The BBC wouldn't be back and it was as if the elements had realised this, and said a noisy and destructive farewell to the camp.

"We only had about 20 supporting artistes turn up on the day after the hurricane so we had to make it look like the usual number by changing costumes and moving them around. I remember trying to arrange with Director Mike Stephens the lifting of a tree off our generator lorry. We had no power that day and could only manage some brief filming." **Roy Gould** *(Production Manager)*

A rapid re-think of the schedule was needed in the wake of this unexpected invasion by Mother Nature. The initial plan to partly record the final scene around the pool was abandoned as the effects of the storm were clearly seen all around and there was no way even the BBC could disguise this. It was decided that the stand-by day [an additional location day allocated in case of unexpected problems but rarely used] on Saturday 18th October would be used to record the final scene in the camp Ballroom. Given what had gone just hours before, the atmosphere was heightened on set especially when it came to singing the farewell song in the Ballroom.

"We got Bert Swanley and the Debonairs to play Goodnight Campers *whilst the cast and crew hummed along to it in order to record the track for playing over the final sequence. Hairs stood up on the back of my neck as I conducted it. It was a very moving moment for us all."*

David Croft

Back in London, with rehearsals re-commencing at the 'Acton Hilton' and several weeks of studio recordings to do, the cast were back to their old jolly selves. The final series kicked off with a slapstick romp *Tell It To The Marines* where Ted challenges the Marine display team to a competition over an assault course. Su Pollard showed off her physical comedy skills to the hilt as the programme showed it was going out with a bang. The television review programme *Did You See?* hosted by Ludovic Kennedy on BBC 2 chose this episode to put under the spotlight with some guest presenters taking a look at Perry and Croft's hit creation. Kenneth Williams likened it to the *Carry On's*, saying that it was a true ensemble effort in the great spirit of the classic film series. Kit Hesketh-Harvey (husband of Catherine Rabett, herself shortly to join the Perry and Croft stable) was more muted in his praise feeling that perhaps the programme had run it's course, whilst Janet Street Porter thought it was 'absolutely brilliant' in comparison to a spate of awful sit-coms that she had seen recently. One of the episodes of the final run, *Let Them Eat Cake*, proved to be a showcase for the vocal talents of Spike Dixon.

"Jimmy Perry had always been on at me to get an act together as an impressionist. There are so many impressionists around though and many are so much better than me. I have got a gift for mimicry and I used to entertain my friends behind the camera, which is fine. But to do it on stage professionally is another matter. So Jimmy wrote this episode of Hi-de-Hi! in which I had to do all the voices. It was a French Revolution tableau and he got me to do Arthur Askey, Burt Lancaster, Alec Guinness, Olivier… So I was forced to do my repertoire in front of millions." **Jeffrey Holland**

The cast assemble for an informal group shot after a day's filming in the ballroom.

'Carnival Time' - Behind the Scenes

In the scripts Gladys marries Clive as the 1960 season draws to a close. After spending the previous three series chasing after all the Yellowcoats, it seemed a bit improbable that Clive should suddenly want to settle down with Gladys. But the end was nigh, and all stories have to have an ending.

The final episode *The Wind Of Change* proved to be one of the most memorable of all 58 in the canon. Joe Maplin reveals that he is doing away with all Yellowcoats and that the camps will have a modern make-over with self catering coming in and certainly no more 'Hi-de-Hi!' It was an eerie foretaste of what happened to the holiday industry in later years. When Ted sits around the pool and says, "They have had the best of it Spike, they'll all go abroad now. They'll have the sun, but without you and me they won't have the fun." It was a summing up of the decline of the holiday camp movement. Finally the day that everybody had been dreading arrived. Friday 27th November 1987 saw the recording of the final episode at TV Centre. As if Joe Maplin had sent out a call to arms, the family was completed by former cast members Simon Cadell and Barry Howard returning to Maplin's to take their place among the studio audience. Very wisely, the action was played out up until the showing of the final 15 minutes which had been deliberately all made at Dovercourt two months previously. David Croft made sure that all the end credits shots of the cast smiling and waving at the camera were taken before the lights were dimmed and the footage was shown to the audience, and all involved with the show, for the first time. There was not a dry eye in the house! The atmosphere became highly emotional and the cast and crew cried and hugged each other as the final strains of 'Holiday Rock' blared out from the monitors. The cast were all given their copies of Joe Maplin's autobiography 'How I Done It' as seen in the last episode. It would take just over two months for the episode to air, and the viewers were rewarded with a funny and ultimately touching episode which allowed 15 million people to say a fond farewell to old friends.

With cast and writers onto new pastures, the staff of Maplin's faded into legend. Perry and Croft have over the years declined several offers of resurrecting the characters for charity fundraisers or television reunion shows. However David Croft did let slip to the Radio Times in 2003 what he thought had become of our friends at Crimpton-on-Sea:

"The only person from Maplin's who did anything with his life was Jeffrey Fairbrother, who went back to Cambridge to pursue his academic career and became a successful Professor. The rest of them hovered on the fringes of show business: they weren't good enough to do anything much in the real world. They were stars in the little enclosed world of the holiday camp, but if they had to face any professional competition they wouldn't have stood a chance. Yvonne and Barry were typical of that: they thought they were the best ballroom dancers in the world, but they were a sad old couple really. There was something quite vicious about the humour in Hi-de-Hi! Gladys married Squadron Leader Clive, and the marriage teetered on for years, although she was always frustrated about her lack of opportunities in life. Ted went back to the second-rate comedy circuit whence he came. Over the years his material became cruder and cruder to keep up with the times, and he ended up like Bernard Manning. As for Peggy: she finally realised her dream of becoming a Yellowcoat, and was a highly regarded member of the Maplin's staff. She was the happiest of the lot."

Memories of a Maplin's 'Camper'

"My first day of filming for Hi-de-Hi! started by meeting up with other supporting artists at Colchester railway station where we were taken by bus up to north Norfolk so we could spend the day getting on and off a steam train. Not knowing a single soul it was all a bit daunting but by the time we reached Norfolk it was as though we had all been friends for years, and that was the way it remained right up to the very last episode four years later.

We certainly went through some experiences together from being cheer leaders (I shouted loudest for the 'Kent' team) in what felt like freezing condition around the 'Olympic Size Swimming Pool' pretending it was the height of summer, but our discomfort was nothing to that of Spike, whom we all agreed should be thrown into the pool on several occasions. There were times when it was even pouring with rain, but you just can't see that on the film. Other very wet underfoot sequences were taken in Friday Wood, Colchester, as we cheered the teams over the Army obstacle course – the wellies were kept out of shot, but were a necessity especially to reach the catering van! Oh - they always did feed us well.

Keep fit with Gladys Pugh was also good fun as we ladies all did our 'I must, I must, I must improve my bust' exercises whilst the camera kept sneaking around to find some unusual angles! Glad I was wearing shorts and a tee shirt that did not require buttons! Others were not quite so fortunate!

Our roles and costumes varied from nightwear and hair curlers as we patiently queued in the early morning for the toilets at the end of the chalet lines (no en-suite back in 1960) to being dressed as Madam Butterfly in the ballroom for the themed evening of 'Famous Lovers.' I had always wanted to wear a kimono and Hi-de-Hi! gave me the chance – though the shoes were not very comfortable – I now know why they take short little steps! Several times I played the role of a disgruntled parent, for example when the Punch and Judy Man upset the children, so I must have had that natural harassed parent look from my own life experiences with my son!

The very last day of filming was highly emotional, and the devastation caused by the hurricane only heightened the sense of real loss for what had been. Trying to be 'all professional' I failed miserably as the tears ran down my face when we sang for the last time Goodnight Campers.

When asked to write a few words about my memories of filming Hi-de-Hi! I really had no idea where to start, there were so many to choose from, but I think the overriding feeling I still have after all these years is the warmth and friendship that was created by all those connected to the programme, and I am sure those genuine sentiments were captured and transmitted to the audience."

Patsy Urquhart

Memories of a Maplin's 'Camper'

❝ To be asked to appear on Hi-de-Hi! was a dream come true. I'd followed the series since the pilot episode, and knew David & Tony, The Webb Twins, via cabaret work. However it was not until David Griffin joined the team that the opportunity arose for me to be a part of this wonderful series. Hi-de-Hi! needed a large supporting cast and so an advert was placed in the local press for Equity members to apply. I have never liked the term 'extras', we were much more than that, as we had to interact with the principals as if we were real holiday makers. I have forgotten the number of times we were asked to shout 'Ho-de-Ho' in response to Ted's 'Hi-de-Hi' only to hear (Paul Shane) reply 'Ted can't hear you - Hi-de-Hi!'. Having been to the same Warner's Camp as a fourteen year old in 1958 I was surprised to find very little had changed. It really was like stepping back in time, the clothes, the short haircut plastered with Brylcreem, the innocence of the 1950s, it was all there. The chalets were the ones used during the Warner's Summer season and each year those taking part in Hi-de-Hi! and who lived outside the area, hired them for the duration. The writers and Principals stayed at The Cliff Hotel in Dovercourt, overlooking the sea, a mile or so away from the location.

For us supporting artistes it was a holiday in every sense of the word, meeting colleagues each year, swapping stories and anecdotes and picking up where we had left off when the previous series 'wrapped'. In a way we had become part of a very special family created by David and Jimmy, but soon it would have to end, Hi-de-Hi! had run its course. By this time David Croft was writing 'Allo 'Allo with Jeremy Lloyd and some of us, myself included, had been offered parts in this new venture. There were also rumours that a new series styled on Upstairs Downstairs was in the pipeline and of course this became You Rang M'Lord?

Having been involved in many of the Holiday Camp 'games', dancing with Peggy in the Hawaiian Ballroom and throwing Spike in the Pool more times than I care to remember, my big chance came during the filming of the final episode entitled The Wind of Change. The writers must have known something in advance because in the early hours of 16th October 1987 Warners Holiday Camp was hit by a hurricane. Filming for that day was cancelled and the cast retreated to The Cliff Hotel where plans were made to film where possible on the following Saturday morning. Many people couldn't even reach the location especially those who had been booked for Friday. I was one of those who could get there. During the filming of the final scenes in the Ballroom, Roy Gould approached me and asked if I would like to do a 'few lines' as he put it. '"Yes" said I, "when do you want me?" 'Now', was his reply and I was taken over to speak with Jimmy Perry who explained what was required. I can still hear him saying 'keep your voice up, keep your voice up', and then those immortal lines, "See you again, next year Ted". At least he didn't call me 'Stupid Boy'. It was a very emotional scene, Su Pollard was in tears as were other members of the cast and crew. Hi-de-Hi! had come to an end. All that was left was a final personalised version of Goodnight Campers written especially for David and Jimmy and sung by us all.

The end of a very special era and one I will always cherish. Thank you David and Jimmy. ❞

Vince Rayner

"See you again next year, Ted"

7 Episode Guide

All episodes written by Jimmy Perry and David Croft

Audience ratings are those supplied by the official ratings agencies JICTAR and BARB to the BBC.

Studio = studio recording date   **TX** = original transmission date   **OOV** = Out of view

Pilot
1. Hi-de-Hi (Titled 'Hey Diddle Diddle' for the DVD release)

Series One
2. Desire in the Mickey Mouse Grotto
3. The Beauty Queen Affair
4. The Partridge Season
5. The Day of Reckoning
6. Charity Begins at Home
7. No Dogs Allowed

Series Two
8. If Wet - in the Ballroom
9. Peggy's Big Chance
10. Lift Up Your Minds
11. On with the Motley
12. A Night Not to Remember
13. Sausages or Limelight

Series Three
14. Nice People with Nice Manners
15. Carnival Time
16. A Matter of Conscience
17. The Pay-Off
18. Trouble and Strife

Series Four
19. Stripes
20. Co-Respondent's Course
21. It's a Blue World
22. Eruptions
23. The Society Entertainer
24. Sing You Sinners
25. Maplin Intercontinental
26. All Change

Series Five
27. Concessions
28. Save Our Heritage
29. Empty Saddles
30. The Marriage Settlement
31. The Graven Image
32. Peggy's Pen Friend
33. The Epidemic

Series Six
34. Together Again
35. Ted at the Helm
36. Opening Day
37. Off with the Motley
38. Hey Diddle Diddle, Who's on the Fiddle?
39. Raffles

Series Seven
40. The Great Cat Robbery
41. It's Murder
42. Who Killed Mr Partridge?
43. Spaghetti Galore
44. A Lack of Punch
45. Ivory Castles in the Air
46. Man Trap

Series Eight
47. Pigs Might Fly
48. The New Broom
49. Orphan of the Storm
50. God Bless Our Family
51. Only the Brave
52. September Song

Series Nine
53. Tell it to the Marines
54. Marry-Go-Round
55. The Perils of Peggy
56. Let Them Eat Cake
57. Wedding Bells
58. The Wind of Change

The production documentation records that the stock footage from the opening titles came from two main sources: The EMI Pathé News Library supplied shots of Nikita Khrushchev and Harold MacMillan (in a White Hat), Fidel Castro and solo shots of Harold MacMillan. Whilst the VisNews Library provided shots of the newly re-elected MacMillan, Elvis in Germany, Archbishop Makarios III returning to Cyprus, Charles De Gaulle installed as President of France, Billy Graham, Dr. Kwame Nkrumah arriving at London Airport, a Hovercraft and the Queen Mary liner, Ban The Bomb protest and the Sputnik satellite launch in 1958.
The closing titles were supplied from stock footage held by EMI Pathé News Library (specifically a Bikini Contest, Spaghetti Eating and Regatta) and Movietone News (assorted shots of holiday camps).

'Lift Up Your Minds' - Episode Guide

PILOT

1. HI-de-HI!

Studio: TC 4 - Friday 26th October 1979 **TX:** 1st January 1980 (edited repeat 19th February 1981), BBC 1
Duration: 40 mins **Audience Rating:** 4.40 million **

The year is 1959 and Maplin's Holiday Camp has a new Entertainments Manager. Jeffrey Fairbrother, a top Archaeology Professor at Cambridge. Whilst on his way to Crimpton on Sea he meets a couple of characters on the train, Ted Bovis and Spike Dixon who unbeknownst to him turn out to be members of his staff. Jeffrey listens with interest as they chat about life at the holiday camp with all the 'crumpet' and 'fiddles'. Jeffrey soon realises that there is more to knobbly knees and glamorous grandmother competitions than he thought. With the rest of the staff already assembling at the camp and looking forward to the new summer season, just what will they make of their new Entertainments Manager? One thing is for sure, Ted and Spike already know that they are going to have to be very careful indeed.

Full Cast:

Jeffrey Fairbrother	SIMON CADELL
Ted Bovis	PAUL SHANE
Gladys Pugh	RUTH MADOC
Spike Dixon	JEFFREY HOLLAND
Mr. Partridge	LESLIE DWYER
Fred Quilly	FELIX BOWNESS
Yvonne Stuart-Hargreaves	DIANE HOLLAND
Barry Stuart-Hargreaves	BARRY HOWARD
Peggy Ollerenshaw	SU POLLARD
Sylvia Garnsey	NIKKI KELLY
Betty Whistler	RIKKI HOWARD
Mary	PENNY IRVING
Stanley Matthews	DAVID WEBB
Bruce Matthews	TONY WEBB
Gary Bolton	TERENCE CREASEY
Marty Storm (Wilf Green)	RICHARD COTTAN
Maud Fairbrother	JOYCE GRANT
Old Man	HARRY MARKHAM
Old Woman	JOSEPHINE ANTOSZ
Hilda	MARIANNE TOLLAST
Passengers on train	EVE AUBREY, ESME DEAR, CHARLIE GRAY
Maintenance man	TREVOR HARTLEY
Security & Maintenance man	KEN CUNNINGHAM

Location filming dates:
15th October - 18th October 1979

Pilot Filming Locations:
Warner's Holiday Camp, Dovercourt.

Featured music: *Little White Bull* and *Singin' The Blues* (Tommy Steele), *Jailhouse Rock* (Richard Cottan), *Sugartime* (Tommy Kinsman and his Orchestra), *Side Saddle* (Russ Conway), *Move It* and *Livin' Doll* (Cliff Richard and The Shadows), *Auld Lang Syne* (BBC Sound Archive)

Pilot Production credits:
Studio Warm Up FELIX BOWNESS. Vision Mixer ANGELA BEVERIDGE. Graphic Design TONY GEDDES. Costume designer MARY HUSBAND. Make Up DAWN ALCOCK. Film Cameraman REMI ADEFARASIN. Film Sound DAVE BRINICOMBE. Film Editor MIKE ROBOTHAM. Studio Lighting PETER WINN. Studio Sound MICHAEL McCARTHY. Production Assistant EVAN KING. Designer GARRY FREEMAN. Produced and directed by DAVID CROFT.

N.B. A 35 minute edit was shown when repeated, and this edit has been seen several times during repeat seasons. The major trims to the episode are of Ted and Spike looking around the camp when they first arrive and the photo montage of Jeffrey Fairbrother during his week at Maplin's. The DVD release features the full 40 minute episode although given the title of *Hey Diddle Diddle*.

** The documentation held by the BBC Written Archive Centre records the Hi-de-Hi! Pilot as having achieved 4.40 million at 7.25pm on New Years Day 1980. This was up against Test Cricket on BBC 2 with 0.70 million and the television premiere of the movie musical *Paint Your Wagon* on ITV with a colossal 20.70 million viewers.

> ❝ I have no recollection of how 'Hey Diddle Diddle' arose as a title. [for the Pilot Episode DVD release] I'm pretty sure it wasn't mine or Jimmy's. I would like to think we would have come up with something more appropriate. ❞ **David Croft**

Series One

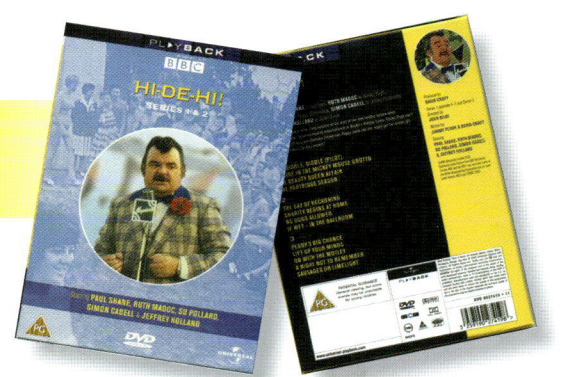

'Lift Up Your Minds' - Episode Guide

Regular Cast:

Jeffrey Fairbrother	SIMON CADELL
Ted Bovis	PAUL SHANE
Gladys Pugh	RUTH MADOC
Spike Dixon	JEFFREY HOLLAND
Mr. Partridge	LESLIE DWYER
Fred Quilly	FELIX BOWNESS
Yvonne Stuart-Hargreaves	DIANE HOLLAND
Barry Stuart-Hargreaves	BARRY HOWARD
Peggy Ollerenshaw	SU POLLARD
Sylvia Garnsey	NIKKI KELLY
Betty Whistler	RIKKI HOWARD
Mary	PENNY IRVING
Stanley Matthews	DAVID WEBB
Bruce Matthews	TONY WEBB
Gary Bolton	TERENCE CREASEY

Location filming dates:
25th September - 11th October 1980

Series One filming locations:
Warner's Holiday Camp, Dovercourt (all episodes). Dovercourt, West End Beach (3 & 5). Dovercourt, West End Point (4). Dovercourt, West End Promenade and Beach Huts (5).

2. DESIRE IN THE MICKEY MOUSE GROTTO

Studio: TC8 - Sunday 19th October 1980   **TX:** Thursday 26th February 1981 at 8pm, BBC 1
Duration: 29 mins 47 secs   **Audience Rating:** 15.45 million

The fun starts here. Ted Bovis the camp host has always had an eye for the ladies. He arranges a secret meeting with Rose, an attractive and curvaceous young girl camper, who is holidaying with her elderly parents. Their romantic evening reaches an abrupt end due to the arrival of Security Staff. In an attempt to avoid detection they unwittingly set suspicions on Jeffrey Fairbrother. Poor Jeffrey finds himself in serious trouble with the girl's father, who just happens to be one of Joe Maplin's personal friends. Word has reached him that his daughter has been involved in a romantic tryst. However Gladys Pugh comes to the rescue with an alibi for the previous night's goings on which the girl's father reluctantly believes. Jeffrey is both amazed and appalled at Gladys's outrageousness. All Jeffrey needs now is confusion about Ted's Bingo figures - they just do not add up.

Guest cast:

Marty Storm	Richard Cottan
Rose's Dad	Derek Benfield
Rose's Mum	Pearl Hackney
Rose	Gillian Taylforth
Camper at Table	Jimmy Mac
Camper in Bar	Keith James
Man in plaster	Gerald Taylor
Large lady camper	Kathleen Heath

Featured music: *Anchor and Star* (Band of The Scots Guards), *The Trolley Song* (Su Pollard unaccompanied), *Chanson De Matin* (Diane Holland unaccompanied), *Good Morning* (Su Pollard unaccompanied), *Love Me Tender* (Richard Cottan), *The Loveliest Night of the Year, Ship Ahoy, Darktown Strutters Ball, The Green Door, Lollipop* (Played by Roy Cloughton, Ron Fenn, Sid McLean, Don Drury, John Malam).

3. THE BEAUTY QUEEN AFFAIR

Studio: TC 3 - Sunday 26th October 1980 **TX:** Thursday 5th March 1981 at 8pm, BBC1
Duration: 29 mins 43 secs **Audience Rating:** 13.55 million

It's the day of the Holiday Princess Competition and all the Entertainments staff at Maplins are busy preparing for it. Ted Bovis wants to show Jeffrey Fairbrother Spike's new funny costume and all eyes are on Spike when he walks into the office as Ollie the Octopus. Ted also has a proposition concerning the Holiday Princess Competition. Ollie the Octopus is in place on the Olympic Sized Pool. Jeffrey gets a tap on the shoulder from a total stranger. He soon discovers that this man is the father of one of the Beauty Queens and worse still is that the man is trying to bribe him in to letting his daughter win the competition. Jeffrey is on the warpath about all the free gifts being handed out to the staff from the campers, he tries so hard to tell them that it is morally wrong to accept gifts in this way - only to find himself the recipient of a magnum of Champagne! And who worse to accept the gift on Jeffrey's behalf but Ted Bovis.

Guest cast:
Harry Plowright	Bobby Dennis
Reg Greenstreet	Ronnie Brody
Hilda	Marianne Tollast
Holiday Princesses	Nita Gavin
	Claire Vousden
	Anita Green
	Mandy Pretty
	Marion Wilson
	Pauline Lesley
	Taryn Kay
	Jill Oliver

Featured music: *You'll Never Walk Alone* (Su Pollard unaccompanied), *A Teenager In Love* (Marty Wilde) *The Post Horn Gallop, I Could Have Danced All Night, Sweet and Lovely* (played by Marianne Tollast on the organ).

4. THE PARTRIDGE SEASON

Studio: TC 3 - Sunday 2nd November 1980 **TX:** Thursday 12th March 1981 at 8pm, BBC 1
Duration: 29 mins 47 secs **Audience rating:** Not Available

Mr Partridge who is a fan of the 'old sauce', goes on one of his seasonal benders which results in him locking himself in his chalet and refusing to come out. With Joe Maplin's orders that the show must always go on, and after careful debate with Gladys checking of the staff rotas, it is decided that only one man is free to do the job - Jeffrey Fairbrother! Jeffrey becomes increasingly worried until Maplin's sexiest Yellowcoat Sylvia offers to help Jeffrey for she can do the voice of Mr Punch very well - much to the chagrin of Gladys, who worships Jeffrey's every move. It's a very tight squeeze in the Punch & Judy booth! All seems to be going well, until Mr. Partridge emerges from his chalet still much the worse for wear, and decides to take over the entertainment...

Guest cast:
Punch and Judy   Professor Guy Higgins (OOV)

Featured music: *Just Like the Ivy I'll Cling to You* and *The Holy City* (Leslie Dwyer unaccompanied).

An early Audience Studio Recording ticket

5. THE DAY OF RECKONING

Studio: TC 8 - Sunday 9th November 1980 **TX:** Thursday 19th March 1981 at 8pm, BBC 1
Duration: 29 mins 14 secs **Audience rating:** 15.55 million

Fred Quilly thinks that racing mobster Big Mac from Brighton has tracked him down to Maplin's Holiday Camp. The staff are on their toes to prevent Big Mac taking his revenge. Spike and Peggy are dressed in a Pantomime Horse but with Fred gone to ground they have to take a newly delivered horse to the stables for Fred. They decide to use the shortcut across the beach. Suspicious newlyweds book into chalet number 10. Jeffrey decides to take evasive action to protect Fred and to stop any trouble on his camp…..even if it might mean swindling the campers out of their spending money. During the evening's entertainments in the Hawaiian Ballroom, Jeffrey offers Big Mac's henchman £200 to leave the camp. A rendezvous at 6 o'clock brings confusion on all sides and nothing works out as it should.

Guest cast:
Ron Armitage	John Bardon
Mrs. Armitage	Doremy Vernon
Horsebox driver	Shaun Curry
Stuntmen in panto horse	Stuart Fell, Derek Ware
Hawaiian barmaids	Val Clover, Julia Gaye, Belinda Lee, Meme Lai
Bert Swanley and the Debonairs	Jason James Bruce Guest Michael Leader Tommy Winward, Albert Welch

Featured music: *A Teenager In Love* (Marty Wilde), *Turkey In The Straw, The Green Door, Lollipop, Have You Met Miss Jones?* (performed by Ron Fenn, Sid McLean, Roy Cloughton, Don Drury, John Malam, John Van Derrick).

6. CHARITY BEGINS AT HOME

Studio: TC 3 - Sunday 16th November 1980 **TX:** Thursday 26th March 1981 at 8pm, BBC 1
Duration: 29 mins 11 secs **Audience rating:** 15.55 million

In Joe Maplin's latest letter he insists that the staff 'smile more'. From now on every Thursday will be 'Sunshine Smiles Day' and Jeffrey wants everyone to pull together despite a lot of hostility from the staff. Ted tells Spike that it will be ideal to start up the Campers Amenity Fund. The Yellowcoats help Ted work his fiddle to collect cash from the campers. Things are going well until Mary makes a blunder by shaking the Amenity Fund tin right under the nose of Jeffrey Fairbrother. It's time for Ted to put his thinking cap on and double quick! And will Spike stick by him regardless when Jeffrey finds out just who is responsible for the petty swindle? A report from the Camp Administration arriving at the same time states that the campers are knocking off too many items including toilet rolls and light bulbs. Jeffrey has an idea that will hopefully solve the problem. But Ted has other ideas himself, once he discovers where Peggy is going to store it all!

Guest cast:
Old man	Harry Markham
Old woman	Josephine Antosz

Featured music: *Sand In My Shoes* (Su Pollard unaccompanied), *Let A Smile Be Your Umbrella* (Reginald Pursglove and his Orchestra with vocal by Ruth Madoc), *When I Fall In Love* (played by Ron Fenn, Sid McLean, Roy Cloughton, Don Drury, John Malam).

7. NO DOGS ALLOWED

Studio: TC 3 - Sunday 23rd November 1980 **TX:** Thursday 2nd April 1981 at 8pm, BBC 1
Duration: 30 mins 28 secs **Audience rating:** 14.15 million

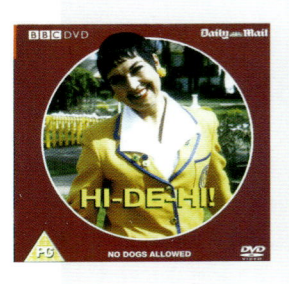

"No dogs are allowed in the Camp" - Joe Maplin's orders. He apparently hates them ever since he kicked one of the Queen's corgis at a Buckingham Palace function! Tongues are wagging all around the camp when strange noises are heard coming from Jeffrey's chalet during the night. Stories about mass orgies, girl campers and a lot of soap suds are doing the rounds until Jeffrey hears of them from a tearful Gladys. He decides to tell Gladys all about a letter he received from his wife and all about Bubbles, his dog. He has had to smuggle the animal on to the camp late at night while everyone was asleep, all except Mr Partridge who was smuggling booze onto the camp and saw him with the dog. He explains to Gladys that he has to try and find a new home for Bubbles. Meanwhile, Ted is furious with Jeffrey over a letter from Head Office that has been read out to all Entertainments Staff informing them that everyone has to wear a Yellowcoat - including Ted. He will do anything to avoid wearing a Yellowcoat and hatches a plan to set Jeffrey up and get him the sack. With the help of a gullible Peggy, her pass key, and a nosey local photographer, a daring strategy is about to be played out.

Guest cast:

Private Detective	Ron Pember
Bubbles	PASA
Voice of Bubbles	Percy Edwards (OOV)
Punch and Judy	Professor Guy Higgins (OOV)

Featured music: *Goodnight Sweetheart* (played by Ron Fenn, Sid McLean, Roy Cloughton, Don Drury, John Malam and sung by staff and campers), *I'm Forever Blowing Bubbles* (Leslie Dwyer unaccompanied), *Born In A Trunk* (Su Pollard unaccompanied).

Series One Production Credits:

Studio Warm Up FELIX BOWNESS. Choreographer MICHELLE HARDY. Rehearsal Pianist ROY MOORE. Punch and Judy Advisor PROFESSOR GUY HIGGINS. Vision Mixer ANGELA BEVERIDGE. Videotape Editors PHIL SOUTHBY, HOWARD DELL. Costume JAN WRIGHT. Make Up JILL HAGGAR. Visual Effects ANDY LAZELL. Film Cameraman MAX SAMETT. Film Sound JOHN GATLAND. Film Editor MIKE ROBOTHAM. Studio Lighting HENRY BARBER. Studio Sound MICHAEL McCARTHY. Production Assistant SUSAN BELBIN. Design GARRY FREEMAN, PAUL ALLEN. Assistant Producer JOHN KILBY (episodes 2 and 3). Director JOHN KILBY (episodes 4 - 7). Director DAVID CROFT (episodes 2 and 3). Produced by DAVID CROFT.

Series Two

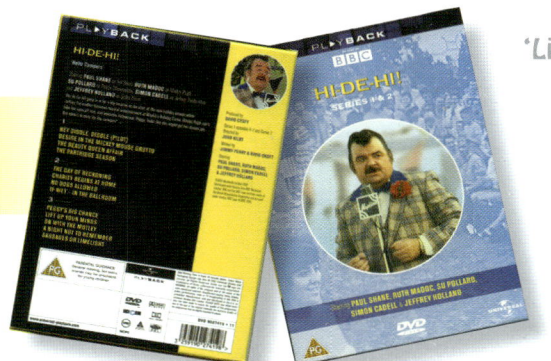

Regular Cast:

Jeffrey Fairbrother	SIMON CADELL
Ted Bovis	PAUL SHANE
Gladys Pugh	RUTH MADOC
Spike Dixon	JEFFREY HOLLAND
Mr. Partridge	LESLIE DWYER
Fred Quilly	FELIX BOWNESS
Yvonne Stuart-Hargreaves	DIANE HOLLAND
Barry Stuart-Hargreaves	BARRY HOWARD
Peggy Ollerenshaw	SU POLLARD
Sylvia Garnsey	NIKKI KELLY
Betty Whistler	RIKKI HOWARD
Val	GAIL HARRISON
Stanley Matthews	DAVID WEBB
Bruce Matthews	TONY WEBB
Gary Bolton	CHRIS ANDREWS

Location filming dates:
28th September - 14th October 1981

Series Two Filmng Locations:
Warner's Holiday Camp, Dovercourt (all episodes). Mistley, The Walls (10, 13). Dovercourt, Beach adjacent to Lighthouse, Boating Lake & Park (13).

8. IF WET - IN THE BALLROOM

Studio: TC 3 - Sunday 25th October 1981   **TX:** Sunday 29th November 1981 at 7.15pm, BBC 1
Duration: 30 mins 33 secs   **Audience rating:** Not Available

The staff are at their wits' end trying to amuse the campers. Rain has been pouring down for days and they have practically exhausted their repertoire of indoor amusements. Jeffrey has called a meeting and asks the staff for suggestions. The Yellowcoats suggest a treasure hunt if Jeffrey can supply some prizes. Yvonne and Barry put forward the idea of tap dancing classes if her head can withstand the noise. Spike tells everybody about Mr Partridge's act from way back - Wizard Willy - and it's not long before Mr Partridge gets talked into doing it all over again. After all it is for the kids! All decked out in his wizard costume and digging out his old tricks he finds himself being heckled by a rather obnoxious child, Charlie Ruckston. Enough's enough and he takes matters into his own hands and nearly suffocates young Charlie. He then finds himself in trouble yet again with Jeffrey and possibly facing the sack for his latest misdemeanour . But Jeffrey comes to the rescue with a surprisingly dodgy plan and the only person he confides in is Spike, as he knows he has strong morals and a good heart. But together they agree not to mention the cunning plan to Ted. As usual nothing works out as it should. So it is left to Ted Bovis to rescue the situation once again and to give the lad a lesson in life.

Guest cast:

Charlie Ruckston 'No. 7'	Sam Smart
Olwen Jones 'No. 8'	Wendy Hall
Ramona	Jean Lear
Olwen's mother	Caroline Cross

Magic advisor for the episode - Lenny Blease

Featured music: *Singin' In The Rain* (The Gypsy Accordion Band), *Tip Toe Through The Tulips* (vocal: Leslie Dwyer, piano: Jean Lear), *It's Magic* (Jean Lear), *An Old Straw Hat* (vocal: Wendy Hall, piano: Jean Lear), *Solid Men To The Front* (Band of Her Majestys Royal Marines).

'Lift Up Your Minds' - Episode Guide

9. PEGGY'S BIG CHANCE

Studio: TC 4 - Sunday 1st November 1981 **TX:** Sunday 6th December 1981, BBC 1
Duration: 29 mins 52 secs **Audience rating:** Not Available

Peggy has always had a burning ambition to be a Yellowcoat and she thinks she's in with a chance when the Entertainments Director is due to visit the camp. However, with another one of Joe Maplin's letters being read by Jeffrey to all the staff, criticizing them all for not making the campers laugh and giving them a great time, something has to be done. A pool wheeze is the suggestion and something sinister in the water is desperately needed to liven things up. With all the staff members otherwise engaged Jeffrey gives Peggy the starring role - a shark. The campers are assembled around the Olympic Sized Pool and all the staff in their various costumes including Spike who is dressed up as a busty dolly bird the fun starts. Peggy has to be rescued herself by two curvaceous shark fighters played by Betty and Sylvia. Peggy still gets her interview with the Entertainments Director but are Peggy's dreams about to be shattered?

Guest cast:
Ramona   **Jean Lear**
Waitresses in the Laughing Cow
                 Janie Love, Linda Kent, Elaine Ford

Featured music: *Friends* (Billy Cotton and his Band), *Dreamboat* (Alma Cogan), *Ma I Miss Your Apple Pie* (vocal: Ruth Madoc, organist: Jean Lear), *Devil's Gallop: The Dick Barton Theme* (Jean Lear).

10. LIFT UP YOUR MINDS

Studio: TC 3 - Sunday 8th November 1981 **TX:** Sunday 13th December 1981 at 7.15pm, BBC1
Duration: 29 mins 3 secs **Audience rating:** Not Available

"Not enough campers attending breakfast" - that is Joe Maplins's orders and it's Jeffrey's duty to tell his staff the good news. Not everyone is happy including old Mr Partridge who hasn't sat in on breakfast for 14 years and Ted informs Jeffrey that the mornings are his quiet times. But as much as Jeffrey sympathises with them all he is adamant that all staff have to be there in the breakfast hall the next morning. And a success it is with Spike entertaining the campers and getting covered in custard pies for his trouble! Jeffrey sees this as a wonderful opportunity to change the campers' views on things - to move away from hedonistic values like eating and drinking towards more cultural pursuits. He thinks that holding a record recital might just do the trick. It could add a bit of sophistication to the camp. But with Shostakovich failing to inspire anybody it leaves Jeffrey feeling completely demoralised and in doing so makes him think about leaving the camp for good. Gladys is worried that the man she loves will indeed walk away from the camp and more importantly from her. Despite the fact that Ted thinks Jeffrey is a complete berk he has no intention of seeing Gladys upset and sets about concocting another plan to keep Jeffrey at the camp. But it will involve another one of his fiddles and one that Jeffrey must never find out about - especially if Gladys has anything to do with it.

Guest cast:
Woman   **Jean Challis**
Second Man   **Roy Heather**

Featured music: *Good Morning* (Tommy Kinsman and his Orchestra), *Sons of the Sea* (Jeffrey Holland unaccompanied), *Land of Hope and Glory* (Paul Shane unaccompanied), extracts from *Symphony No. 7 (opus 60)* by Shostakovich and *Symphonic Dances (opus 45)* by Rachmaninoff (London Philharmonic Orchestra).

11. ON WITH THE MOTLEY

Studio: TC 6 - Sunday 15th November 1981   **TX:** Sunday 20th December 1981 at 7.15pm, BBC 1
Duration: 29 mins 2 secs   **Audience rating:** 16.1 million

Jeffrey Fairbrother is extremely angry with Ted for insulting him in front of the campers and intends to severely reprimand him. Meanwhile Ted is sitting in the Laughing Cow milk bar when Peggy bursts in to tell him he has had a telephone call from his Agent and that he must 'phone back immediately. Ted is being booked at a posh do in Clacton and is convinced he is finally on his way at last, particularly when he learns that an *Opportunity Knocks* talent scout will be there. But he must let Jeffrey know all about it and that he knows will mean eating a bit of humble pie. Mr Fairbrother excepts his apology much to Gladys's annoyance. Ted spins Jeffrey a yarn informing him that it could involve a further 11 Sundays off, giving Spike his chance in the ballroom. Jeffrey says that he will get onto Head Office to see if he can clear the time off and luckily for Ted they agree. Taking Peggy with him for moral support the evening is an absolute disaster and Ted's jokes and toilet humour do not go down well with the Clacton set. The very next day Peggy lets slip to Mr Fairbrother all about Ted's big chance, and tells him that he very nearly didn't get paid for his efforts either. Ted realises that he is better off among the deadbeats and the has-beens, and the campers who really worship him.

Featured music: *I Believe* and *Be Sincere* (Paul Shane accompanied by Don Drury, Roy Cloughton, John Malam, Syd McLean, Colin Woolway), *Just Walking In The Rain* (performed by Don Drury, Roy Cloughton, John Malam, Syd McLean, Colin Woolway), *Pickin' A Chicken* (Eve Boswell with Glen Somers and his Orchestra), *Sing Little Birdie* (Teddy Johnson and Pearl Carr).

12. A NIGHT NOT TO REMEMBER

Studio: TC 3 - Sunday 22nd November 1981   **TX:** Sunday 27th December 1981, BBC 1
Duration: 28 mins 42 secs   **Audience rating:** 13.7 million

It's Egyptian night in the Hawaiian bar and all the staff are dressed up for the event. Even Jeffrey Fairbrother is wearing a fez, which according to Gladys makes him look like a true gentleman. However as soon as he enters the bar he is bombarded by a group of male campers who want to buy him drinks. Not wanting to offend the men he accepts their offer, without realising that they are in fact lacing his drink with spirits. One drink leads to another and then another and by the end of the evening Jeffrey is completely oblivious to everything going on around him. Gladys guides him back to his chalet after 'Goodnight Campers', and with the gossip mongers at Maplin's already spreading rumours about her spending the night with Mr Fairbrother, it is down to Gladys to set the record straight. Peggy finds one of Gladys's bras in the Professor's chalet - hidden under a book of 'The Ruins Of Petra', setting the gossip tongues wagging. Gladys is determined to set the record straight so she gathers the entertainments staff and with the help of a Sergeant in the Metropolitan Police explains what happened on that fateful night in the Hawaiian Ballroom. But maybe all is not as it would seem.

Only Gladys knows the full truth - and she isn't telling anyone!

Guest cast:
Mr. Pritchard	David Troughton
Bert	Nigel Williams

Featured music: *Singin' The Blues*, *The Snake Charmer of Old Baghdad*, *Goodnight Campers (aka Goodnight Sweetheart)* (performed by Roy Cloughton, Don Drury, John Malam, Syd McLean, Colin Woolway), *Solid Men To The Front* (Band of Her Majesty's Royal Marines), *Don't Laugh At Me* (Norman Wisdom).

13. SAUSAGES OR LIMELIGHT

Studio: TC 4 - Sunday 29th November 1981 **TX:** Sunday 3rd January 1982 at 7.15pm, BBC 1
Duration: 30 mins 30 secs **Audience rating:** Not Available

When Joe Maplin sends another one of his stylish letters to the camp to tell the staff that the campers are eating far too much grub and not being entertained enough by the 'M & F' Yellowcoats, Jeffrey has to sort it out and quick. Joe Maplin has already instructed that all staff must greet the campers off the trains in full uniform, which does not go down too well. With Spike away visiting his girlfriend in the Midlands it falls upon Peggy to take his place but Gladys is having none of it and threatens to tell her Supervisor Miss Cathcart. Ted tells Jeffrey that only sex and greed will stop the campers from eating and it is decided that a 'Goldrush' is what is needed to coax the campers away from the dining hall. Ted can arrange for some cheap rings as prizes, so the next morning the first Goldrush is staged in the dining hall. When Ted suddenly announces the magic words "There's gold in them there hills" there is a huge dash to a specially installed haystack and Mr Fairbrother finds himself nearly crushed in the excitement. Meanwhile Spike has to make a decision about his future - does he leave Maplin's forever to settle down to wedded bliss and butchery or does he stay in the job that he truly loves? Will the smell of the greasepaint win him over?

Guest cast:

Brenda	Julie-Anne Blythen
Edna	Janie Love
Man with revolting manners	Pete Sturgeon
Woman in treasure hill who finds the ring	Lisa Anselmi

1981 Audience Studio Recording ticket featuring an illustration by Jeffrey Holland and showing all the main cast.

Series Two Production Credits:

Studio Warm Up FELIX BOWNESS. Production Team ROBIN CARR, BERNADETTE DARNELL, CLARE GRAHAM, SUZANNE PINTO. Vision Mixer ANGELA BEVERIDGE. Costume JAN WRIGHT. Make Up SHIRLEY CHANNING WILLIAMS. Visual Effects ANDY LAZELL. Senior Cameraman GARTH TUCKER, JOHN DAILLEY. Film Cameraman MAX SAMETT. Film Sound TERRY ELMS, JOHN PAINE. Film Editor MIKE ROBOTHAM. Studio Lighting DUNCAN BROWN. Studio Sound LAURIE TAYLOR. Production Manager SUSAN BELBIN. Directed by JOHN KILBY. Produced by DAVID CROFT.

Series Three

Regular Cast:

Jeffrey Fairbrother	SIMON CADELL
Ted Bovis	PAUL SHANE
Gladys Pugh	RUTH MADOC
Spike Dixon	JEFFREY HOLLAND
Mr. Partridge	LESLIE DWYER
Fred Quilly	FELIX BOWNESS
Yvonne Stuart-Hargreaves	DIANE HOLLAND
Barry Stuart-Hargreaves	BARRY HOWARD
Peggy Ollerenshaw	SU POLLARD
Sylvia Garnsey	NIKKI KELLY
Betty Whistler	RIKKI HOWARD
Tracey Bentwood	SUSAN BEAGLEY
Stanley Matthews	DAVID WEBB (except episode 17)
Bruce Matthews	TONY WEBB (except episode 17)
Gary Bolton	CHRIS ANDREWS (except episode 17)

Location filming dates:
28th April - 13th May 1982

Series Three filming locations:
Warner's Holiday Camp, Dovercourt (all episodes). Dovercourt, West End Beach & Lane (15). Flatford, Willy Lott's House (Flatford Mill) (14). Mistley, (formerly) Dairy House Farm (17).

14. NICE PEOPLE WITH NICE MANNERS

Studio: TC 4 - Friday 25th June 1982 **TX:** Sunday 31st October 1982, BBC1
Duration: 28 mins 46 secs **Audience rating:** Not Available

Barry and Yvonne are organising a party but only want a select few invited. Barry asks Peggy to deliver the hand written invitations personally after she has finished her work and she puts them somewhere safe. Meanwhile Jeffrey has to break the news to the staff that all of them must take part in the camp's most popular contest entitled 'That's Your Bum'. Gladys asks Peggy to take her place in the line up as she is Management and Peggy is more than happy to do. If only she had not drank so many milkshakes beforehand. Later Peggy sees beds outside the dancer's chalet and asks Barry what's going on. When he mentions their party she immediately realises that she has mislaid the invitations. In a blind panic she rushes to Mr Fairbrother to explain what is happening. He tells her to go round to all the staff and get them to Barry and Yvonne's chalet as soon as possible so as not to disappoint them. What will they say however, when everyone gatecrashes their party? Particularly with most of the staff in their night clothes! Will it be Mantovani or will Elvis rule the day?

Guest cast:
Ramona   Jean Lear

Featured music: *Jezebel* (Su Pollard unaccompanied), *Boom Why Does My Heart Go Boom* (vocal: Ruth Madoc, organist: Jean Lear), *Charmaine, Tulips From Amsterdam* and *I May Never Pass This Way Again* (Mantovani and his Orchestra), *Jailhouse Rock* (from the Music For Pleasure LP *Smash Hits Presley Style*).

15. CARNIVAL TIME

Studio: TC 8 - Friday 4th June 1982   **TX:** Sunday 7th November 1982, BBC 1
Duration: 29 mins 39 secs   **Audience rating:** 10.50 million

Ted and Spike are summoned to Jeffrey's office as a matter of urgency. Another letter has arrived from Joe Maplin informing them that the Wild West costumes are on their way to the camp, in time for the Carnival in nearby Crimpton on Sea. All the entertainments staff are taking part on floats. A list of who is to play which parts has to be drawn up. Gladys is in line to play the White Virgin and Mr Partridge is going to be Chief Sitting Bull, hopefully sober! Hugo Buxton, Dean of Cambridge University, arrives at the camp on a mission to take Jeffrey back to Cambridge where he is needed. Jeffrey is of course thrilled to see his old friend but is absolutely adamant that he will not be returning to his old academic life. At the rehearsal everybody is decked out in their Wild West costumes and bunting is draped around the floats. However, things go wrong when Ted tries to get the fire burning near the wigwam where Gladys is tied to a post and suddenly a real blaze breaks out. The noises from the fire begin to frighten Fred's horses, and Mr Toby (the coalman's horse) takes off with Fred and Peggy clutching onto the reigns. Barry and the Yellowcoat lads pull the float into the Olympic Sized Pool to put the fire out and all the entertainments staff follow. But this goes to show Hugo Buxton once and for all just how much Jeffrey is enjoying himself at Maplin's working with people who are now his friends.

Guest cast:
Hugo Buxton	John Le Mesurier
Maud Fairbrother	Joyce Grant
Ramona	Jean Lear
Stuntmen with Sorrel (Mr. Toby)	Stuart Fell and Derek Ware

Featured music: *Thanks A Million* (Dick Powell from The Dick Powell Songbook with vocal by Ruth Madoc), *The Boys In The Backroom* (Jean Lear).

16. A MATTER OF CONSCIENCE

Studio: TC 4 - Friday 11th June 1982   **TX:** Sunday 14th November 1982, BBC1
Duration: 28 mins 16 secs   **Audience rating:** 12.20 million

The local Council is planning to build a Hospital next to the camp. Joe Maplin wants the plan to be thwarted and the staff must do as he asks in order for him to get his own way. "Lots of noises and lots of smells" are what is required from one and all. Jeffrey is so appalled as are most of the Yellowcoats, who actually feel that a Hospital is a good thing. Jeffrey intends telling Joe Maplin that he will not have anything to do with such a plan but seeing as he is the Boss it seems he has no choice especially when Mr. Maplin gets personal - implying that he and Gladys are more than work colleagues! Ted tells Jeffrey to leave it to him and that he will do all that Joe Maplin wants, as he pays his wages. He has a cunning plan and one that will involve making Peggy a Yellowcoat for the day. All he needs to do is tell her a few white lies involving talent scouts from the BBC and Hollywood visiting the neighbouring field which means she will have to make lots of noise with the campers. Peggy thinks she is doing good - until she finds out the truth.

Featured music: *Swedish Rhapsody* (Mantovani and his Orchestra).

17. THE PAY-OFF

Studio: TC 4 - Friday 18th June 1982   **TX:** Sunday 21st November 1982, BBC 1
Duration: 29 mins 29 secs   **Audience rating:** 10.85 million

The local Council is still determined to build the Hospital next to the camp. Joe Maplin sends a shoe-box containing £1000 to Jeffrey with strict instructions that he is to bribe the Councillors. He is outraged and appalled at Mr Maplin's behaviour and decides to pack his things and leave the camp for good. Gladys is devastated and gets Ted to somehow talk to him and stall him. He informs Jeffrey that he will return to money to Joe Maplin personally, as he went to school with him and understands him more than anyone. Another one of Ted's lies as he didn't even go to school! He tells Spike he intends taking the money to the Councillors to bribe them whilst also creaming some of the money for himself. Spike is of course horrified and wants nothing to with it. However, Ted's plan fails miserably and he ends up at the Police Station for questioning. Only when he returns to the camp to see Jeffrey does he come clean about the whole sorry affair and tells him that he has told a "little white lie" involving Mr. Fairbrother in an absolutely outrageous way.

Guest cast:
Inspector Palmer	Roy Heather

Featured music: *Horsie Horsie* (The Revellers with vocal by Ruth Madoc).

18. TROUBLE AND STRIFE

Studio: TC 3 - Friday 2nd July 1982   **TX:** Sunday 28th November 1982 at 7.15pm, BBC 1
Duration: 29 mins 17 secs   **Audience rating:** 10.85 million

Ted Bovis's ex-wife turns up at Maplin's and introduces herself to Jeffrey Fairbrother. She has come to see Ted demanding the arrears of her maintenance. A Bailiff issues Ted with a writ and explains that failure to pay could result in him being sent to Prison. He tells Spike that he must get working on all the fiddles he can remember in order to raise the money as quickly as possible. Ted must get the spare chalet key from Peggy and concoct yet another story. This time about a poor Orphan who is in need of a holiday. With a new intake of campers just arriving off the buses, all the staff are on hand to mention various deals and privileges that they can arrange for them. Free tennis balls, special dance lessons, bigger breakfasts. They're all at it. Ted manages to fool the campers and collect nearly all the money for his ex-wife - but will she agree with the final sum?

Guest cast:
Hilary Bovis	Rikki Lee
Mrs. Brown	Leni Harper
Mr. Brown	Sion Probert
Bailiff	John D. Collins

Featured music: *Lollipop* (Gary Miller), *I'm Gonna Sit Right Down And Write Myself A Letter* (Russ Conway), *Medley: Lollipop / Wear My Ring Round Your Neck / Kewpie Doll* and *Side Saddle* (Russ Conway).

Series Three Production Credits:

Studio Warm Up FELIX BOWNESS. Production Assistants BERNADETTE DARNELL, WILLA HANCOCK. Assistant Floor Managers ROBIN CARR, COLIN FAY. Vision Mixer ANGELA BEVERIDGE. Senior Cameraman PETER HILLS. Costume MARY HUSBAND. Make Up CAROLYN PERRY. Film Visual Effects COLIN MAPSON. Properties Buyer ROGER WOOD. Cameraman MAX SAMETT. Film Sound GRAHAM HARE. Film Editor MIKE ROBOTHAM. Studio Sound LAURIE TAYLOR, MICHAEL FELTON. Studio Lighting DUNCAN BROWN. Production Manager SUSAN BELBIN. Design GARRY FREEMAN. Directed by JOHN KILBY (except episode 15 directed by DAVID CROFT). Produced by DAVID CROFT.

'Lift Up Your Minds' - Episode Guide

Series Four

Regular Cast

Jeffrey Fairbrother	SIMON CADELL
Ted Bovis	PAUL SHANE
Gladys Pugh	RUTH MADOC
Spike Dixon	JEFFREY HOLLAND
Mr. Partridge	LESLIE DWYER
Fred Quilly	FELIX BOWNESS
Yvonne Stuart-Hargreaves	DIANE HOLLAND
Barry Stuart-Hargreaves	BARRY HOWARD
Peggy Ollerenshaw	SU POLLARD
Sylvia Garnsey	NIKKI KELLY
Betty Whistler	RIKKI HOWARD
Tracey Bentwood	SUSAN BEAGLEY
Stanley Matthews	DAVID WEBB
Bruce Matthews	TONY WEBB
Gary Bolton	CHRIS ANDREWS

Location filming dates:
23rd September - 5th October 1982

Series Four filming locations:
Warner's Holiday Camp, Dovercourt (all episodes). Dovercourt, Facing Beach Huts (20), Hall Lane (19), West End Beach (20, 23), West End Lane (19).

19. STRIPES

Studio: TC 4 - Sunday 24th October 1982 **TX:** Sunday 5th December 1982, BBC1
Duration: 29 mins 34 secs **Audience rating:** 12.5 million

Joe Maplin reckons that all the Yellowcoats are 'slummocky' and need sorting out. In order to show her authority Gladys sews two extra rings on to the sleeve of her jacket, which angers many of the staff including Barry, Yvonne and Fred Quilly. Ted decides to take matters into his own hands - and shows everyone who is boss. As the campers arrive off the buses Gladys notices someone she does not want to see. She confides in Spike and tells him that her half brother Gareth has arrived and that he has no business here. He has a bad reputation and an eye for the ladies. Gladys reckons that he could spoil everything for her and confronts him immediately, she will be watching his every move. A peeping-tom is on the loose around the camp and scaring the girl Yellowcoats late at night. Gladys instructs Spike to help her brother pack his bags. But alas, next day Gladys finds out from Jeffrey that security apprehended the culprit - and it could not have been her brother after all. How wrong could she have been? Could she also be wrong about the extra rings on her sleeve?

Guest cast:

Gareth Davies	Talfryn Thomas
Ramona	Jean Lear
Holiday Princess	Lorraine Porter
Chauffeur	John Maxim junior
Joe Maplin	John Maxim senior

Featured music: *Swedish Rhapsody* (Mantovani and his Orchestra), *Petite Fleur* (Chris Barber's Jazz Band), *Oh You Beautiful Doll* (Joe 'Mr. Piano' Henderson).

'Lift Up Your Minds' - Episode Guide

20. CO-RESPONDENT'S COURSE

Studio: TC 8 - Sunday 31st October 1982   **TX:** Sunday 12th December 1982 at 7.15pm, BBC 1
Duration: 29 mins 10 secs   **Audience rating:** 12.40 million

Mr. Fairbrother instructs the male members of staff that he will have a word with Mr. Glover the Head of Entertainment when he arrives at the camp, about the Window Dressing Competition. This competition is not popular and is not fair on people like Barry, Fred and Mr. Partridge who all have to dress up in silk bonnets and tight corsets. When Jeffrey receives a letter from his mother begging him to return home as his wife is making a fool of him, he rushes off to make a 'phone call. Gladys, Ted and Spike check out the letter to find out what made Jeffrey react in such a way. Later in the day, Peggy tells a mystery gentleman - thought to be Mr Glover - to take a seat in Mr Fairbrother's office. But when Jeffrey returns to his office he finds out it is in fact Max Tewksbury, his wife's new boyfriend. asking him to divorce her.

However, he refuses to play ball and is unwilling to co-operate. Max must then dig for evidence to try and besmirch Jeffrey's honour and where better to start than with a potty chalet maid. Peggy is bribed and asked to sign a sworn statement saying she has seen both Jeffrey and Gladys in a compromising position…

Guest cast:
Max Tewksbury	John Fortune
Clive, solicitor	John Horsley
Mr. Glover	David Beale
Irene Hazlehurst	Joan Dainty
Ramona	Jean Lear

Featured music: *Putting On The Style* (Joe 'Mr. Piano' Henderson), *Swedish Rhapsody* (Mantovani and his Orchestra).

21. IT'S A BLUE WORLD

Studio: TC 8 - Saturday 13th November 1982   **TX:** Sunday 19th December 1982 at 7.15pm, BBC 1
Duration: 29 mins 8 secs   **Audience rating:** Not Available

Barry and Yvonne are voicing their issues with Mr. Fairbrother in his office after the 'Ugly Bug Ball'. They are adamant that Jeffrey will have to have words with Ted regarding his 'mucky jokes'. Jeffrey is in full agreement with them and intends to tell Ted - gently! Meanwhile Ted is offered the chance to hire an "artistic adult film" from a shady character in the Laughing Cow Milk Bar, to show to the male campers late at night when everybody is asleep. He tracks down Peggy and tells her another feeble tale saying he wants the key to the bar after dark. The Yellowcoats have agreed to hold a pyjama party on the same night in the Laughing Cow. Ted is busy selling raffle tickets on camp but only to the male campers, and with Jeffrey and Gladys becoming suspicious it looks like the Laughing Cow is going to be a bit crowded! Spike stumbles on a reel of film on Ted's bed and takes a look. Later, with the male campers taking their seats in the milk bar and Fred on door duty to keep out uninvited guests. Spike warns Ted to stop the showing of the film immediately. With the Police arriving at any minute what will happen to Ted and what will Jeffrey say when he sees what film is actually to be shown?

Guest cast:
Ron Griffin	Freddie Earlle
Inspector Sutcliffe	Ian Collier
Police Sergeant	Richard Bates
Police Constable	Harry Fielder

Featured music: *Love Me Tender* (from the Music For Pleasure LP 'Smash Hits Presley Style'), *Dance Of The Cuckoos* (Ronnie Hazlehurst).

22. ERUPTIONS

Studio: TC 4 - Saturday 6th November 1982, Sunday 7th November 1982, BBC1
TX: Sunday 26th December 1982 **Duration:** 45 mins 16 secs **Audience rating:** 9.55 million

Mr. Fairbrother has had a call Mr. Partridge into his office yet again about his drinking, this time for being drunk whilst entertaining the children. A report will have to be written and Mr. Partridge tries to talk his way out of it. Ted is also angry about what is going on whilst he does his act, too many distractions and he tells Jeffrey straight. Either it stops or he will not go on. Joe Maplin has installed a model volcano in the ballroom, to be staged during Hawaiian Night. It erupts during one of Ted's songs making matters ten times worse. Even Barry and Yvonne are upset when the campers rush across the dance floor to see The Mighty Mountain of Pitzpalou during their performance. Ted is not prepared to tolerate it anymore and with the help of Spike, Fred and Peggy they set about in the dead of night to sabotage the device and get rid of it once and for all. Even Barry and Yvonne are roped in - holding the ladder and hiding it from view of Security. However, Mr Partridge gets wind of the scheme and hopes that by telling Mr. Fairbrother, it will show him in a new light and possibly clear him of being reported for being drunk on duty. Jeffrey wakes Gladys up and they go to investigate. Mr Partridge leads them to a short cut but unfortunately for Jeffrey and Gladys they manage to get locked in the Three Bears Cottage. Rumours start to circulate around the camp the next day concerning Jeffrey and Gladys. That evening with the entertainment in full swing and the Fire Chief present to check out fire safety, has Ted's plan worked - or will Joe Maplin have the last laugh?

Guest cast:
Fire Chief	Michael Redfern
Security Guard	Paul Toothill
Punch and Judy	Professor Guy Higgins (OOV)

Featured music: *The Book* and *Today I Love Everybody* (Paul Shane), *Sweet Leilani'*, *Green Door*, *Mexican Hat Dance* (Roy Cloughton, Don Drury, Don Sandford), *Chestnut Tree* (Joe 'Mr. Piano' Henderson).

23. THE SOCIETY ENTERTAINER

Studio: TC 4 - Saturday 27th November 1982 **TX:** Sunday 1st January 1983 at 7.15pm, BBC 1
Duration: 29 mins 58 secs **Audience rating:** 12.45 million

A new intake of campers are arriving at Maplin's. Jeffrey decides that a change of voice on Radio Maplin would be a good thing but Gladys is completely against the idea, arguing that she is Radio Maplin. Jeffrey is adamant however that a change is needed and they will start the next day with Sylvia. Of course things do not go to plan, thanks of course to Gladys. She tells Peggy to clear all the paperwork away from the tannoy whilst clearing up in the Radio room - including the itinerary for the day! Spike meanwhile meets a nice sophisticated Scottish girl and her Mother who are amongst the new arrivals, which results in him falling out with Ted. All the staff are aware that Spike has become a bit haughty and distant towards them when he is with the girl. He doesn't even want to socialise with them any more. Even the campers think his act is becoming dull and his popularity seems to be waning. It is a very worrying time particularly for Mr Fairbrother. It is left to Ted to sort the problem out and he informs Jeffrey that his plan is drastic and that Spike will not like it one little bit but something has got to be done. Ted employs Peggy to help him in the act and Spike is receiving the 'belters' again, but it comes at a cost. A cost that will offend his new love, her mother and the entire Scottish nation! But it will be worth it in the end - it will put Spike back where he belongs.....a big hit at Maplin's once again.

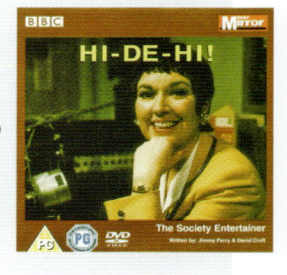

Guest cast:
Doris Ogilvy	Iris Russell
Francoise Ogilvy	Jennifer Black
The Hulk	Arthur Bostrom
Matronly Woman	Jean Challis

Featured music: *Cocktails For Two* and *Road To The Isles* (Jeffrey Holland).

24. SING YOU SINNERS

Studio: TC 4 - Saturday 20th November 1982 **TX:** Sunday 9th January 1983 at 7.15pm, BBC 1
Duration: 30 mins 49 secs **Audience rating:** 10.60 million

Jeffrey Fairbrother is holding a very important meeting with the camp Padre, who is sorry to have to tell him that he just cannot go on with the Sunday 'half hour' slot. Not enough money is being put in the collection these days to maintain his Church, and with Joe Maplin putting on extra pressure he feels that enough is enough. Jeffrey immediately 'phones Head Office about a replacement but is told to get on with it himself. Despite Jeffrey's best efforts the Sunday Service is a complete disaster. Mr. Partridge tells Ted about his days the in the Deep South in America where the collections taken during worship were bountiful. Jeffrey approaches Ted and asks him to please do him a favour - by taking over the 'half hour' slot – Ted jumps at the chance. Is it divine intervention or is Ted looking to make a fast buck? All the staff are drafted in for a Gospel extravaganza, the like of which Maplin's has never seen before…

Guest cast:
The Reverend Fulljames	James Ottaway
Ramona	Jean Lear

Featured music: *Oft In Danger, Oft In Woe, Onward Christian Soldiers* (Roy Cloughton with 4 musicians), *The Saints* (The company), *Little Curly Hair In A High Chair* (Ruth Madoc), *The Garden Of Eden* (Jeffrey Holland), *Delilah and Hava Nigila* (Perry Duke with 4 musicians).

Put Your Hand In Your Pocket was written by Roy Moore, David Croft and Jimmy Perry and performed by Paul Shane and the Company.

25. MAPLIN INTERCONTINENTAL

Studio: TC 4 - Saturday 4th December 1982 **TX:** Sunday 16th January 1983 at 7.15pm, BBC 1
Duration: 29 mins 19 secs **Audience rating:** 13.40 million

It's that time of the year again when the campers have to vote for their favourite female Yellowcoat and Ted tells Jeffrey that it's a waste of time really as Gladys has won five years running. An urgent letter arrives from Joe Maplin informing him that the winner of the Best Yellowcoat prize is to work at his new camp in the Bahamas there is great excitement. Gladys is in two minds about the competition this season, particularly as she wants to stay on with Jeffrey at Maplin's. Peggy asks Mr. Fairbrother if she can be considered to replace the winner and he thinks it is a fabulous idea and promises to do everything he can. Even Yvonne wants to enter this years' competition much to Barry's annoyance. However when Jeffrey gets a personal 'phone call from Joe Maplin himself to say he may send him over to the new camp in the Caribbean as Entertainments' Manager Gladys changes her mind and decides to get cracking in order to win the competition yet again. There is great excitement is in the Ballroom as the votes are being counted and it is left to Jeffrey to make the casting vote as two of the Yellowcoats are tying for first place. However a tropical storm serves the hand of fate to both Sylvia and Peggy.

Guest cast:
Newsreader	Colin Ward-Lewis
Ramona	Jean Lear
Guitarist	Dave Lingard (OOV)

Featured music: *Alone* (Russ Conway), *Be My Love* (vocal: Tony Webb with Jean Lear and Dave Lingard).

26. ALL CHANGE

Studio: TC 3 - Saturday 11th December 1982 **TX:** Sunday 23rd January 1983 at 7.15pm, BBC 1
Duration: 29 mins 22 secs   **Audience rating:** 13.95 million

Barry and Yvonne are to separate and further more Yvonne wants Barry out of her chalet. With the imminent arrival of Joan Wainwright, a Supervisor that Joe Maplin has appointed to look over the Yellowcoats, he has to act fast. She will of course want a chalet all to herself and that gives him a further problem - where is Gladys going to sleep? He decides to put Barry in with Ted and Spike and Gladys will have to share with Yvonne. Things go from bad to worse. Miss Wainwright has a vendetta against Gladys ridiculing everything she does, Ted knows who Joan Wainwright is - or was - and decides to intervene.

Guest cast:
Joan Wainwright   **Cheryl Murray**

Fetaured music: *Swedish Rhapsody* (Mantovani and his Orchestra).

Series Four Production Credits:

Studio Warm Up FELIX BOWNESS. Rehearsal Pianist ROY MOORE Production Team:. ROBIN CARR, BERNADETTE DARNELL, ROY GOULD, SUZANNE PINTO. Vision Mixer ANGELA BEVERIDGE. Senior Cameraman GARTH TUCKER, RON PEVERALL, RON PERCIVAL. Costume MARY HUSBAND. Make Up JILL HAGGER. Properties Buyer ROGER WOOD. Videotape Editor PHIL SOUTHBY. Visual Effects ANDY LAZELL, EFFECTS ASSOCIATES. Film Cameraman MAX SAMETT. Film Sound TERRY ELMS. Film Editor MIKE ROBOTHAM. Studio Sound LAURIE TAYLOR. Studio Lighting DUNCAN BROWN, JOHN GREEN. Production Manager SUSAN BELBIN. Design GARRY FREEMAN. Directed by JOHN KILBY (except episodes 22, 23, 24, 25 directed by DAVID CROFT). Produced by DAVID CROFT.

Series Five

Regular Cast:

Jeffrey Fairbrother	SIMON CADELL
Ted Bovis	PAUL SHANE
Gladys Pugh	RUTH MADOC
Spike Dixon	JEFFREY HOLLAND
Mr. Partridge	LESLIE DWYER
Fred Quilly	FELIX BOWNESS
Yvonne Stuart-Hargreaves	DIANE HOLLAND
Barry Stuart-Hargreaves	BARRY HOWARD
Peggy Ollerenshaw	SU POLLARD
Sylvia Garnsey	NIKKI KELLY
Betty Whistler	RIKKI HOWARD
Tracey Bentwood	SUSAN BEAGLEY
Stanley Matthews	DAVID WEBB
Bruce Matthews	TONY WEBB
Gary Bolton	CHRIS ANDREWS

Location filming dates:
26th September - 22nd October 1983

Series Five filming locations:
Warner's Holiday Camp, Dovercourt (all episodes). Great Oakley, Stone's Green Road (Builder's Yard) (28). Hitcham, 2 Laurals Cottages (28). Stone's Green, Junction of Colchester Road/Stonehall Road (28). Little Oakley, Earlham's Marshes & Beach (32).

27. CONCESSIONS

Studio: TC 4 - Friday 28th October 1983 **TX:** Sunday 27th November 1983 at 7.15pm, BBC 1
Duration: 29 mins 26 secs **Audience rating:** 10.30 million

Ted is pretending to be ill and he is getting Spike to do his slot in the Ballroom later that evening, even lending him his best material, but Spike has his own ideas. Ted has agreed to do a turn at the Chamber of Commerce dinner up the road and he is taking Mr. Partridge with him to play the piano and even gets Peggy a job as a Waitress for the evening. All of which means Spike has got to lie to Jeffrey, something he hates doing. All is going well for Ted until Jeffrey and Gladys decide they will check up on him and take him a whisky. They are taken aback to discover a dummy in his bed. Back in the Ballroom, Spike is making a dummy of himself, dressed as Pinocchio and telling jokes about Wood and String! It is not going down at all well. Peggy is picking up bread rolls off the floor and she overhears a bent Councillor talking about ruining Joe Maplin and thwarting his plans to extend his camp. Later when they get back to camp Peggy relates to Ted and Spike what she overheard.

Ted decides to act on it straight away and visit the Councillor but his plans go awry. Peggy, however saves the day by telephoning Joe Maplin personally to warn him about the plot. All Ted needs to do now is confess to Jeffrey about why he lied. And what will Ted say when he finds about Spike's jokes about wood and string?

Guest cast:

Charlie Dawson	Johnny Allen
Head Waiter	Eric Longworth
Percy, Dawson's ally	Martin Gordon

Featured music: *L'Apres Midi D'une Faune*, *Waltz No. 1 in Eb*, (performed by Roy Cloughton, Don Drury with 3 musicians), *I'll String Along With You* (Jeffrey Holland), *Today I Love Everybody* (vocal: Paul Shane, pianist: Roy Moore).

28. SAVE OUR HERITAGE

Studio: TC 3 - Friday 4th November 1983 **TX:** Sunday 4th December 1983 at. 7.15pm, BBC 1
Duration: 29 mins 14 secs **Audience rating:** 10.30 million

Its Vicars and Tarts night in the Hawaiian Ballroom Jeffrey is dressed as a Cardinal and all the other members of staff are dressed accordingly, all except Spike who has come as a Strawberry Tart! Jeffrey becomes concerned when a local cottage is faced with destruction and its owner Mrs. Baxter threatened with eviction to make way for an extension to Joe Maplin's camp. He visits the cottage himself with Ted and when he sees it for the first time realises that it is an absolute gem and well worth saving. He then decides to rally round the staff to get them to join him in sabotaging Joe Maplin's plans. They agree. First thing they must do is hide the bulldozer. Fred's horse 'Flight' and all the staff are pulling ropes to get the vehicle moving. They work as quietly as possible so the night-watch man does not hear what's going on - that is until Peggy informs them he isn't even there! They all set off with the bulldozer, Ted at the helm.

When a Police siren is heard in the distance the staff start to panic. Thinking they have been rumbled they run into the bushes to hide. All except Jeffrey who is stranded in the bulldozer arm. Can they save Mrs. Baxter's cottage and avoid trouble with the law?

Guest cast:
Mrs. Baxter	Lally Bowers
First Vicar	Tim Swinton
Real Vicar	Michael Lomax
Police Sergeant	Martyn Read
Police Constable	Jeffrey Stewart
Police Constable (driving)	Gary Raynsford

Featured music: *In A Monastery Garden* (Roy Cloughton, Don Drury with 3 musicians), *You'll Never Walk Alone* (Paul Shane).

29. EMPTY SADDLES

Studio: TC 1 - Friday 11th November 1983 **TX:** Sunday 11th December 1983 at 7.15pm, BBC 1
Duration: 27 mins 31 secs **Audience rating:** 9.60 million

On Joe Maplin's orders Fred's lame horses must be sent to the 'knackers yard' and it falls upon Mr. Fairbrother to break the bad news. When Fred is shown the letter he just gets up quietly and leaves - absolutely heartbroken. Mr. Partridge is telling all the entertainments staff that Fred has nicked one of his bottles of Scotch and is now drunk! Jeffrey insists that he is taken to the sick bay. Ted comes up with a great idea that will not only save Fred's horses but will show Mr. Maplin in a different light. It will involve a naïve Chalet Maid writing a letter to the HM The Queen and contacting the local newspaper telling them all that Joe Maplin is opening up a home for retired horses. Nobody is quite prepared for the immediate reaction.

Guest cast:
'Memsahib' Lady	Madeleine Christie
'Colonel' Gent	Ballard Berkeley
Receptionist	Karen Hodson

Featured music: *When You're Smiling* (The Webb Twins).

30. THE MARRIAGE SETTLEMENT

Studio: TC 3 - Friday 18th November 1983 **TX:** Sunday 18th December 1983, BBC 1
Duration: 29 mins 49 secs **Audience rating:** 9.80 million

Maplin's favourite competition is taking place in the Ballroom - the legendary 'Who Can Stuff The Most Spaghetti Down Their Trousers Competition'. Things are going well until Peggy hands Gladys a note to say that Mr. Fairbrother and his wife Daphne are in his office. Gladys is so shocked she rushes over there to catch them leaving and mishears what is being said. She is convinced that Jeffrey is about to go back to his wife. However, he has agreed to give his wife grounds for divorce which will involve him hiring a professional Co-respondent. For this he will need Peggy's help and tracks her down immediately to explain what he will want her to do. Peggy is flustered and very confused by Mr. Fairbrother's instructions but will go along with the plan anyway. He of course swears her to absolute secrecy. Because Gladys is so sad at the thought of losing Jeffrey forever, Peggy decides to put her out of her misery and informs her of what Jeffrey has planned. Unbeknown to Jeffrey, all the entertainments staff soon get to hear about what is going on via the Maplin's grapevine. Jeffrey arranges to meet up with a young lady from the agency and on arrival takes her out to dinner at Tony's Trattoria in the High Street. Thanks to some dodgy scampi things don't quite work out as Jeffrey would like.

Guest cast:
Daphne Fairbrother	Claire Oberman
Jenny Maitland	Susan Jameson
Ramona	Jean Lear
Kent House team	Robert Briggs, Chris Drake, Lorraine Turner
Gloucester House team	Jo Croydon, Mark Kelly, Bryan Thurlow

Featured music: *Here We Are Again* (Paul Shane and the Yellowcoats), *O Sole Mio* (Jeffrey Holland), *Finiculi, Finicula* (vocals: Ruth Madoc and Su Pollard, organist: Jean Lear), *Singing The Blues* (Tommy Steele), *Sugar Time* (Su Pollard), *As Time Goes By* (Carroll Gibbons and the Savoy Hotel Orpheans).

31. THE GRAVEN IMAGE

Studio: TC 1 - Friday 25th November 1983 **TX:** Sunday 8th January 1984 at 7.15pm, BBC 1
Duration: 29 mins 39 secs **Audience rating:** 10.75 million

It falls upon Jeffrey Fairbrother to inform his entertainments staff that Joe Maplin has ordered the unveiling of a statue of himself at the camp. The staff are not happy about it one bit, especially Mr Partridge who quotes from the Bible that there shall not be any graven images. But Jeffrey knows that Joe Maplin must be obeyed. Problems arise when Ted takes Spike on one of the Campers' Mystery Tours and he gets very drunk. Spike then decides to liven up the statue that night, on the eve of the unveiling ceremony. In the morning Jeffrey asks Ted to go through the practice run with him and on pulling the cord to unveil Mr Maplin gets the shock of his life. The statue has been painted over and now resembles a clown. He is absolutely horrified and calls for an urgent meeting in the staff room. At the meeting Spike owns up remorsefully expecting everybody to turn on him. He is surprised to find that all the staff think it is an improvement and that it shows Joe Maplin for what he really is. However with the ceremony getting closer, it is a mad dash to put it right again particularly as Joe's hatchet man Harold Fox will be arriving for the unveiling. It's on with the overalls and armed with paintbrushes to see if they can get it painted in time. But with rain clouds looming overhead, will the ceremony be a success?

Guest cast:
Harold Fox	Gavin Richards
Gatekeeper	Rex Lear
Photographer	Stuart Rayner
Bert Swanley and The Debonairs	Bruce Guest, Andrew Pearson, Jason James, Michael Leader, Tommy Winward
Coach driver	Joe Long
Harold Fox's chauffeur	John Brown

Featured music: *Dambusters March, Egyptian March from Aida, When The Guards Are On Parade* (performed by Roy Cloughton, Don Drury with 3 musicians), *The Drinking Song* (Paul Shane and Jeffrey Holland), *The Diplomat* (The Band of HM Royal Marines).

32. PEGGY'S PEN FRIEND

Studio: TC 4 - Friday 2nd December 1983 **TX:** Sunday 15th January 1984 at 7.15pm, BBC 1
Duration: 31 mins **Audience rating:** 12.55 million

Ted is sitting in the Laughing Cow Milk Bar with Peggy and is learning all about her new boyfriend Monty. She is very excited about a forthcoming visit from her long term pen-friend and decides to show both Ted and Spike his actual photo. She says he is a little bit older - 45. However on seeing the photo, they realise he is quite a bit older than 45. Not wanting to spoil her excitement though, Ted and Spike inform Jeffrey of Peggy's date and also of the fact that Monty is an old man. They all become concerned for her welfare. The arranged picnic is to take place in the sand dunes and the some of the staff become very suspicious of his motives and decide to follow them. Gladys and Jeffrey sit armed with binoculars, Ted and Spike hide in the sand dunes and Fred is on one of his horses. All keeping watch over the gullible and very impressionable Peggy. But is heartbreak around the corner for the Chalet Maid?

Guest cast:
Monty	Morris Barry
Edna (Waitress)	Liz D'Esterre

Featured music: *Stagecoach* (Eric Winstone and his Band with vocal by Ruth Madoc), *Love Is A Many Splendoured Thing* (Frank Chacksfield with vocal by Ruth Madoc), *Legend of the Glass Mountain* (performed by Roy Cloughton, Don Drury and 3 musicians).

33. THE EPIDEMIC

Studio: TC 3 - Friday 9th December 1983 **TX:** Sunday 22nd January 1984 at 7.15pm, BBC 1
Duration: 27 mins 44 secs **Audience rating:** 12.75 million

A plague of graffiti has broken out at Maplins with Chads appearing all over the Holiday Camp. What is worse, Joe Maplin is expected at the camp with Gilbert Harding for a lecture. A Chad has appeared on the wall of the Wagtail Club. Barry is given the job of cleaning it off. As he is scrubbing the wall, he puts his back out and is in great pain. He is carried back to his chalet and will be indisposed for a while. Yvonne, being aware of the problem, telephones an old dancing partner of hers - Julian Dalrymple-Sykes to fill the gap. Later in the Ballroom, all the staff notice that they dance so well together - all because Yvonne still fancies him. Hundreds of Chads are cropping up all over the camp. The staff are fighting a losing battle and with Joe Maplin's visit approaching drastic action has to be taken. Cue Ted's broadcast over Radio Maplin telling the harrowing story of Fred Quilly during the war. News even to Fred Quilly.

Guest cast:
Julian Dalrymple-Sykes	Ben Aris

Featured music: *Ma, He's Making Eyes At Me, Green Door, Crazy Rhythm* (performed by Roy Cloughton, Don Drury and 3 musicians), *There'll Always Be An England* (The Band Of The Life Guards).

Series Five Production Credits:

Studio Warm Up FELIX BOWNESS. Choreographer KENN OLDFIELD Production team: BERNADETTE DARNELL, ROY GOULD, STACEY ADAIR, NIKKI COCKCROFT. Costume JACKIE SOUTHERN Make Up JILL HAGGER. Camera Supervisor KEN MAJOR, GARTH TUCKER, JOHN DAILLEY. Videotape Editor ROGER MARTIN, JOHN PAROUSSI. Vision Mixer ANGELA BEVERIDGE. Properties Buyer ROGER WOOD. Film Cameraman MAX SAMETT. Film Sound TERRY ELMS. Film Editor MIKE ROBOTHAM. Studio Lighting DUNCAN BROWN. Studio Sound BOB FOLEY. Production Manager SUSAN BELBIN. Design BERNARD LLOYD-JONES. Executive Producer DAVID CROFT. Produced and directed by JOHN KILBY.

Series Six

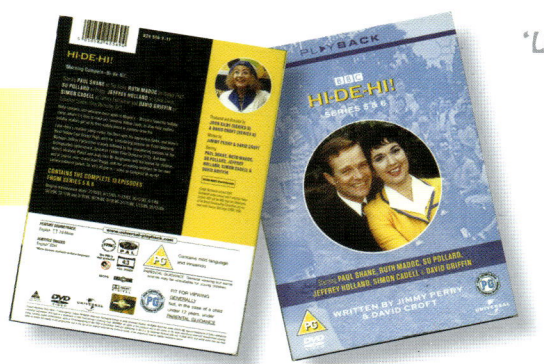

Regular Cast:

Ted Bovis	PAUL SHANE
Gladys Pugh	RUTH MADOC
Spike Dixon	JEFFREY HOLLAND
Peggy Ollerenshaw	SU POLLARD
Squadron Leader Clive Dempster DFC (from episode 35)	DAVID GRIFFIN
Mr. Partridge (episodes 36, 37, 38)	LESLIE DWYER
Fred Quilly	FELIX BOWNESS
Yvonne Stuart-Hargreaves	DIANE HOLLAND
Barry Stuart-Hargreaves	BARRY HOWARD
Sylvia Garnsey	NIKKI KELLY
April Wingate (from episode 35)	LINDA REGAN
Dawn Freshwater (from episode 35)	LAURA JACKSON
Babs Weaver (from episode 35)	JULIE-CHRISTIAN YOUNG
Stanley Matthews	DAVID WEBB
Bruce Matthews	TONY WEBB
Gary Bolton	CHRIS ANDREWS

Location filming dates:
24th September – 15th October 1984

Series Six Locations:
Warner's Holiday Camp, Dovercourt (all episodes). Dovercourt, West End Beach and Promenade (39). North Norfolk Railway (34). Weybourne Station and Approach Road (34, 36).

34. TOGETHER AGAIN

Studio: Friday 26th October 1984 **TX:** Saturday 3rd November 1984, BBC 1
Duration: 28 mins 24 secs **Audience rating:** 14.10 million

It is 1960 and a new season at Maplin's Holiday Camp is about to commence. Ted, Spike and Peggy are all travelling together by train. They meet up with the rest of the staff at Moulton Junction. Maplin's is looking sad and forlorn but already Spike is looking forward to being thrown into the Olympic Sized Pool. Gladys has a shock when she goes to the office expecting to see Jeffrey Fairbrother. The office is still a mess from the end of season party and there is a letter waiting for her. It is a farewell note from Jeffrey. He explains he has taken a post in Wisconsin and just wanted to say goodbye to all the staff, especially Gladys and to thank them all for everything. Gladys is left heartbroken, but with Fairbrother out of the way Ted thinks he may be about to be offered the vacant post.

Guest cast:
Station Master	Jan Harding
Station Announcer	Brenda Cowling (OOV)

Featured music: *Rock Island Line* (Jeffrey Holland unaccompanied).

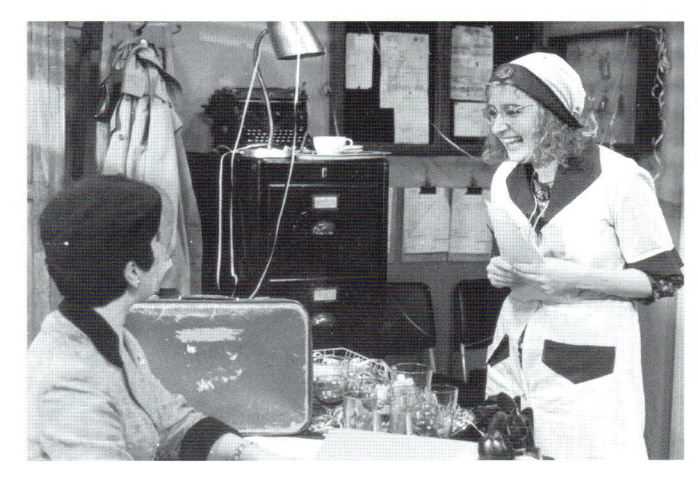

35. TED AT THE HELM

Studio: Friday 2nd November 1984 **TX:** Saturday 10th November 1984 at 8pm, BBC 1
Duration: 28 mins 21 secs **Audience rating:** 14.60 million

Ted thinks he is about to be offered the job of Entertainments Manager when he gets a summons to Head Office in London. Ever excited, he gets Spike to help him get ready and tells Peggy to bring along his suit. When he gets to London he is called in by Harold Fox and is shocked to be issued with a tax bill for £180! When he enquires about the vacant post of Entertainments' Manager at Maplin's he is told that Squadron Leader Clive Dempster DFC is taking the job. On his arrival back at Maplin's, Ted heads straight for Gladys's chalet to share the news and for a friendly shoulder to cry on. How can he face everybody now, especially after bragging that the job was his? Three new girl Yellowcoats join the staff leaving Peggy feeling increasingly fed up and wondering if she will ever get her dream job. When Mr. Fairbrother's replacement Clive zooms into the camp a few days later in his little sports car, he takes everybody by surprise. Clive insists on all the entertainments staff joining him in the pub down the road to celebrate his arrival but with no money on him, he asks Ted for some readies. Ted begins to recognise the signs of a con man...

Guest cast:
Harold Fox   **Gavin Richards**

Featured music: *Chick, Chick Chicken* and *Flamingo* (Jeffrey Holland unaccompanied).

36. OPENING DAY

Studio: TC 6 - Friday 9th November 1984 **TX:** Saturday 17th November 1984, BBC1
Duration: 29 mins 50 secs **Audience rating:** 15.55 million

It's opening day at Maplin's and it is always a busy day. Gladys, Fred, Bruce and Stanley have been up since 5am testing out all the loud speakers around the camp - but was it such a good idea getting Peggy involved? And with a whistle? Peggy has had an even bigger problem waking Clive Dempster from a deep sleep. All the Yellowcoats and entertainments staff have been told that they must head down to the Railway station to meet the first intake of campers off the trains. Mr. Partridge and Mr. Punch manage to upset the station master by wanting to collect all the railway tickets from the campers, Barry and Yvonne moan to Gladys once again and just where is Sylvia? Ted tells Spike that he is not happy about Clive owing him money but when Clive drives up at the Station, in his Sports car with Sylvia alongside him, he hands Ted the money he owes him. Ted has also collected a handsome sum from the Staff Gratuities Box and is thrilled - that is until Clive somehow manages to borrow it. Ted is left to wonder about Clive's financial situation and he realises he will have to work even harder to keep the money away from Clive's grasp!

Guest cast:
Station Master   **Jan Harding**
Punch and Judy   **Professor Guy Higgins (OOV)**

Featured music: *Well Keep A Welcome, Sospan Fach, Men Of Harlech* (Ruth Madoc unaccompanied), *Dambusters March* (The Band of the Royal Marines), *The Irish Washerwoman* (Paul Shane unaccompanied), *Jolly Good Company* (Paul Shane and the Yellowcoats with Roy Cloughton and band).

37. OFF WITH THE MOTLEY

Studio: Friday 16th November 1984   **TX:** Saturday 24th November 1984 at 8pm, BBC 1
Duration: 28 mins 55 secs   **Audience rating:** 15.35 million

Spike and Ted are getting a bit concerned about the new Entertainments Manager due to his habit of borrowing money from various people around the camp. He is so different from Mr. Fairbrother. Clive's next victim is Gladys, who coughs up £10 for him to lend to Yvonne, another of Clive's lies. But concerns have to be put to one side as it is 'Drown Your Granny' competition and Ted is announcing the staff who are to take part as Grannies. Barry and Yvonne are horrified at being included and so is Sylvia when Gladys tells her she is to be one too! Peggy is told by Clive that she has an appointment in the Admin Block and that it sounds important. Is she in trouble? It's quite the opposite as she has been promoted to Deputy Supervisor Of Cleaning which will mean more money and more responsibility for her. When all the staff are having fun around the Olympic Sized Pool and getting soaking wet with the campers, she is on the other side of the camp being bombarded by towels and toilet rolls! Peggy has to decide where her heart lies.

Su Pollard with her stunt double in 'Off with the Motley', Denise Ryan.

Guest cast:
Plumber	Ronnie Brody
Rose	Lucy Gould
Mavis	Pamela Manson
Enid	Lisa Bluthal
Ramona	Jean Lear
Peggy's Double (swimming pool sequence)	Denise Ryan
Chalet maid	Rosemary Banks
Partridge's Double	Cyril Cook (film only)

Featured music: *Blaze Away* (The Grand Massed Bands of Fairey, Fodens and BMC), *I'm Dreaming Of A White Christmas* (Frank Chacksfield and his Orchestra with vocal by Ruth Madoc), *Happy Days Are Here Again, Startime, Little Old Lady, Be A Clown* (Jean Lear), *I Cover The Waterfront* (vocal: Ruth Madoc, organist: Jean Lear), *Miners Dream Of Home* (vocals: Entertainments staff, organist: Jean Lear), *Civilisation* (vocal: Paul Shane, organist: Jean Lear).

38. HEY DIDDLE DIDDLE, WHO'S ON THE FIDDLE?

Studio: TC 1 - Friday 23rd November 1984   **TX:** Saturday 1st December 1984 at 8pm, BBC 1
Duration: 28 mins 35 secs   **Audience rating:** 15.05 million

Clive asks Peggy to take his jacket to the cleaners for him, but beforehand she calls on Spike to ask him for her scissors back. Together they discover a letter in Clive's jacket pocket. Spike assumes it is Joe Maplin's letter that was read out that morning – but they discover it isn't. It is a far more sinister letter implying that Clive has been given the job of Entertainments Manager to spy on the rest of the staff. Spike is even more upset when he reads on the envelope 'Private & Confidential' and sets out on a mission to protect everybody on the staff and to conceal their fiddles from Joe Maplin and from Clive. He manages to break up Ted's Bingo drum and nearly gets a thump for his efforts. Peggy can't just sit back and let Spike take the blame for his actions, not when he is only trying to protect them all. She shows Ted the letter that they found and he decides that Clive must be confronted and that they must take along the letter as proof.

Guest cast:
Christine	Angela Graham-Jones
George	Paul Wilce

Featured music: *Alone* (Jimmy Gregor & The Lower Strings with vocal by Ruth Madoc), *Quando Calienta El Sol (Love Me With All Of Your Heart)* (Robert Delgado and his Orchestra with vocal by Ruth Madoc).

'Lift Up Your Minds' - Episode Guide

39. RAFFLES

Studio: TC 4 - Friday 30th November 1984 **TX:** Tuesday 25th December 1984 at 6.05pm, BBC 1
Duration: 30 mins 6 secs **Audience rating:** 14.85 million

Clive is up to his neck in debt. He confides in Gladys and tells her how it all occurred, prompting her to feel sorry for him. However, the next day he buys champagne for the staff as he has just received a big cheque from his Father. A Debt Collector arrives at Maplin's demanding £200 with menaces. Meanwhile Fred tells Ted that he will have to move an old car out of the stables as he has some new horses arriving and he needs the space. Ted has a wonderful idea - another way of ripping off the campers and making pots of money - a Raffle to win a car. His clapped out old banger of course not Clive's swanky motor. But the cars are identical and with a bit of polish to Ted's car, a daring fiddle is on.

Guest cast:

Plumber	**Ronnie Brody**
Debt Collector	**Geoffrey Leesley**
Matronly camper	**Brenda Cowling**
Lady car winner	**Peggyann Clifford**
Heavy	**Les Henry**

Featured music: *As Time Goes By* and *He'd Have To Get Under, Get Out and Get Under* (performed by Roy Cloughton, Don Drury and 3 musicians) *Wot Cher!* and *The Lambeth Walk* (Roy Cloughton, Don Drury with 3 musicians, vocals: Diane Holland and Barry Howard).

Series Six Production Credits:

Studio Warm Up FELIX BOWNESS. Punch and Judy advisor PROFESSOR GUY HIGGINS. Dances staged by KENN OLDFIELD. Production Team NIKKI COCKCROFT, ROY GOULD, LINDSAY CHAMIER, OLWYN SILVESTER. Costume Designer JOAN WADGE. Make Up Designer CAROLINE NOBLE. Camera Supervisor KEN MAJOR. Videotape editor ROGER MARTIN, PHIL SOUTHBY, JOHN PAROUSSI. Vision Mixer HILARY WEST, ANGELA BEVERIDGE. Studio lighting DUNCAN BROWN. Studio sound LAURIE TAYLOR. Visual effects COLIN MAPSON. Properties buyer THERESA KEAVENEY. Film cameraman MAX SAMETT. Film sound MICHAEL SPENCER. Film editor COLIN JONES. Production managers SUSAN BELBIN, MARTIN DENNIS. Designer BERNARD LLOYD-JONES. Produced and directed by DAVID CROFT.

'Lift Up Your Minds' - Episode Guide

Series Seven

Regular Cast:

Ted Bovis	PAUL SHANE
Gladys Pugh	RUTH MADOC
Spike Dixon	JEFFREY HOLLAND
Peggy Ollerenshaw	SU POLLARD
Clive Dempster	DAVID GRIFFIN
Fred Quilly	FELIX BOWNESS
Yvonne Stuart-Hargreaves	DIANE HOLLAND
Barry Stuart-Hargreaves	BARRY HOWARD
Sylvia Garnsey	NIKKI KELLY
April Wingate	LINDA REGAN
Dawn Freshwater	LAURA JACKSON
Babs Weaver	JULIE-CHRISTIAN YOUNG
Stanley Matthews	DAVID WEBB
Bruce Matthews	TONY WEBB
Gary Bolton	CHRIS ANDREWS

Location filming dates:
23rd September - 17th October 1985

Series Seven filming locations:
Warner's Holiday Camp, Dovercourt (all episodes). Dovercourt, West End Beach (42). Dovercourt, Cliff Hotel, exterior and interior (bar) (43). Harwich, (formerly) Three Cups PH, Church Street (43). Dovercourt, Promenade and Beach (44).

40. THE GREAT CAT ROBBERY

Studio: TC 6 - Friday 6th December 1985 and Saturday 7th December 1985
TX: Wednesday 25th December 1985 at 6.30pm, BBC 1 **Duration:** 57 mins 55 secs
N.B. Some satellite repeats have shown this episode in two halves. **Audience rating:** 14.0 million

Peggy has been asked to be a South Sea Island Virgin in the legendary 'South Sea Island Leg Over Race' alongside Yvonne and she is absolutely delighted when she and her partner Fred win the race to get their knickers up the flagpole first. Later Ted is busy reading an article in the local paper about his act and is bragging to the staff about being described as a 'knockout'. Peggy takes a look at the paper and says that she recognises a face. A man who stayed at the camp last season. He is a known Cat Burglar and has stolen a diamond necklace worth a princely £10,000 and the staff get excited at the thought that the loot could actually be buried under the floorboards somewhere on the camp. With a bit of careful deduction Peggy remembers which line of chalets the man had stayed in and narrows it down further to three chalets. Ted and Clive instigate a plan to retrieve the diamonds. Barry and Yvonne have chosen not to do anything dodgy but they have agreed to lend Ted some of Yvonne's 'Obligon' tablets - the ones that help her sleep. The campers who occupy the three chalets to be searched will be given mugs of cocoa laced with the tablets, and Peggy must make sure that they drink it. Then the search can begin! With the campers now fast asleep, the moving out of furniture, floorboards and beds - complete with campers - can take place and the staff can get to work searching for the necklace.

Guest cast:

Elderly Man	John Rutland
Marjorie	Jeanne Mockford
Steve	Richard Speight
Eunice	Lucy Gould

Featured music: *Aloha, Happy Days Are Here Again* (Jean Lear), *Hawaiian War Chant* (vocal: Ruth Madoc, organist: Jean Lear) *Moonlight Fiesta* (Winifred Atwell with Cyril Ornadel and His Orchestra), *Portrait Of My Love* (Victor Silvester and his Ballroom Orchestra), Anniversary Waltz (Jeffrey Holland), *Goodnight Campers* (performed by Roy Cloughton and 4 musicians and sung by the company).

41. IT'S MURDER

Studio: TC 8 - Friday 25th October 1985   **TX:** Sunday 5th January 1986, BBC 1
Duration: 30 mins approx.   **Audience rating:** Not Available

At the morning staff meeting Barry and Yvonne want everybody to sign their petition to get rid of Mr. Partridge as he fell asleep whilst drunk, and in Barry's bed too. It is the final straw as far as they are concerned. Word soon gets round that Mr. Partridge is causing chaos down at the Punch & Judy booth, he has upset both parents and kids. Not only was he drunk yet again but he was also using violence. Clive is called in to calm the parents down, but his solution to the problem involves taking them off to one of the camp bars to buy them all drinks. Later on at an emergency staff meeting Clive informs everybody that Mr. Partridge has already put in complaints about each and every one of them. Ted's act is far too blue, Spike is boring and Fred is walking round in ladies underwear! Old Partridge cannot be found anywhere. They think he has left the camp, until late at night a shocking discovery is made in the Olympic Sized Pool.

Guest cast:
Mr. Thompson	Billy Burden
Angry Parent	Bill Pertwee
Peggy's Boy in Ballroom	Barry Birch

Featured music: *Calling All Workers* (from the Decca LP 'Those Wonderful Radio Years'), *The Darktown Strutters' Ball* (Fred Elizade and His Music), *My Yiddishe Momme* (vocal: Paul Shane with Roy Cloughton and 4 musicians).

42. WHO KILLED MR. PARTRIDGE?

Studio: TC 8 - Friday 1st November 1985   **TX:** Sunday 12th January 1986 at 7.15pm, BBC 1
Duration: 28 mins 37 secs   **Audience rating:** Not Available

With Ted and Spike discovering Mr. Partridge's body floating face down in the pool and a knife sticking out of his back, they have to think fast. They knock on Peggy's chalet door and tell her what's happened. They also ask her to go round to all the staff chalets to wake everyone up immediately and tell them that Ted has called an important meeting in the staff room and their presence is required. Meanwhile Ted 'phones Joe Maplin in London and is awaiting further instructions from him. The next thing that is needed is to stop the campers from seeing the body and the only way to do that is to turn the lights off round the pool - but Fred manages to fuse the whole camp! Worse to come though is when a restless camper out walking sees the body but before he has a chance to raise the alarm he is bundled away by Fred and the Twins. Things are not looking too good and with Joe Maplin not telephoning back with instructions, Clive finally decides to telephone the Police. All the staff are now in serious trouble. The situation is not helped by Joe denying all knowledge of the goings on at Crimpton-on-Sea!

Guest cast:
Male Camper	Robin Parkinson
Inspector Phillips	Michael Lees
Police Constable	James Gow
Police Sergeant	Philip Kendall
Superintendent	Len Lowe (OOV)
Police photographer	Martyn Townsend
Policeman carrying dummy	Nicholas Donovan

43. SPAGHETTI GALORE

Studio: TC 4 - Friday 8th November 1986 **TX:** Sunday 19th January 1986 at 7.15pm, BBC 1
Duration: 31 mins 34 secs **Audience rating:** 12.90 million

Fred informs Clive that it is Gladys's birthday soon so Clive decides to take her out for a romantic evening. Tomorrow is his day off and he is going to London but he tells Gladys that he will get back to the camp later and waiting in a nearby pub for her. With a letter arriving in camp from Harold Fox from Head Office to say that he is visiting the camp; it is left to Gladys to deal with him as Clive will not be around. Mr. Fox arrives and is not too pleased with what he finds but is aware that it is Gladys's Birthday and insists on taking her out for dinner. Gladys is worried that she will now be forced to miss her date with Clive, but it is Peggy to the rescue with her quick thinking. She intends to ride a motorbike and drive Gladys to both dates. However things do not quite go to plan, when Harold Fox and Clive have the same idea - a slap up meal at Tony's Trattoria.

Guest cast:
Tony	Graham Stark
Harold Fox	Gavin Richards
Chauffeur	Stan Young
Girl on tennis court	Sarah Jones-Parry
Stunt double for Peggy	Tracey Eddon
Keep fit campers	Sherry Adelaide, Marjorie Butters, Bernadette Cavanagh
2nd Girl on tennis court	Debbie Riordan

Featured music: *Wheels* (Joe Loss and his Orchestra), *Manhatten Beach* (Band of HM Royal Marines), *La Scala, Caterina, Fonta Musica* (archive recordings).

44. A LACK OF PUNCH

Studio: TC 1 - Friday 15th November 1985 **TX:** Sunday 26th January 1986 at 7.15pm, BBC 1
Duration: 29 mins 30 secs **Audience rating:** Not Available

Gladys reads out a letter from Joe Maplin letting the staff know that there will be no replacement for Mr. Partridge. To add to their surprise they are told that they will have to take it in turns to entertain the children. Joe Maplin has recruited his girlfriend Poppy Maxwell to write some short stories in which they will act. Barry and Yvonne are up first in a playlet entitled *Tuffet Tantrums*. Barry is Percy the Pixie and Yvonne will play Miss Muffet. Gladys is next up and she has to be Old Mother Hubbard, Spike will be Wee Willy Winky and poor Ted has to play Humpty Dumpty. This is the final straw for Ted and he tries hard to think of a way of getting out of future productions. On their next day off Ted and Spike visit Grapethorpe, a local seaside town, and they notice a smelly old tramp entertaining children on the beach. Ted knows that he has found the answer to the staffing problem. They take 'Uncle Sammy' back to the camp with promises of a warm chalet, clean clothes and plenty of grub. However Sammy was not anticipating a hot bath containing sheep dip and being scrubbed raw.

Guest cast:
Uncle Sammy Morris	Kenneth Connor
Police Sergeant	Paul Toothill
Ramona	Jean Lear

Featured music: *Be My Love* (Mantovani and his Orchestra with vocal by Ruth Madoc), *Dance of the Sugarplum Fairy* (L'Orchestrede La Suisse Romande), *Percy The Pixie* (vocal: Barry Howard, pianist: Jean Lear).

45. IVORY CASTLES IN THE AIR

Studio: TC 1 - Friday 22nd November 1985 **TX:** Sunday 9th February 1986 at 7.15pm, BBC 1
Duration: 29 mins 52 secs **Audience rating:** 13.65 million

Joe Maplin is sending down representatives from two of his favourite companies. The staff are to participate in the competition for the best 'Fluorabrite Couple'. They are all to pair off and smile at the judges and whoever has the brightest smile will be the winners. Gladys will partner Spike which will not please April. Peggy is given the title of Miss Sanikill 1960. Clive gets a sudden visit at Maplin's from his very favourite Uncle who tells him that his father needs him back at Dempster Hall as soon as possible to help run things. Clive however, is reluctant as he is enjoying his cushy time at Maplin's. But he does think that Gladys would be the ideal candidate to run Dempster Hall. He soons invites Gladys to meet his father and to show her round the family home. Whilst visiting she becomes hooked and actually thinks that Clive is going to pop the big question. The local paper is soon running a story about Spike and Gladys finding love which may well scupper Gladys's dreams.

Guest cast:
Uncle Charles	Dennis Ramsden
Jerry Price	Ronnie Stevens

Featured music: *The White Cliffs Of Dover* (Geraldo and his Orchestra with vocal by Ruth Madoc), *Skyliner* (performed by Roy Cloughton and 4 musicians), *Apache* (The Shadows).

46. MAN TRAP

Studio: TC 4 - Friday 29th November 1985 **TX:** Sunday 16th February 1986 at 7.15pm, BBC 1
Duration: 31 mins 4 secs **Audience rating:** 13.75 million

Whilst dusting Clive's office Peggy takes a telephone call from Clive's father. He tells Peggy that he liked Gladys very much when she visited the Hall but he has decided on an Australian girl who has experience with Kangaroos. Clive explains how his father wants someone to run his business for him. Peggy is mortified and lets Ted and Spike know about Clive's deceitfulness. They all know that Gladys will be humiliated when she finds out the real reason for visiting Dempster Hall. All is not well with Yvonne and Barry either. Yvonne oversteps the mark with her constant criticism of Barry and sparks fly. Ted tells Clive he must get engaged to Gladys so as not to hurt her. He can break it off later. Expensive champagne is ordered for the announcement to the rest of the staff. Peggy is the only one not in the mood for celebrating as she knows that Gladys truly loves him. She sets out to do something about it and telephones the East Coast Gazette, to spread the news a bit further.

Featured music: *Ac-cent-tchu-ate The Positive* (Su Pollard unaccompanied), *Summer Place* (Norrie Paramor and his Orchestra), *Hit And Miss* (John Barry Seven), *Starry Eyed* (Michael Holliday).

Series Seven Production Credits:

Warm Up Man FELIX BOWNESS. Production team: BERNADETTE DARNELL, ROY GOULD, DUNCAN COOPER. Costume JACQUELINE PARRY. Make Up GILLIAN THOMAS. Properties Buyer THERESA STEVENS. Visual Effects COLIN MAPSON, STEVE BOWMAN. Camera Supervisor KEN MAJOR. Videotape Editor MALCOLM WARNER, PHIL SOUTHBY. Vision Mixer ANGELA BEVERIDGE. Film Cameraman MAX SAMETT. Film Sound MICHAEL SPENCER. Film Editor MIKE ROBOTHAM. Dubbing Mixer MIKE NARDUZZO. Studio Lighting DUNCAN BROWN. Studio Sound LAURIE TAYLOR, MICHAEL McCARTHY. Production Managers ROBIN CARR, MARTIN DENNIS. Design ANDRE WELSTEAD-HORNBY. Produced and Directed by DAVID CROFT (except episodes 44, 45 and 46 directed by DAVID CROFT and ROBIN CARR).

'Lift Up Your Minds' - Episode Guide

Series Eight

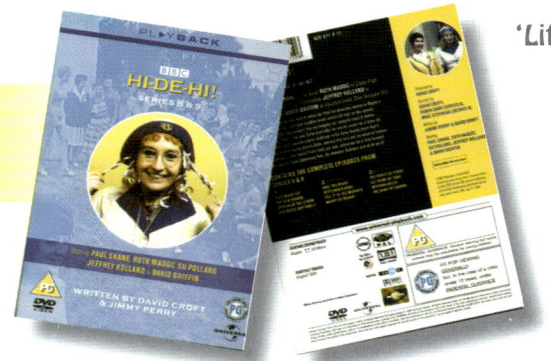

Regular Cast:

Ted Bovis	PAUL SHANE
Gladys Pugh	RUTH MADOC
Spike Dixon	JEFFREY HOLLAND
Peggy Ollerenshaw	SU POLLARD
Clive Dempster	DAVID GRIFFIN
Sammy Morris (from episode 48)	KENNETH CONNOR
Fred Quilly	FELIX BOWNESS
Yvonne Stuart-Hargreaves	DIANE HOLLAND
Julian Dalrymple-Sykes	BEN ARIS
Sylvia Garnsey	NIKKI KELLY
April Wingate	LINDA REGAN
Dawn Freshwater	LAURA JACKSON
Stanley Matthews	DAVID WEBB
Bruce Matthews	TONY WEBB
Gary Bolton	CHRIS ANDREWS

Location filming dates:
23rd September - 16th October 1986

Series Eight filming locations:
Warner's Holiday Camp, Dovercourt (47, 48, 49, 50, 52). Dovercourt, Boating Lake Lower Marine Parade, West End Beach and Cliff Hotel (51) Harwich, outside 1912 Centre and the Electric Palace Cinema (internal & external) (51). Lawford, Units 13 & 14 Commerce Way (51). Manningtree Railway Station and Approach Road (49). Mount Bures, Withers Farm (47, 52).

47. PIGS MIGHT FLY

Studio: TC 4 - Friday 24th October 1986. **TX:** Saturday 8th November 1986 at 7.35pm, BBC 1
Duration: 29 mins 27 secs   **Audience rating:** 14.2 million

Clive is getting worried about going along with Ted's plan and his imminent marriage to Gladys - especially as Gladys is buying wedding magazines! But with other pressing and more important things to do at Maplin's, Spike is feeling confused as he realises that he has feelings for Gladys. Yvonne has locked herself away in her chalet since Barry walked out on her and she doesn't want to see anybody. All the staff are worried about her state of mind. Whilst she sneaks out to the camp washrooms, shrouded in a blanket, Peggy and Fred run into her chalet and steal all her sleeping tablets and Barry's farewell note. Concerned about the entertainments programme, Gladys takes the initiative and sends for Yvonne's substitute dance partner - Julian Dalrymple-Sykes. Knowing how much Yvonne thinks of him Gladys is certain that he will be able to help. Just as well, as Clive has just received a letter from Joe Maplin telling them all that he is sending a new Camp Controller to check what's going on. They had better take care as he has the power to hire and fire.

Guest cast:

Alec Foster	Ewan Hooper
Mr. Turner	Billy Burden
Henry, the gatekeeper	Gordon Peters

Featured music: *If I Can Help Somebody* (The Morris Concert Band), *Who's Wonderful, Who's Marvellous? Miss Annabelle Lee* (performed by Roy Cloughton and 4 musicians).

48. THE NEW BROOM

Studio: TC 4 - Friday 31st October 1986 **TX:** Saturday 15th November 1986 at 7.40pm, BBC 1
Duration: 29 mins 44 secs   **Audience rating:** 12.7 million

With Alec Foster making enemies of everybody and sacking staff all over the camp, his attention falls on the entertainments staff. He asks to see Clive at 9 o'clock but is extremely angry when he turns up late. Clive is not an early riser, after all. Alec tells Clive to sharpen up his act or he will get his cards. When Sammy Morris arrives back at Maplin's with a letter from Joe Maplin announcing that he is the new Children's Entertainer the staff decide that Clive must sort it out and quick. Peggy asks Foster if she could be considered as a Yellowcoat in the future. He tells her to come to his chalet later that evening after 'Goodnight Campers' and he will interview her personally. Foster's intentions are more sinister and when Peggy cottons on, he threatens her and the rest of the staff with the sack if she breathes a word.

Guest cast:
Alec Foster   Ewan Hooper

49. ORPHAN OF THE STORM

Studio: TC 8 - Friday 7th November 1986 **TX:** Saturday 22nd November 1986 at 7.40pm, BBC 1
Duration: 29 mins 25 secs   **Audience rating:** 13.2 million

Ted is busy doing his 'Famous People on the Toilet' routine in the Ballroom and all the entertainments staff are assembled at the bar when Alec Foster appears and tells them all to jump to it and dance with the campers. All except Peggy who he tells to leave the Ballroom at once. The very next day he gives Peggy the sack for allegedly pinching soap from the storeroom. Peggy is heartbroken as she loves working at the camp. It's agreed that Clive will pay Alec Foster a visit to try and persuade him to give Peggy her job back. Peggy decides that she has caused enough trouble and leaves for the station immediately. But all is not lost as she is saved by an unexpected rescuer...

Guest cast:
Alec Foster   Ewan Hooper
Boy in ballroom   Peter Waddington

Featured music: *La Cumbasita, I Want To Be Happy, A Room With A View, He's A Fine Old English Gentleman*, (performed by Roy Cloughton with 4 musicians) *Shake Hands With A Millionaire* (vocal: Paul Shane), *Guitar Boogie Shuffle* (Bert Weedon).

Series eight, cast and production crew photo shoot taken on location at Warner's Holiday Camp, Dovercourt. The cast appear to be in costume for the episode *September Song*.

'Lift Up Your Minds' - Episode Guide

50. GOD BLESS OUR FAMILY

Studio: TC 4 - Friday 14th November 1986 **TX:** Saturday 6th December 1986 at 7.40pm, BBC 1
Duration: 29 mins 29 secs   **Audience rating:** 10.4 million

Ted finds it more and more difficult sharing his chalet with Spike and Julian especially as they keep waking him up early. "If only Yvonne would have me" says Julian. Whilst Peggy is waiting for a new delivery of toilet rolls at the main gate, Clive's posh relatives suddenly arrive demanding to come on to the camp as day visitors. They are intent on trying to persuade Clive to return home to his father where he belongs. They also intend to put Gladys firmly in her place. Clive gets a huge shock later when he walks in and finds his family sitting there drinking frothy coffee. So it's back to his office, where the family have their say only to find Gladys is not such a pushover. She tells them that she loves Clive implicitly but she will agree not to marry Clive and hands back his engagement ring. Just as Gladys has finally played into his hands, an outburst from his own mouth shocks even Clive.

Guest cast:
Charles Dempster	Dennis Ramsden
Winifrid Dempster	Mavis Pugh
General Sir Claud Dempster	Peter Fontaine
Vice-Admiral Neville Dempster	Iain Anders
Bishop Simon Dempster	Fred Bryant
Henry, the gatekeeper	Gordon Peters
Lorry driver	Bryan Burdon

Featured music: *In a Golden Coach* (Billy Cotton and his Band), *Tallahassie Lassie* (Freddie Cannon) - this was replaced in later broadcasts by *Hit and Miss* performed by the John Barry Seven.

51. ONLY THE BRAVE

Studio: TC 8 - Friday 21st November 1986 and Saturday 22nd November 1986
TX: Saturday 13th December 1986 at 7.50pm, BBC 1 **Duration:** 29 mins 48 secs **Audience rating:** 10.3 million

With all the entertainments staff organising a Children's Teddy Bears' Picnic on the camp, Spike informs everybody that it's soon to be April's birthday and he would like to organise a surprise party for her. Everybody seems keen on the idea but the next day Peggy takes a phone call from Head Office informing her that staff parties are now banned due to trouble at another camp. Ted comes up with a brilliant idea. He arranges a late night trip to a local cinema for all the staff to see April's favourite film, *Bambi*. But a mix up with the projectionist results in the showing of a war film instead, *A Few Came Back*. April is very disappointed but calms down providing she can snuggle up to Spike. Clive has brought some specially mixed Martinis for him and Gladys. They fall asleep with Gladys dreaming of heroic deeds of wartime heroes.

Guest cast:
Mr. Watson, cinema manager	Len Howe
Charles, RAF Officer	Andrew Collins
Mary, WRAF Officer	Sorel Johnson
Jack, projectionist	Freddie Earlle
Double for Gladys	Tracey Eddon
Double for Clive	Tip Tipping
Cinema usherettes	Bernadette Cavanagh, Terry Cavanagh, Alison Howard

Featured music: *Salute To Freedom, Pas Daction* (from the LP Archive Series Vol 4.), *Roll Out The Barrel* (vocals: Entertainments staff, pianist: Roy Moore), *Cornish Rhapsody* (Roy Moore on piano / National Philharmonic Orchestra conducted by Elgar Howarth), *It's In The Air* (Su Pollard unaccompanied), *The Teddy Bears Picnic* (Donald Thorne).

'Lift Up Your Minds' - Episode Guide

52. SEPTEMBER SONG

Studio: TC 8 - Friday 28th November 1986 **TX:** Saturday 27th December 1986 at 7.50pm, BBC 1
Duration: 43 mins 51 secs. **Audience rating:** 13.4 million

All the entertainments staff are gathered in the staff room and not very happy about Joe Maplin's proposal of a Circus Night in the Hawaiian Ballroom. Ted is especially grumpy and walks out of the meeting. Later on he apologises to Gladys and comes clean saying he is getting married. He tells all the staff that he has fallen head over heels in love with a brilliant young pianist called Betty Barlow who is on holiday at Maplin's. He is even hoping to set up an act called 'Bovis & Barlow'. An unexpected visit from Betty's mother with some home truths spells heartbreak for Ted…

Guest cast:
Betty Barlow	**Caroline Dennis**
Mrs. Barlow	**Toni Palmer**
Mr. Turner	**Billy Burden**

Featured music: *Passing Strangers* (vocals: Paul Shane and Caroline Dennis, pianist: Caroline Dennis with overdubbed strings conducted by Ronnie Hazlehurst), *Be A Clown* (vocals: Paul Shane, piano: Roy Moore with Roy Cloughton and 4 musicians).

God Bless Our Family. Spike impersonates Peggy, although he hasn't gone so far as to tear his right-hand pocket..

Series Eight Production Credits:

Studio Warm Up FELIX BOWNESS. Choreographer KENN OLDFIELD. Production team VALERIE LETLEY, LAURA MACKIE, JANICE THOMAS, SHARON PORTER. Costume ANNA BURUMA, VALERIE WHITE. Make Up DENISE BARON. Properties Buyer JUDY FARR. Camera Supervisor KEN MAJOR. Videotape Editor CHRIS WADSWORTH, PHIL SOUTHBY. Vision Mixer ANGELA BEVERIDGE. Film Cameraman MAX SAMETT. Film Sound MICHAEL SPENCER. Film Editor MIKE ROBOTHAM. Studio Lighting HOWARD KING. Studio Sound MICHAEL McCARTHY. Production Manager MARTIN DENNIS. Design CHRIS HULL, MARTIN METHVEN. Directed by ROBIN CARR (except episodes 47, 50, 51 directed by ROBIN CARR and DAVID CROFT, episode 52 directed by DAVID CROFT). Produced by DAVID CROFT.

Series Nine

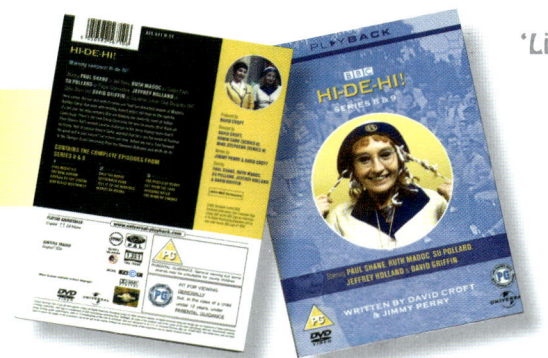

'Lift Up Your Minds' - Episode Guide

Regular Cast:

Ted Bovis	PAUL SHANE
Gladys Pugh	RUTH MADOC
Spike Dixon	JEFFREY HOLLAND
Peggy Ollerenshaw	SU POLLARD
Clive Dempster	DAVID GRIFFIN
Sammy Morris	KENNETH CONNOR
Fred Quilly	FELIX BOWNESS
Yvonne Stuart-Hargreaves	DIANE HOLLAND
Julian Dalrymple-Sykes	BEN ARIS
Sylvia Garnsey	NIKKI KELLY
April Wingate	LINDA REGAN
Dawn Freshwater	LAURA JACKSON
Stanley Matthews	DAVID WEBB
Bruce Matthews	TONY WEBB
Gary Bolton	CHRIS ANDREWS

Location recording dates:
23rd September - 18th October 1987

Series Nine filming locations:
Warner's Holiday Camp, Dovercourt (all episodes). Ardleigh (roads around the area) (57). Dovercourt, Room in Michaelstowe Hall, Ramsey Road (57). Dovercourt, West End Beach (55). Colchester, Friday Wood (53). Lawford, St Mary's Church, Church Hill (57).

53. TELL IT TO THE MARINES

Studio: TC 8 - Friday 23rd October 1987 **TX:** Saturday 26th December 1987 at 6pm, BBC 1
Duration: 45 mins 23 secs **Audience rating:** 14.6 million

Gladys announces on Radio Maplin that there will be a Royal Marine Display Team in action at Maplin's Holiday Camp and urges people not to miss it. The cocky Sergeant likes throwing his weight around and it falls upon Peggy to play the organ for the display. When the Sergeant starts shouting at her, Ted intervenes and starts mocking the Marines. Ted challenges the visitors to a race over an assault course - Maplin's versus the Royal Marines . In earshot is a local Bookie who stands to make lots of money on the outcome so Ted decides to even up the odds with a few fiddles. With Gary out of action, Peggy is lured to take part providing she can put on a deep voice and replace him. Spike, Julian and a reluctant Clive all agree to take part. Also taking part is one of the Twins, or maybe both, thanks to Ted's cunning plan. The scene is set, the plan is in action and now it's all go, go, go!

Guest cast:

Marine Sergeant	Brian Gwaspari
Trevor	Perry Benson
Charlie	Timothy Bateson
Trevor's Dad	Michael Burns
Trevor's Mum	Su Elliot
Ramona	Jean Lear

5 members of Assault course team and 14 members of the Gymnastic Display Team led by Major John Quinn

Featured music: *A Life On The Ocean Wave* (The Band of Her Majestys Royal Marines with vocal by Ruth Madoc), *A Life On The Ocean Wave* and *In The Mood* (Jean Lear), *Freight Train* and *Dambusters March* (performed by Roy Cloughton and 4 musicians) *Man of Mystery* (The Shadows).

139

54. MARRY-GO-ROUND

Studio: TC 8 - Friday 30th October 1987 **TX:** Saturday 2nd January 1988 at 6.20pm, BBC 1
Duration: 30 mins   **Audience rating:** 13.2 million

Spike is dressed up in one of his funny costumes and trying to make people laugh but the campers just don't seem to be laughing. A letter has arrived from Joe Maplin informing Spike that complaints have been made about him from the campers saying he is just not funny any more. Clive tells him not to worry too much but Spike is distraught and very worried. The only person who Spike feels he can talk to about his problem is Gladys. She doesn't seem to mind being woken up and soon reassures Spike telling him that his problem lies with something on his mind. It must be April. He realises that he must marry April and then everything will be okay again. As he leaves Gladys's chalet he is seen by Yvonne who in the morning starts telling the staff – including Clive. Yvonne feels that as he is engaged to Gladys he has a right to know what is going on. Clive is angry and decides to confront Gladys immediately, even though deep down inside he knows she is innocent and that nothing occurred in her chalet. But he does see it as a great opportunity to get out of his engagement.

Guest cast:
Parent	Mike Carnell
1st Woman	Pauline Jefferson
2nd Woman	Helen Dorward
Man	John Fernley

Featured music: *Slow Boat To China*, *Dream Lover* and *Our Love Affair* (performed by Roy Cloughton with 4 musicians), *Apache* and *Man Of Mystery* (The Shadows).

55. THE PERILS OF PEGGY

Studio: TC 6 - Friday 6th November 1987   **TX:** Saturday 9th January 1988
Duration: 30 mins 9 secs   **Audience rating:** 13.3 million

After finally being rejected by Gladys, Clive realises that he has made a mistake and decides after a day at his family's home that he does want to marry her after all. He asks for Ted's help again. Chocolates and flowers don't work. During the 'Crossing the Line' ceremony around the Olympic Sized Pool a plan is set for Clive to dive in and save Peggy from drowning. He is too slow off the mark however and Gary comes to the rescue instead. There is just one more plan that Ted can think of and it will involve Peggy once more. This time a hole is made in the sand dunes and Peggy is to climb in, up to her neck along with buckets of water and a lot of mud provided by Sylvia and the Yellowcoats, to make it look like quicksand. But behind the deception lurks real danger…

Guest cast:
Boy with glasses	Gary Rice
Ramona	Jean Lear
Double for Peggy	Tracey Eddon

Featured music: *What Kind Of Fool Am I?* (Paul Shane), *The Happy Wanderer* (unaccompanied sung by Ramblers), *Side Saddle* and *Toy Balloons* (Russ Conway).

1987 Audience Studio Recording ticket. Jeffrey Holland updated his illustration to include Uncle Sammy, Julian Darlrymple-Sykes and Clive Dempster.

'Lift Up Your Minds' - Episode Guide

56. LET THEM EAT CAKE

Studio: TC 8 - Friday 13th November 1987   **TX:** Saturday 16th January 1988 at 6.20pm, BBC 1
Duration: 29 mins 31 secs   **Audience rating:** 10.4 million

Clive has also received another one of Joe Maplin's letters informing him that people are not booking their holidays for next season and it's all because certain competitions have been dropped from the roster. Joe Maplin wants a floodlit tableau around the pool. It has been decided that the French Revolution will be the theme. Yvonne will not be Marie Antoinette this time as she has one of her heads. Peggy is delighted to stand in. Alec Foster arrives back at Maplin's and Ted sees his chance to ask for a pay rise. Foster sacks Ted and employs an up and coming comic who has appeared on *Opportunity Knocks*. A forlorn Ted is instructed to introduce his replacement Jimmy Jasper on his last night in the Ballroom. But will the campers take to the new face?

Guest cast:
Alec Foster	Ewan Hooper
Jimmy Jasper	Brian Godfrey
Percy	Paddy Ward
Betty	Laura Allen

Featured music: *Kon-Tiki* and *Theme For Young Lovers* (The Shadows), *Snow Coach* (Russ Conway).

57. WEDDING BELLS

Studio: TC 1 - Friday 20th November 1987   **TX:** Saturday 23rd January 1988 at 6.20pm, BBC 1
Duration: 29 mins 39 secs   **Audience rating:** 13.3 million

All the talk around the camp is of Clive and Gladys's wedding and preparations are underway. Ted will be Clive's Best Man and Spike will be giving Gladys away. The champagne has been ordered and Clive has been to see the Archbishop of Canterbury regarding a special marriage licence. April is not pleased at hearing this because she wants Spike to get one for them too. The only fly in the ointment could be Yvonne secretly telephoning Clive's rich relatives informing them of the details of the wedding. However, Nora the Maid at Dempster Hall lets Clive know that his family intends to sabotage the wedding. With all the Maplins staff arriving at the church, along with Gladys's mother, the excitement is mounting. The Vicar is getting increasingly worried however about the lateness as he has another wedding to perform. Clive's family are on their way to the church. But they seem to be having all kinds of trouble reading the road signs. Will they get to the church on time and put a stop to Gladys and Clive's happiness?

Guest cast:
Roger	Michael Robbins
Doreen	Barbara New
Winifrid Dempster	Mavis Pugh
Nora	Brenda Cowling
Charles Dempster	Dennis Ramsden
General Sir Claud Dempster	Peter Fontaine
Vice-Admiral Neville Dempster	Iain Anders
Bishop Simon Dempster	Fred Bryant
Vicar	Frank Williams
Village native	Anthony Benson
Groom	Nick Mercer
Verger	Colin Bean
Mrs. Pugh	Patricia Hughes
Bride	Debbie Riordan

Featured music: *It's Only Rock and Roll 2 and 3* (Tim Renwick, from the LP *The Guitar Story*), *Anniversary Song* performed by Roy Cloughton with 4 musicians and vocal by Paul Shane.

'Lift Up Your Minds' - Episode Guide

58. THE WIND OF CHANGE

Studio: TC 1 - Friday 27th November 1987 **TX:** Saturday 30th January 1988 at 6.20pm, BBC 1
Duration: 33 mins 35 secs **Audience rating:** 15.0 million

Marriage has certainly made Gladys happy, and with her serenading everybody over Radio Maplin it is clear to Ted and Spike that she is truly in love with Clive. The end of the season is looming so all that remains is to find out where everybody will be for next season. Dawn has been taken to Hospital with appendicitis, a replacement has to be found pronto. Head Office in London has no-one available and leaves the decision in Clive's capable hands. Who can he give the job to? Peggy is the obvious choice and he leaves it to Gladys to break the news to her and to hand over her Yellowcoat. Peggy is ecstatic and is soon entertaining the campers non stop. In fact like no other Yellowcoat before. Within days she is temporarily joining Dawn in the local Hospital, suffering from nervous exhaustion. Back at camp the staff are putting their names down on the list to return for the next season at Maplin's when Alec Foster arrives with bad news. Next season there will be no knobbly-knees competitions, no funny chicken and certainly no "Hi-de-Hi". Joe Maplin is going up market and instead of chalets and fish and chips, there will be self catering leisure facilities. When the final 'Goodnight Campers' rings out in the Hawaiian Ballroom the staff realise the wind of change has blown through Maplin's. It's the end of an era and things will never be the same again.

Guest cast:

Alec Foster	Ewan Hooper
Mr. Turner	Billy Burden
Matron	Kathleen Bidmead
Ramona	Jean Lear
Double for Peggy	Tracey Eddon
Camper in ballroom	Vince Rayner
Waitress	Laura Allen

Featured music: *It's Only Rock and Roll 2 and 3* (Tim Renwick, from the LP *The Guitar Story*) *Love Is The Sweetest Thing* (Ted Heath with vocal by Ruth Madoc), *They Were Only Playing Leapfrog* (vocal: Su Pollard, organist: Jean Lear), *You'll Never Walk Alone, Who's Taking You Home Tonight?*, Goodnight Sweetheart (Roy Cloughton with 4 musicians).

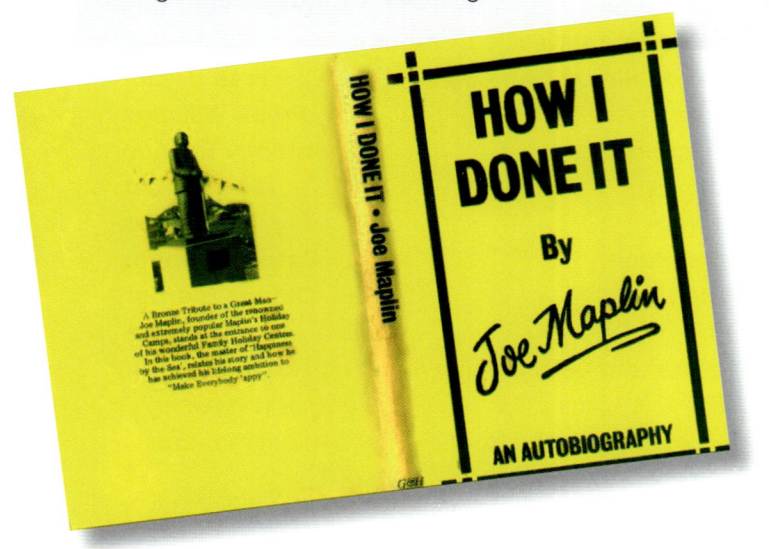

The flyleaf for Joe Maplin's autobiography handed out by Alec Foster.
All the cast members were able to keep their copy as a souvenir. This copy belongs to Jeffrey Holland.

Series Nine Production Credits:

Studio Warm Up FELIX BOWNESS. Production team VALERIE LETLEY, JUDITH BANTOCK, FRANCESCA GILPIN, YVONNE O'GRADY. Costume LYN AVERY. Make Up MARTHA LIVESLEY. Visual Effects COLIN MAPSON. Properties Buyer PAULINE SEAGER. Camera Supervisor KEN MAJOR. Videotape Editor ED WOODEN, ROGER MARTIN. Vision Mixer ANGELA BEVERIDGE. Technical Co-ordinator RAY HIDER. Film Cameraman MAX SAMETT. Film Sound MICHAEL SPENCER. Film Editor MIKE ROBOTHAM. Studio Lighting MARTIN KISNER. Studio Sound GRAHAM WILKINSON. Production Manager ROY GOULD. Design SANDRA WELSTEAD-HORNBY. Executive Producer DAVID CROFT. Directed by MIKE STEPHENS (except episode 53 produced and directed by DAVID CROFT).

8 Maplin's on TV
Cast appearances outside the camp

Below we list some of the television shows which have featured the Maplin's gang over the years.

Cheggers Plays Pop
TX BBC1, 1st June 1981
Paul Shane (with Ruth Madoc) sings 'Holiday Rock' on Keith Chegwin's pop-quiz show.

It'a a Knockout
TX BBC1, 19th June 1981
Paul Shane, Ruth Madoc and Su Pollard help score the fun in Luton.

This is Your Life: Paul Shane
TX ITV, 16th December 1981
Eamonn Andrews surprises Paul Shane in Covent Garden. Among the guests are veteran variety comic Sandy Powell and Paul's great friends Ronnie Dukes and Rikki Lee.

Russell Harty
TX BBC 2, 17th December 1981
Jimmy Perry, David Croft, Paul Shane and Ruth Madoc join Harty to chat about the success of the series.

Hi There 1982
TX BBC1, 31st December 1981
A special variety show from the BBC's Pebble Mill studios featuring Paul Shane, Ruth Madoc, Jeffrey Holland, Leslie Dwyer and Barry Howard in costume chatting and joking throughout the programme.

Saturday Superstore
TX BBC1, 6th November 1982
Keith Chegwin goes behind the scenes of Hi-de-Hi!, looking at rehearsals for the Christmas special "Eruptions" in the studio next door to Superstore. All the cast are in the studio with Chegwin asking them questions on the series.

Jim'll Fix It
TX BBC1, 25th December 1983
Elizabeth Newton gets her wish to be a Maplin's Yellowcoat in a special sketch featuring Simon Cadell, Paul Shane, Ruth Madoc, Jeffrey Holland, Su Pollard, Felix Bowness and The Webb Twins.

This is Your Life: Ruth Madoc
TX ITV, 28th November 1984
Eamonn Andrews surprises Ruth with the big red book. Guests include the Ros Male Voice Choir.

This is Your Life: Felix Bowness
TX ITV, 11th December 1985
Among those paying tribute to Felix are Wendy Richard, Mollie Sugden, Ernie Wise, Doris Waters, Ken Dodd plus the cast of Hi-de-Hi!

Les Dawson's Blankety Blank: Hi-de-Hi Special
TX BBC1, 26th December 1986
Special themed edition of the popular game show with the panellists consisting of Jeffrey Holland, Ruth Madoc, David Griffin, Linda Regan, Paul Shane and Su Pollard

Open Air Goes Christmas Crackers
TX BBC1, 20th December 1987
A filmed insert showing behind the scenes during the making of 'Tell It To The Marines' precedes a live interview with Su Pollard dressed as Aladdin.

This is Your Life: Su Pollard
TX ITV, 1st March 1989
Recorded on the stage of the Richmond Theatre, Surrey. The cast of Hi-de-Hi! and Jimmy Perry pay tribute to Su along with family and friends.

'Open Air' recording in October 1987 for their Christmas Special. Compare this image to that on page 91.

Omnibus: Perry & Croft – The Sitcoms
TX BBC 1, 18th April 1995
A celebration of the work of Perry and Croft featuring many of the cast members from their television shows. Those interviewed include Jimmy Perry, David Croft, Clive Dunn, Bill Pertwee, Ian Lavender, Don Estelle, Melvyn Hayes, Michael Knowles, Donald Hewlett, Simon Cadell, Paul Shane, Jeffrey Holland and Su Pollard.

This is Your Life: David Croft
TX BBC1, 20th December 1995
Simon Cadell, Su Pollard, Jeffrey Holland, Felix Bowness and Paul Shane are among those paying in this long overdue tribute to David. Others making an appearance included Clive Dunn, Bill Pertwee, Frank Williams, Windsor Davies, Melvyn Hayes, Mollie Sugden, Wendy Richard, John Inman, Gorden Kaye, Carmen Silvera, Jeremy Lloyd and Jimmy Perry.

Hi-de-Hi Selection Box
TX BBC1, 23rd July 1997
Celebrity fans including Nicholas Parsons, Tony Blackburn, George Melly, Linda Lusardi, Jimmy Tarbuck and Jim Bowen pick out their favourite moments from the series.

Stars Reunited: Hi-de-Hi!
TX BBC1, 8th July 2003
Dale Winton hosts this reunion show which brings together Paul Shane, Ruth Madoc, Su Pollard and Nikki Kelly with a surprise appearance by Barry Howard. NB A shortened 30 minute version of this programme was repeated on 29th June 2004.

Comedy Connections: Hi-de-Hi!
TX BBC1, 9th August 2004
Featuring interviews with Jimmy Perry, David Croft, Paul Shane, Ruth Madoc, Jeffrey Holland, David Griffin, Felix Bowness and Nikki Kelly.

The Paul O'Grady Show
TX Channel 4, 13th November 2007
Paul O'Grady welcomes Paul Shane, Ruth Madoc, Jeffrey Holland and Su Pollard onto his show to reminisce about their time at Maplin's.

Eggheads
TX BBC2 2009
A Hi-de-Hi! team consisting of Jimmy Perry, Paul Shane, Jeffrey Holland, Barry Howard and Nikki Kelly take on the resident brainy Quiz and Game Show champions in a special edition of the cult BBC2 show.

Another clip from the 'Open Air' programme recording in the Staff Room.

Happy Campers

IAIN ANDERS b1933 – d1997

Iain Anders - real name Iain Anders Robertson - was probably best known to television viewers as Superintendent Jack McVitie – 'The Biscuit' – in the drama series *Taggart*, a role he played from 1985 up until his death.

His early career in acting saw him in stage seasons at the Byre Theatre, St. Andrews, the Gateway Theatre, Edinburgh and the Salisbury Playhouse. Iain's television career encompassed a wide variety of roles in *Z Cars*, *The Avengers*, *Dixon of Dock Green*, *Softly Softly*, *Shoestring*, *Juliet Bravo* and *A Horseman Riding By*. Aside from his work as an actor, Iain worked as a legal executive to a leading south London firm of criminal lawyers preparing briefs for the barristers defending clients in court.

Iain made two appearances in Hi-de-Hi! as Clive's uncle Vice-Admiral Neville Dempster, in the episodes 'God Bless Our Family' and 'Wedding Bells'.

TIMOTHY BATESON b1926 - d2009

A very busy character actor, Timothy's appearances were numerous. On stage he had played the Butler in *Wild Orchids* at Chichester, Mr. Dodsworth in Alan Bennett's *Office Suite* at the West Yorkshire Playhouse, *Tango At The End Of Winter* at the Edinburgh Festival and *Jumpers* at the Aldwych Theatre in the West End among many others. His television credits encompass *The Bill*, *Casualty*, *The Sculptress*, *As Time Goes By*, *Brookside*, *The Good Life*, *Doctor Who*, *Last Of The Summer Wine* and *Worzel Gummidge*. On film he can be seen in *Les Miserables*, *101 Dalmations*, *Our Man in Havana*, *A Christmas Carol* and *A Handful of Dust*. His entry into Maplin's comes in the special 'Tell It To The Marines' when he plays Ted's bookie, Charlie Rose, who has bets riding on the outcome of the obstacle course race between the Yellowcoats and the Army.

JOHN BARDON b1939, Brentford, London

John Bardon - real name John Jones - originally trained to be an industrial Designer before finding his way into showbusiness. Among his many television credits are Les in *Birds Of A Feather*, Bernie Sweet in *Get Back*, Fred Timson in *Rumpole* and Mr. Jarvis in *Johnny Jarvis*. On the big screen John's appearances have included *East Is East*, *Fierce Creatures*, *Clockwise* and *84 Charing Cross Road*. John won an Olivier Award in 1988 for his role in the musical *Kiss Me Kate*. His first connection with Perry and Croft was when he was cast as the spiv Private Walker in the successful West End stage version of *Dad's Army* and also a small role in the television episode 'Ring Dem Bells'. In Hi-de-Hi! he appears as small time crook Ron Armitage who plans to ransack the chalets in the episode 'The Day Of Reckoning'. Today John is best known as Dot's long suffering husband Jim Branning in *EastEnders*.

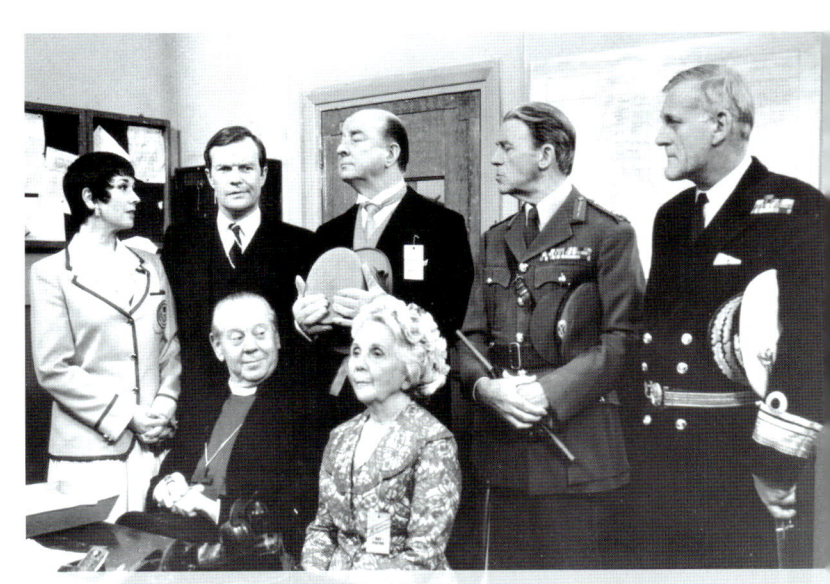

The Dempster family. Left to Right from Clive; Denis Ramsden, Peter Fontaine, Iain Anders with Fred Bryant and Mavis Pugh (sitting).

'Nice People with Nice Manners' - Happy Campers

MORRIS BARRY b1937 - d2000

Originally from Northampton, Morris became a highly regarded television Director and Producer. Among the shows he either directed or produced are *Count Dracula, Z Cars, Poldark, Angels,* several episodes of *Doctor Who* with Patrick Troughton and the early ITV soap *Compact*. As an actor he has been seen in *Blake's 7, Are You Being Served?, Doctor Who* opposite Tom Baker, *All Creatures Great and Small, Tales of The Unexpected* and *Nanny*. He is seen in Hi-de-Hi! as Peggy's penfriend, Monty, who lures her to the sand dunes followed by most of the entertainment staff.

COLIN BEAN b1926 - d2009

As Private Sponge, Colin was a regular cast member of *Dad's Army*. Colin worked for Jimmy Perry at Watford before becoming Private Sponge in the Home Guard. Among Colin's other television appearances are Lord Russell in *The First Churchills, Z Cars, Up Pompeii, The Liver Birds, Are You Being Served?, Michael Bentine's Potty Time* and *Lady Killers.* He turns up with fellow refugee from Walmington-On-Sea, Frank Williams, when he is verger to the church where Clive and Gladys marry in 'Wedding Bells'.

Colin was acutely aware that he might be compared unfavourably with another Verger in Walmington On Sea. "I deliberately set out to make him different to Teddy Sinclair. Teddy was quite aggressive as Mr. Yeatman, so I made my Verger a much more timid creation so that comparisons couldn't easily be drawn." In 1997 Colin published his autobiography, *Who Do You Think You Are Kidding?*. Colin made is last public appearance at the Dad's Army 40th Celebrations in Thetford in the Summer of 2008.

DEREK BENFIELD b1926 - d2009

Derek is perhaps best remembered as Bill Riley in 92 episodes of the BBC drama serial *The Brothers* in the 1970s but has more recently been seen as Patricia Routledge's husband Robert in *Hetty Wainthropp Investigates*. Other television credits include *Z Cars, Dixon Of Dock Green, Yes Minister, Rumpole of the Bailey* and two series of *The First of The Summer Wine*.

As a successful Playwright his comedies have been produced all over the world. Some of his most successful plays have been *Caught on the Hop* (in which he appeared with his *Brothers* co-stars Richard Easton and Margaret Ashcroft), *Beyond A Joke* (starring Arthur Lowe), *Touch And Go* (starring Trevor Bannister and Henry McGee) and *Bedside Manners* (starring John Inman). Derek says "As an actor - especially one who has been around as long as I have - you meet many other actors in various productions with whom you work briefly and then pass on to the next engagement. So inevitably your memory of long-gone TV shows is sometimes short. Not in the case of Hi-de-Hi! however! I still recall with pleasure the filming of 'Desire in the Mickey Mouse Grotto'. My role as 'Rose's Dad' was good fun, and it was a delight to act with the lovely Gillian Taylforth and the late great Simon Cadell. I found the whole cast were very friendly, the working atmosphere happy and relaxed, and I was honoured to take part in an early episode of a series which subsequently became so deservedly successful. My only regret was that my character did not re-appear!"

BALLARD BERKELEY b1904 - d1988

Ballard Berkeley is best known as batty Major Gowen in both series of *Fawlty Towers*, thus ensuring him worldwide recognition.

He once played retired Colonel Freddie Danby in Radio 4's *The Archers*. His film career began in 1930 and encompassed such movie gems as *In Which We Serve*, Hitchcock's *Stage Fright*, *See How They Run* in addition to small screen appearances in *The Adventures of Robin Hood, Dixon of Dock Green*, *To The Manor Born* as Uncle Greville as Guy Penrose in *Fresh Fields, That's My Boy, Terry and June* and as a fisherman in an early *Are You Being Served*. His brief foray into the world of Maplin's comes at the end of 'Empty Saddles' when a colonial Colonel type arrives intent on leaving his favoured equine in Joe Maplin's home for retired horses.

146

'Nice People with Nice Manners' - Happy Campers

Colin Bean as the Verger standing next to Frank Williams as the Vicar on location for the penultimate episode 'Wedding Bells'.

JENNIFER BLACK

Originating from Scotland, Jennifer's television credits include *Tinsel Town*, *Taggart: Angel Eyes*, *The Bill*, *I Saw You*, Gill Templer in *Rebus* and Bill Forsyth's *Local Hero*. On the stage she has been seen as Ruth in *Blythe Spirit*, Mrs. Darling in *Peter Pan* and Blanche in *A Streetcar Named Desire* among numerous appearances. As Francoise Ogilvy, she bewitches Spike and allows her Mother to get Spike to change his vulgar comedy act much to the horror of Ted Bovis in the episode 'The Society Entertainer'.

LALLY BOWERS b1917 - d1984

Veteran actress Lally delighted in playing eccentrics. Her small screen appearances include Mrs. Dalton in *A Fine Romance*, Arthur Askey's wife in *Love and Kisses*, Mrs. Maybury in *My Name Is Harry Worth*, Harriet in *Potter* opposite Arthur Lowe, *The Duchess of Duke Street* and *The Avengers*. Her best known television role was arguably as Dolly Love with Peggy Mount and Pat Coombs in the retirement home comedy *You're Only Young Twice*. Lally's distinctive husky voice was often her greatest asset and brought a saucy presence to the movies *Up Pompeii* and *Up The Chastity Belt* with Frankie Howerd, Miss Flodden in *Our Miss Fred* with Danny La Rue and as the Queen in *The Slipper and the Rose*. As Mrs. Baxter in the episode 'Save Our Heritage', her cottage is in danger of being demolished until Jeffrey Fairbrother and the rest of the Maplin's staff leap to her rescue.

RONNIE BRODY b1918 - d1991

Ronnie Brody was a veteran of many British comedy shows, always providing stalwart support to regulars. The son of variety performers Bourne & Lester, Ronnie has been seen in films such as *A Funny Thing Happened on the way to the Forum*, *Superman III* as well as a couple of the *Carry On* series. Ronnie made several notable appearances in *Hi-de-Hi!* The first being in the episode 'The Beauty Queen Affair' when as Reg Greenstreet, a well meaning father of a entrant in the Maplin's beauty contest, he attempts to bribe Jeffrey into letting her win. He later turns up in the show as the whinging plumber Sid in two episodes. Over the years Ronnie proved a favourite of David Croft who used him in supporting roles in all his hit series.

FRED BRYANT b1929 Bristol

Upon leaving school, Fred worked as a Blacksmith until he joined the RAF. Rising to the rank of Sergeant, Fred spent 22 years in active service travelling all over the world. Following his retirement from the RAF, Fred took up acting. He worked extensively in repertory theatre including Eastbourne, Birmingham and Leicester. Touring extensively, his roles include Dr. Chausible in *The Importance of Being Ernest*, Joe Horn in *Rain*, Boniface the Innkeeper in *The Baeux Stratagem*, Mr. Micawber in *David Copperfield* and Sir Timothy Farrer in *Hindle Wakes*.

Television work has seen Fred in *Softly, Softly*, *Black Arrow*, *Lorna Doone*, *Life of Shakespeare*, *Rumpole of the Bailey*, *Bus'n'Ches*, *Me and my Girl*, *Never the Twain* and *Poirot*. On film, Fred can be seen in *For Your Eyes Only*, *Quadrophenia*, *The Wild Geese* and *The Tall Guy*.

Fred's string of David Croft appearances have seen him as Clive's uncle Bishop Simon Dempster in *Hi-de-Hi!*, a German Officer in *'Allo 'Allo*, the Bishop's Butler in *You Rang, M'Lord?* In addition to being part of the cast of the stage farce *Hi-de-Hi Spirits*.

BILLY BURDEN b1914 - d1994

Billy Burden was a familiar face in several David Croft productions. He was born in Dorset and developed a variety act based around the old yokel Farmer character that was to be the mainstay of his professional appearances throughout his career.

He topped the bill on Moss Empire variety bills on many occasions and became a well respected figure on the comedy circuit. His first appearance for David Croft was in *Oh Happy Band* as Mr. Sowerby. His most famous role was undoubtedly as Mr. Moulterd, another yokel who helps the former Grace Brothers employees look after their inheritance in *Grace & Favour*. Billy was first seen in *Hi-de-Hi!* as an irate parent in 'It's Murder' but made a further two appearances as Mr. Turner who helped Julian Dalrymple-Sykes run his pig farm.

BRYAN BURDON

Bryan Burdon has appeared in nearly every branch of entertainment. He began his showbusiness career at the age of twelve touring in variety and revue with his father, Comedian Albert Burdon, working in all the major music halls. On leaving his father's act he joined a number of variety companies to gain experience in the legitimate theatre. Soon after he became a member of the famous *Fol De Rols* summer show where he stayed for three seasons sharing the comedy with the late Leslie Crowther. He has been principal Comedian in summer shows at all the famous seaside resorts. Straight roles in the theatre have included the farce *Chase Me Comrade*, *Seagulls Over Sorrento*, *Flare Path* and the lead in the West End run of *Strippers* at the Phoenix Theatre. During the Rock & Roll era Bryan compared many major pop tours. Musicals have included *Hit the Deck*, *Irma La Douce*, a tour of *Bud 'N' Ches* in which he played one of the Crazy Gang, *Sugar Babies* at the Savoy with Mickey Rooney and Ann Miller and the British premiere of Stephen Sondheim's *Follies*. Bryan holds the unique record of having co-written and starred in the prestigious Theatre Royal Windsor's pantomime for 25 years. His television credits include Sapper Binns in *Danger UXB*, *The Secret Diary of Adrian Mole*, *Emmerdale Farm*, *Sunday Night at The London Palladium*, *A Xmas Lantern* with Wayne Sleep, *Midsummer Murders* and *Victoria Wood - As Seen on TV*. In addition he has guested on a number of *Sooty* shows and hosted the final two series of *Pinky and Perky*. In *Hi-de-Hi!* Bryan has the relatively small role of a Van Driver in the episode 'God Bless Our Family'.

MICHAEL BURNS b1950, Middlesborough

Mike Burns is best known as the devoted Handyman Colin in seven series of the BBC's sports centre comedy, *The Brittas Empire*. Among Mike's other television credits are Farmer Matthews in *Emmerdale*, Percy Williams in *Lovejoy*, Ray Clegg in *Auf Wiedersehen Pet II*, Fletcher in *Blott on the Landscape* and *Sink or Swim*. He has an impressive list of theatrical credits to his name which include a national tour of *The Hitch-Hiker's Guide to the Galaxy* as Arthur Dent, Mr. Bloo in *The Rise and Fall of Little Voice*, Gary Le Jeune in *Noises Off* and Graham in Alan Bennett's *Talking Heads*. In *Hi-de-Hi!*, Mike is seen as Dad to young Trevor in the Christmas special 'Tell It To The Marines'. Mike has one particular memory from Maplin's which causes him embarrassment everytime he thinks of it. "On the first day of shooting, I was standing by some of the chalets with Felix Bowness and some donkeys. I was extremely nervous about doing my scene later in the day. I noticed a chap standing next to me and I casually said 'Who are you?' The reply came 'David Croft.' It didn't register with me because I was so wrapped up in my own nervousness. 'What do

'Nice People with Nice Manners' - Happy Campers

you do?' I asked without thinking. 'I write it and usually direct it as well.' Suddenly the penny clicked, and I have never lived it down. To think I never recognised one of the great legends of British comedy writing."

JEAN CHALLIS b1934, Cheadle Hulme

Jean Challis is a staple of British comedy programmes. Her theatre credits are also extensive and include the national tour of *Singin' In The Rain* with Tommy Steele, *Oliver!* in Sheffield, Matron in the national tour of *Doctor on the Boil*, *Canterbury Tales* at the Phoenix Theatre and *Animal Crackers* at the Lyric Theatre, Shaftesbury Avenue. Her most recognisable roles in television comedy have been in *Nearest & Dearest*, *Terry & June*, Mrs. Rumbold in *Are You Being Served?*, *Alas Smith and Jones*, Mrs. Arnott in two series of *Dear John*, Mildred in *One Foot In The Grave* and *Goodnight Sweetheart*. Jean lived in Cyprus for a number of years but more recently has returned to the UK and been seen in *Casualty*, *The Bill*, *Deuce Bigolo European Jigolo* and in the *Doctor Who* adventure 'The Idiot's Lantern'.

Jean has two appearances in Hi-de-Hi! to her credit, in each of them playing campers. Her first is as the wife of Roy Heather in the 1981 episode 'Lift Up Your Minds. She subsequently was seen in 1983 kissing Simon Cadell in 'The Society Entertainer'.

PEGGY-ANN CLIFFORD b1921 - d1984

Peggy was born in Bournemouth and went on to become a familiar face on British comedy programmes. She was seen opposite Tony Hancock in several of the popular television *Hancock's Half Hour* programmes, *Bless This House* with Sid James, *Are You Being Served?*, *'Allo 'Allo*, *Oh Happy Band*, *The Churchill Said To Me* with Frankie Howerd and *George and Mildred*. On the big screen credits include *Kind Hearts and Coronets*, *Doctor at Large*, *Sparrow's Can't Sing*, Willa Claudia in *Carry On Cleo*, *Far From The Madding Crowd* and *Murder By Decree*.

Shortly before her death Peggy plays the camper who wins a car in Ted's raffle but cannot claim her prize because she is too large to fit into the driver's seat, in the episode 'Raffles'.

IAN COLLIER d2008

Ian Collier made a name for himself during the 1970's in many high profile television programmes of the time. These included *The Sweeney*, *Duchess Of Duke Street*, *Return of the Saint* and *Minder*. Featured roles have included George Travis during the second series of *Howards' Way* and Colonel Lipscoombe in the *Rules of Engagement*. His CV reads like a history of popular programming in the 70's and 80's and encompasses *The Sweeney*, *A Fine Romance*, *Are You Being Served?*, *Keeping Up Appearances*, *Bergerac*, *Juliet Bravo*, *EastEnders*, *Boon*, *All Creatures Great and Small* and *Jeeves and Wooster*. He was particularly well known to *Doctor Who* fans. Ian first appeared in the 1972 story 'The Time Monster' with Jon Pertwee but was best known for his role as Omega, a powerful exiled Time Lord, in the 1983 story 'Arc Of Infinity' with Peter Davison. Ian re-created his role as Omega for an audio adventure by Big Finish Productions in 2003.

Ian arrived at Maplin's playing Inspector Sutcliffe in 'It's A Blue World' where he would discover an illicit film showing in the Laughing Cow Milk Bar.

SHAUN CURRY b1937, Herne Hill, London

Shaun Curry is one of Britain's busiest television actors. He is probably best remembered in comedy circles as Vince's dad in the John Sullivan penned *Just Good Friends*. His television credits are vast and include *May To December*, *Divided We Stand*, *Up Pompeii*, *Terry and June*, *Then Churchill Said to Me* with Frankie Howerd, *To The Manor Born*, *Bergerac*, *The House of Elliott*, *London's Burning*, *Mind Your Language*, *The Professionals*, *Minder*, *The Sweeney* and *Very Big Very Soon* with Paul Shane. His stage work

'Nice People with Nice Manners' - Happy Campers

has encompassed seasons with the Royal Shakespeare Company and the National Theatre, *Privates on Parade* in the West End, the national tour of *42nd Street* and *The Iceman Cometh* at the Abbey Theatre in Dublin. Shaun appears briefly in Hi-de-Hi! as the Horsebox driver in the series one episode 'Day Of Reckoning'.

CAROLINE DENNIS

Born into a theatrical family, Caroline's first stage appearance was at the age of three and was featured in children's television programmes both in England and Australia. She trained at the Leeds College of Music in classical and jazz piano. She followed this with a stint in 'Theatre Vanguard', the touring wing of the Sheffield Crucible Theatre. Combining her skills as a musician with a natural flair for performing has made Caroline a much sought after artist. She co-starred with Les Dennis and Dustin Gee in *The Laughter Show* for the BBC and also alongside Bobby Davro for TV South. Other television appearances include Josephine in two series of Carla Lane's *Leaving*, *The Bill*, *Holby City*, *Crown Court*, *Three Up, Two Down* and as April Lipman (Gracie Fields' musical director) in the Yorkshire TV movie *Pride of our Alley*. On stage she has played Vi Petty in *Buddy* at the Victoria Palace, Cynthia Lennon in *Imagine* at the Liverpool Playhouse, *Noises Off*, *Wait Until Dark*, *Godspell* (in a production directed by it's creator John Michael Tabelak), *What the Butler Saw*, Glenda in *Last of the Summer Wine* at the Pier Theatre, Bournemouth and in the West End season of *Jailhouse Rock* at the Piccadilly. Caroline has also been seen frequently in pantomime playing Principal Boy at Chichester, Richmond and Wimbledon. Caroline's appearance in Hi-de-Hi! as Betty Barlow, the pianist with whom Ted falls in love in the episode 'September Song', follows a family tradition. Her father the comedian and actor Bobby Dennis was seen in the 1981 episode 'The Beauty Queen Affair' playing laugh-a-minute camper Harry Plowright. Caroline has a clear recollection of getting involved in the Perry and Croft repertory company. "I originally auditioned for David Croft to be a French Prostitute in 'Allo 'Allo." Caroline remembers. "When we were shooting 'Allo 'Allo I found myself sitting next to David at dinner and we started talking and I told him all about my piano playing. I really thought nothing of it. Then a couple of months later I got a call from the BBC Wardrobe Department asking what my bust size was. 'Whatever do you want to know that for?' I asked. They told me I was going to be in Hi-de-Hi! playing Betty Barlow. I didn't know anything about it. My agent hadn't mentioned anything. I was engaged for a five week period as the episode that I was in was a Christmas special and as such there was a longer recording period. Betty was squeaky clean, a bit naive. Paul Shane was wonderful I thought. He gave a very touching performance. It made the whole situation seem very real. I played the piano live in that scene and they later overdubbed the strings onto it."

As a cabaret performer Caroline is now much sought after on five star cruise ships. "I have my own show which is a mixture of jazz, swing and classical. Nowadays the cruise ships are the top work for light entertainment acts and I can have the luxury of a grand piano and seven piece band which you wouldn't find anywhere else."

FREDDIE EARLLE b1924 – d2007

Glaswegian Freddie originally trained as an apprentice Barber, but his natural flair and gift at making people laugh caused many of his customers to advise him to take up showbiz professionally. This he subsequently did, and he acquired a partner in the comedy act Mundy and Earlle touring all the music halls and variety palaces, appearing on the same bill as such legends as Laurel & Hardy, Frank Sinatra, Gypsy Rose Lee and Tommy Cooper. The closure of the music halls saw Freddie up and move his family to a kibbutz in Israel for a time, but once showbusiness is in your blood it is very difficult to stay away. He returned and carved a niche for himself as a supporting actor and made fine appearances in some of the best television shows of the era: *Bergerac*, *Dad's Army*, *It Ain't Half Hot Mum*, *Coronation Street*, *Clochemerle*, *London's Burning* to name a few. He retired to southern Spain where he passed away aged 83. Freddie is chiefly remembered in Hi-de-Hi! for his appearance as Ron Griffin, who sells Ted some films of an adult nature in the episode "It's a Blue World", and also as cinema projectionist Jack in the war time movie spoof "Only The Brave".

PERCY EDWARDS MBE. b1908 - d1996

Percy began imitating the wild creatures of his native Suffolk and was soon doing this as a party piece in his early teens. He made his first broadcast in 1930 on the BBC radio programme *Vaudeville*. He became a household name through his bird impressions on *Ray's a Laugh* with Ted Ray and subsequently was in huge

'Nice People with Nice Manners' - Happy Campers

demand for his services. It was said that he could acurately impersonate 600 species of bird, Percy was a keen ornathologist all his life. In addition to his bird noises, Percy also developed a talent for being able to recreate a plethora of animals large and small. Percy provided the 'voices' for a host of popular programmes including *On The Buses*, *The Good Life*, *Sorry!*, *Hilary* and perhaps most famously in the movies as the title role in *Alien*. His contribution to Hi-de-Hi! was in the first series episode 'No Dogs Allowed' as the voice of Jeffrey Fairbrother's excitable dog Bubbles.

SU ELLIOTT b1950, Newcastle-upon-Tyne

Su trained at the Guildhall School of Speech and Drama. Her stage appearances include Doreen Slater in *The Secret Diary of Adrian Mole* and *Can't Pay Won't Pay* in the West End. Su repeated the role of Doreen Slater in the popular television series *Secret Diary of Adrian Mole* and subsequently *Growing Pains of Adrian Mole*. Her best known role is as Marjorie Osbourne, long suffering wife of tearaway Oz, in the first two series of *Auf Wiedersehen Pet*. Su can also be seen in episodes of *When The Boat Comes In*, *Minder*, *The Worst Witch*, *Poirot*, Julie Dewhurst in *Coronation Street*, *Casualty*, *The Bill* and Maggie Gibson in *This Life*. Su plays Trevor's Mum in the Hi-de-Hi! episode 'Tell It To The Marines'.

PETER FONTAINE b1920

Peter studied drama at the London School of Dramatic Art and after a break in the army when he served in the Far East as a Signals Officer with the RWAFF, he returned to the theatre. He has appeared in his younger days in over 200 plays in repertory theatres all over the country, very often playing twice nightly. He also appeared in the West End in at least another ten productions including the controversial *Fallen Angels* at the Ambassadors Theatre with Hermoine Baddeley and Hermoine Gingold. Peter has appeared in more than 100 films and had a five year stint in Hollywood where he once had the amusing experience of dubbing Frank Sinatra's voice into English! TV credits include *Secret Army*, *Gangsters*, *Z Cars*, *Crossroads*, *The Liver Birds* and *Being Dom Joly*.

Peter played General Sir Claud Dempster in two episodes of Hi-de-Hi! and was Barker in 'The Wounds of War', an episode of *You Rang, M'Lord?* He toured in the Perry-Croft farce *Hi-de-Hi Spirits* in 1986.

JOHN FORTUNE b1939

Today best known for his satirical programmes with John Bird and Rory Bremner, John Fortune was educated at Bristol Cathedral School and King's College, Cambridge. John directed the Footlights Revue in his second year and wrote sketches and performed for it in his third. On leaving University John was one of the founders of *Peter Cook's Establishment Club* where he wrote and performed sketches with Eleanor Bron and John Bird. The group toured America in 1962/63, settling in New York for nine months. Returning to the UK he provided material and performed in BBC satirical shows: *Not So Much a Programme...*, *BBC3* and *The Late Show*. Since then he has co-written and appeared in many BBC comedy series including *Birds and Well Anyway* with John Bird; *On The Margin* with Alan Bennett; *Where Was Spring* with Eleanor Bron; *The End of The Pier Show*, and *In The Looking Glass* with John Wells and Carl Davis. He has written two BBC TV comedy series *Roger Doesn't Live Here Anymore* and *Round and Round*. His novel, *A Melon for Ecstacy,* was co-written with John Wells. In 1984 the American film director, John Landis, commissioned two screenplays for Universal and Paramount Pictures. John Fortune's appearance in Hi-de-Hi! saw him as Max Tewksbury. Max is the new boyfriend of Jeffrey Fairbrother's wife Daphne who comes to Maplin's to try and persuade Jeffrey to grant his wife a divorce.

BRIAN GODFREY b1948

Brian Godfrey is one of Britain's top pantomime performers, each Christmas he can be found appearing as an Ugly Sister in *Cinderella*. He comes from a family of variety artists - his grandmother was a leading lady at the Old Surrey Theatre. Aged fourteen Brian appeared in *I Could Go on Singing* with Judy Garland and further

'Nice People with Nice Manners' - Happy Campers

film appearances include *Stand Up Virgin Soldiers*, *A Bridge Too Far* and *Gandhi*. On stage his appearances have included many seasons in *Run For Your Wife* with Les Dawson, *The Mating Season* with Sid James and the role of Gunner 'Nosher' Evans in the stage version of *It Ain't Half Hot Mum* in Scarborough and on tour. As Jimmy Jasper in 'Let Them Eat Cake' he is the recent winner of television's *Opportunity Knocks* who thinks he can replace Ted and cut the mustard with the tough Maplin's ballroom audience.

JOYCE GRANT b1924 – d2006

Born in Bloemfontein, South Africa, Joyce grew up with her two brothers on a farm. She came to London to train at the Central School of Speech and Drama prior to returning to South Africa. Moving back to the UK in the 1950s Joyce began to make a name for herself in the theatre including the Soho Theatre Company's production of Sheridan's *St. Patrick's Day* in 1972 and Joe Orton's *The Good and Faithful Servant* at the King's Head, Islington in 1974. Joyce also toured the UK in Noël Coward's *Present Laughter* with Peter Wyndgarde. Among her West End appearances are Helga in *Deathtrap*, Mrs. McGee in *Corpse*, Miss Prism in *The Importance of Being Earnest* at the Old Vic and Princess Olga in *Fathers and Sons* for the National Theatre. One of her favourite stage roles was as Aunt Em / Glinda, the good Witch, in the Royal Shakespeare Company's version of *The Wizard of Oz* and played on Broadway in *Rockerfeller and the Red Indians* with Frankie Howerd. Joyce began her television career in 1965 with *Gideon's Way* and went on to appear in such series as *The Professionals*, *The Liver Birds*, *Doctor at Large*, Mrs. Hockridge in *Pardon My Genie*, Norah in *Keep it in the Family* and in a 1973 adaptation of *Pygmalion*.

Her two appearances in Hi-de-Hi! were in the small but important role of Mrs. Maud Fairbrother, Jeffrey's mother. In the pilot episode she berates her son for taking the job at Maplin's with "hoards of Teddy Bear boys" and later in a 'phone conversation with John Le Mesurier during 'Carnival Time' she admits she hasn't heard from her son for weeks.

BRIAN GWASPARI

Brian spent two seasons with the Royal Shakespeare Company and the Bristol Old Vic before deciding to go to drama school at the Webber Douglas Academy. Following a tour of *Fiddler on the Roof*, Brian spent several years appearing with Britain's leading repertory companies in Stoke, Bristol, Birmingham, Sheffield and Greenwich. Brian appeared in many Shakespeare adaptations at the Open Space in London and toured in the play *Friends Like This* with Barbara Dickson and Roy Hudd. His best known television work was a regular role opposite Jill Gascoine in the drama *The Gentle Touch*. Other television appearances include *Van Der Valk*, *Yes Prime Minister*, *Ever Decreasing Circles*, *Soldier Soldier*, *EastEnders* and *Screaming* by Carla Lane. Film credits include *The Sweeney 2*, *A Bridge Too Far* and *Hercule Poirot's Christmas*. In 'Tell It To The Marines' Brian is seen as the cocky Army Sergeant who goads Ted into pitting the Maplin's staff against the military over an assault course.

PEARL HACKNEY b1919, Burton On Trent

Married to actor Eric Barker, Pearl Hackney often appeared with her husband in radio and on stage. Having trained as a Ballet Dancer, Pearl started her career at the Windmill Theatre in London and moved to Liverpool to further her acting career in repertory. Among her small screen credits are Mrs. Carr in *Oh Father* with Arthur Lowe, Mrs. Grainger in *Are You Being Served?*, *Z Cars*, *The New Avengers*, *Coronation Street*, *All Creatures Great and Small* and *Bergerac*. Pearl also had roles in films including *There's a Girl in my Soup*, *Stand Up Virgin Soldiers*, *Hound of the Baskervilles* and *Yanks*. Pearl also played the part of Mrs Pike in the radio versions of *Dad's Army*. She is the mother of Petronella Barker, who was later Anthony Hopkins' first wife. Pearl retired from acting in 1994. In Hi-de-Hi! Pearl plays the stern Mum of wayward daughter Rose in the episode 'Desire In The Mickey Mouse Grotto'.

LENI HARPER

Leni is a former Scottish Tap Champion and is a widely experienced Singer and Comedienne. On stage she has appeared in *The Best Little Whorehouse In Texas* at the Theatre Royal, Drury Lane, as the Usherette and Magenta in *The Rocky Horror Show* at the Comedy Theatre, *The Meg & Mog Show* at the Arts Theatre and *Meet Me at the Gate* at the King's Head Theatre. Leni was a Co-presenter with Noel Edmonds on *The Late, Late Breakfast Show* for the BBC and has also been seen as Kelly's PA in *The Kelly Monteith Show*, Mrs. Mcallister in *Chucklevision*, Madeleine Dunnock in *Me and My Girl* with Richard O'Sullivan and Tim Brooke-Taylor, Sharon Love in *High Road* and an episode of *Casualty*. Her brief appearance as the Brummie Camper in the episode 'Trouble And Strife' sees Leni as a girl looking for an illicit holiday with her boyfriend. Upon entering a chalet she exclaims "Look Lionel, they've got bunks!" on seeing the sleeping arrangements. It is of course all part of Ted Bovis' ploy to con some more money out of the pair.

ROY HEATHER b1935, Stoke Poges, Bucks

Roy is today best known as the cafe owner Sid in *Only Fools and Horses* a role he has played since 1985. He became an actor after being made redundant from his job as a Warehouse Manager in 1978. His first job for Croft and Perry was a small role as a Colonel in the final series of *It Ain't Half Hot Mum*. Roy's debut in Hi-de-Hi! is as a camper who thinks he has come to hear a talk on mountaineering by Jeffrey Fairbrother in 'Lift Up Your Minds' but then leaves to take part in the 'Who's got the wrong trousers on?' competition. Subsequently Roy was seen as Inspector Palmer in the episode 'The Pay Off'. Roy has also appeared in such series as *Just Good Friends*, *Big Deal*, *A Fine Romance*, *Birds of a Feather*, *The Edge of Darkness* and *Time Gentleman Please*. Among his stage appearances are productions with the Royal Shakespeare Company and a favourite role as Billy Cotton in *Wakey Wakey* at the Belgrade Theatre. Roy can clearly remember his first appearance in the Hawaiian Ballroom, during Jeffrey Fairbrother's talk on Shostakovich. "Paul Shane, Jeffrey Holland and I just couldn't stop laughing." he says. "It was a lot of fun. After my second appearance on Hi-de-Hi! I didn't see Jeff Holland again until about fifteen years later when I was at an Awards dinner with the *Fools and Horses* gang. Jeff was on another table. I thought he wouldn't remember me but during the evening he came over and said 'I hope you've got the right trousers on'. I couldn't believe he had remembered me after all that time." It was working for David Croft in *It Ain't Half Hot Mum* that Roy had to thank for his ongoing career as Sid. "In the bar after recording the show, Windsor Davies and Melvyn Hayes introduced me to Producer Ray Butt. It was through that introduction that I was cast as Sid." More recently Sid has been promoted to running the Nag's Head pub following the death of Kenneth MacDonald who played Landlord Mike. "It was very sad losing Ken. I never dreamed though that I would be his replacement. One day my wife took a call from John Sullivan and I thought it was John Challis who plays Boycie larking about. Sure enough the call was from John Sullivan who told me they had been talking about it and they all felt that Sid should be the one to run the pub, to keep it in the family as it were. The strange thing was I later found out that Ken MacDonald had given an interview some years before in which he was asked who he thought should run the pub if his character Mike didn't do it anymore and he had said 'Sid'. So I feel as if in a way I have had Mike's blessing to take over at the Nag's Head."

EWAN HOOPER b1935, Dundee

Ewan's credits as an actor include *The Avengers*: *What The Butler Saw*, *Heartbeat*, *Casualty*, *Peak Practice*, *Boon*, *Poirot*, *Wire in the Blood* and *Coronation Street*. He can be seen in the movies *How I Won The War*, *Dracula Has Risen From The Grave*, *Julius Caesar* and as Julie Walter's father in *Personal Services*. Ewan campaigned tirelessly fund raising to build the Greenwich Theatre

'Nice People with Nice Manners' - Happy Campers

and he became its first Artistic Director in 1969. As the vicious Camp Controller Alec Foster he is seen in no less than five episodes of Hi-de-Hi! He is first seen sacking a Gate Guard in 'The New Broom' and proceeds to get rid of anyone whom he dislikes - which turns out to be most of the entertainment staff. Alec is very fond of sacking people and gives both Clive and Spike a black eye when they try to stand up to him. He even makes a pass at Peggy in his chalet late one night. He comes a cropper several times most notably when he sacks Ted and tries to install a new young Comic in his place.

SUSAN JAMESON b1944, Worcestershire

Susan Jameson's television career is dominated by her roles as Myra Booth in *Coronation Street* and Jessie Seaton in *When The Boat Comes In*, the latter with her husband James Bolam. Other series in which Susan has appeared include *Take Three Women*, *Band of Gold* and in the films *All Creatures Great & Small* and *International Velvet*. Susan has very vivid memories of her time at Maplin's and inparticular her co-stars. "I was lucky enough to do an episode of this marvellous show. I played Jeffrey Fairbrother's hired co-respondent, the woman named as the 'guilty party' in Jeffrey's divorce. This meant I had the huge pleasure of playing several scenes with my chum, the wonderful Simon Cadell." Susan showed a professional admiration for Simon's portrayal of the introverted academic. "His fantastic blend of truth and humour made the poor man's confusion and embarrassment so touching, and hilarious. We were supposed to stay in his chalet all night and be caught there together. We played cards, and sat in awkward silences and my character was extremely bored by the whole situation, and by Jeffrey himself. And inevitably, Gladys got to know about it! For me personally it was delight, and we spent the whole time either laughing or discussing good food and fine wine, subjects in which Simon took an enormous interest. Then, too, I got to meet all my favourite characters from the show. How cleverly they were used, and how we looked forward to seeing them all each week (especially the wonderful, irascible Leslie Dwyer who I completely fell for at rehearsals!). One of my happiest show business memories."

RIKKI LEE b1938 - d1986

As a cabaret duo, Rikki Lee and her husband Ronnie Dukes established themselves as one of the most popular double acts on the northern club circuit. Possessing a belter singing voice which would contrast nicely with Ronnie's talent for comedy, Dukes and Lee would pack out clubs wherever they appeared. Ronnie from Rotherham, met Rikki when she was still a schoolgirl, and together they formed a song and dance act. Rikki's mother, Violet, became part of the act as their pianist when she filled in one night when their regular pianist failed to show up. Their sons Dean and Perry signed on as soon as they were old enough as Drummer and Guitarist respectively. They became natives of Barnsley, living in a large house in the village of Cawthorne. Although they had a villa in Majorca and a boat on the River Trent, demand for their services at home and abroad was overwhelming and they were often to be seen guesting on television variety

Susan Jameson as Jenny Maitland joins Simon Cadell in the episode The Marriage Settlement.

Ted faces up to his ex-wife Hilary (Rikki Lee) as she threatens legal action to get him to pay his maintainence arrears in Trouble and Strife.

spectaculars. Dukes and Lee appeared in the 1975 Royal Command Performance on a bill that also included the cast of *Dad's Army*. Tragedy struck for the Dukes in 1981 when Ronnie collapsed on stage and died in Jersey where they were appearing, aged just 49. Rikki continued a solo career until her untimely passing in 1986, aged 48. In the *Hi-de-Hi!* episode 'Trouble and Strife', Rikki gives a wonderful performance as Hilary Bovis, Ted's estranged wife, who turns up at Maplin's demanding the arrears of her maintainence. Dean and Perry Dukes were part of the on stage band ('Bert Swanley and the Debonairs') for the entire run of the *Hi-de-Hi!* stage musical.

JOHN LE MESURIER b1912 - d1983

John Le Mesurier is the epitome of the English upper class gentleman. He will be forever remembered as the well meaning Sergeant Arthur Wilson in *Dad's Army*. "How awfully nice" became his catchphrase as he tries to drill the Walmington-on-Sea Home Guard platoon with a rod of velvet. Le Mesurier appeared in countless films and television series, never straying too far from the English gent with which he is most associated and he worked with many Comedians including Tony Hancock, Frankie Howerd and The Goodies. He won a BAFTA award for his role in Dennis Potter's 1971 play *Traitor*. John's entry into Maplin's came in the episode 'Carnival Time' as Hugo Buxton, the Dean of Jeffrey Fairbrother's university. He has come to persuade Jeffrey to return with him and take up a senior position in the Archaeology Department. John's wonderful sense of timing in his scenes with Simon Cadell are a highlight of the episode. John's final line in a Perry-Croft comedy "Round spherical objects!" seals a fifteen year association with the writing legends. John was married for a time to actress Hattie Jacques.

ERIC LONGWORTH b1918 - d2008

Eric's career spanned over 50 years and included managing theatres in Oldham and Guildford. During the Second World War he served with the Army in Bombay and resumed his acting career upon demob. Eric first appeared for Jimmy Perry in his ATV sitcom *Lollipop Loves Mr. Mole* which in turn led to his role as Town Clerk, Claude Gordon, in several episodes of *Dad's Army*. He was also Understudy to Arthur Lowe in the West End stage production, although Eric always remained grateful that Arthur never missed a performance! He has featured in *Coronation Street* (opposite fellow Walmington citizen James Beck) and in the films *Tom Jones* and *No Sex Please, We're British*. He appears in *Hi-de-Hi!* as the Head Waiter in 'Concessions' as Ted attempts to bribe a local councillor. Eric was proud of his connections with *Dad's Army* and shortly before passing away joined other cast members to celebrate the shows 40th anniversary at the Imperial War Museum in 2008.

JEANNE MOCKFORD b1931, London

Having trained at RADA, Jeanne's television appearances encompass such series as *Little Britain*, *My Hero*, *Last of the Summer Wine*, *One Foot in the Grave*, *Keeping Up Appearances* and *Dear John*. Her best known appearances came as Senna the Soothsayer opposite Frankie Howerd in both series of *Up Pompeii*. She plays Marjorie, one of the campers who is put to sleep with Yvonne's Obligon sleeping tablets in the hour long special 'The Great Cat Robbery.'

CHERYL MURRAY b1952, Liverpool

Real name Cheryl Frayling-Wright, Cheryl studied dance in her native Liverpool before embarking on a course at LAMDA. She is probably best known as Suzie Birchall, the bane of Elsie Tanner's life, in *Coronation Street*, a role she played for some six years. Cheryl has also been seen as Jungle Jillian opposite Ronnie Corbett in *Sorry!*, *Billy Liar*, *Brookside* and *Zigger Zagger*. As Joan Wainwright - Joe Maplin's girlfriend and Supervisor of Yellowcoats - she injects some venom into the camp and takes an instant dislike to Gladys

'Nice People with Nice Manners' - Happy Campers

Pugh in the episode 'All Change'. Help is at hand when Ted recognises her as Beryl Green, a Magicians Assistant from his past who has a secret to hide. Cheryl still makes the occassional acting appearance, but her career has been curtailed by the onset of Multiple Sclerosis.

CLAIRE OBERMAN b1956

Born in Holland and educated in New Zealand, Claire won a scholarship to the National Drama School aged just 16, in Wellington. Her small screen appearances include *The Two Ronnies*, *Trainer*, *Doctors*, *Bugs* and in the feature film *Patriot Games*. Claire makes an appearance in Hi-de-Hi! as Jeffrey Fairbrother's wife Daphne who is seeking a divorce. When Gladys claps eyes on her in the episode 'The Marriage Settlement' she is struck dumb by the beauty and sophistication of Fairbrother's spouse. Claire is recognised chiefly as nurse Kate Norris in three series of the acclaimed drama *Tenko* for the BBC as well as the feature length special *Tenko Reunion* in 1985.

TONI PALMER b1932, London

Antonia - Toni - Palmer was part of Joan Littlewood's Theatre Workshop in Stratford East with Jimmy Perry. Her association with Littlewood led to major West End successes in *Fings Ain't What They Used To Be* and Lionel Bart's *Blitz*. She has also been seen on stage as The Courtesan in *The Comedy Of Errors* for the Royal Shakespeare Company and Madam Giry in her husband Ken Hill's adaptation of *The Phantom of the Opera*. On television she has specialised in comedy roles including a notable appearance as Blossom in *Only Fools and Horses* and one episode of *The Rag Trade*. Films include *Personal Services* as Aunty Winny. Her appearance in 'September Song' is as Mrs. Barlow, the mother of a young pianist whom Ted wants to marry.

ROBIN PARKINSON b1920, Coventry

Robin entered showbusiness in 1958 and has been a stalwart in television supporting roles ever since. He can be seen in episodes of *Whatever Happened to the Likely Lads*, *On The Buses*, *Dad's Army*, *The Young Ones*, *Shelley*, *Girls About Town* and as Monsieur Leclerc in three series of *'Allo 'Allo*. Robin also played the role in the *'Allo 'Allo* stage production at the London Palladium. As the camper who discovers Mr. Partridge's apparent murder in the episode 'Who Killed Mr. Partridge?', he is tied up and gagged by the staff in order to stop him broadcasting the news to the rest of the holiday makers.

RON PEMBER b1934, Plaistow, London

Raised in Dagenham, Ron began his career by performing Shakespeare in Durham pubs! He spent 25 years as an actor / writer / director with Bernard Miles at the Mermaid Theatre, working with companies that included Timothy Dalton, Spike Milligan, Barry Humphries and Tom Baker. He was part of Lord Olivier's first National Theatre Company appearing in such legendary productions as *Othello*, Zeferrelli's *Much Ado About Nothing* and the world premiere of Tom Stoppard's *Rosencrantz and Guildenstern Are Dead*. In addition he has written the music for numerous stage productions and co-authored a play on Jack The Ripper which transfered to the Ambassadors Theatre in the West End. On television he has been seen in *The Two Ronnies*, *The Fall and Rise Of Reginald Perrin*, *Secret Army*, *The Avengers* and *Dear John*. His appearance in Hi-de-Hi! comes in the first series episode 'No Dogs Allowed' playing a Private Detective trying to get a photo of Jeffrey Fairborther secretly keeping his pet dog Bubbles in his chalet. The recording featured a familiar face for Ron: "Simon Cadell, bless his heart, was an old friend of mine and we appeared together again at the National Theatre, directed by Alan Ayckbourn in his own play *Small Family Business*. As for Hi-de-Hi! I remember it took us hours enticing the dog who went everywhere but through the fence." Following a stroke in 1992, Ron retired from acting and now lives in Southend-on-Sea.

GORDON PETERS b1935, County Durham

Veteran actor Gordon Peters has been the backbone of supporting performances in many television comedies over the years. He is a stalwart of Croft-coms having appeared in *Dad's Army*, *You Rang, M'Lord?*, *Grace & Favour* and *Are You Being Served?* He is perhaps best

156

'Nice People with Nice Manners' - Happy Campers

recognised as Ronnie, Victor and Margaret Medrew's friend from hell, in *One Foot in the Grave*. In 1973 Gordon starred in his own BBC sitcom *The Gordon Peters Show*, guests in the series included Frank Thornton, Bill Pertwee and Gorden Kaye. In Hi-de-Hi! Gordon made two appearances as Henry, the Gate Keeper, who is sacked by Alec Foster for being asleep on duty.

SION PROBERT b. Swansea

Leni Harper and Sion Probert as the victims of one Ted's scams

As an actor Sion Probert has been seen in 20 episodes of *Pobol Y Cwm* for BBC Wales, *Our Friends in the North*, *Next of Kin*, *The Bill*, *Casualty*, *Thicker Than Water*, *The Tempest*, *How Green Was My Valley*, *The Sweeney*, *Jackanory Playhouse*, *How's Business*, *The Landlord* and *Without Motive*. A much in demand classical actor he has appeared in *Henry V* and *Richard III* for the Royal Shakespeare Company. Sion's appearances with the English Shakespeare Company have included *The War of the Roses*, *Richard II*, *Henry IV Parts I & II*, *Henry V* and *Richard III*. As the Brummie camper who falls foul of Ted's fiddles in Hi-de-Hi!, he exclaims to Leni Harper "I did ask for a double bed!"

DENNIS RAMSDEN b1918, Leeds

Dennis was de-mobbed from the RAF where he had been an Armourer straight into Dundee Repertory Company. He has made many West End appearances starting with *The Happiest Days of Your Life* with Margaret Rutherford followed by *Seagulls Over Sorrento* with William Hartnell and *A Sign of the Times* with Kenneth More. As a noted theatrical director he scored a "hat trick" when three of his productions were running simultaneously in the West End, as he was also appearing in a play he had the rare distinction of being billed outside four London theatres. Among his credits as an actor are *No Sex Please, We're British* with Michael Crawford and David Jason. On television Dennis has been seen in *To The Manor Born* as Aubrey Fforbes-Hamilton's solicitor and in *Only Fools and Horses: A Hole In One* playing a Judge. As a Butler in The Two Ronnies' silent comedy *The Picnic* Dennis has an arrow fired at his forehead. Dennis went on to direct the stage play *Hi-De-Hi Spirits*. Dennis remembers that the play "Wasn't very successful" but has lasting memories of an incident when the play was on tour in Blackpool. "I got to the theatre one morning and there were large display boards outside showing pictures of the cast in the show. I heard two old ladies muttering to each other looking at the photos. 'Look, it's that lot from Hi-de-Hi!' I heard one say. 'Shall we go and see them?' The other replied 'Better sit at the front in case it's a small screen!' You couldn't write dialogue like that." Dennis made three appearances as Clive Dempster's Uncle Charles in the television series, "It was a lovely job." Dennis recalls. "I remember for one of them I was appearing at Eastbourne in a summer season and had to drive to the location for early Sunday morning. I hardly had a wink of sleep but somehow managed to remember the lines and look vaguely noble."

MICHAEL REDFERN b1943, Middlesex

Having trained at the Corona Stage School Michael became best known as the Dad in the Oxo family with Lynda Bellingham in the famous series of commercials in the 1980s. Among his television appearances are *The Bill*, *Sorry!*, *In Sickness and in Health*, *Bottom*, *Between The Lines*, *EastEnders*, *Doctors*, *London's Burning* and *The Detectives*. In the episode 'Eruptions', he is the strict Fire Chief who comes to Maplin's to oversee the effects of Joe Maplin's new display in the ballroom, the Mighty Mountain Of Pitzpalu.

'Nice People with Nice Manners' - Happy Campers

GAVIN RICHARDS b1946, London

Gavin Richards is most familiar to television viewers as the long suffering Terry Raymond in *EastEnders* although his screen credits are quite vast. Trained at Bristol Vic Theatre School he has worked as an actor, director and writer in theatre, television and film for over 40 years. His television credits include *Coronation Street, Lovejoy, Inspector Morse, Minder, Pie in the Sky* and *Between the lines*. He is known to fans of *'Allo 'Allo* as the Italian Captain Alberto Bertorelli, a role he played for two series. Gavin also performed in the stage production at the London Palladium Theatre, which also toured New Zealand and Australia.

In Hi-de-Hi! he turns up as "the smiling viper" Harold Fox. First seen in the show at the unveiling of Joe Maplin's statue in 'The Graven Image', Fox is seen twice more as Maplin's General Manager when he calls Ted to Head Office to hand him his long overdue tax demand. Finally he takes Gladys Pugh out for her birthday to Tony's Trattoria in Crimpton-on-Sea for a slap-up meal and gets left there on his own and is ridiculed by his own driver. Gavin now resides in New Zealand.

MICHAEL ROBBINS b1930 - d1992

Michael Robbins is still remembered by millions as the work shy Arthur married to Anna Karen's horrendous Olive in forty nine episodes of ITV's *On The Buses* from 1969-72. He also appeared in the trilogy of feature films based on the series that followed.

Primarily a comedy actor, Michael has also appeared in *One Foot in the Grave, In Sickness and in Health, The New Statesman* in addition to several 'straight' roles in *The Sweeney, Minder, The Avengers, Dixon of Dock Green* and *Doctor Who*, most notably *Doctor Who: The Visitation* with Peter Davison. As Roger the overbearing husband to Barbara New's Doreen in 'Wedding Bells' he makes his first appearance in a Perry-Croft production. One of his final television roles was as James Twelvetrees' father in 'Stranger In The Night', an episode of *You Rang, M'Lord?*, where it is revealed that James' father isn't the Lay-Preacher he would have everyone believe but a petty criminal on the run from the law. Michael was married to actress Hal Dyer.

IRIS RUSSELL b1922, Kuala Lumpur, Malaysia

Iris has a wealth of theatrical experience to her credit. She started her career in Donald Wolfit's Shakespearian company before joining ENSA. She has played opposite Yul Bryner in *Lute Song* and been seen as Mrs. Pearce in *My Fair Lady* in Manchester, Mrs. Bedwin in *Oliver!* in the West End and on tour and Marina in *Two Dozen Red Roses* in Dundee.

Her television pedigree is equally impressive having been seen in *The Avengers, Crossroads, Taggart, Fanny By Gaslight, Grange Hill* and *The Ruth Rendell Mysteries*. Her soft Edinburgh accent was heard in the Hi-de-Hi! episode 'The Society Entertainer' as the overbearing mother Doris Ogilvy, who along with daughter Francoise, tries to persuade Spike Dixon to ditch the vulgar comedy style for a more sophisticated approach. Like many guest artists on the show, Iris has fond memories of joining the Maplin's team. "When I was asked to appear in *Hi-de-Hi!* I was very apprehensive, as I'd never played that kind of comedy on television before." Iris recalls. "I was worried about over-acting and playing for laughs. But after I had finished a long speech on my first entrance, I looked up and David Croft was standing near me with a broad grin on his face. I remember sighing with relief and thinking 'That was all right then.' After the episode was finished there was a party. We had to guess the name and type of wine. No-one could solve the problem. It turned out to be Pear wine! I also remember the resident cast being very nice and friendly. Not always the case in regular shows."

SAM SMART b1967, Ladbrook Grove, London

Sam Smart trained at the Anna Scher Theatre School and was a child actor. He appeared as Georgie, a regular in *Grange Hill*. Among his other credits are episodes of *Poirot, Lovejoy, 2 Point 4 Children, The Bill* and *EastEnders*. His movie appearances include *Love, Honour and Obey* and *Wilt*. Sam is seen in Hi-de-Hi! as Charlie Ruckston, a precocious young lad who is tied up and gagged by Mr. Partridge when Charlie tries to

Michael Robbins and Barbara New as Roger and Doreen in the episode Wedding Bells.

heckle his wizard Magician act in the episode 'If Wet – In The Ballroom'. "The reason Hi-de-Hi! sticks in my mind is that it was my first proper TV gig," Sam recalls today. "I remember going up to Wood Lane to the BBC, Croft and Perry's office was on the top floor. I just went in and read for it, a couple of days later I was offered the job. They wanted a cheeky kid… and I was a cheeky kid! I had a very strict chaperone but of course I wanted to be drinking with the cast until midnight. I had most of my scenes with Leslie Dwyer. He was a lovely old guy and he had been around for years and years. I think he liked working with us, the kids. Lots of energy. I was very excited at being in something so high profile. I don't think Perry and Croft ever worked with kids. I can't remember any of their shows having kids in them. David Croft was a tough man. I don't think any of the cast were all that famous when I made my episode, but they all quickly became household names. Simon Cadell I remember quite fondly, and I used to see him from time to time around London. He had that great ability that some actors are born with it, it isn't taught. Su Pollard was unique! As I was only making Hi-de-Hi! for about a week my schooling never suffered. Later on when I was making Grange Hill I would have a special Tutor who would teach me in the morning, then I would work on the show and go back to my lessons later in the day. Mind you I wasn't really an academic, by then I had been distracted by acting. There was a repeat of Only Fools and Horses on recently, I had never seen the episode that I had done. I couldn't remember a thing about it, what I did or said. I was around 17 at that time, but your first job you ALWAYS remember and I will always remember Hi-de-Hi!"

GRAHAM STARK b1922, Wallasey, Merseyside

Graham Stark established himself as one of Britain's busiest character actors. His first professional engagement was in a pantomime at the Lyceum Theatre, London, when he was just 13 years old. In 1939 he enrolled at RADA and made his first movie appearance in *The Spy is Black*, starring Conrad Veidt. After volunteering for the RAF during World War II, Graham joined Ralf Reader's famous Gang Show and entertained troops all over the world. His friendship with Peter Sellers, forged during that time, lasted until Sellers' untimely death in 1980. He was awarded the Bucket and Spade Oscar in Cromer for best comic in the summer season of 1954! Graham Stark's 99 films have encompassed such all time greats as the *Pink Panther* series of films, *Alfie*, *Casino Royale* and *Watch It Sailor*. On radio he has been heard in *Educating Archie, Ray's a Laugh, The Goon Show* among many credits. Following the death of James Beck, Graham played Private Walker in several radio episodes of *Dad's Army*. Graham has supported just about every major comic on television: Ken Dodd, Spike Milligan, Jimmy Tarbuck, Benny Hill - the list is endless. His guest appearance in Hi-de-Hi! features a bravura performance as Tony, the owner of Tony's Trattoria, who caters for "Miss Pag" - alias Gladys - on her birthday thrice over in the episode 'Spaghetti Galore'. In 2003 Graham published his autobiography 'Stark Naked'.

RONNIE STEVENS b1925 – d2006

Ronnie Stevens' career has been notable mostly in British feature films. These include *Doctor in Clover*, *Carry On Cruising*, *San Ferry Ann*, *I'm All Right Jack*, *Dentist in the Chair* and *Goodbye Mr. Chips*. On television he has been seen in *Only When I Laugh*, *Yes Minister*, *Fresh Fields*, *Terry and June*, *May to December*, *As Time Goes By*. In the theatre he started in revue including *Intimacy at 8.30* and *The Lord Chamberlain Regrets* before progressing to such productions as *84 Charing Cross Road*, the revival of *A Funny Thing Happened on the Way to the Forum* with Frankie Howerd, *As You*

Ruth Madoc and David Griffin share a joke while Graham Stark looks on in a scene from the episode Spaghetti Galore.

'Nice People with Nice Manners' - Happy Campers

Like It and *Lettice & Lovage*. His guest appearance in *Hi-de-Hi!* is as Jerry Price, the marketing man from Fluorabrite toothpaste in 'Ivory Castles in the Air'. Supervising the competition for the brightest smile, he encounters Yvonne and Barry. "Blimey they are scraping the bottom of the barrel with you two ain't they?" he tells them.

JEFF STEWART b1955, Aberdeen, Scotland

Jeff Stewart is best known to television viewers as the well meaning Reg Hollis in *The Bill*, a character he has played for over twenty years. His other television work includes Harry Fellows in *Crossroads*, Dukka in *Doctor Who*, Jenkins in *Reilly: Ace of Spies*, *Minder*, *Lytton's Diary*, *Roots* and *The Nightmare Man*. In the series five episode 'Save Our Heritage' Jeff can be seen in *Hi-de-Hi!* playing the Police Constable who is eager to get back to the station for his break.

GILLIAN TAYLFORTH b1955, London

Gillian Taylforth is now known nationally as Kathy Beale, a member of the original *EastEnders* cast from 1985. She trained at the Anna Scher Theatre School before landing a part in the remake of *The Rag Trade* with Miriam Karlin and Peter Jones. She appeared in the second episode of *Hi-de-Hi!* 'Desire in the Mickey Mouse Grotto'. Rose is a femme fatale who is up to no good with Ted, however her suspicious mum and dad think that Jeffrey Fairbrother is the man preying on their daughter. Kathy is often remembered for hosting the quiz programme *On Safari* with Christopher Biggins but more recently has been creating waves once again in the trashy soccer drama *Footballers' Wives*.

TALFRYN THOMAS b1922 - d1982

A widely respected Welsh character actor, Talfryn appeared in television shows with Ken Dodd and Ronnie Barker before being more widely recognisable as Mr. Cheeseman, the newspaper Reporter who for a time joined Captain Mainwaring and the Home Guard for several episodes of *Dad's Army*. He also turned in a memorable performance in the disturbing Terry Nation drama *Survivors*. As Gareth Davies, Gladys Pugh's half-brother, Talfryn delivers a finely tuned performance as the odd ball brother who is not as sinister as his sister seems to think. Talfryn sadly passed away before the broadcast of the episode 'Stripes'.

DAVID TROUGHTON b1950, London

The son of actor Patrick Troughton, David is now a hugely respected member of the Royal Shakespeare Company. His television credits are numerous and include the King Of Peladon in *Doctor Who* with Jon Pertwee, Bob Buzzard in *A Very Peculiar Practice* and King George V in *All The King's Men* opposite David Jason and Dame Maggie Smith. David plays Mr. Pritchard, the Policeman in love with Gladys Pugh, who allegedly helps put the drunken Mr. Fairbrother into bed in the episode 'A Night Not To Remember'.

NIGEL WILLIAMS

Nigel won the William Pool Shakespeare Prize and the Caryl Brahms Musical Award while training at RADA. He has appeared in many theatres throughout the UK in addition to London appearances in *Oscar* at the King's Head Theatre, Lord Evelyn Oakley in *Anything Goes* at the Prince Edward Theatre, Rizzoli in Stephen Sondeim's *Passion* at the Queen's Theatre and *Assassins* at the Hampstead New Theatre. Nigel also toured the UK as Viv Nicholson's father George in the musical *Spend Spend Spend* with Barbara Dickson. He has over a hundred television appearances to his credit including sixty episodes as Douglas Brady in *Crossroads*, *Keeping Up Appearances*, *Secret Army*, *Fanny By Gaslight*, *Up The Elephant and Round the Castle*, *Home James*, *The River*, *Emmerdale Farm*, *Grange Hill*, *Red Dwarf* and *The Last Salute*. As the rugby player Bert who laces Jeffrey Fairbrother's drinks - "It's only tomato juice!" - in the episode 'A Night Not To Remember', Nigel sets in motion a string of events which leads to an embarrassing loss of memory for the Cambridge Professor.

10 Holiday Rock
The theme tune

One of the most memorable items in all of Jimmy and David's hit shows has been the signature tunes. These have been composed by Jimmy and a couple of collaborators.

The recording of 'Who Do You Think You Are Kidding, Mister Hitler?' by the great variety star Bud Flanagan, which was recorded for *Dad's Army,* earned Jimmy and his Co-composer Derek Taverner an Ivor Novello Award. The song so perfectly captures the flavour of the patriotic, anthemic compositions of the 1940s that to this day there are many people who believe it is an actual song of the period, not a faithful tribute recorded in 1968 shortly before Flanagan's death. Perry and Taverner also came up with a 'gang show' feel to 'Meet the Gang', the jaunty opening to *It Ain't Half Hot Mum.* (Later Jimmy would team up with Roy Moore to write the *You Rang, M'Lord?* theme.) "I'm a pasticher." Jimmy concedes. "David is a better musician than I am but when people turn on my shows they must know at once what it is all about. It sets the scene in 30 seconds." Jimmy's signature tune for Hi-de-Hi! is the only song he is credited as sole Composer. The song 'Holiday Rock' captures the dawn of the rock and roll era to perfection, you can instantly imagine a dance-hall full of Teddy Boys rocking away the night to just such a melody. It sounds very like an Elvis recording from the late '50s which is of course just exactly how it was supposed to sound. "When I had finished writing 'Holiday Rock' I took it to Ronnie Hazlehurst. He laughed and said 'Wait a minute, this sounds like the Elvis Presley song Blue Suede Shoes…' I said, ' You try and make that stand up in court!'" The veteran musician and composer Ronnie Hazlehurst

Holiday Rock

Well, if you're feeling lonely, and getting in a stew
Just bend your ear, come over here, and,
Man, here's what you do.
If you got the blues, I got some news,
Join in the fun in your blue suede shoes and…

CHORUS:
Do the holiday rock (holiday rock)
Do the holiday rock (holiday rock)
Hi-de-hi-de-hi
Ho-de-ho-de-ho
Go, go, go do the holiday rock

Summertime comes, work's such a bore,
Get on the train with the one you adore and…

REPEAT CHORUS

Summon the crowd, shout it out loud
Tell the world you're feeling proud and…

REPEAT CHORUS

Mamas and papas, get in the swing,
Now's the time you can have your fling and…

REPEAT CHORUS

I said hi-de-hi (ho-de-ho)
I said hi-de-hi (ho-de-ho)
I said hi-de-hi (ho-de-ho)
I said hi-de-hi (ho-de-ho)
Hi-de-hi-de-hi
Ho-de-ho-de-ho
Go, go, go, do the holiday rock

Can't get a chick, don't know the trick,
We're on the way you can take your pick and…

REPEAT CHORUS

You got the blues, I got some news,
Join in the fun in your blue suede shoes and…

REPEAT CHORUS

I said hi-de-hi (ho-de-ho)
I said hi-de-hi (ho-de-ho)
I said hi-de-hi (ho-de-ho)
I said hi-de-hi (ho-de-ho)
Hi-de-hi-de-hi
Ho-de-ho-de-ho
Go, go, go, do the holiday rock

I said hi-de-hi (ho-de-ho)
I said hi-de-hi (ho-de-ho)
I said hi-de-hi (ho-de-ho)
I said hi-de-hi (ho-de-ho)
Hi-de-hi-de-hi
Ho-de-ho-de-ho
Go, go, go, do the holiday rock

I said hi-de-hi-de-hi
Ho-de-ho-de-ho
Go, go, go, do the holiday rock
I said hi-de-hi-de-hi
Ho-de-ho-de-ho
Go, go, go, do the holiday rock

N.B. Text in italics are extra verses written for the stage musical

Words and music by Jimmy Perry
Published by Veronica Music Limited / Heath Levy Music Co Ltd.
Reproduced with permission

'September Song' - Holiday Rock

(1928–2007) had become the Musical Director for the Light Entertainment Department at the BBC by the late 1970s and as such was responsible for overseeing all such recordings for comedies and variety shows. Ronnie is perhaps best known today for his music on the epic saga of Yorkshire folk *Last of the Summer Wine*, he also provided the melody to the cash register opening of *Are You Being Served?* among his countless familiar compositions.

A team of seven session musicians were gathered at the BBC's Lime Grove Studios on Monday 22 October 1979 to record 'Holiday Rock' for the first time. Ronnie conducted the band which included his regular musicians Judd Proctor on guitar and Eddie Mordue on tenor sax. The backing vocals were performed by The Ladybirds. The vocal harmony group consisted of Maggie Stredder, Ann Simmons and Laura Lee. The Ladybirds pretty much worked solidly on TV throughout the '60s and '70s backing all manner of artists. Stredder and Simmons had in fact been in The Vernons Girls, the famous choir that had emerged from Vernon Pools Social Clubs. The Vernons Girls went on to have some minor chart hits at about the time that Hi-de-Hi! was set and had become a regular act on the legendary Jack Good pop show *Oh Boy!* The important lead Elvis sound-a-like vocal was taken by singer Ken Barrie. This original version was only used on both the opening and closing titles of series one and the pilot episode.

Ken Barrie aka Postman Pat!

WHO IS KEN BARRIE?

Ken was born in 1933 as Les Hulme in Tunstall, Stoke on Trent. He started singing with dance bands part time in his native Stoke, whilst working as a compositor for a printing firm. Moving south to Uxbridge and following National Service in the RAF, Ken landed a position as resident Vocalist with the Lou Preager Orchestra at the Hammersmith Palais, one of the premier ballrooms in the country at that time.

Changing his professional name to Ken Barrie (after one of his wife's brothers) he was signed to Embassy Records, an inexpensive label for the Woolworths chain producing cover versions of Elvis, Roy Orbison and other chart acts of the day. Embassy Records billed him as Les Carle but the name wasn't to last. Giving up dance band work in 1969 due to ill health, Ken joined The Mike Sammes Singers in addition to also being a member of The Cliff Adams Singers and The Maggie Stredder Singers. A vast amount of session recording work also came in, backing artists of the calibre of Barbara Streisand, Frankie Laine, Bing Crosby and Perry Como. In fact Ken released an entire album of Como covers on the Music for Pleasure label in 1976. Ken worked extensively for composer Barry Gray in the 1960s recording versions of popular Gerry Anderson series themes such as *Fireball XL5* and *Stingray*. In addition Ken also worked as a Backing Vocalist on many television shows including *Top of the Pops, The Ken Dodd Show, Seaside Special, The Generation Game* to name but a few. Ken also provided the distinctive whistling on the theme tune to the popular BBC series *My Family And Other Animals*.

In 1980 Writer and Guitarist Bryan Daly encouraged Ken to send a sample of his character voices to a company providing music for a new animated children's television series called *Postman Pat*. The rest is history. Ken became the voice of the nation's most famous Postman and still voices the character nearly thirty years later. His recording of the *Postman Pat* theme became a chart hit and is among the most fondly remembered TV themes to this day.

"Although Paul Shane ended up doing the pop single, I am pleased to have been the original voice on Hi-de-Hi!" says Ken. "I was doing backing vocals for an edition of *The Generation Game* once. Paul Shane and some of the others were on the show. During a break I went up to him and said, 'I sang the theme tune at the beginning of your show.' Paul called the others over and introduced me to Ruth Madoc and Jeffrey Holland. They were very nice to me. Although nobody would ever know it's me, I am proud of having my singing going into millions of homes at the start of such a classic comedy."

After the broadcast of the first series and with meteoric ratings success assured, EMI Records arranged for Paul Shane to record his own version of the theme for a 7 inch single release (catalogue number EMI 5180). The song was introduced by Ruth Madoc as Gladys Pugh whilst the B-side sported a new rock and roll track *Juke Box Saturday Night*. The single version was produced by Paul Greedus, whose successes have included hit singles for Dana, Celine Dion, 1982 Eurovision winner Nicole's *A Little Peace* and 1980s smash *I Eat Cannibals* by Toto Coelo. In his book *Tough In The Middle* Paul remembers re-creating the Hi-de-Hi! theme.

"I was chatting to Mike Fletcher, an old publishing colleague who handled the songwriting side of Jimmy Perry and David Croft's business affairs. As usual, Jimmy had written the theme tune to his new series Hi-de-Hi!, although on this occasion, the version used in the pilot episode was felt to be slightly luke warm and disappointing. It was a very poor rip-off of 'Blue Suede Shoes'. Some form of 1950s rock and roll parody had always been the requirement for the theme, but it just wasn't catchy enough for a hook-line like 'Holiday Rock' so I told Mike they should be looking at a beefier music track with maybe an answer / repeat style chorus that would catch on with viewers and radio listeners alike and could make a good sing-along record if the series took off."

"I agreed to take Jimmy's basic song and try to improve on it. Now it needs to be explained here that transforming a song in this way does not necessarily constitute co-writing, as it already exists. So although I took it completely apart structurally and rebuilt it as a catchy theme song, it was still Jimmy's original idea and as such, I was classed as a mere Arranger (and Arrangers are Arrangers and not Writers or creators, therefore they get no writing royalties.). Everyone involved was so pleased with my 're-work' of the theme that I was offered the job of producing the official version for EMI Records / BBC TV and allowed to write the B-Side (which in those days meant a very healthy share of any record sales royalties). We recorded the tracks in EMI's Abbey Road Studio 2, where most of the famous Beatles tracks were cut in the early 60s with George Martin at the controls. In those days, Sound Engineers like George were exactly that – Engineers – and as such even wore long white coats just like their counterparts in the more scientific fields. Check out the very early recording photos of the Beatles. You'll see him there, looking for all the world like a serious Doctor or Surgeon consulting with his hirsute patients."

The EMI single sleeve.

"In truth, I would have done that job for free just for the honour of sitting and working at the very same mixing desk that the Fab Four had stood around.

On one of the recording days for 'Holiday Rock', I got to the studio a little earlier than usual to find no-one was in yet. I ambled down the long staircase that leads from the control room into the huge 'live' area of the studio below and just stood there in reverence for I don't know how long. I swear through the total silence I could hear the echoes of the celebrity choir singing 'All You Need is Love' still reverberating around the enormous room 15 years on. It made my back tingle. The EMI record Holiday Rock *by Paul Shane & The Yellowcoats was released to coincide with the first BBC series and was solidly championed by DJs Terry Wogan and Gloria Hunniford on their daily BBC radio shows. They had already become big fans of the show and through their support and numerous airplays, it leapt straight into the charts at number 37 in May 1981. Everyone involved instinctively knew that all it needed was one single* Top of the Pops *appearance to ensure enough increased singles sales to become a massive hit, as the TV show was rapidly taking off in a big way by now. We were duly booked to appear on the show that week. I say 'we' as I had now roped myself in as Guitarist for the band just for the 'craic' as the Irish say (not to mention the TV appearance fees the backing band got…)"*

"Now try and appreciate this - I am a lifelong fan of Tottenham Hotspur Football Club and will have not a word said against them. Insult them at your peril if I am around. However, I curse them to this day for failing to beat Manchester City in the Saturday FA Cup Final of 1981, as the live broadcast replay on the following Wednesday caused Top of the Pops to be cancelled and along with it, our almost-guaranteed 40,000 extra record

'September Song' - Holiday Rock

sales. Yet still it couldn't stop us and thanks to increased airplays the record went up 6 places though still remained outside the top 30. We were again promised a TOTP slot the following week. I am talking about the very same 'following week' that Paul Shane received a legal injunction from a chain of Northern Working Men's Clubs announcing that, if he did not fulfil his contractual obligations by performing his stand-up comedy routine from Monday through Saturday that week in Doncaster as per their 6 month old signed agreement, he would (in legal terminology) 'Have the pants sued off him.' He was left no viable option but to fully comply and as such was forced to pull out of his TOTP recording spot. No Paul Shane = No TOTP."

"The frustrated Producer of the BBC show promised one final time that we would definitely appear the following week, always providing the record went up again in the charts. Quite how many more 'following week' chances we were going to get, I could only hazard a guess at! Can you believe it? Such are the vagaries of record sales collated that the damn thing dropped one single place in the charts and our guaranteed TV spot was cancelled. End of Hi-de-Hi! story (as far as the record was concerned)."

The single was re-released on the BBC Records label (catalogue number RESL103) the following year. A piano sheet music version was also published by Music Sales Ltd in 1981 to tie in with the single release. The closing titles would be adorned by Paul Shane's version from the second series until the final episode. A lesser known version of the song is by The Webb Twins – David and Tony – who included it on their 1985 album. (Catalogue number SRT5KL511). A karaoke backing track was produced by staunch Perry and Croft fan Joe Blackie of Zoom Entertainments in Hull, East Yorkshire, on their 2006 *Classic TV Themes Vol.1* release (Catalogue number B000LZ6DGE).

The BBC single sleeve.

'The Pay Off' - Camp Shop

11 Camp Shop
Programme merchandise

Merchandising is today a major part of any promotion for a television comedy series. A glance at the racks of your local HMV or W.H.Smith reveals an unlimited array of spin-off products on virtually any modern television show you can name - and in some cases not so modern. It was quite different back in the early 1980s when Hi-de-Hi! was reaching its peak.

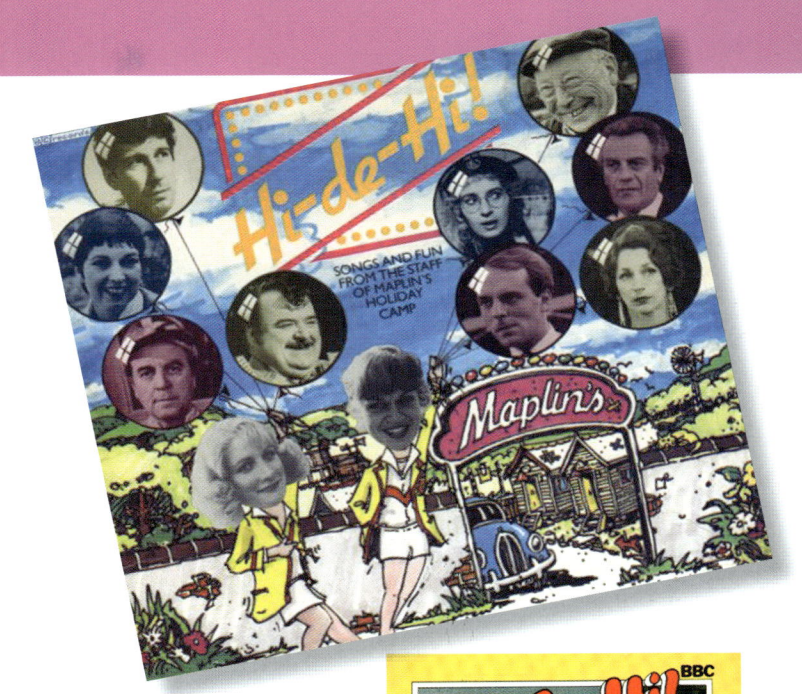

Audio Recordings
The theme music was issued as a single (see the 'Holiday Rock' chapter 10 for further details) paving the way for a selection of Maplin's Memorabilia to hit the shelves. The BBC's commercial arm wasn't the mighty corporate machine it is now, but nevertheless a small amount of products associated with the show did eventually appear. The first of these was a long playing record (remember those?) entitled *Hi-de-hi! - Songs And Fun From The Staff of Maplin's Holiday Camp* (Catalogue REC 436 vinyl, ZCM 436 cassette). The cast were gathered together to record tracks in character from the period. The theme song was of course included and highlights of the disc would be Mr. Partridge's *Tip Toe Through The Tulips*, Gladys and Jeffrey declaring *Baby It's Cold Outside*, Peggy yearning to lead *The Big Parade*, Barry and Yvonne going *Dancing In The Dark* and Fred Quilly's spirited rendition of *The Next Horse I Ride On*.

The cover picture of the Hi-de-Hi! novel was taken on the set of the Stage Musical.
Very noticable are the actor's tanned looks.
Paul Ableman has written several TV novels, including *Porridge, Last of the Summer Wine, Waiting for God, Shoestring* in addition to the novelisation of the *Dad's Army* feature film.

Reading Matter
A paperback book published by the BBC written by Paul Ableman and novelising five scripts from the 1983 series. The narrative was delivered by a mysterious senior camper Charlie Binns and was a brave stab at putting over the broad humour in written form. With a cover price of £1.50 it was a bargain! Two annual books appeared, the 1983 annual was issued by Stafford Pemberton Publishing (£2.50) and the rarer 1984 annual by Purnell books (£2.95). Both featured an assortment of illustrated stories and comic strips centring around Maplin's characters. The team was immortalised in a comic strip as part of the short lived TV Tops magazine with the first strip appearing in the August 1982 issue. The Hi-de-Hi! strip continued until the demise of the magazine in late 1982. The Heineken lager brand ran a campaign in 1984 with the slogan Hi-de-

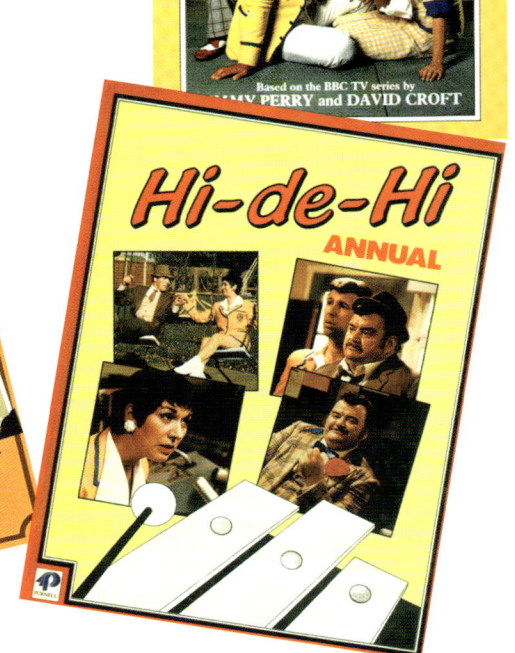

165

'The Pay Off' - Camp Shop

Heineken and issued six promotional postcards in the style of Donald McGill featuring a character looking very much like Ted Bovis.

A fan magazine 'Hello Campers' was produced by Rob Cope between 1994 and 1998. Altogether seven bumper issues were produced and would include reviews, articles and interviews with many of the stars of Hi-de-Hi! as well as other Perry and Croft shows.

Video Releases

1988 saw the release of the first Hi-de-Hi! commercial video by the BBC (BBV 4155) containing the first three episodes of the show. Two boxed sets of Hi-de-Hi! Videos were released in America in 2001 covering the first two series, the same episodes were released as VHS and DVD boxed sets in the UK. A problem with copyright blighted the first attempt to release the sets in the UK by Universal-Playback in August 2002. It was discovered by the BBC that clearance to use the song 'Love Me Tender' (sung by Marty Storm in the episode 'Desire In The Mickey Mouse Grotto') hadn't been obtained and all copies were recalled just three days before the release date. They were eventually issued in March 2003 with the sequence featuring the troublesome music edited out. However a few copies of the original discs did make it onto the market making them much sought after collectors' items among fans. A second set of videos and DVDs (Series Three and Four) were released in the UK in March 2004. Further releases on DVD only covering the Fifth and Sixth series of Hi-de-Hi! were issued in 2006 and the remaining episodes in 2008. British newspaper the Daily Mail gave away free copies of the episodes 'The Partridge Season' and 'No Dogs Allowed' whilst the Daily Mirror readers' freebie was 'The Society Entertainer', part of a BBC comedy related promotion in 2005.

Model Bus

Lledo models of Enfield issued a collection of vehicles based on BBC comedies in 1993 and this included a Maplin's Holiday Bus. It was a fine recreation of the vintage bus that fetched the campers from the train to the camp in a bright yellow livery. Another £4.99 bargain.

'The Pay Off' - Camp Shop

Board Game
A Hi-de-Hi! Board Game was issued in 1984 by Waddingtons, the object of which was to take part in each camp contest on the playing board and the one with the most points after eight games is declared the winner. The player could choose to be either Gladys, Jeffrey, Ted or Peggy. Although a likeness of Spike does appear on the box.

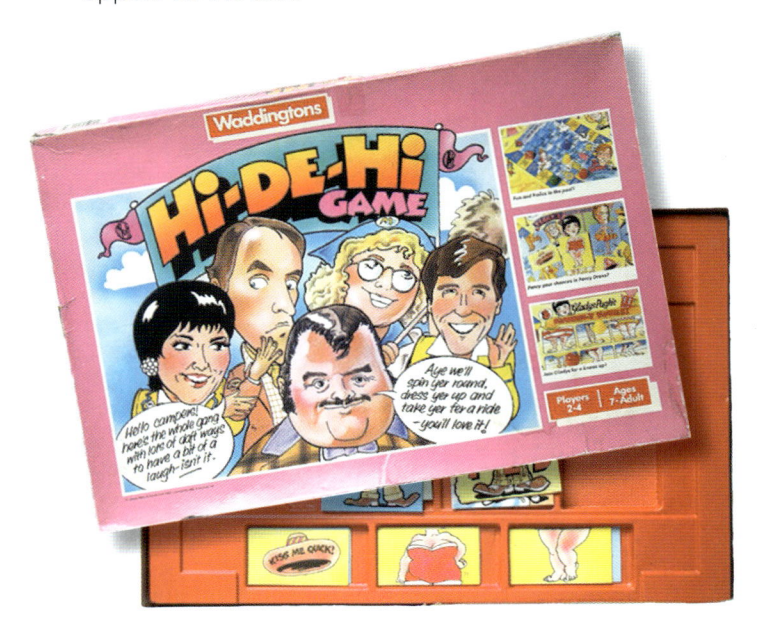

Promotional Badge
Handed out during the 1982 pantomime season at Bristol featuring four of the Hi-de-Hi cast. These plastic badges are very highly sought after. Based on a cartoon by Jeffrey Holland featuring Gladys, Ted, Spike and Barry.

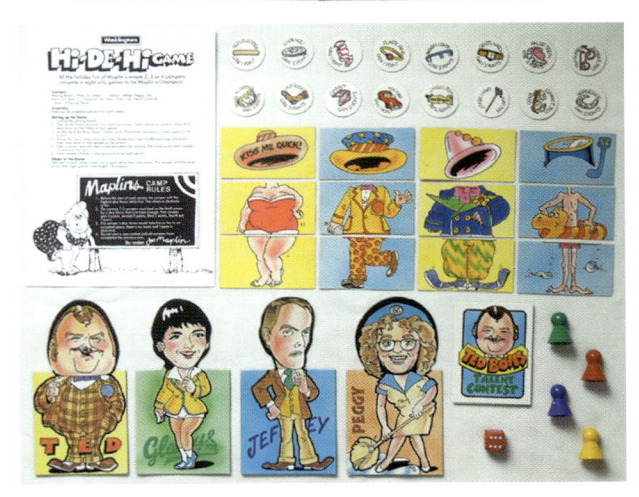

Published Scripts
No scripts of the show have ever been published, unlike other popular comedy shows of the era. However an authorised stage adaption by Paul Carpenter and Ian Gower featuring several stories is available from Samuel French Theatrical Publishers.

167

'The Wind of Change' - Crimpton-on-Sea

12 Crimpton-on-Sea
Then and Now by Tony Tarran

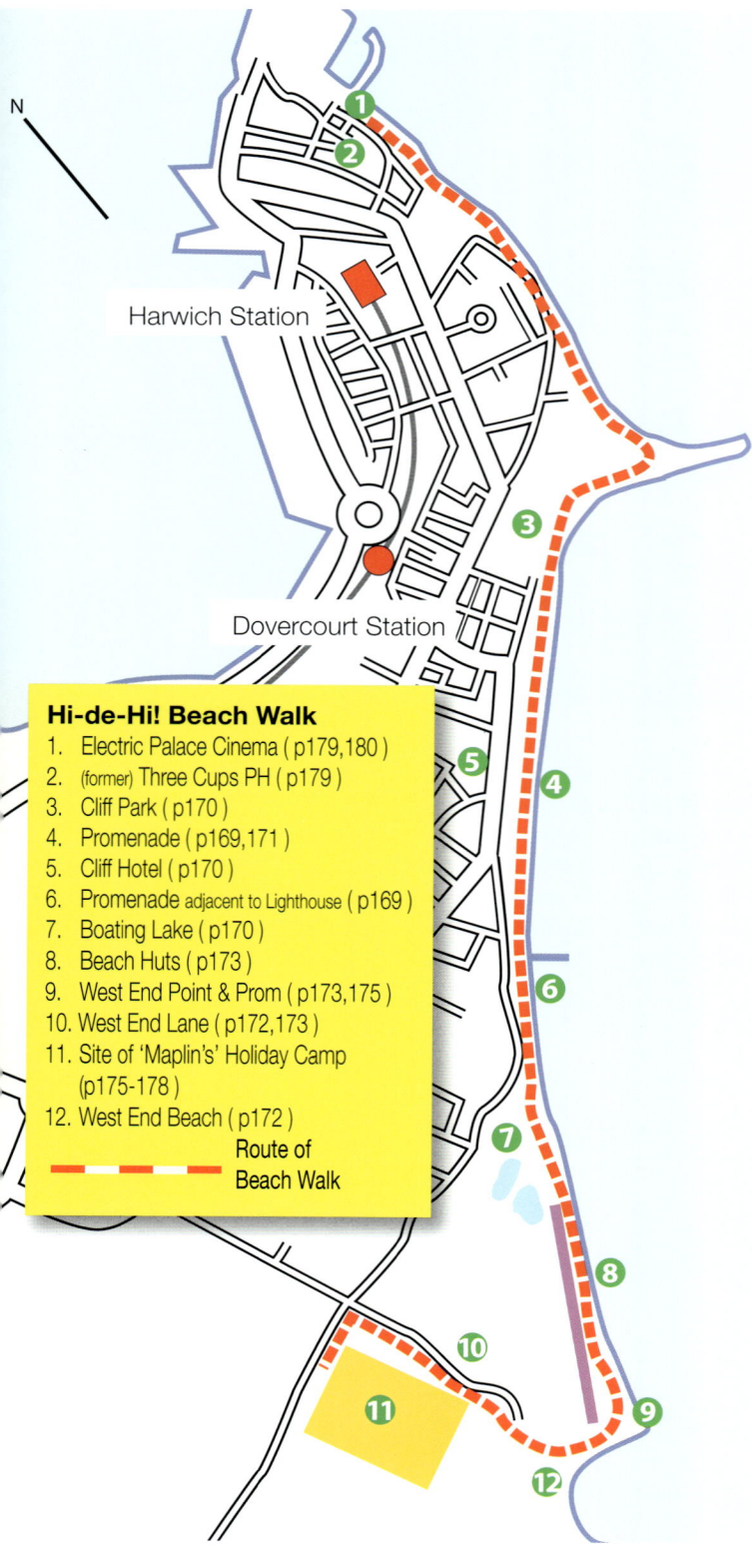

Hi-de-Hi! Beach Walk
1. Electric Palace Cinema (p179,180)
2. (former) Three Cups PH (p179)
3. Cliff Park (p170)
4. Promenade (p169,171)
5. Cliff Hotel (p170)
6. Promenade adjacent to Lighthouse (p169)
7. Boating Lake (p170)
8. Beach Huts (p173)
9. West End Point & Prom (p173,175)
10. West End Lane (p172,173)
11. Site of 'Maplin's' Holiday Camp (p175-178)
12. West End Beach (p172)

Route of Beach Walk

The filming locations were an important and integral part of Hi-de-Hi! and would normally account for about 25% of the running time for each episode, certain episodes excepted, eg 'Tell it to the Marines' where extensive location work was used.

Warner's Holiday Camp at Dovercourt was established as the main location from day one, where the majority of filming could be done in controlled conditions (it was used in all but one of the 58 episodes). Numerous areas within the camp were utilised principally the 'Olympic sized' swimming pool, the Ballroom, the Chalet Lines and the Reception Area but the Dining Hall, the Entrance Gate, the Approach Drive, Pets' Corner and Playing fields, amongst others, were used when called upon.

Today there are no distinguishable features of the former camp in existence; only some of the mature Poplar trees remain although they are gradually being removed. The trees Harry Warner planted to the front of the swimming pool have survived the redevelopment of the Northern part of the site for housing. The remainder of the site between the housing and West End beach remains undeveloped and overgrown. Some of the photographs on the following pages indicate the complete transformation of the site.

The locations to the rear of the camp namely West End beach and promenade also featured on more than one occasion. Other nearby locations were used for filming as it was important in terms of timescale and budgets not to have to travel too far from the main location, exceptions to this was filming at Mount Bures on the Essex / Suffolk border, Friday Wood in Colchester, Hitcham in Suffolk and a week spent on the North Norfolk Railway at Weybourne.

This chapter has expanded upon the 'Hi-de-Hi! Beach Walk' leaflet produced in 2007 which was the first attempt at listing the film locations used in the programme. The locations have been identified, photographed and matched as close as possible with scenes from the programme. The exercise has also proven fruitful in obtaining anecdotes and behind the scenes photographs from people who owned properties that were used.

To find these locations has taken considerable time and whilst most were already known, to find others required clues from local people, crew and cast all of whom, along with all those who allowed access to their properties, I would like to take this opportunity to thank. David Webb deserves a special mention for his assistance in finding the elusive Mistley, Lawford and Hitcham locations.

It must be noted that many of the locations are on private land or property and no right of access must be assumed or implied.

'The Wind of Change' - Crimpton-on-Sea

Ardleigh, junction of Waterhouse Lane/Morrow Lane.
The Prop sign to Buxton Magna was in the same position as the current sign.

Colchester, Friday Wood.
[Used as the Marine's Assault Course]
Friday Wood is a large open space owned by the MOD but open to the public. The assault course was created especially for the episode *Tell it to the Marines*.

Dovercourt, beach adjacent to Lighthouse.
Sea defence works are now in evidence

Dovercourt, beach opposite Cliff Hotel.
[Used as Grapethorpe Beach]

169

'The Wind of Change' - Crimpton-on-Sea

Dovercourt, Boating Lake.

Dovercourt, Cliff Hotel
The interior bar was used as The Fisherman's Rest. The hotel has changed very little, however, the balcony and the 'Tartan Bitter' sign have been removed.

Dovercourt, Cliff Park

Dovercourt, Hall Lane (opposite West End Lane).

'The Wind of Change' - Crimpton-on-Sea

Dovercourt, Michaelstowe Hall, Ramsey Road.
[Used as Dempster Hall]
Filming only took place using the interior, but the building itself certainly looks the part.

Dovercourt, Promenade opposite Cliff Hotel.
[Used for Grapethorpe Promenade]
The building in the background has lost one of its chimneys!

Dovercourt, Promenade opposite Cliff Hotel.
[Used for Grapethorpe Promenade]
The Cliff Hotel can clearly be seen in the background.

Dovercourt, Promenade opposite Cliff Hotel.
[Used for Grapethorpe Promenade]
One of the Dovercourt Lighthouses can be seen clearly in the background.

'The Wind of Change' - Crimpton-on-Sea

Dovercourt, West End Beach.

Dovercourt, West End Beach.

Dovercourt, West End Lane.
The row of chalets on the left have since been replaced by housing on the same location.

Dovercourt, West End Lane

172

'The Wind of Change' - Crimpton-on-Sea

Dovercourt, West End Lane (Northern end).

Dovercourt, West End Promenade & Beach Huts.

Dovercourt, West End Promenade & Beach Huts.
Sea defence works have been undertaken, these were carried out during the run of the programme and are visible on later episodes.

Dovercourt, West End Promenade & Beach Huts.

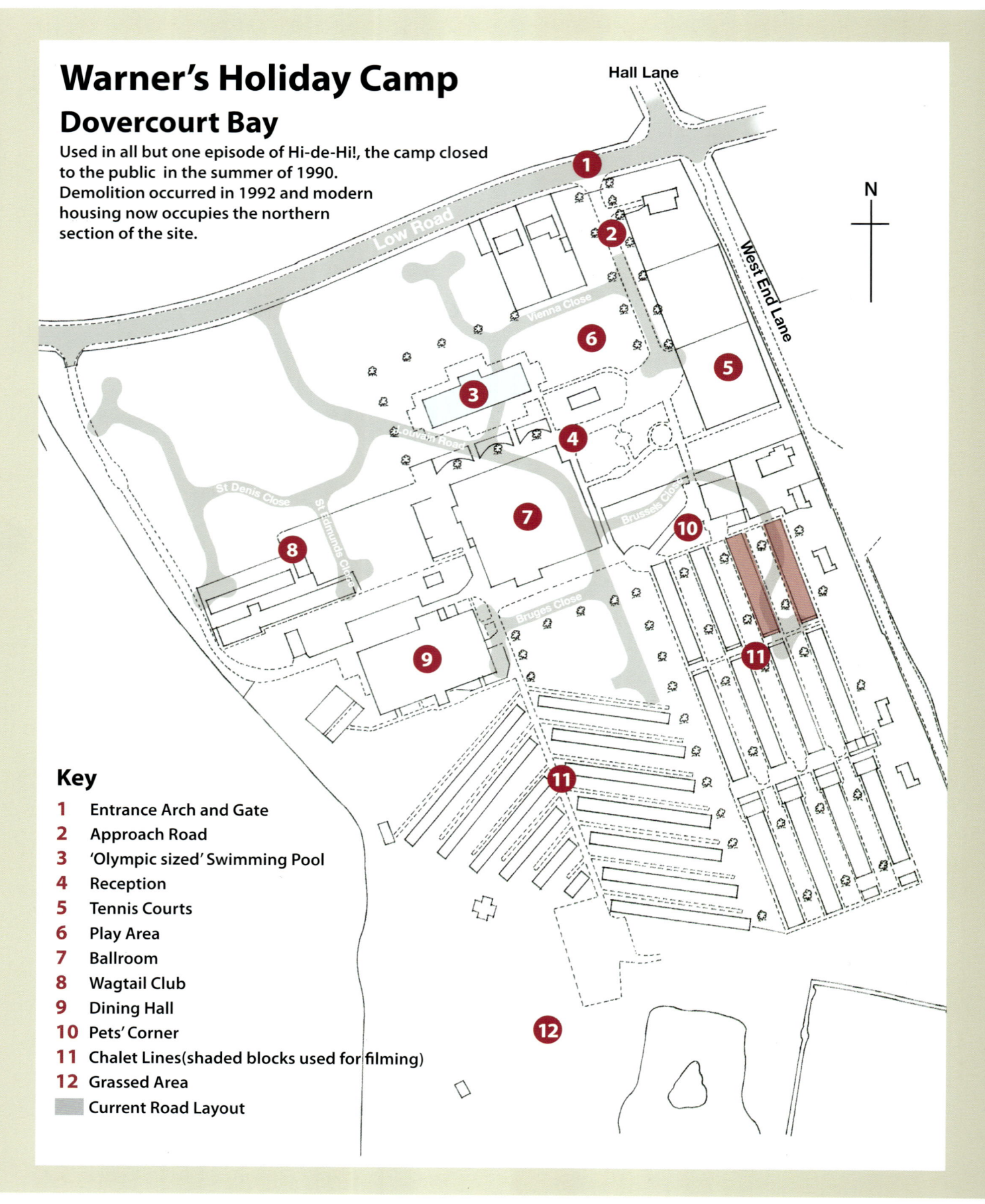

Warner's Holiday Camp
Dovercourt Bay

Used in all but one episode of Hi-de-Hi!, the camp closed to the public in the summer of 1990. Demolition occurred in 1992 and modern housing now occupies the northern section of the site.

Key

1. Entrance Arch and Gate
2. Approach Road
3. 'Olympic sized' Swimming Pool
4. Reception
5. Tennis Courts
6. Play Area
7. Ballroom
8. Wagtail Club
9. Dining Hall
10. Pets' Corner
11. Chalet Lines (shaded blocks used for filming)
12. Grassed Area
- Current Road Layout

'The Wind of Change' - Crimpton-on-Sea

'The Wind of Change' - Crimpton-on-Sea

Dovercourt, West End Point.

Dovercourt, Warner's Holiday Camp now Vienna Close.
The estate road is on the same alignment as the approach drive to the former camp.

Dovercourt, Warner's Holiday Camp now Vienna Close.
The kerb to the footpath is in the same position as the whitened stones to the left of the picture.

Dovercourt, Warner's Holiday Camp now Brussels Close.
The Poplar tree featured in the episode *Pigs Might Fly* has survived the development.

'The Wind of Change' - Crimpton-on-Sea

Dovercourt, Warner's Holiday Camp now Vienna Close/Louvain Road.
The stage by the swimming pool would have been in a position that straddles the road junction, footpath and front garden to the right.

Dovercourt, Warner's Holiday Camp.
Rear of camp adjacent to West End Lane.

Dovercourt, Warner's Holiday Camp, now Bruges Close.
This view faces the exterior of the dining hall with the entrance doors in the same position as the white double garage doors in the middle. The haystack in *Sausages or Limelight* would have been where the last house on the left now stands.

Dovercourt, Warner's Holiday Camp.
The same location today

'The Wind of Change' - Crimpton-on-Sea

Dovercourt, Warner's Holiday Camp, Low Road.
Any evidence of the former camp entrance has now disappeared.

Dovercourt, Warner's Holiday Camp now Vienna Close.
The tennis courts were to the left of the picture.

Dovercourt, Warner's Holiday Camp.
Joe Maplin's statue stood proud in a position that lines up with the left handcorner of this property (also see page 86).

Dovercourt, Warner's Holiday Camp.
The footpath to the left of the tree corresponds with the position of Ted sitting on his suitcase in the last episode *Wind of Change*.

'The Wind of Change' - Crimpton-on-Sea

Dovercourt, Warner's Holiday Camp, now Louvain Road.
The picture (left) is taken from the position of the car in the background of the picture above, looking towards the cast.

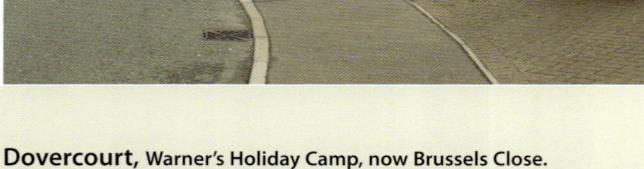

Dovercourt, Warner's Holiday Camp, now Brussels Close.
Looking down the former chalet lines, the far Poplar tree [arrowed] is still in position but the near one has been removed.

Dovercourt, Warner's Holiday Camp, grassed area to rear of camp.
This area has completely overgrown, but illustrates the difficulty in establishing the locations used.

Flatford, Willy Lott's House (Flatford Mill).
No change at this location made famous by John Constable, although the water is not so clear!

'The Wind of Change' - Crimpton-on-Sea

> ❝ My father agreed to let the BBC use the yard [below] and was paid £100 for the privilege. I was excited about watching the filming but got called out to work on the day and by the time I returned all filming was over. Susie Belbin took me down the pub for a drink at the end of the day to make up for it. I remember Felix Bowness wanting to buy the tiles off the barn roof but father never did sell them and they are still on there today. If I remember rightly the BBC had to get the bulldozer from a company some 40 miles away. ❞
>
> **Bob Deex**

Great Oakley, Stone's Green Road.
[Used as a builder's yard]
The dilapidated hut has since been demolished but the adjoining hut and oak tree remain.

Harwich, formerly Three Cups PH, Church Street.
[Exterior used as Tony's Trattoria]
Little change to this listed building. Gladys would have entered the building by the left hand door.

Harwich, Electric Palace Cinema (Exterior).
A Grade 2* listed building built in 1911 and is one of the oldest working cinemas in the country. Filming was carried out over three days.

'The Wind of Change' - Crimpton-on-Sea

Harwich, Electric Palace Cinema (interior).
[Used as Crimpton-on-Sea Electric Palace Cinema]
Essentially the same with subtle changes including new seating and signage.

Hitcham, 2 Laurels Cottages.
[Used as Mrs Baxter's Cottage]
Very little has changed. The bird table just visible above Gladys' head is still in place.

Hitcham, 2 Laurals Cottages
[Used as Mrs Baxter's cottage]
The cottage still retains its charm and original features.
Note the false door on the side elevation (above).

Lawford, St Mary's Church, Church Hill.
The church was used for both internal and external shots

'The Wind of Change' - Crimpton-on-Sea

Lawford, St Mary's Church, Church Hill.

Lawford, St Mary's Church, Church Hill.
Entrance to Church Yard

> My sister Lucy and I were given time off school to play the part of two bridesmaids in 'Wedding Bells'. It was all very exciting and afterwards we were given the dresses to keep. As my father David Webb was a yellow coat in the show, I had grown up knowing the cast and was thrilled to appear in an episode. I am now a news reporter for ITV/Anglia and was able to cover the Hi-de-Hi! Reunion event in 2007 and meet up again with some of the cast.
>
> **Victoria Webb**

Manningtree, Station Approach Road.
[Used as approach road to Crimpton-on-Sea Station]

'The Wind of Change' - Crimpton-on-Sea

Manningtree Station
[Crimpton-on-Sea Station]
The entrance has changed very little however the canopy has been removed.

Mistley, The Walls
This spot was used for the final scene in two episodes of series two.

Mistley, (Formerly) Dairy House Farm.
[Used as Fred Quilly's stables]
A tight squeeze for cast and crew, but clever camera work secured the scenes. This picture was taken looking in the same direction as the cast.

Mistley, (Formerly) Dairy House Farm.
[Used as Fred Quilly's stables]
The stables have long gone and the site is now a swimming pool.

182

'The Wind of Change' - Crimpton-on-Sea

Mount Bures, Withers Farm.
{Used as Julian Dalrymple-Sykes' Pig Farm]
The post with the prop 'phone attached is still in position. The doorway now leads into a cloakroom.

Mount Bures, Withers Farm.
{Used as Julian Dalrymple-Sykes' Pig Farm]
The approach road has changed little, and the manure has long gone!

> ❝ We needed a dilapidated farm to use as Julian's pig farm and it was proving difficult to find a farmer that was willing to let us film. The farmer who owned Withers farm at Mount Bures [above] called regularly at Warner's camp to collect the food waste for pig swill and it was suggested by the Camp Manager Alan Catten that we approach him. So we visited and agreed to use the farm as it fit the bill even though it was about 30 miles from Dovercourt. ❞
>
> **Roy Gould, Production Manager.**

Stones Green, junction of Colchester Road/Stonehall Road.
Kerb stones and road markings are now in evidence and the previously concealed cottage has been renovated and is now visible from the road.

13 Maplin's on stage
The Holiday Musical & Hi-DE-Hi! Spirits

Transferring television hits onto the stage has long been a popular past-time with theatre producers. Both David Croft and Jimmy Perry had a firm pedigree in the theatre so it was inevitable that their shows would find a home on the stage. By the time Hi-de-Hi! aired for the first time Perry and Croft had already scored big hits with *Dad's Army* in the West End (1975) and a summer season of *It Ain't Half Hot Mum* in Bournemouth (1979). David Croft had also had a sell out run of *Are You Being Served?* at the Winter Gardens, Blackpool (1976). Producer Duncan C. Weldon headed a team of producers for the Triumph-Apollo organisation in presenting the stage version of Hi-de-Hi! which was subtitled *The Holiday Musical*.

One by one the stars of the show were signed up to re-create their roles in front of a live theatre audience. Notable exceptions were Leslie Dwyer who did not feel at the age of 77 he could cope with twice daily performances, likewise Diane Holland declined the invitation due in part to the arthritis she suffered. Mandi Martin was cast as the stage Yvonne for the show's premiere at the Birmingham Alexandra Theatre on 7th June 1983. A new role was created to fill the gap left by Mr. Partridge; children's entertainer Uncle Benjamin played by showbiz veteran Ben Warriss. Warriss had been part of the double act Jewell & Warriss with his cousin Jimmy Jewell, major radio and television stars in the 1950s. With the TV series at it's peak in popularity the theatre box office was booming as holidaymakers at the Pavilion Theatre, Bournemouth - where a three month summer season beckoned - queued up to see Ted, Spike, Gladys and the rest give them the holiday of a lifetime, albeit crammed into two hours plus an interval!

The Holiday Musical - Synopsis
Act One

The show opens on the set of Jeffrey Fairbrother's study at Cambridge University in 1966 where he is addressing an informal meeting of his students. Lots of hippies with long hair and covered in beads litter the floor. "What pretty hair." Jeffrey says to a student upon entering only to discover the long haired beauty is in fact a man. He starts to recount the tale of how he got the job at Maplin's which is interrupted by the bing-bing-bong of Gladys Pugh over the tannoy with a "Hi-de-hi!" as we are transported back to 1959. Ted Bovis takes centre stage with a showstopping rendition of 'Hi-de-hi (Holiday Rock)' who then introduces the Yellowcoats, Yvonne and Barry, Uncle Benjamin, Fred Quilly, Spike Dixon and finally Gladys Pugh. They all join in with a reprise of 'Holiday Rock' before departing the stage to make way for Jeffrey who has arrived at Maplin's, suitcase in hand. The first thing he hears are bells and horns - it's Peggy's trolley and the Chalet Maid mistakes Jeffrey for a camper. "This camp holds the record - over 500 people go into the pool" she enthuses. "Oooh, you are the University Professor... The whole camp is buzzing." Giving him some very confusing directions to his new office Jeffrey Fairbrother eventually finds the staff rooms where he encounters Stanley and Bruce and eventually Gladys. It is love at first sight - for Gladys at least. As the staff assemble to meet their new Entertainments Manager, Ted tells Spike he is not bothered who the new Manager is because he has auditioned for a new rock and roll show and is just waiting to be called up. Fred is determined to get his Jockey's licence back and Uncle Benjamin is "just filling in" whilst old Partridge is away. Yvonne and Barry are busy rehearsing when Gladys announces over the

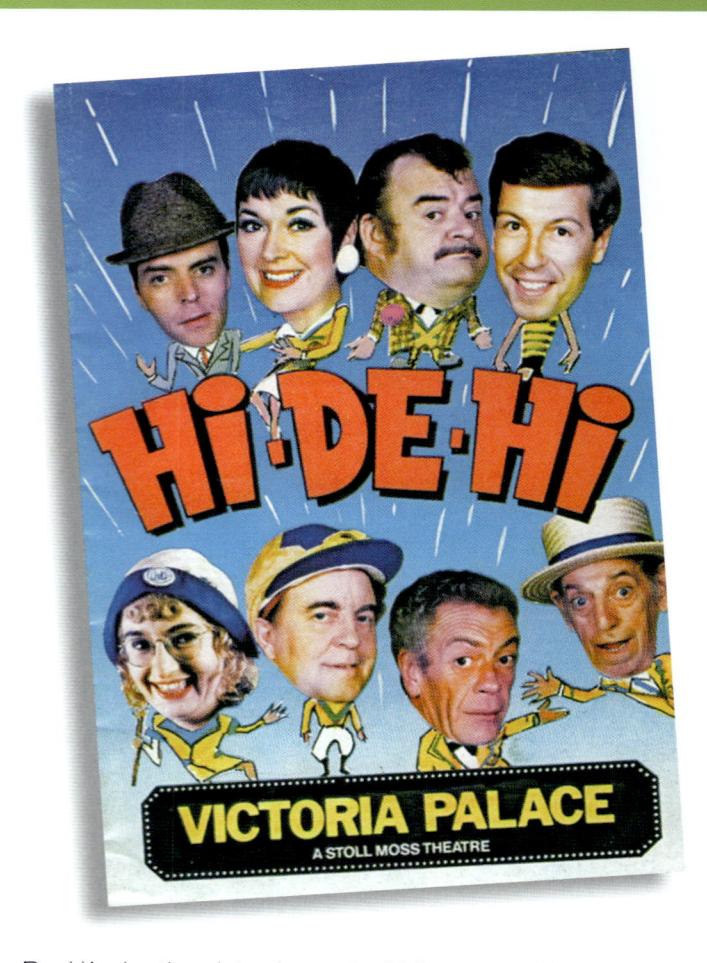

'Together Again' - Maplin's on Stage

Tannoy that all Yellowcoats are to assemble in the staff room but they are busy making plans to take part in the heats for the World Ballroom Championship after which "we won't have to do another season at this grotty place, offers will come flooding in" says Barry. The action cuts to Peggy on the 'phone to her mother, she has reversed the charges and just has time to tell her Mum that she has put in an application to be a Yellowcoat. Meanwhile Ted is explaining to Jeffrey the basics of "Musical Po's", the new competition at Maplin's which is along the same lines as Musical Chairs but with chamber pots. Yvonne and Barry are incensed but Gladys is adamant: what Joe Maplin says goes. So Fairbrother is forced to explain to the bewildered audience in his own awkward manner the rules of the game. Ted has to leap in and save the day and the game of Musical Po's begins. Peggy gets a po' stuck on her head and the scene ends with sirens wailing in the background. "That was my first encounter with holiday camp humour," says Jeffrey. He reasons that the British laugh at four things when on holiday a) domestic china i.e. chamber pots, b) big bottoms, c) large female chests and d) "little things". A giant saucy postcard is projected onto a screen and Jeffrey proceeds to give a very serious analysis of its contents which the theatre audience find hysterical, marvelling at the discomfort as Jeffrey is struggling to explain the rude connotations of the picture. Simon Cadell's brilliant portrayal of Fairbrother comes into its own as he painfully reaches the final catagory. Next up is "Listen With Gladys" for the children as she launches into the 'Ugly Bug Ball' song dressed as a Ladybird. "Lord Stick Insect and Lady Preying Mantis" arrive looking suspiciously like a distressed Yvonne and Barry. Fred is dressed as a maggot, Uncle Benjamin is a spider and Peggy trails feet galore as a caterpillar. Just as the Ugly Bug Ball is getting into full swing two rural characters arrive - which are Ted and Spike doing their rendition of yokel Farmers - with

Photocall for the cast during rehearsals, with Jimmy Perry and David Croft

some insecticide. But they decide not to spray and join in with the final chorus of the song in a glorious riot of colour. Back in the office Jeffrey tells Gladys that he has been short-listed for an important historical dig in the Holy Land which will be filmed by the BBC. Gladys is immediately worried that Jeffrey will be leaving. She sets about flirting with him but is interrupted by Peggy with her application to be a Yellowcoat. Gladys turns on the Chalet Maid telling her that she has little chance of achieving her ambition. Rejected Peggy turns to the audience saying that her secret is to 'Look For The Silver Lining' as Su Pollard delivers a heart warming rendition of the classic song. She gets the audience to join in with her, "I feel ever so much better now, thanks ever so," she says before leaving to a tumultuous round of applause. Uncle Benjamin is next under the spotlight, explaining to young Spike the best way to end a turn is

Ted Bovis and Spike Dixon on stage with Childrens Entertainer Uncle Benjamnin, played by Ben Warriss.

185

Images from the Stage Show;
Top left: Paul & Jeff's excellent Laurel & Hardy impression.
Right: Felix Bowness sings.
Bottom left: The big production number at the end of act one.

with a bit of "walloping" ie: tap dance. Ted tells them that being a turn is the best thing to be, that 'straight' actors would give their right arm to be a variety artiste. *They Want To Be Turns* sings Ted which is a cue for the rest of the staff to pay tribute to some showbusiness greats. Felix Bowness arrives giving his rendition of *Give Me The Moonlight* in a tribute to Frankie Vaughan. Su Pollard becomes Gracie Fields singing *Sally* then Paul Shane and Jeffrey Holland are Laurel and Hardy on the *Trail of the Lonesome Pine* with a stunning recreation of the legendary duo's most famous movie sequence. Wilson, Keppel and Betty doing their famous Sand Dance is provided by Barry Howard, Ben Warriss and 'Yvonne' after which Simon Cadell pays tribute to Noel Coward with *Mad Dogs and Englishmen* delivered at break-neck speed. Suddenly the mood changes and Ruth Madoc is the beautiful Madame Butterfly surrounded by Geisha girls delivering Puccini's finest opera. She is interrupted by Paul Shane striding on as a Canadian Mountie, a refugee from Rose Marie. "When I'm calling yoooooo...." he belts out. "Why are you dressed as a member of the Canadian Mounted Police?" sings Gladys. "I might ask you the same question, why are you dressed up as a Japanese tart?" chants Ted before the charms of *Nessun Dorma* grip them for a spectacular finish. *Any Old Iron* is given the Shane / Madoc treatment before the entire cast return for a reprise of the song *They Want To Be Turns* bringing the curtain down on act one in true showbiz fashion.

Act Two

After the interval the gang return with one of Maplin's sing-a-long anthems *Here We Are Again (Happy As Can Be)* which has the audience joining in and ready to enter the world of Joe Maplin once more. The singing continues with the Maplin's national anthem *Sons Of The Sea (Bobbing Up And Down)* and *Just Once More Chance* during which Ted encourages everyone to wave hankies and programmes in the air. Ted launches into a game of bingo but Jeffrey decides that he would like to have a go. Naturally he is terrible: "Two fat ladies: 33" he shouts, "On its own: 41, unlucky for some: 19". "Why is 19 unlucky for some?" asks Ted "Well if they haven't got it on their cards it is unlucky for them," Fairbrother reasons. Peggy wins but is disqualified for being staff the audience barrack on her behalf and she is allowed to win! Barry and Yvonne want to change their day off to compete at the Royal Albert Hall in the World Ballroom Championships. On the same day Peggy is going for her Yellowcoat interview, Fred is being called before the board of the Jockey Club and Ted is off to see his agent. Gladys despairs when Jeffrey says he has written to Joe Maplin telling him he might have to quit the camp to go and work as an Archaeologist again. Joe Maplin is quick to reply:

"Get this sonny. No-one walks out on me in the middle of the season. Not even some clever dick Teacher. Stroll on, have you gone bonkers? May I remind you that you have a contract with me to keep the campers happy not swan off to the desert to dig up mouldy Arabs who have been dead 2,000 years!"

As it turns out Joe Maplin is forcing Fred to send a forged note to Gladys inviting her to Jeffrey's chalet and when she is there Fred is to take a photo of them together in their night attire which Joe will then use to blackmail Jeffrey into staying for the rest of the season. But before this it's South American night in the ballroom with the entire company decked out in carnival attire. This is of course a cue for a big production number. *They've Got an Awful Lot of Coffee in Brazil* they sing as the night in the ballroom draws to a close. Fred is wracked with guilt about having to help Joe Maplin blackmail Fairbrother, but Gladys is over the moon to receive a note of passion seemingly from her beloved Jeffrey and heads off to the Entertainments Manager's chalet. She rushes into the chalet but the cruel deception is soon discovered leaving Gladys broken hearted and she rushes back to her own chalet.

Benjamin and Fred make a right hash of getting the photo as Fred keeps rushing in and out of the chalet taking pictures and trying to find Gladys who isn't there! Gladys meanwhile is yearning for her love and sings a passioned *If It Takes Forever, I Will Wait For You*. Soon Thursday has arrived. Barry and Yvonne set off to the Ballroom Championships as Ted, Peggy and Fred all await their big day too. Spike is dressed as a comedy fairy godmother, he wishes he could fix it for all their dreams to come true. Suddenly the wand takes on real magical powers and we are transported into a fantasy world where Fred is in the Derby final "Get out of the way Piggott or I'll belt you one!" He shouts as he romps home to win the race by a length. The scene then switches to the Albert Hall as Barry and Yvonne take the floor, wowing the judges with their dazzling display of dancing. Next Gladys is transported to the jungle in pursuit of Jeffrey on his archaeological dig. She is captured by natives and is rescued by Jeffrey who carries her off in his arms declaring undying love. Peggy is at Buckingham Palace where Her Majesty The Queen awards her the coveted Yellowcoat as she descends a staircase singing *We'll Build A Stairway to Paradise*. Finally Ted is seen as Elvis rocking and rolling to *Kid Creole* and further Presley hits, as the girls scream at this latest pop idol. Alas the power of the wand fades and we see the reality of the situation. Fred doesn't get his Jockey licence, Barry and Yvonne haven't attained the standard needed to compete in the Ballroom Championships, Peggy's application to become a Yellowcoat has been refused and Gladys has received a goodbye note from Jeffrey who has gone off to dig up some more fossils. "You were a damn good right hand man," he writes. We return to 1966 as Jeffrey concludes the tale. "I often look back on that summer of 1959 with great affection. I wonder also where they all are and what they are doing now..." He pauses and looks around but his students have disappeared. "I think I'll go for a drive," he informs us. "For a dig. Not to look for fossils but some old and very dear friends." The haunting strains of '*Goodnight Campers* echo around the theatre as we go back to the Maplin's Ballroom. As the song reaches its climax "Hello Gladys," says a voice. "Jeffrey!" she cries as Gladys is reunited with her beloved Jeffrey and the curtain comes down on the show. Goodnight campers, goodnight.

'Together Again' - Maplin's on Stage

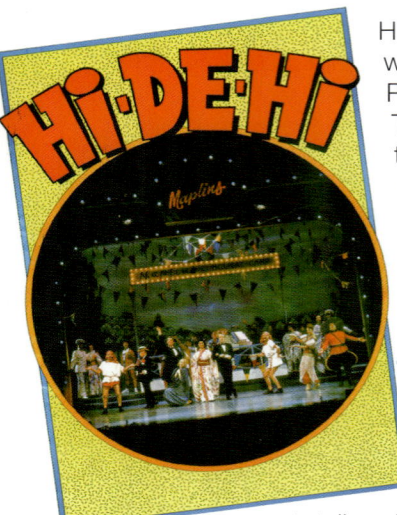

Hi-de-Hi! *The Holiday Musical* was a dazzling success at the Pavilion Theatre, Bournemouth. The show was performed twice nightly with a first house at 6.10pm and a later show at 8.40pm. This was to allow audiences to attend following dinner sittings at guest houses throughout the resort. Ticket prices ranged from £2 up to £4. A holiday bargain indeed. The Daily Express commented, "The show, though not lavishly set, is well rehearsed and totally enjoyable." It did have criticisms though, "The first half ends with the splendid Ugly Bug Ball. But the finale splutters to a conclusion: not so much a climax, more an epitaph. And Simon Cadell should slow down during his rendering of 'Mad Dogs And Englishmen'." However, The Stage newspaper was quick to commend Simon on his 'word perfect' rendition of the song and to recognise Su Pollard's 'powerful voice'. The Stage summarised: "Thanks to the versatility of the cast, David Croft and Jimmy Perry have been able to make an excellent holiday musical out of Hi-de-Hi! at the Pavilion, Bournemouth and if the same cast can be kept together it should become an attraction at many other resorts in the years to come."

With box office receipts high and audience reaction to the show always euphoric, plans were immediately laid to take it to the heart of London's theatre land, at the Victoria Palace, where the success was repeated once again. This time a best seat in the stalls or circle might set you back up to £7.50, whilst an upper circle seat could be snapped up for as little as £4. This was the second West End show to have this title, Hi-de-Hi! was presented at the Palace Theatre in 1943 starring Flanagan and Allen, Monsieur Eddie Gray and Wilson, Keppel and Betty. Rather spookily the great sand dance variety act Wilson, Keppel and Betty were also included in the variety tribute section of The Holiday Musical exactly forty years later! Despite many performances being sold out, the London theatre critics didn't welcome the show onto their turf very warmly.

Charles Spencer, The Standard: "The storyline is conspicuous only by its absence and much of the evening consists of the cast doing variety turns and party pieces. Old songs abound and there is a Music Hall atmosphere, greatly enhanced by the arrival of veteran comedian Ben Warriss who performs the most dignified of tap dances…. Simon Cadell emerges as the undoubted star - his performance as the hesitant, cruelly embarrassed Fairbrother is a subtle and truly perceptive comic creation…As always Su Pollard attracts more than her fair share of the limelight as the delightfully gormless Chalet Maid Peggy, while Ruth Madoc smoulders with hilarious sexuality as Gladys Pugh, the sharp tongued girl from the valley's whose passion is doomed to remain unrequited."

Michael Billington, The Guardian: "…I find it difficult to be nostalgic for tat; and for the most part this show asks us to be woozily indulgent to bad gags and wobbly impressions."

John Connor, City Limits: "I wasn't expecting it to be such dross. End of the pier production numbers, done with suitable professionalism but boring as hell, a paltry script even by panto / sit-com standards and laughs based on catchphrases only."

Steve Grant, Time Out: "… its only real thrust seems to be revealing Su Pollard's Peggy is a more gifted singer than the bona-fide Maplin's Yellowcoats and that Paul Shane's superb Teddy Boy comic, Ted Bovis, isn't just a tit 'n' bum 'n' farts merchant."

Eric Shorter, Daily Telegraph: "In effect, this is a revue which consists of turns by people who may be pleasant enough on the small selective screen but who tend to look in the flesh and on the boards of a playhouse, which once housed the Crazy Gang, less than adequate… It was, one gathers, a summer show. This is easy to believe, and the star is Simon Cadell who seems to win everyone's heart, like Su Pollard as the revered Margaret (sic)."

The lofty reviews certainly didn't dent the box office at the Victoria Palace where standing ovations were a regular feature at the curtain call.

In what appears to be a Christmas photo opportunity, the cast line up outside the Victoria Palace Theatre, London on a damp day.

Mid-way through the season, Simon Cadell bade farewell to the role of Fairbrother. His commitments to playing Hamlet in Birmingham meant that he would never play Fairbrother again following his final performance at the Victoria Palace. To fill the gap in the show, a David Croft veteran stepped in. Michael Knowles had been a guest artist in *Dad's Army*, played a major role in *It Ain't Half Hot Mum* and now stepped up to the challenge of giving his own take on Jeffrey Fairbrother. Audiences continued to give Knowles the same enthusiastic reception as they had to Cadell. The show managed good business until early May when the cast were ready for a break, the Victoria Palace said farewell to Hi-de-Hi! *The Holiday Musical* having hosted yet another theatrical hit.

Finally the seaside beckoned yet again as the northern show business mecca, Blackpool, prepared for the Maplin's invasion to its massive 3,000 seater Opera House. Michael Knowles continued to be Jeffrey whilst Felix Bowness decided to return to his position as warm up comedian for some of television's biggest shows and was replaced by respected actor and comic Joe Black. Once again the Daily Express were on hand to offer a review. "Every kid in the house identifies with Su Pollard. The fact that she sings like an angel is an unexpected bonus. Yet I warm more readily to the delicious Ruth Madoc, as Gladys, Vamp from the Valleys. To hear her hiss the word "trowsserss" is to know lust at its most elemental." The Express summarised that the show "Is all rather old fashioned, but then so is Hi-de-Hi!" Again great value with seat prices ranging from £1.50 to £4, a programme would set you back 40p. The audience continued to love the show and when the curtain fell on the final night in Blackpool many thousands had witnessed the magic that the staff of Maplin's had created on stage. It remains a very memorable encounter with the television legends to all who witnessed *The Holiday Musical*. Alas no video footage exists as an archive of the show, but audio recordings were made and are in the hands of the cast or collectors.

Simon Cadell hands over 'Jeffrey Fairbrother' to Michael Knowles. They pose for the press at the Victoria Palace Theatre, London.

HI-DE-HI! THE HOLIDAY MUSICAL

Cast:

Jeffrey Fairbrother	Simon Cadell
	Michael Knowles*
Ted Bovis	Paul Shane
Gladys Pugh	Ruth Madoc
Spike Dixon	Jeffrey Holland
Fred Quilly	Felix Bowness
	Joe Black*
Peggy Ollerenshaw	Su Pollard
Barry Stuart-Hargreaves	Barry Howard
Yvonne Stuart-Hargreaves	Mandi Martin
	Marie Lorraine*
Uncle Benjamin	Ben Warriss
Chesterman	Ben Warriss / Len Lowe* / Barry Craine*
Stanley	David Webb
Bruce	Tony Webb
Yellowcoats	Roslyn Cole
	Lisa-Dawn Hart
	Felicity Lee
	Debbie Riordan
	Cathy Stevens
	Tim Swinton*
	Christine Jackman*
	Karen Kent*
	Angie Lloyd*
	Diane Neeser*
	Liz Stark*
	Julie Whitehill*
Bert Swanley and the Debonairs	David Hale keyboards
	Peter Parkinson tenor sax / flute
	Perry Duke bass guitar
	Dean Duke percussion
	Trevor Dunford guitar

* parts taken over during the Victoria Palace and Blackpool seasons

Staged by	Tudor Davies
Costumes by	David Blight
Original Maplin's costumes and Ugly Bug Ball costumes by	Mary Husband
Musical Director	David Hale

Written and Directed by Jimmy Perry and David Croft.

World premiere at Alexandra Theatre, Birmingham 7 - 11 June 1983, it subsequently ran for a season at the Pavilion Theatre, Bournemouth from 13 June 1983 through to 24 September 1983. A West End run at the Victoria Palace Theatre commenced 22 December 1983 through to 5 May 1984 and finally at Blackpool Opera House from 13 July until 22 September 1984.

'Together Again' - Maplin's on Stage

Hi-DE-Hi Spirits

A second stage presentation manifested itself a couple of years later, this time not a musical but a stage comedy featuring four Hi-de-Hi! stars re-creating their roles. Well known theatrical producer Mark Furness persuaded Jimmy Perry and David Croft to write a script featuring the staff outside the holiday camp setting of the series. Paul Shane and Ruth Madoc were tempted back to top the bill as Ted and Gladys whilst two of the newer staff members were seen live on stage for the first time in their Maplin's guises. David Griffin was well established as Clive Dempster by this point and Linda Regan as April was also familiar to television viewers from the latest episodes, so the box office of the venues where the show appeared were booming with fans queuing up to witness the four stars in action. The production was directed by Dennis Ramsden who was seen in the television series as Clive's uncle. The production also featured Fred Bryant as Charles, the Bishop of Ely, and Peter Fontaine as Freeman, both of whom would be seen as members of Clive's family in future television episodes.

Play Synopsis

The setting of the play is a warehouse on the banks of the Thames that has been converted into a photographer's studio and flat. It is the autumn of 1960, the camp has shut and Ted is staying with Clive who is looking after the flat for his friend Adrian, a glamour photographer. Gladys has been invited but turns up with April in tow. The warehouse is the scene of a vodka smuggling operation and when a Policeman arrives just as a consignment of illicit vodka is to be delivered by Russian seamen the action becomes fast and furious.

Although the play did very good box office figures wherever it played, it has never been a favourite with the writers. David Croft partly blames the constraints of the staging. "Hi-De-Hi Spirits was written to order. It worked quite well in Bournemouth but we weren't proud of it. We had a small area to work with in terms of the set so we [the audience] couldn't see outside of the warehouse setting. Paul Shane was encouraged to ad lib throughout and it went well after that." Paul Shane himself is typically forthright in his assessment of the production. "They came into my dressing room in Bournemouth, threw the script on the table and said 'There are the bones, get on with it.' The script is nothing like the show. I changed it all. We had them walking down that Pier wetting themselves with laughter - they [the audience] didn't know what at. I put the meat into it with ad-libs and routines I devised. It took me a month to turn it around." Jimmy Perry perhaps sums up the piece, "It wasn't the best thing we've done."

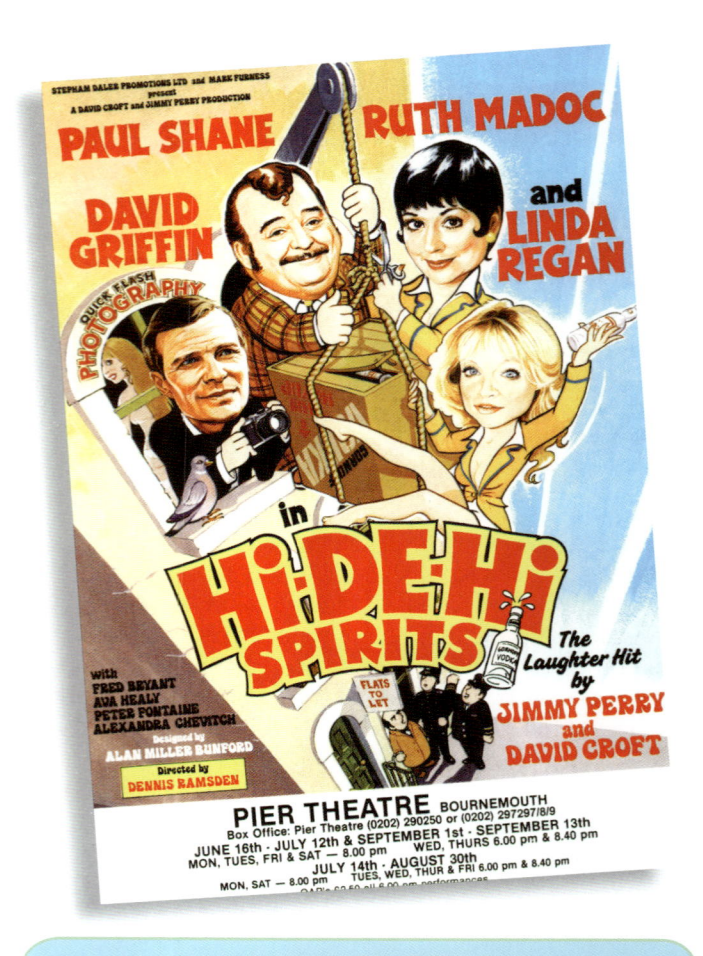

HI-DE-HI SPIRITS

Cast in order of appearance:

Squadron Leader Clive Dempster	David Griffin
Ted Bovis	Paul Shane
Gladys Pugh	Ruth Madoc
April Wingate	Linda Regan
Samantha	Ava Healy
Charles, Bishop of Ely	Fred Bryant
Freeman	Peter Fontaine
Captain Pullicoff	Alexandra Chevitch
Russian Seaman	Clive Chenery
Customs Officer	Chris Merrick

Written by Jimmy Perry & David Croft
Directed by Dennis Ramsden

World premiere at the Alexandra Theatre, Birmingham (19th - 24th May 1986). Subsequent tour dates: Darlington Civic Theatre (26th - 31st May 1986), His Majesty's Theatre, Aberdeen (2nd - 7th June 1986), Grand Theatre, Blackpool (9th - 14th June 1986) and finally for a summer season at the Pier Theatre, Bournemouth (16th June - 13th September 1986).

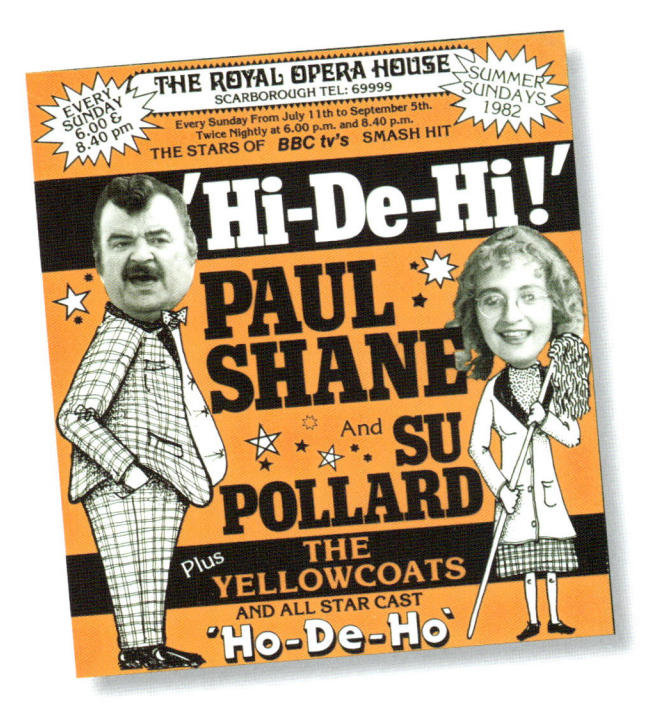

The Paul Shane and Su Pollard Show, Scarborough

A year before the Hi-de-Hi! *The Holiday Musical* was premiered, Paul Shane and Su Pollard had both been booked to appear for several Sundays in a row at the Opera House Scarborough from July to September 1982. Producer Nick Thomas had the posters printed showing them both as their television characters, with a headline stating 'The Stars of BBCTV's Smash Hit 'Hi-De-Hi! Paul Shane and Su Pollard' and at the bottom 'plus The Yellowcoats.'

Perry and Croft were not amused. Solicitiors were summoned and it looked for a time as if legal wrangling over the billing would end up in the court room. This was not a Hi-de-Hi! production after all. At the last moment, an agreement was reached and hundreds of happy holidaymakers got to see the two stars live - Su Pollard even appeared as Peggy for a short sketch during the evening.

Amateur Productions

The UK amateur premiere of Hi-de-Hi! The Holiday Musical occurred at the Garrick Playhouse, Altrincham in December 2005 in a production directed by professional actor Alan Rothwell. The original script had been obtained from Jimmy Perry.

A new stage production of Hi-de-Hi! based on several of the television scripts was adapted by Paul Carpenter and Ian Gower and premiered by the Tring Festival Company at the Court Theatre, Tring in June 2007. Jimmy Perry found time to attend one of the performances.
This version has now been published for amateur performance by Samuel French Ltd.

Jimmy Perry and Jeffrey Holland meet the cast at The Court Theatre, Tring.

Staff room scene from the play at The Court Theatre

The Cliff Hotel, Dovercourt was chosen as the cast and crew stayed there during location filming and John Wade the Manager at the time was still there so it seemed a good choice.

The time had come to unveil the commemorative plaque, everybody crowded into the foyer along with the two film crews and Jimmy and David duly did the honours after a word from the Mayor of Harwich.

At last the programmes link with the town of Dovercourt had been recognised. Su at this point took me to one side and asked me if she could dress up as 'Peggy' to make her entrance for the evening, do you need to ask I thought!

The evening's entertainment consisted of several sketches from our own Jeffrey Fairbrother and Gladys Pugh, a viewing of rare out-takes, supplied by Jeff Holland, a charity auction and raffle with the evening ending with a celebrity led rendition of 'Goodnight Campers'.

The doors reopened again on Sunday to reveal the Hawaiian Ballroom which overnight had been cleared and the displays set up, the queue of people waiting to come was evident and pleasing. All our VIPs were on hand for a signing session and to talk to the fans. At lunch time the children were entertained by Punch & Judy, alas Mr Partridge was not available but his stand in coped admirably.

Maplin's Reunion 2007

Maplin's Reunion 2007

I approached David Croft about the possibility of organising a Hi-de-Hi! event during a chat with him at the Bell Hotel in Thetford in May 2004, it was the Monday morning after the annual Dad's Army weekend. I said to him that it was 25 years since the pilot episode of Hi-de-Hi! and wouldn't it be good to celebrate the programme in some way possibly with an event in Dovercourt where the location filming took place, which coincidentally is my home town. He agreed with the idea in principle without hesitation. After several discussions with my wife Joanne over the next 2 years, we came to the conclusion, that we should aim to do an event in 2007 which would coincide with the 20th anniversary of the final episode.

On Saturday the 17th October the VIPs arrived one by one; Jimmy Perry, Jeff Holland, David Webb, Tony Webb, Nikki Kelly and Mary Husband. I had to go to Dovercourt station to pick up Su Pollard and I was very relieved and excited when she got off the train. (Su was also reacquainted with Charlie the parrot, who she taught to swear during her filming days. He had to be bought in for the special day as he had retired from the hotel some years ago.) Early evening saw the arrival of David Croft who had just got back into the country and had come directly to Dovercourt from the airport.

About 500 people came through the doors during the day. Our VIPs kindly stayed on until tea time before they departed, after which we just collapsed in a heap in the hotel bar feeling absolutely exhausted.

I would like to take this opportunity to again thank all the VIP guests who attended - David Croft, Jimmy Perry, Su Pollard, Jeff Holland, Nikki Kelly, David Webb, Tony Webb, Mary Husband and Charles Garland. A warm thank you again to all our helpers over the weekend - our colleagues from the Dad's Army Appreciation Society team, Rob Cope and my daughter Nichola, who was a Yellowcoat for the day in Su's costume lent to us by Mary Husband. Last but not least, I'd like to thank my wife, Jo.

Tony Tarran

Hi-de-Hi!
During location filming
of BBC TV's hit comedy
Hi-de-Hi!
the cast & writers stayed
here at the Cliff Hotel
1980 - 1987
Presented by
Jimmy Perry OBE & David Croft OBE
on
13th October 2007

together, focused on *Hi-de-Hi!* and in an hour long special managed to get Paul Shane, Ruth Madoc, Su Pollard, Nikki Kelly and Barry Howard to recall their camp frolics in 2003.

2007 brought the first public *Hi-de-Hi!* Reunion at the Cliff Hotel, Dovercourt organised by Jo and Tony Tarran to commemorate 20 years since recording finished on the series. Jo and Tony had grown up in the shadow of the camp, with Jo having had a Saturday job making the chalet beds for Warner's, and their memories of the BBC invading their town each Autumn ensured that they had a very special place in their hearts for *Hi-de-Hi!* The weekend in October 2007 had Jimmy Perry and David Croft as guests of honour, they unveiled a plaque in the foyer of the hotel commemorating the 'home' of the BBC for the making of the series. Cast members who were on hand for the special reunion meal were Jeffrey Holland, Su Pollard (dressed as Peggy Ollerenshaw!), Nikki Kelly, David and Tony Webb plus costume designer Mary Husband and Charles Garland. Also on hand courtesy of the Court Theatre, Tring's production of *Hi-de-Hi!* some months previously were Stephanie Bedwin as Gladys Pugh and Andy Faber as Jeffrey Fairbrother, superbly recreating the Maplin's legends culminating in the reading of a letter from Joe Maplin himself. The Marine Suite of the hotel was expertly converted into Maplin's Hawaiian Ballroom by the Tarrans and the celebrations lasted into the early hours of the morning despite a rousing rendition of *Goodnight Campers* at 11pm!

The Autumn of 2007 had Paul O'Grady celebrating *Hi-de-Hi!* on his enormously popular daytime chat show. Paul, Ruth, Jeff and Su were invited on the programme with O'Grady declaring himself a huge *Hi-de-Hi!* fan. He often presents his show dressed in a replica Maplin's Yellowcoat, and admitted to going to see the *Hi-de-Hi!* stage show at the Victoria Palace many times during its run.

A website devoted to Hi-de-Hi! and You Rang, M'Lord? was launched in May 2008 at www.hi-de-hi.net by Rob Cope, Tony & Jo Tarran, as an ongoing information service to fans of the shows and also selling exclusive merchandise.

A return to the Cliff Hotel beckoned for the 30th Anniversary Celebrations over a weekend in October 2009. Writers, fans

Paul O'Grady with Ruth Madoc (note upside down blazer badge) on his late afternoon show in 2007. Paul Shane, Jeff Holland and Su Pollard were also there.

and cast all came together to mark three decades of *Hi-de-Hi!* in addition to 21 years of *You Rang, M'Lord?* Magician Matt Grindley and former Supporting Artiste on the show, Vince Rayner, provided cabaret. Following a Saturday night of fun and frolics in the Hawaiian Ballroom, a special Sunday luncheon was held to celebrate both series attended by cast (including original Yellowcoat Terence Creasey who had flown from his home in Perth, Australia, to be there) and of course, Jimmy Perry and David Croft whose genius gave us the shows.

2010 and a major new theatre tour of the *Hi-de-Hi!* stage musical featuring Barry Howard and Nikki Kelly as Barry and Yvonne Stuart-Hargreaves with the former lead singer of The Nolans, Bernie Nolan, in the role of Peggy Ollerenshaw with popular actor and panto star Damian Williams in the role of Ted Bovis. Presented by Bruce James Productions, it is further proof that the enduring appeal of the series continues.

The laughter that *Hi-de-Hi!* gave a nation cannot be underestimated. For all the cast of the show, the programme was something special. For we viewers, it is a comedy classic that will not be forgotten and the refrain 'Ho-de-Ho!' will spring to our lips whenever the show is mentioned. Jimmy Perry and David Croft made sure Britain's finest hour was honoured in the iconic *Dad's Army*, but they were not slow in reminding us that beyond that conflict the people of Britain owed so much to the many entertainers, domestic staff and ancillary workers who worked very hard to ensure millions of families had a holiday they would remember for the rest of their lives. Although it might well be something of a social history lesson now, Hi-de-Hi! stands tall in showing a post-war Britain having the fun it truly deserved.

directorial duties whilst Charles Garland took the producer's mantle. Sherrie Hewson's return to *Coronation Street* prevented her from resuming the role of May Skinner, so in stepped Julia Deakin, a vastly experienced theatre actress who had played a lead role in the Granada TV comedy *Mother's Ruin* with Dora Bryan and Roy Barraclough. The pilot was re-recorded with Julia and given the title 'All Change' to herald the start of a full series of nine episodes which went to air in the summer of 1996. A further series of ten episodes were commissioned for 1997 but this proved to be the end of the line for the residents of Hatley Station. Erratic scheduling meant that viewers never knew when the programme would be on and this had an detrimental effect on viewing figures. The result meant that the BBC's axe fell on the show swifter than Beeching's had originally done on the little branch lines. It was truly the end of an era. The final episode 'Ton Up' saw Windsor Davies return to the Croft fold with a guest appearance as a local Mayor. Although nobody knew it at the recording of the final episode in August 1997, the last episode of *Oh Doctor Beeching!* would also be the final entry into David Croft's legendary roster of programmes for the corporation. He had written over 400 episodes of nostalgic comedy, most of them with his two long term writing partners, Jimmy Perry and Jeremy Lloyd.

Producer Charles Garland observes: "After only two series *Oh Doctor Beeching!* was dropped. Although it had, by today's standards, a huge audience of enthusiastic and loyal viewers. But it wasn't trendy enough for the new style BBC comedy, crammed with young stand-up performers writing their own material. Hard for a Head of Comedy to boast in a Soho wine bar that he'd just re-commissioned *Oh Doctor Beeching!* Even new comedy stars like Mac McDonald didn't help raise our profile, and so the curtain fell on the David Croft office. Room 4045 at BBC Television Centre itself ceased to exist too. Our little room was absorbed into an open plan office with nasty little cubicles, where everyone can hear what you say. Everyone makes mistakes but we were always able to rectify them before production started, and no-one ever needed to know. 'The Croft Office' was essentially an autonomous production company, left alone, pretty much - except when budgets were discussed - to do what we did best, make television comedy programmes. Not for ourselves or our peers, but for audiences world-wide. I think we all did very well."

David's production company Worldwide Theatrix financed a pilot programme in 2008 entitled *Here Comes The Queen* The show was co-written with Jeremy Lloyd and concerned a brother and sister who find they are sole heirs to a small European Principality. Originally conceived as a vehicle for John Inman and Mollie Sugden some years before, the idea was resurrected and filmed with Wendy Richard, Les Dennis, Ian Lavender and Phillip Madoc playing the leading roles. Although not broadcast, the production was eventually released on DVD through David's own website. Jimmy chose to retire from scriptwriting to concentrate on his autobiography.

The comedy classics that Jimmy and David have created continue to have lives beyond terrestrial or satellite repeats. The advent of the DVD disc has ensured high quality copies of all their shows are available in the High Street. Occasionally the *Hi-de-Hi!* gang are brought back together. In November 1999, a private reunion arranged by former Yellowcoat David Webb, was held at the Variety Artistes' Federation in central London where Joe Maplin's former employees got together for a night of catching up and unashamedly nostalgic good humour. *Stars Reunited*, a BBC daytime show that specialised in getting casts of popular television programmes back

The Maplin's Staff Reunion of 1999 held at the Variety Artistes Federation in central London, to celebrate 20 years since the pilot episode.

Beeching and Beyond

Following the struggle to get the final series of You Rang, M'Lord? to the screen, it looked as though David Croft's comedies were not wanted at the BBC. Although the corporation were quite happy to repeat Dad's Army in a prominent spot, any talk of new programmes from the Croft empire were quickly dispelled. David and his other writing partner Jeremy Lloyd took their latest idea Which Way To The War, following a group of soldiers lost in the Libyan desert during the Second World War, to Yorkshire Television where a pilot was made and transmitted in August 1994. Not happy that one of their most celebrated comedy writers had effectively jumped ship, the BBC were suddenly keen to woo David back and asked him if he had any ideas for future comedies. As it happened he had. David had been approached by broadcaster and sometime actor Richard Spendlove about a comedy he had devised set in 1963 when Dr. Richard Beeching's axe had fallen heavily on Britain's railway network. Spendlove had worked for 35 years for British Rail and had managed to go from Porter to Station Master within a 17 month period. David liked the sound of the proposal and figured it would work as a vehicle for his company of regular players. Spendlove and Croft took the idea to Jimmy Perry, and whilst initially interested, Jimmy backed out citing his lack of knowledge of life on the railways. Spendlove and Croft then began writing together in earnest and wrote a pilot they originally called Puff Puff Puff but was later renamed Oh Doctor Beeching!

David turned heavily to the actors he had worked most successfully with in his previous two shows with Jimmy Perry. Paul Shane was engaged to play the Porter Jack Skinner, Su Pollard became Booking Office Clerk, Ethel Schumann and Jeffrey Holland the stern new Station Master, Cecil Parkin. Further refugees from 'You Rang' came onboard: Barbara New swapped Mabel's tatty clothes to become Railway widow and village gossip Vera Plumtree. Ivor Roberts went from Foreman in Lord Meldrum's factory to Engine Driver Arnold, with Apprentice Driver Ralph played by Perry Benson, formerly Bootboy Henry. Two comedy names new to the David Croft company were hired. Coronation Street star Sherrie Hewson was to play Jack's wife May Skinner and On The Buses legend Stephen Lewis would bring shades of Blakey to his role as dour faced Signalman Harry Lambert. The rest of the cast comprised of young actors new to television: Lindsay Grimshaw (Jack and May's daughter Gloria), Paul Aspen (Ethel's dopey son Wilfred), Terry John (train guard Percy) and Tara Daniels (teenager Amy Matlock). The recording of the pilot took place at Television Centre on 12th May 1995, following location filming at Arley Station, near Kidderminster, on the beautiful Severn Valley Railway line.

Su Pollard sang the jaunty theme tune, a re-working of the Music Hall classic Oh Mister Porter, and the entire pilot was deemed a great success. Over 10 million viewers saw the much publicised return of David Croft and his strolling players, more than enough for the BBC to commission a full series the following year. Roy Gould returned to handle the

Oh Doctor Beeching! - Jeff Holland as Cecil Parkin, Paul Shane as Jack Skinner and Su Pollard as Ethel Schumann.

Scene 4.

Ivy is at the front door. Four 'theatricals' come into the hall. Ivy tells them that they are not supposed to be here yet as she's not spoken to Mr. Twelvetrees. James comes from the dining room and asks what it is that she hasn't spoken to him about. Ivy gabbles off a story about these people who had been booked into some digs by the Stage Manager of the Pier Pavilion Theatre only to find that there were cockroaches crawling up the wall… 'And,' interposes one of the group, 'It was so damp, I swear I saw a goldfish swimming across the bedroom carpet.'

James takes Ivy to one side. He is furious. 'Do I understand from all this that you have let rooms to people working at the Pier Pavilion when I expressly said that I did not want anything to do with theatricals?' He fumes.

'Yes, James' returns Ivy, biting her lip.

'I thought we were partners Ivy. I thought we discussed things.' He continues.

'You didn't discuss sacking Nora with me this morning.' She retorts. James stops and looks at her and backs down. Ivy is over the Moon. She turns back to the four theatricals who in turn ask her if she's got any grub. She tells them to go in the dining room. They move off noisily into the dining room. James tells them to keep the noise down as there are other guests to consider.

'What other guests?' asks Ivy.

'Mrs. Beaton.'

'Who?'

'The Widow, Ivy.'

James tells Ivy that it is no good, taking in theatricals will lower the tone of the whole establishment and they must think of a way of getting hold of some money. Peeved, Ivy tells him that he could always go and see Mrs. Dobson, the Butcher's widow… 'I'm sure she wouldn't refuse you a favour, seeing as how handsome you are.'

Ivy runs up the stairs in tears, leaving James to muse.

© Robin Carr and Roy Gould
(Reproduced with permission)

Ivy tells her that if it was up to her then Mabel could stay as long as she liked, but she was afraid James would not have the same attitude. Mabel begs her not to send her away. Ivy, being the kind hearted soul that she is, tells her of course she won't and that they will think of something so she can stay.

MIX TO:

Scene 2.

James returns from the bank downcast.
Ivy is finishing a conversation on the 'phone. We can hear her say 'Send them round' and that she will talk to Mr. Twelvetrees.
Replacing the receiver she greets James sheepishly and asks whether he's got the chops. He tells her he hasn't. Ivy asks what they are going to do?
'I don't know Ivy, this could mean the end of everything' says James.
'Oh it's not as bad as all that James,' says Ivy, 'We could always have bread and jam'.
'Whatever are you talking about, Ivy?' asks James.
'For tea.' answers Ivy.
James scolds her and says he's talking about the money the Bank have refused to lend him. This could mean the business folding. They would have to sell up and move off; the end of the partnership. Ivy says that she's got something to tell him.
It is at this point that James hears the clattering of a knife and fork on crockery. He peers through the glass in the door that adjoins the kitchen with the dining room and sees the back of a woman dressed in widows weeds. (Mabel in disguise). She is tucking into egg on toast.
Ivy informs James that she is Mrs. Beaton, a widow that has lost her husband. She has just booked in. James says that he will go and welcome her; Ivy tried to stop him but to no avail.

CUT TO:

Scene 3.

Mabel is gorging herself as James comes up behind her. From over her shoulder he greets her. The fork is halfway to her mouth; it freezes; the other hand quickly brings down the veil. Coming round in front of her, James asks if she is enjoying her meal. Mabel puts on her "posh voice" and says 'It h'aint 'alf bad'. Bemused James is about to investigate further when the door bell rings, and loud common voices are heard.

corner. James is baffled to know why she requires to know; 'Well,' she says, 'the one on the corner is better than the one on the hill, since the owner of the one on the hill, Mr. Dobson, died and there's more meat in his sausages'. James asks her what in heavens name she is talking about. 'Besides,' continues Ivy, 'Mr. Dobson's widow, Mrs. Dobson, thinks you're very handsome; I overheard her say so to Mrs. Turner, the Undertakers widow. James tells her that he cannot stand there all day listening to tittle-tattle overheard from widow-women. He goes.

Ivy sits with her back to the window and starts to thumb through Mrs. Beaton.

A wrinkled face appears at the window. It is Mabel, the Char from the Meldrum household. She sees Ivy and her eyes brighten. She taps on the window; Ivy stops reading and looks up; she decides she's hearing things and goes back to her reading; Mabel taps again, Ivy looks up, shrugs and goes back to her book. Mabel is now determined and knocks harder; the pain of glass falls out and crashes into the sink; in horror Mabel ducks down. Shocked, Ivy goes to the sink and examines the broken glass; she peers into the hole in the window;, at the same time Mabel comes from below on the other side; the two of them are by now nose to nose; they both jump back in fright. Mabel comes back to the window and peers in again.

'Is that you Ivy?' she asks. Ivy sheepishly returns and recognising her, greets her through the glass. Mabel asks if she can come in. Ivy lets her in the back door.

'What are you doing here?' Ivy asks. Mabel tells her that her old man has died.

'He was standing at the bar in the Red Lion when he ordered drinks all round. Well the Landlord knew something was up from that second. Anyway they got the round in and when the Guv'nor told him the amount he wanted, my old man keeled over and snuffed it.'

'That's awful.' says Ivy.

'It gets worse Ivy', says Mabel, 'When they searched through his pockets, they found he didn't have a farthing on him. Now the Landlord's wife is livid 'cos the till's two pound five and three pence halfpenny down on the takings, and the Landlords livid 'cos he's getting an ear 'ole bashing from his old lady for allowing my old man to buy a round in the first place when he knows that he's never paid for a drink in his entire life.'

Mabel goes on to tell Ivy that she's had to run away from London because the creditors are after her and the only person she felt she could turn to was Ivy. (It transpires that Ivy has been writing to her every week with news of the Boarding House).

James and Ivy

Following the end of You Rang, M'Lord?, efforts were made to continue the saga of three of its most popular characters Just as *Upstairs, Downstairs* had spawned its own spin off following the Footman and the Maid, *Thomas And Sarah,* so Robin Carr and Roy Gould tried to interest the BBC in a spin-off from 'You Rang' entitled *James and Ivy* which would follow Lord Meldrum's Footman and Maid into their seaside Boarding House venture that they had joined together to run at the end of the final episode. Alas the BBC were not interested in continuing the characters and so the project came to nought. However several pages of an outline were completed by Carr and Gould so here is a little glimpse of what might have been for James, Ivy and an unexpected visitor from the Meldrum household…

PILOT EPISODE: MONEY TALKS

We open the series in Nineteen Twenty-Nine, in a Boarding House situated on the front at Seabourne, a typical seaside town built in the Victorian era.

JAMES TWELVETREES and IVY TEASDALE who, up until eighteen months previous had been Footman and Maid, respectively, at the London house of Lord George Meldrum, now run 'Palmerston House', a Boarding House for respectable clientele.

SCENE 1.

James is in the kitchen going over the books as Ivy enters. She asks where Nora the Cook is; James tells her that he has had to dispense with her services. Ivy is cross with him for not consulting her first as they are meant to be partners in this venture. James explains that the books are not balancing and that he had to let her go, besides which, he tells her, she is a kind hearted soul and he knew that if he asked her first, she would never have agreed to get rid of Nora. Ivy concedes the point. Ivy then wonders that if they do not have a Cook who will do all the cooking; James tells her that she will. Ivy protests that she can't even boil an egg let alone cater for 20 guests. James takes down from the shelf a copy of Mrs. Beaton's fine book on cookery; besides which if trade went on the way it has there would be no-one to cook for anyway.

Putting on his coat James tells Ivy he is just off to see the Bank Manager to ask whether he will loan the money required to continue in business. If he is successful he tells her then he might consider popping into the Butchers to buy a chop each for their tea. Ivy asks if the Butchers he's referring to is the one up the hill or the one on the investments for Lord Meldrum. George's wealth is now seriously depleted. Agatha tells him that she caught Sir Ralph performing an occult ceremony, George is then convinced he is cursed. News then arrives that the crop at his Lordship's rubber plantation in Malaya has been blighted by the dreaded Bang Go Khan Beetle. Ivy is sent to fetch the Bishop for an exorcism. Fearing poverty beckons, Poppy is forced to accept Jerry's proposal of marriage. Realising his brother's hold over him is at an end, Teddy finally declares his love for Rose.

Guest cast:

Jerry	John D. Collins
Rose	Amanda Bellamy
Mr. Barnes	Ivor Roberts
Jock	Stuart McGugan
Mr. Foster	Michael Lees
Secretary	Fred Bryant
Robin, Chaplain	Robbie Barnett

Featured music: *Louise* (Michael Knowles unaccompanied)

26. WELL, THERE YOU ARE THEN...!

Studio: D Elstree, Friday 20th November 1992.

TX: Saturday 4th April 1993 at 6.10pm.

Duration: 49 mins 31 secs   Audience rating: 7.50 million

With the American Stock Market crash and the ravages of the Bang Go Khan Beetle at the factory, George is facing financial ruin. Christie's arrive at the house as the Meldrum's are forced to discreetly sell some of their antiques. Alf, James and Ivy worry for the future and Mrs. Lipton announces her marriage to Constable Wilson. A lifeline arrives in the shape of Lady Lavender's jewels. Cissy thinks she knows a way of keeping the factory open. Agatha delivers a devastating blow to George and Madge finally realises that Teddy has no intention of marrying her. By 1928, the lives of everyone have been irrevocably changed…

Guest cast:

Jerry	John D. Collins
Jock	Stuart McGugan
Mr. Barnes	Ivor Roberts
Mr. Foster	Michael Lees
Rose	Amanda Bellamy
Agnes	Suzy Cooper
The Jolly Follies	David Webb
	Tony Webb
	Sarah Jones-Parry
Pianist	Roy Moore
Christie's Man	Gordon Peters

Featured music: *Nellie Dean* (played by Roy Moore), *Chick Chick Chick Chicken*, (Played by Roy Moore, performed by the cast) *Jolly Follies* (composed and played by Roy Moore, performed by the cast)

Series Four Credits: Studio Warm Up FELIX BOWNESS. Costume Designer MARY HUSBAND. Make-Up Designer JILL HAGGER. Properties Buyer PAULINE SEAGER. Graphic Designer ANDY CARROLL. Visual Effects ROGER TURNER. Camera Supervisor JOHN VINCENT. Resource Co-ordinator ANDREW BREAKS. Videotape Editor STEVE JAMISON. Visual Effects ROGER TURNER. Vision Mixer HILARY WEST. Assistant Floor Managers BECCY FAWCETT, STEVE DUNN. Production Assistant PIPPA SMITH. Production Secretary KATIE TYRRELL. Sound Supervisor MICHAEL McCARTHY. Lighting Director DUNCAN BROWN. Production Managers JEREMY CONNOR, CHARLES GARLAND. Designer GWEN EVANS. Directed by ROY GOULD. Produced by DAVID CROFT.

Guest cast:

Penelope Barrington-Blake	Sorel Johnson
Viscount Dudley Thetford	Christopher Luscombe
Lady Marigold	Nicola Van Dam
Earl of Swaffham	Richard Vernon
Dobson, the tailor	Jeffrey Gardiner
Mr. Pearson	Felix Bowness
Rupert	Eli Woods
Parrot Voice	Jeffrey Holland (OOV)

Featured music: *Boys Of The Old Brigade, Bird Songs At Eventide* (vocals: the cast, organist: Charles Hamel-Cooke), *He's A Jolly Good Fellow* (sung by cast)

The entire House of Meldrum attend the funeral of Lady Lavender's parrot, Captain.

23. COME TO THE BALL

Studio: D Elstree, Friday 9th October 1992.

TX: Saturday 3rd April 1993 at 8.30pm.

Duration: 49 mins 25 secs   Audience rating: 9.52 million

Lord Meldrum decides to inspect the servant's quarters, starting with Mrs. Lipton's room. Mabel has found a purse in the street containing £5, and wonders what to do with her good fortune. Sir Ralph throws a lavish ball for the servants. Ivy wonders if James will consent to escort her. Miss Poppy however has plans to keep James all to herself for the evening. Teddy is alarmed to find that Madge has forgiven him for his indiscretions.

Guest cast:

Rose	Amanda Bellamy
Selfridge	Hugh Lloyd
Lady Hampshire's Maid	Gillian Tompkins
Mr. Perkins	Norman Mitchell
Musicians at Ball	Selwyn Fitcher, Cyril Bass, Derek Raymond, Peter Griggs, Len Rudd, Eric Courtney

N.B. Copies distributed for overseas showings include a small section of dialogue cut from the UK broadcast when Lord Meldrum inspects Ivy's room.

Featured music: *Yes Sir, That's My Baby, I Wonder Where My Baby Is Tonight, When You And I Were 17, I Love My Baby (My Baby Loves Me), Sleepy Time Gal* (performed by Roy Moore and musicians)

24. THE TRUTH REVEALED

Studio: D Elstree, Friday 23rd October 1992.

TX: Saturday 10th April 1993 at 6.10pm.

Duration: 48 mins 11 secs   Audience rating: 7.73 million

Sir Ralph sacks Selfridge, his drunken Butler. In a fit of peak, Selfridge tells him of the long standing affair between his wife and George Meldrum. Selfridge rushes to the Meldrum house and reveals to the servants the turn of events. Alf and James know of Ralph's reputation and are sure that he will try and harm his Lordship. When Sir Ralph invites George down to his country house for the weekend, Ralph's strange behaviour is just a smokescreen for his dark intentions towards his old friend…

Guest cast:

Selfridge	Hugh Lloyd
Rose	Amanda Bellamy

Featured music: *Arrival at Ralph's, Night Music, The Chase, Link Music* (all specially composed by Roy Moore)

25. FALL OF THE HOUSE OF MELDRUM

Studio: D Elstree, Friday 6th November 1992.

TX: Saturday 17th April 1993 at 8.30pm.

Duration: 50 mins 3 secs   Audience rating: 7.35 million

The Star Spangled Finance Corporation shares have plummeted. The company dealt with all the American

20. A DAY IN THE COUNTRY

Studio: D Elstree, Friday 29th November 1991.

TX: Sunday 22nd December 1991 at 7.15pm.

Duration: 49 mins 15 secs   Audience rating: 9.12 million

When Lord Meldrum learns that Sir Ralph and Lady Agatha are taking their servants on a day out to Peabody Hall, he arranges a similar trip for his own servants with a view to spending some time in the bushes with Agatha. Mabel wonders if a casual worker who works from 7.30am to 11.30pm is included in the trip. With Constable Wilson driving the charabanc, His Lordship instructs that the servants must sit with the family. Peabody Hall proves to be a day of great reflection for the staff and the family.

Guest cast:

Selfridge	Hugh Lloyd
Chauffeurs	Fred Tomlinson, John Maxim senior
Maid	Yolande Palfrey

Featured music: *The Smoke Goes Up The Chimney* (sung by cast), *Old Folks At Home* (sung in vision by Fred Tomlinson and John Maxim Senior who also played harmonica), *Charabanc Holiday* (specially composed by Roy Moore)

Series Three Production credits: Studio Warm Up FELIX BOWNESS. Music composed by ROY MOORE. Costume Designer MARY HUSBAND. Make-Up Designer JILL HAGGER. Properties Buyers JAYNE LIBOTTE, NICK BARNETT. Graphic Designer ANDY CARROLL. Visual Effects Designer COLIN MAPSON. Camera Supervisor JOHN VINCENT. VT Editor PETER BIRD. Resource Co-ordinator ANDREW BREAKS. Vision Mixer HILARY WEST. Production Assistant CHRISTINE MELLOR. Assistant Floor Managers JEREMY CONNOR, BECCY FAWCETT. Studio Sound MICHAEL McCARTHY. Lighting Director DUNCAN BROWN. Production Manager CHARLES GARLAND. Designer GWEN EVANS. Directed by ROY GOULD. Produced by DAVID CROFT.

SERIES FOUR

Location filming dates: 27th July - 13th August 1992.

21. YES SIR, THAT'S MY BABY

Studio: D Elstree, Friday 18th September 1992.

TX: Saturday 20th March 1993 at 8.30pm.

Duration: 47 mins 58 secs   Audience rating: 7.85 million

The Bishop is preaching the deadly sins during Sunday Service. It's Self Denial Sunday and the Meldrum's are sitting down to meat and fish paste sandwiches whilst the servants make sure a nice roast is on the table downstairs. Miss Cissy leads the house into helping out at the local soup kitchen for the poor. Teddy is still trying to escape the romantic clutches of Madge Cartwright. This time Alf thinks he had the perfect solution. He traces all of Teddy's illegitimate children and brings them to the house to confront Madge.

Guest cast:

Hortense Anstruther	Angela Easterling
UWP Man (Osbert)	Peter Whitbread
Chinaman	Basil Ho Yen

Choir in Church during scene 1 from Norwich Cathedral. Director Neil Taylor.

Featured music: *Praise My Soul* (sung by cast and choir), Incidental organ voluntary (Charles Hamel-Cooke)

22. REQUIEM FOR A PARROT

Studio: D Elstree, Friday 25th September 1992.

TX: Saturday 27th March 1993 at 8.30pm.

Duration: 48 mins 14 secs   Audience rating: 7.93 million

George is still determined that Teddy will be sent to Malaya, and he is fitted for tropical outfits from the Army & Navy Store. When Alf hears that the Earl of Swaffham's son Dudley is unable to provide the family with an heir, he sets about surreptitiously offering the services of James for the task… Lady Lavender's parrot Captain has died. The family feel obliged to attend the bizarre funeral arrangements that Lavender has organised for her feathered friend. When Ivy discovers it is James birthday, she buys him real pewter cufflinks. But once again Miss Poppy thwarts Ivy's kindness.

Guest cast:

Miss Potter	Judith Fellows
Man	Norman Bacon
Dickie Metcalfe	Robin Lermitte
Parrot Voice	Jeffrey Holland (OOV)

17. MEET THE WORKERS

Studio: D Elstree, Friday 25th October 1991.

TX: Sunday 1st December 1991 at 7.15pm.

Duration: 49 mins 25 secs   Audience rating: 8.87 million

Lord Meldrum is intent on being invited onto the Board of Governors of the BBC. He needs to show he is in touch with the ordinary man in the street. To prove this he invites Jock, Barnes and Foster from the United Jack Rubber Company to dinner. Mrs. Lipton is instructed to provide fish and chips and bottles of brown ale. His workers have a more lavish evening in mind. Miss Poppy announces her engagement to Dickie Metcalfe. Alf suspects he may be a confidence trickster. Lady Lavender invites the servants to the wedding of her parrots.

Guest cast:

Dickie Metcalfe	Robin Lermitte
Jock	Stuart McGugan
Mr. Barnes	Ivor Roberts
Mr. Foster	Michael Lees
Parrot Voice	Jeffrey Holland (OOV)

Featured music: *Blue Heaven* from *The Desert Song* (Edith Day, Harry Welshman with the Drury Lane Theatre Orchestra), *The Foggy Foggy Dew* (vocal: Frank Williams, harmonium: Roy Moore)

18. GRETNA GREEN OR BUST

Studio: D Elstree, Friday 8th November 1991.

TX: Sunday 8th December 1991 at 7.15pm.

Duration: 48 mins 33 secs   Audience rating: 8.41 million

The family go to Covent Garden to see the ballet. When Poppy tells Agatha the name of her fiancé, it turns out that she has been blackmailed by Dickie Metcalfe in the past. Poppy secretly elopes with Metcalfe, they set off at dawn to drive to Gretna Green, planning to get married. When the rest of the house learns of Metcalfe's past they follow in hot pursuit to try and save Poppy from the clutches of the bounder.

Guest cast:

Dickie Metcalfe	Robin Lermitte
Rose	Amanda Bellamy
Mr. Pearson	Felix Bowness
Landlord	Bryan Burdon
Petrol attendant	Peter Simmo
Osbert	Peter Whitbread
Hortense Anstruther	Angela Easterling

Clip of Bolshoi Ballet 200th season *The Nutcracker* obtained from Film Research & Production Services Ltd, London.

Featured music: *Dance of The Snow Flakes* from *The Nutcracker* by Tchaikovsky, *Bang Goes The Bride* (specially composed by Roy Moore)

19. THE NIGHT OF RECKONING

Studio: D Elstree, Friday 22nd November 1991

TX: Sunday 15th December 1991 at 7.15pm, BBC 1

Duration: 49 mins 15 secs   Audience rating: 10.19 million

Mabel's husband has pawned the bed clothes and has been using the rent money to drink at the Red Lion. If she doesn't pay the rent arrears by Friday she will be evicted. Lady Agatha invites James for an interview to be the new Butler for Sir Ralph. Agatha has an ulterior motive and when Poppy finds out about the job offer, she delivers Agatha an ultimatum. Lady Lavender finally traces Captain Dolby who proves to be just as eccentric as Lavender. In a desperate bid to get Madge off his back, Teddy is persuaded to spend the night with her and prove himself to be a flop in the bedroom…

Guest cast:

Captain Dolby	Maurice Denham
Maid	Yolande Palfrey
Hortense Anstruther	Angela Easterling
Jerry	John D. Collins

Featured music: *The Red Flag* (sung by the cast)

SERIES THREE

Location filming dates: 27th July - 14th August 1991.

14. PLEASE LOOK AFTER THE ORPHANS

Studio: D Elstree, Friday 9th September 1991.

TX: Sunday 10th November 1991 at 7.15pm.

Duration: 49 mins 15 secs

Alf is being pestered by Mrs. Lipton to finalise his divorce so he gets his old Music Hall partner, Myrtle, to pose as Mrs. Stokes. Meanwhile he has a brain wave to make some money by fooling Mrs. Lipton into baking some cakes she thinks are destined for the local Orphanage. Sir Ralph enlists George's help in secretly following Agatha whom he suspects is up to no good.

Guest cast:

Myrtle	Barbara Windsor
Miss Potter	Judith Fellows
Mr. Pearson	Felix Bowness
Rose	Amanda Bellamy
Young Man	Brogden Miller
Penelope	Sorel Johnson
Jerry	John D. Collins
Parrot voice	Jeffrey Holland (OOV)

Featured music: *Let's All Go Down The Strand* and *Boiled Beef And Carrots* (BBC archive), *Sunny - Who* (Binne Hale, Jack Buchanan with the Novelty Orchestra)

15. CURRENT AFFAIRS

Studio: D Elstree, Friday 20th September 1991.

TX: Sunday 17th November 1991 at 7.15pm.

Duration: 49 mins 2 secs

With Sir Ralph staying in the guest room, Ivy is confused when she takes up the breakfast trays and Lady Agatha seems to be taking turns to sleep with both her husband and Lord Meldrum! Mrs. Lipton is hard at work baking for the Orphanage. Is it a complete coincidence that The Sunshine Pantry finds itself a new supplier of pastries and cakes from the Stokes Cake Company? Myrtle arrives at the house pretending to be Mrs. Stokes.

Guest cast:

Penelope	Sorel Johnson
Jerry	John D. Collins
Miss Potter	Judith Fellows
Percy	Joseph Swash
Dorothy	Karen Salt
Myrtle	Barbara Windsor
Assistant in Sunshine Pantry	Kay Schell
Customer in Sunshine Pantry	Roy Stephens
Children in Kitchen	
Ben Farrer, Daniel Costelloe, Sophie Flinder, Luke Kent	

Barbara Windsor makes two brief appearances as Myrtle, who Alf Stokes persuades to act as his estranged wife.

16. MRS. LIPTON'S NASTY TURN

Studio: D Elstree, Friday 11th October 1991.

TX: Sunday 24th November 1991 at 7.15pm.

Duration: 49 mins 25 secs

Mrs. Lipton has finally lost her temper with Alf, and thrown his Lordship's crockery at him. With 14 plates, 3 saucers and 5 cups to be paid for Blanche thinks she is going to get the sack. Things go from bad to worse when Lady Lavender sends for the Cook… George finds out that his daughter Cissy is standing for election - unfortunately it is for the United Workers Party. Standing by her principles, Cissy packs her bags and leaves the house. Miss Poppy introduces her new boyfriend, Dickie Metcalfe. James and Ivy visit the Sunshine Pantry where Ivy learns the truth about the Stokes Cake Company.

12. STRANGER IN THE NIGHT

Studio: D Elstree, Friday 16th November 1990.

TX: Sunday 16th December 1990 at 7.15pm.

Duration: 49 mins 42 secs   Audience rating: 8.54 million

James is embarrassed when his father arrives at the house on the run from the Police. Far from being the lay-Preacher that James made him out to be, he is a Petty criminal on the run from both the Police and a gang of robbers. The servants decide to hide him until they can arrange for him to flee the country, but can they keep the fugitive out of sight from the Meldrums?

Guest cast:

Dad Twelvetrees	Michael Robbins
Seaman	Buster Waeland
Captain	Harry Landis
Lady Lavender's double	Denise Ryan
Parrot voice	Jeffrey Holland (OOV)

Michael Robbins as James Twelvetrees' father, a petty criminal wanted by the Police.

13. ROYAL FLUSH

Studio: D Elstree, Friday 30th November 1990.

TX: Sunday 23rd December 1990 at 7.15pm.

Duration: 49 mins 15 secs   Audience rating: 9.12 million

Excitement runs through the household when it is announced that the King Boris and Queen Isabella of Dalmatia are coming to dinner. Miss Poppy upsets Mrs. Lipton when she tells her that Fortnum And Mason will be doing the catering. In addition Noel Coward is expected to join them after the opening night of his new play. George decides to invite Sir Fred Kendal, owner of Kendal's Kut-Price Kemists, as he is keen for him to stock products from the Union Jack Rubber Company!

Guest cast:

Jerry	John D. Collins
Voice in Sauna	Don Smoothey (OOV)
Noel Coward	Guy Siner
Robin, Chaplain	Robbie Barnett
Penelope	Sorel Johnson
Sir Fred Kendal	Geoffrey Hughes
Lady Flo Kendal	Hilda Braid
King Boris	Davy Kaye
Queen Isabella	Deddie Davies
Count Max Zarkoff	Barry Howard
Mr. Pearson	Felix Bowness (edited out of broadcast)

Featured music: *The Girlfriend* (from the LP The Great British Dance Bands Play The Music of Rodgers and Hart), *Long Live Dalmatia* (music by Roy Moore, words by Perry and Croft), *Samson's Song* from Samson and Delilah (vocal: Yvonne Marsh, piano: Roy Moore), *Narcissus and The Lost Chord* (Roy Moore on piano)

Series Two Production credits: Studio Warm Up FELIX BOWNESS. Music composed by ROY MOORE. Choreographer KENN OLDFIELD. Costume Designer MARY HUSBAND. Costume Assistant LIZ NICHOLLS. Make-Up Designer JILL HAGGER. Properties Buyers GILLIAN FARR, HILARY NASH. Graphic Designer ANDY CARROLL. Visual Effects Designer PERRY BRAHAN. Camera Supervisor JOHN VINCENT. VT Editor PETER BIRD. Technical Co-ordinators RAY HIDER, STEVE LOWRY, PHILIP DEAN, PAUL THACKRAY, MIKE ENDERSBY. Vision Mixer HILARY WEST. Film Cameraman BARRY McCANN. Film Sound CHRIS KING. Film Editor MIKE ROBOTHAM. Production Assistant CHRISTINE MELLOR. Assistant Floor Managers NICK WOOD, ANNA WACHSTEIN. Studio Sound MICHAEL McCARTHY. Studio Lighting DUNCAN BROWN, ALAN JEFFERY. Production Managers ROY GOULD, CHARLES GARLAND. Designer GWEN EVANS. Directed by DAVID CROFT (except 'The Wounds of War' Directed by DAVID CROFT and ROY GOULD). Produced by DAVID CROFT.

Guest cast:

Girl	Eve Bland
Jock	Stuart McGugan
Jim	Nicholas Pickard
Bert	Peter Simmo
Elizabeth	Beccy Booth
Mr. Foster	Michael Lees
Sergeant	Ben Aris
Stanley Baldwin	Patrick Blackwell

Featured music: *Miss Annabelle Lee* (Jack Smith and The Whispering Orchestra)

9. MONEY TALKS

Studio: D Elstree, Friday 5th October 1990.

TX: Sunday 25th November 1990 at 7.15pm.

Duration: 48 mins 28 secs   Audience rating: 9.26 million

Eccentric Lady Lavender throws her money out of the window and into the street when an organ grinder comes to play at the house. There is a frenzy as staff and passers-by race to retrieve the fortune. Alf sees an opportunity to get rich quick and manages to smuggle some of the cash into his pockets and deposit it into an old vase that is stood outside Lavender's room. But the problem is, how to get the money out again?

Guest cast:

Organ-grinder	Paddy Joyce
Rough man	Harry Jones
1st Woman	Jae Jemain
2nd Woman	Jane Goodall
Robin, Chaplain	Robbie Barnett

Featured music: *All The Nice Girls Love A Sailor, Goodbye Dolly I Must Leave You, The Honeysuckle and the Bee, The Man Who Broke the Bank at Monte Carlo, Charmaine, Antonio and his Ice Cream Cart* (recorded on street piano on location)

10. THE MELDRUM VASES

Studio: D, Elstree Friday 19th October 1990.

TX: Sunday 2nd December 1990 at 7.15pm.

Duration: 49 mins 15 secs

Alf has hidden some money in one of his Lordship's vases. He is working out how to get the money out, when His Lordship decides to donate the vase with the money in - plus two identical vases - to the Bishop's charity auction for Distressed Gentlewomen. He will have to buy the vases at the auction to keep hold of the stolen cash. Alf works quickly to con some money out of Mrs. Lipton she thinks will help finalise Alf's divorce. James and Ivy guess what is going on and follow Alf to the auction.

Guest cast:

Jerry	John D. Collins
Robin, Chaplain	Robbie Barnett
Jerry	John D. Collins
Penelope	Sorel Johnson
Parrot voice	Jeffrey Holland (OOV)
Photographer	Joe Phillips
Maid	Susan Goode

Featured music: *Easy To Remember* and *Mountain Greenery* (from LP 'The Great British Dance Bands Play The Music of Rodgers and Hart')

11. THE WOUNDS OF WAR

Studio: D Elstree, Friday 2nd November 1990.

TX: Sunday 9th December 1990 at 7.15pm.

Duration: 49 mins 53 secs

To protect his employer, Alf tells Sir Ralph that Meldrum was wounded in the artillery. Ivy is over the moon when James agrees to take her to the pictures. Mrs. Lipton is convinced that Alf's divorce is being held up by his wife.

Guest cast:

Rose	Amanda Bellamy
Young man	Brogden Miller
Barker	Peter Fontaine
Cinema Usherette	Carole Hancock
Parrot voice	Jeffrey Holland (OOV)

Extract from the film 'The Ring' (1927) directed by Alfred Hitchcock shown on cinema screen, with music specially composed and played by Roy Moore

Featured music: *Aint She Sweet* (played on ukelele and sung by Jeffrey Holland and Susie Brann), *What'll I Do* (Su Pollard unaccompanied)

Guest cast:

Goblin man	Mike Carnell
Mr. Fisher	Iain Mitchell
Aubrey Wilmsloe	Stuart Harrison
Francesca Dyke-Hardie	Harriet Eastcott
Hamish Kintyre	Philip Fox
Lucille Penhalligan	Eluned Hawkins
Jerry	John D. Collins
Penelope Barrington-Blake	Sorel Johnson
Lady Maud Sainsbury	Aimee Delamain
Emma, Maid	Jackie D. Broad
Parrot voice	Jeffrey Holland (OOV)

Series One Production credits: Studio Warm Up FELIX BOWNESS. Choreographer KENN OLDFIELD. Costume Designer MARY HUSBAND. Make-Up Designer JILL HAGGER. Properties Buyer ROGER WILLIAMS. Graphic Designer BILL WILSON. Camera Supervisor JOHN VINCENT. Videotape Editor PETE BIRD. Technical Co-ordinators TONY MUTIMER, RAY HIDER. Vision Mixer HILARY WEST. Film Cameraman BARRY McCANN. Film Sound JOHN PARRY. Film Editor MIKE ROBOTHAM. Production Assistant PENNY THOMPSON. Assistant Floor Managers TAMARA HENRY, WILLIAM CAMPBELL. Studio Sound MICHAEL McCARTHY. Studio Lighting DUNCAN BROWN. Production Managers ROY GOULD, SIMON SPENCER. Designer DAVID BUCKINGHAM. Produced and Directed by DAVID CROFT.

Kenneth Connor appeared in two episodes as Lady Lavender's psychiatrist. Unfortunately his scene was cut from 'Love and Money'.

SERIES TWO

Location filming dates: 23rd July - 4th August 1990.

7. LABOUR OR LOVE

Studio: D Elstree, Friday 7th September 1990.

TX: Sunday 11th November 1990 at 7.15pm.

Duration: 48 mins 53 secs   Audience rating: 9.55 million

Lord Meldrum gives Teddy an ultimatum - marry Madge Cartwright or be sent to work in his factory. Teddy thinks it's a bluff but finds that his brother means every word. Alf discovers that Lady Lavender has got money hidden under the bed and schemes to relieve her of the burden. Lord Meldrum sends for a Psychiatrist to assess Lady Lavender, but Professor Von Mannheim seems more interested in Teddy's problems.

Guest cast:

Rose	Amanda Bellamy
Professor Heinrich Von Mannheim	Kenneth Connor
Man (ext. Rubber company)	Patrick Burke
Mr. Foster, Manager	Michael Lees
Jock	Stuart McGugan
Jim	Nicholas Pickard
Mr. Barnes, Foreman	Ivor Roberts
Cyril, Worker	Don Smoothey

8. TROUBLE AT MILL

Studio: D Elstree, Friday 21st September 1990.

Transmission: Sunday 18th November 1990 at 7.15pm.

Duration: 49 mins 15 secs   Audience rating: 8.86 million

Mr. Teddy is causing havoc at the Union Jack Rubber Company. When he presses his attentions on the factory girls, the entire workforce walk out and Teddy has to be locked into the office for his own protection. His Lordship is called to the Factory to sort out the problem. However, the clock is ticking away as the Prime Minister is expected to dinner. It falls to Alf to negotiate with the workers in order to stop a riot and get His Lordship back home in time for his dinner date.

should benefit from Ivy's windfall. In another twist Lavender then instructs the shares be left to Alf himself…

Guest cast:

Mr. Franklin, the Solicitor	John Clegg
Parrot voice	Jeffrey Holland (OOV)

4. LOVE AND MONEY

Studio: D Elstree, Friday 27th October & Friday 3rd November 1989.

TX: Sunday 28th January 1990 at 7.15pm.

Duration: 49 mins 20 secs

Mr. Franklin, the Solicitor, suggests to Lord Meldrum that he has Lady Lavender assessed by a psychiatrist in order to stop her giving away her shares in the Union Jack Rubber Company. When James finds out Lavender has agreed to give her shares to Alf, he is determined that his old sparring partner will not benefit from the old lady. Ivy threatens to leave if Mr. Teddy doesn't stop pestering her. Mrs. Lipton suggests they swap rooms in order to shame Teddy if he tries a visit to Ivy's room in the dead of night. Cissy holds a fancy dress party which means that both staff and family will have to be on their best behaviour. However when Sir Ralph turns up Ivy puts her foot in it…

Guest cast:

Mr. Pearson	Felix Bowness
Jerry	John D. Collins
Penelope Barrington-Blake	Sorel Johnson
Parrot voice	Jeffrey Holland (OOV)

TRIVIA: Kenneth Connor appeared as Professor Heinrich Von Mannheim in this episode but due to the episode over running its allotted time his appearance had to be edited out.

Featured music: *Don't Bring Lulu* (Jan Garber and his Orchestra), *The Charleston* (The Savoy Orpheans), *If You Knew Susie* (Jack Shilkret and his Orchestra)

5. FAIR SHARES

Studio: D Elstree, Friday 10th & Friday 17th November 1989.

TX: Sunday 4th February 1990 at 7.15pm.

Duration: 49 mins 36 secs   Audience rating: 12.32 million

The aftermath of Cissy's fancy dress party is still being felt the next morning. Ivy is at the centre of the scandal with Sir Ralph declaring she has told him that he saw Lady Agatha in bed with Lord Meldrum. Alf sees the dilemma as being a way to start a bidding war between Meldrum and Shawcross for the shares he has been promised by Lady Lavender. When Alf visits Mr. Fisher, the Pawn Broker, he discovers that Fisher still has the emerald from Teddy's ring that he had pawned after the war. Meanwhile Lady Lavender has given Henry a piece of paper…

Guest cast:

Jerry	John D. Collins
Mr. Fisher, Pawnbroker	Iain Mitchell
Radio announcer	Colin Ward-Lewis (OOV)
Telephone operator	Eluned Hawkins (OOV)
Milkman	Lee Ryan

Featured music: *Love Divine, All Loves Excelling* (London Crusader Choir), *Pale Hands I Love* (Michael Knowles unaccompanied)

6. BEG, BORROW OR STEAL

Studio: D Elstree, Friday 24th November & Friday 1st December 1989.

TX: Sunday 11th February 1990 at 7.15pm.

Duration: 49 mins 56 secs   Audience rating: 9.40 million

With Lady Lavender's parrot having eaten the shares certificate, Alf has seen his windfall disappear. Mr. Fisher is blackmailing Alf into letting him come and burgle the Meldrum's safe. When Cissy arranges for a poetry evening with Aubrey Wilmsloe and his Singerfone, it seems the perfect opportunity for Fisher to rifle the safe. Teddy thinks he has arranged a clandestine meeting with Rose, Madge Cartwright's Maid, but things don't go to plan. As events spiral out of control, Ivy has to make a confession to James in order to try and save the day. But has she done the right thing?

Featured music: *Pack Up Your Troubles* and *Battle Music* (Roy Moore on piano), *Ragtime Cowboy Joe*, *Home on the Range*, *Moonstruck*, *Skaters Waltz* (Band Of The Life Guards, conducted by Roy Moore)

Pilot Production credits: Period banquet etiquette advisor IVOR SPENCER. Poodles supplied by ROBERTS' BROTHERS CIRCUS

Pilot Show Production credits Costume Designer MARY HUSBAND. Make-Up Designer JILL HAGGER. Properties Buyer PAULINE SEAGER. Graphic Designer JANE WYATT. Visual Effects Designer COLIN MAPSON. Camera Supervisor JOHN VINCENT. VT Editor CHRIS WADSWORTH. Vision Mixer ANGELA BEVERIDGE. Film Cameraman MAX SAMETT. Film Sound JOHN PARRY. Film Editor MIKE ROBOTHAM. Production Assistant BERNADETTE DARNELL. Assistant Floor Manager SHARON PORTER. Studio Sound MICHAEL MCCARTHY. Studio Lighting DUNCAN BROWN. Production Managers ROY GOULD, FRANCESCA GILPIN. Designers DAVID BUCKINGHAM, PAUL CROSS. Produced and Directed by DAVID CROFT.

A BBC Production in association with the Severn Network, Australia.

For overseas sales and DVD releases, BBC Worldwide issued a re-edited version running at 49 mins 3 secs. The major trim was right at the beginning of the episode which opens in a projection room of an old cinema during 1918 showing silent news reel footage of the First World War. A piano player is accompanying the footage with *Pack Up Your Troubles*. Captions appear in between the footage on the big screen; "THE VICTORIOUS ALLIED ARMIES ADVANCING ON ALL FRONTS", "The battlecry is FORWARD FORWARD TO VICTORY!" This then cuts to a longer edit of the French battlefields sequence where we find James and Alf on the front line. The sequence in the music hall with Alf and Ivy is the subject of some cuts as is the dressing room scene.

SERIES ONE

Location filming dates: 20th - 29th September 1989.

2. THE PHANTOM SIGN WRITER

Studio: D Elstree, Thursday 5th and Friday 6th October 1989.

TX: Sunday 14th January 1990 at 7.15pm.

Duration: 49 mins 24 secs   Audience rating: 10.52 million

It's Ivy's first full day in the service of Lord Meldrum. Her first duty is to deliver the breakfast trays. However, there seems to be some confusion when delivering Lady Agatha's breakfast. There is a lump in her bed. Could it be his Lordship? Mabel is late for work and has thru'pence deducted from her wages whilst Alf is getting very friendly with the Cook, Mrs. Lipton. Agatha warns George that her husband Sir Ralph suspects their affair. Later in the day The Bishop comes to call. It is discovered that someone has written an obscenity on the side of his Lordship's Rolls Royce. When The Bishop wants to use the vehicle, the servants have to be very quick witted to make sure he doesn't see the slur on their employer.

Guest cast:

Mr. Pearson, the Grocer	Felix Bowness
Parrot voice	Jeffrey Holland (OOV)

3. A DEED OF GIFT

Studio: D Elstree, Friday 13th & Friday 20th October 1989.

TX: Sunday 21st January 1990 at 7.15pm.

Duration: 49 mins 6 secs   Audience rating: 10.61 million

Ivy is growing increasingly worried about Mr. Teddy's efforts to get into her room late at night. She also finds out that Lady Lavender has a peculiar trait with her food… Miss Poppy enjoys flirting with James Twelvetrees, and Ivy is in trouble for wearing make-up put on her by Miss Cissy. Lady Lavender secretly sends for her Solicitor, Mr. Franklin. It turns out she intends to gift her controlling shares in the Union Jack Rubber Company to Ivy. Lord Meldrum is incensed, but the family find they have to be very nice to their Maid just in case she should become a share-holder in the Rubber Company. When Alf finds out about Lady Lavender's plan, he is determined he

Episode Guide

All episodes written by Jimmy Perry and David Croft

TX = original tranmission dates (UK) OOV = out of view

All episodes originally screened on BBC1

Regular cast:

Alfred Stokes, the Butler	PAUL SHANE
James Twelvetrees, the Footman	JEFFREY HOLLAND
Ivy Teasdale, the Maid	SU POLLARD
Lord George Meldrum	DONALD HEWLETT
The Honourable Teddy Meldrum	MICHAEL KNOWLES
Lady Lavender Southwick	MAVIS PUGH
Blanche Lipton, the Cook	BRENDA COWLING
Police Constable Wilson	BILL PERTWEE
Mabel Wheeler, Daily Woman	BARBARA NEW
Henry Livingstone, Bootboy	PERRY BENSON
Cecile (Cissy) Meldrum	CATHERINE RABETT
Poppy Meldrum	SUSIE BRANN
Lady Agatha Shawcross	ANGELA SCOULAR

(except episodes 3, 5, 6, 7, 9, 12, 16, 17)

Sir Ralph Shawcross	JOHN HORSLEY

(except episodes 3, 5, 6, 7, 9, 12, 16, 17)

Charles, The Bishop	FRANK WILLIAMS

(except episodes 3, 4, 5, 6, 7)

Madge Cartwright	YVONNE MARSH

(except episodes 2, 3, 5, 6, 7, 9, 14, 17, 22)

PILOT

Location filming dates: 14th - 19th November 1988.

1. YOU RANG, M'LORD?

Studio: TC 6 - Saturday 3rd & Sunday 4th December 1988.

TX: 29th December 1988, repeated 7th January 1990.

Duration: 55 mins 58 secs   Audience rating: 10.30 million

In the battlefields of France, 1918, Alf Stokes and James Twelvetrees discover the apparently lifeless body of Teddy Meldrum. Alf robs the corpse of an emerald set in Meldrum's ring, but when the body stirs he opts to carry the wounded Soldier back to the field hospital as an excuse to retreat from the front line.

London, 1927: Alf Stokes and his daughter Ivy are given the boot from their jobs on the music halls. Alf decides he has no other option but to go back into service as a Butler. When he arrives at the residence of Lord Meldrum some familiar faces await him. Alf manages to get himself and Ivy a job in the residence of his Lordship but he has to quickly teach Ivy the duties of a Maid to a large house.

Guest cast:

Ward Sister	Sarah Mortimer
Mr. Challon	Ken Morley
Call-Boy	Alf Pearson
Maggie (Maid)	Karen Westwood
Squiffy's Chauffeur	Robert Appleby
Major Squiffy Withers	Cameron Stewart
Jerry	John D. Collins
Parrot voice	Jeffrey Holland (OOV)
Pianist in Cinema	Rose Granville
Cinema Projectionist	Dane Alexander
Stretcher Bearers	Kevin Horan, Jack Street
Conductor in music hall	Evan Ross
Stagehand in music hall	Michael Leader
Electrician in music hall	Terry Duran
Coalman in Street	Paul Weakley
Delivery Driver	E.D. Thomas
Amy Pratt	Helen Gaume
Bella Sidebottom	Rose Hunter
Nurses	Judith Cox, Penny Lambirth
Patients in beds	Michael Elliott, Tom Johnson, Steve Amber
Soldier on stretcher	Andrew Rose
Stretcher bearers	Jack Street, Bob Turson
Private with cigarette	Chris Andrews
Nanny in street	Judith Blakstad

Mitchell, in *EastEnders*. Film credits include *The Belles of St. Trinians, Sparrows Can't Sing, Crooks In Cloisters, Chitty Chitty Bang Bang* and *The Boy Friend*.

Barbara's association spans almost the length of Perry and Croft's writing partnership. She played showgirl Laura La Plaz in the 1968 *Dad's Army* episode 'Shooting Pains' and returned to the fold 23 years later as another showgirl Myrtle, former stage partner of Alf Stokes in You Rang, M'Lord ?

ELI WOODS Rupert

(b. Jack Casey) Best known as 'Our Eli', a stage partner of the now legendary comedian Jimmy James. Eli is in fact Jimmy James' nephew and when his famous uncle died in 1965 Eli went solo playing clubs and holiday camps, TV and radio. A long association with the late Les Dawson began with four series of *Sez Les* for Yorkshire Television and continued on BBC television, radio and in pantomime. Michael Parkinson invited Eli, Roy Castle (who had been in Jimmy James' act for two years in the fifties) and Jim Casey (Jimmy's son) to recreate the 'Animals In A Box' sketch for the BBC chat show. Such was the impact the trio were asked to do it again for the *Royal Variety Performance* in November 1982 at the Theatre Royal, Drury Lane. In addition to many variety and pantomime appearances Eli has also had screen roles in Alan Bennett's *A Private Function*, Eric Sykes' *Mr. H Is Late, Little Dorrit, Heartbeat*, several episodes of *Last of the Summer Wine* and *Distant Shores*. In 1987 Eli appeared with Paul Shane and Su Pollard in *Aladdin* at the Alhambra Theatre in Bradford.

in *The Sandbaggers*, Major Toby Smith-Barton in *The Duchess of Duke Street*, with Dick Emery in *Legacy for Murder*, Sir Desmond Glazebrook in *Yes, Minister* and *Yes, Prime Minister*, Lord Bartelsham in *Ripping Yarns* and in the 1965 Morecambe and Wise vehicle *The Intelligence Men*. His final screen appearance was as an elderly Professor in the 1996 movie *Loch Ness* with Ted Danson.

FRANK WILLIAMS   Charles, Bishop of Dunford

(b.1931, London) Frank Williams made a name for himself in the popular comedy series of the 1950s *The Army Game* as Captain Pocket, a role for which he is still remembered today. Frank first encountered Jimmy Perry when he worked at the Palace Theatre in Watford both as a playwright and an actor. Frank's biggest success as a writer has been the thriller *Alibi For Murder* which has been produced in theatres all over the country. He is best known as the slightly bad tempered Rev. Timothy Farthing in *Dad's Army*, a role he played from 1969 until the show's demise in 1977, indeed, Frank was a lay member of the General Synod of the Church of England for many years.

A theatre actor of great versatility, and until recently Frank appeared each year in pantomime usually sporting the Dame's frocks. In *Hi-de-Hi!* Frank again dons a dog collar to conduct the wedding service of Gladys and Clive in the episode 'Wedding Bells'. It was a welcome return to the Croft & Perry repertory company which would see a promotion to Bishop when Frank became a regular in You Rang, M'Lord? In 2002 Frank Williams published his autobiography *Vicar To Dad's Army* and in 2009 a TV documentary was made of his life and career entitled *Dad's Army and Beyond: The Frank Williams Story*.

BARBARA WINDSOR MBE   Myrtle

(b.1937, Shoreditch, London) Barbara Windsor is an icon of British show business, being forever in the public consciousness for her appearances in nine *Carry On* films. Beginning with *Carry On Spying* in 1964, her most famous scene being the campsite exercises in *Carry On Camping* (1968) where her bra flies off into Kenneth Williams' face. However, the *Carry On's* only form a small part of Barbara's extensive career encompassing all aspects of the profession. On stage she went to Broadway with Joan Littlewood's production of *Oh What A Lovely War*, gained amazing revues as Marie Lloyd in the musical *Sing A Rude Song*, was part of the flop Lionel Bart musical *Twang*, played with Danny La Rue in *Come Spy With Me*, appeared opposite Vanessa Redgrave in *The Threepenny Opera*, *Carry On London* at the Victoria Palace, landlady Kath in Joe Orton's *Entertaining Mister Sloane*, Miss Adelaide in *Guys and Dolls* and in countless pantomimes throughout the country. Barbara television career has been equally impressive having first made an impact as Judy in *The Rag Trade*, Nymphia in *Up Pompeii*, Saucy Nancy in *Worzel Gummidge*, Mabel Fletcher in *Bluebirds*, Millicent in *One Foot in the Grave* and since 1994 landlady of the Queen Vic, Peggy

Frank Williams

Barbara Windsor

Eli Woods

The Mulberry Bush, Doctor In Trouble and *Great Catherine* with Peter O' Toole.

Angela's television career has encompassed Juliet in *Romeo and Juliet,* Cathy and her daughter Catherine in *Wuthering Heights,* Evelyn (A Play For Today), *The Avengers, Coronation Street, Crown Court, Penmarric* and *As Time Goes By.*

GUY SINER   Noel Coward

(b.1947, New York) Guy is best known for his portrayal of Lieutenant Gruber, one of the original and enduring characters of 85 episodes of *'Allo 'Allo* which is one of the most successful comedy series the BBC has ever produced and is still shown in more than 80 countries.

Guy was born in Manhattan to an American father and an English mother. He was educated in England and trained for the stage at the Webber Douglas Academy in London where he won the Rodney Millington Award for his performance as MC in *Cabaret.* In a career of some 30 years he has become a household name in the UK both in theatre and television. In recent years he has spent much of his time working in the film industry in Los Angeles but is now based in London where he juggles two careers - actor and writer/producer.

Guy made his first London appearance in the highly acclaimed *Cowardy Custard* at the Mermaid Theatre. He twice toured Australia with the stage show of *'Allo 'Allo* which also enjoyed a record-breaking UK tour and long West End runs both at the Prince of Wales and the London Palladium.

Television work in London includes *I Claudius, Doctor Who: 'Genesis of the Daleks', Life at Stake, Z Cars, Softly Softly, The Secret Army, The Brittas Empire, Doctors* and of course *'Allo 'Allo.* In LA: *Seinfeld, Martial Law, Diagnosis Murder* (with Dick van Dyke), *Zoe, Babylon 5, When Billie Beat Bobbie* (with Holly Hunter and Goldie Hawn), *That's My Bush* (with the writers of *South Park*), *The Agency* and *Star Trek: Enterprise.*

Guy's experience and contacts in all aspects of film-making are widespread. Features include *The Disappearance of Kevin Johnson, Great Harry and Jane, Lost Highway* (written and directed by David Lynch), *Leprechaun 4, Bug, Return to the Secret Garden, The Second Front* (with Todd Field), *Megiddo* (with Michael York), *Vlad* (with Billy Zane), *Provoked* and *Pirates of the Caribbean* (with Johnny Depp and Geoffrey Rush)

Visit Guy's own website at **www.guysiner.com.**

RICHARD VERNON   The Earl of Swaffham

(b.1925 d.1997) Reading born Richard became one of British acting's most respected character actors. An early leading role was as wartime agent-turned-criminologist Edwin Oldenshaw in the television series *The Man In Room 17* and its sequel *The Fellows.* He was Colonel Smithers in *Goldfinger* with Sean Connery and a man sharing a carriage with The Beatles in their film *A Hard Day's Night.* Science fiction fans remember him fondly as the designer of fjords Slartibartfast in the 1981 television version of Douglas Adams' *The Hitchhiker's Guide To The Galaxy.* Other credits include Sir James Greenley ("C")

Angela Scoular

Guy Siner

Richard Vernon

her debut stage performance with music hall comedian Ernest Lotiga in *My Wife's Family* on tour. A West End debut beckoned as Beth in a production of *Little Women* at the Westminster Theatre. Having worked her way around many repertory companies in the United Kingdom including working for Jimmy Perry at Watford Palace she met her husband John Clegg and they married in 1959. A formidable stage partnership with Hugh Paddick was formed across many theatres in various farces, each trying to out shine the other with hilarious ad-libs throughout the play. Mavis made her television debut as Lady Maltby in a 1974 episode of *Dad's Army*, 'The Captain's Car'. She is one of only a handful of performers who can claim to have had roles in all four Perry-Croft comedies. In *It Ain't Half Hot Mum* she was seen as Chief Commander Crisp in the episode 'Ticket To Blighty' appearing with her husband John Clegg (Gunner Graham). As Lady Winifred Dempster she guest stars in two episodes of *Hi-de-Hi!* as Clive's upper crust aunt. Other notable television appearances include Mrs Chase in *Fawlty Towers:* The Kipper And The Corpse, *Spooner's Patch*, three episodes of *Are You Being Served?* and *Sorry!*

CATHERINE RABETT   Miss Cissy Meldrum

(b.1960, London) Catherine's career in theatre has included Alice Fitzwarren in *Dick Whittington* at the Theatre Royal, Brighton, Lufthansa Hostess in a tour of *Boeing Boeing*, Daphne Stillington in *Present Laughter* at Windsor, Gwendolyn in *The Importance of Being Ernest* at Leatherhead, Bianca in *Taming of the Shrew* for the Barbados Shakespeare Festival, Sheila in *Dial M For Murder* in the West End and Pamela Arbroath in *39 Steps* on a major tour.

Television appearances are Carol Pringle in *Auf Wiedersehen Pet 2*, *Chance In A Million*, Anna in *Capital City*, Jane in *Bergerac*, Louise in *Minder*, Marion in *A Year In Provence*, Lydia Lee in *Poirot*, Mrs. Lewis in *Pilgrim's Rest*, Carla Adlem in several episodes of *Doctors* and Pam Montclare in *Emmerdale* and presenter of 13 episodes of Home for Anglia TV. Film appearances include *The Living Daylights* and *Maurice*.

IVOR ROBERTS   Mr. Barnes

(b.1925 d.1999) Originating from Nottingham, Ivor was the son of a Welsh man who had performed a trapeze act before the First World War. Ivor became an Assistant Stage Manager with the Regency Players at the Theatre Royal, Leicester before joining the Royal Navy. Upon demob in 1946 he made his comeback in *Robinson Crusoe* in Aberystwyth and gained valuable repertory experience with Harry Hanson's Court Players. A stint as a continuity announcer at TWW (Television West And Wales) until it lost its franchise in 1968 led to a career on the small screen as an actor. His numerous credits include *Six Days of Justice, Coronation Street, Secret Army, Bergerac, Doctor Who: Genesis of the Daleks, Born and Bred, George and Mildred, Minder, Sorry!* and Eric Sykes' *The 19th Hole*. Ivor had a stint with the National Theatre in 1985 appearing in *The Government Inspector* and *Pravda* and also appeared in the pop video to Barbra Streisand's single "Emotion".

His final performances were for BBC Radio Wales as farmer Donald Evans in the soap opera *Station Road*. His first appearance for David Croft was foreman Mr. Barnes at the factory of The Union Jack Rubber Company. Ivor went on to play engine driver Arnold, a regular in *Oh Doctor Beeching!*

ANGELA SCOULAR   Lady Agatha Shawcross

(b.1945, London) Trained at RADA, Angela's theatre experience includes repertory seasons at Leicester, Birmingham and Glasgow, also *The Price of Experience* at the Traverse in Edinburgh. *The Tempest* with Hugh Griffith in France, *On Approval* in Canada, *The Rivals* in Chichester, *Holmes and the Ripper* on tour and London seasons of *Black Comedy*, *Hamlet* with Alan Bates, *Absurd Person Singular*, *Sextet* with her husband Leslie Phillips and *Little Lies* with Sir John Mills.

Angela is a former Bond girl, having appeared opposite David Niven in *Casino Royale* and subsequently as Ruby Barlett with George Lazenby in *On Her Majesty's Secret Service*. Further film credits are Charlie Chaplin's *Countess From Hong Kong* with Marlon Brando, *The Adventurers, Here We Go Round*

came in a television advertising campaign for Vicks Sinex Nasal Spray during the 1980s. "I played a mother whose catchphrase 'Course you can Malcolm' was mimicked a lot. There is even a rap CD with me on" Barbara points out proudly.

Theatre appearances have been as diverse as *Bedroom Farce* (King's Head), *Equus* (Haymarket, Leicester), *Emu In Pantoland* (Shaftesbury Theatre), *Travelling Light* (Prince of Wales Theatre), *The School Mistress* (Savoy Theatre), *Salad Days* (Vaudeville Theatre), *Waltz of the Torreadors* (Criterion Theatre) and *Summertime* (Apollo Theatre). Barbara's film credits are *Anna Karenina*, *Witness for the Prosecution*, *Edward II* and *Ali G In Da House*.

For David Croft, Barbara was seen as the meek Doreen opposite Michael Robbins as her husband Roger in the *Hi-de-Hi!* episode 'Wedding Bells' and later as railway widow Vera Plumtree in *Oh Doctor Beeching!*

BILL PERTWEE MBE Constable Wilson

(b.1926, Amersham, Bucks.) Bill Pertwee hails from a theatrical family that includes screen writer Roland Pertwee, actor/comedian Jon Pertwee and playwright Michael Pertwee. Bill's career started in a concert party in Bognor Regis but quickly found its niche in radio where he became a regular with Kenneth Horne in his radio shows *Beyond Our Ken* and *Round The Horne*.

In the theatre Bill has appeared in *There Goes the Bride* (Criterion Theatre), *Don't Just Lie There Say Something* (UK tour), *Worzel Gummidge* (Wimbledon and Southampton), *Habeas Corpus* (UK tour), *It Runs in the Family* (Playhouse Theatre), *Funny Money* (Playhouse Theatre) and *Die Fledermaus* (Guildford). Bill has also appeared in countless Summer shows and pantomimes throughout the UK during his 50 years in show business.

His most famous role is of course as Air Raid Warden Hodges in *Dad's Army*, on television, on film and on stage. In addition he has appeared in *Worzel Gummidge*, *Woof*, *Harry Hill*, *The Generation Game*, *We'll Meet Again*, *Blankety Blank*, *Spy Trap* and in 1999 the subject of *This Is Your Life*. On the big screen Bill has been seen in two *Carry On's*, *Confessions Of A Pop Performer*, *From Bed To Nurse* and *Psychomania*.

As a writer, Bill Pertwee has published several best selling books: *Promenades and Pierrots*, *By Royal Command*, *Dad's Army - The Making of a Television Legend*, *Stars in Battledress*, *The Station Now Standing*, *Beside The Seaside* and his autobiography *A Funny Way to Make a Living*.

Aside from an appearance in the last episode of *It Ain't Half Hot Mum*, Bill also played an irate father in the *Hi-de-Hi!* episode 'It's Murder'.

MAVIS PUGH Lady Lavender Southwick

(b.1914 d.2006) Mavis Gladys Fox Pugh was born in Croydon, the daughter of a London solicitor, she won a scholarship to the International School of Acting and started her professional life in repertory at Amersham. 5 feet 1 inch tall Mavis made

Mavis Pugh

Catherine Rabett

Ivor Roberts

would frighten me to death after years of looking out into the darkness!" and the comic Dickie Henderson,. "Again a lovely man, he would offer me so much advice on stage technique and how to engage an audience. He was terribly kind."

STUART McGUGAN Jock McGregor

(b.1944, Stirling, Scotland) Stuart is best known as Gunner 'Atlas' Mackintosh, a member of the Royal Artillery Concert Party in *It Ain't Half Hot Mum*. He was also a presenter of the legendary BBC children's series *Play School*. Having trained at RADA, among Stuart's theatre credits are *Golden Girls* (Leeds Playhouse), *Robin Hood* (Glasgow), *The Memory of Water* (Vaudeville Theatre), *Tunes of Glory* (tour), *The Living Quarters* (Royal Lyceum Theatre, Edinburgh). His TV experience is extensive: *Dad's Army* (as the Scottish Sergeant in 'Number Engaged'), *Tutti Frutti, Taggart, Hamish Macbeth, The Bill, Heartbeat, Casualty, Footballer's Wives, Doctors, Silent Witness, Boy Meets Girl* and regular roles in *Wish Me Luck* and *Family Affairs*.

KEN MORLEY Mr. Challon, Theatre Manager

(b.1943, Chorley, Lancashire) Still recognised from his long stint as grocer Reg Houldsworth in *Coronation Street* between 1989 and 1995, Ken Morley is an experienced character actor on stage and television. He was a regular in *'Allo 'Allo* for three years playing General Leopold von Flockenstuffen and has had roles in *Little Dorrit,* as Mr. Wobbler, *The Fall and Rise of Reginald Perrin, Woof, Red Dwarf, The Grand* and the short lived sitcom *Hardware*. Ken appears regularly in stage farces and pantomime.

BARBARA NEW Mabel Wheeler, the Charlady

(b.1933, Hampstead, London) Barbara New's first television appearance was in *Pride & Prejudice*. Since then she has graced *London's Burning, The Victoria Wood Show, Softly Softly, The Dora Bryan Show, The Good Companions, Juliet Bravo, The Bill, Shine On Harvey Moon, Ripping Yarns* and a regular in a BBC children's programme with Rod Hull. "*Emu's Broadcasting Company* went on for six years" says Barbara. "Rod Hull, Billy Dainty and I had a wonderful time together. We couldn't have been more different the three of us yet somehow we managed to have so much fun. Every year at Christmas we used to do a big theatre pantomime together as well. The show was set in Emu's own television studio and I was the cleaner who used to have to read the news and act in some spoof of a real television show." Barbara has worked extensively with Ronnie Barker, "I'd known Ronnie Barker for years and years, even before I met my husband Michael [Barrington, who played the Prison Governor in *Porridge*]. We were both in our first West End play together with Dirk Bogarde and Geraldine McEwan. Ronnie was a struggling actor like the rest of us. I had a marvellous time working with The Two Ronnies over the years." Barbara's best known role with Barker and Corbett is as the Maiden Aunt in their silent seaside classic *By The Sea*. One of Barbara's most famous guises

Ken Morley

Barbara New

Bill Pertwee MBE

Anthony Hopkins to appear in his adaptation of Chekhov's *Uncle Vanya*, retitled August, on both film and stage. Hugh's autobiography *Thank God For A Funny Face* was published in 2002.

YVONNE MARSH   Madge Cartwright

(b.1932, London) Yvonne proved to be a natural show off as a child. So much so that a family friend paid for her to attend the Helen Wills School of Dance in Golders Green. Such was Yvonne's talent at an early age in ballet and tap that she found herself being entered for three exams on a single day! This led in turn to her father and mother enrolling her into the prestigious Ada Foster School of Performing Arts. It was from this well known theatrical training ground that Yvonne found herself the lead character in the 1948 movie *The Little Ballerina* directed by Lewis Gilbert which would also feature Dame Margot Fonteyn and Anthony Newley. This led to further appearances on the big screen; *Come Dance With Me*, *The Story of Gilbert and Sullivan*, *Street Corner* and *Casino Royale*. Prior to this her West End stage debut had been as Mary Mary, Quite Contrary, in *The Land of the Christmas Stocking* at the Duke Of York's Theatre in 1945. It marked the start of many appearances on the London stage most notably *Round About Piccadilly* with Max Bygraves and *The Water Babies* with Jessie Matthews. "*The Water Babies* was a lovely show," recalls Yvonne. "But we suffered because we were not allowed to do any advertising. The infamous nude revue *Oh Calcutta* was playing nightly at the Royalty Theatre, and we were doing mornings and matinees with *The Water Babies*, a family show. As a result it didn't run too long, but it should have succeeded. A great pity." Yvonne appeared many times with Hughie Green and even recorded a live LP at Butlin's in Bognor with the legendary presenter.

Many happy years were spent touring with her own variety act, singing standards and ballads in theatres nationwide. Yvonne is however still remembered as one of Britain's finest ever principal boys in pantomime. "Pantomime is the very first experience children ever have of the theatre so it's terribly important to do it properly," she says. "My first West End panto was as *Goody Two Shoes* at the London Casino (1950) with a wonderful cast: Charlie Cairoli, Little Jimmy, Leon Cortez… so many fine performers." Yvonne played principal boy in many major pantomimes all over the country, winning great acclaim wherever she appeared. During one record breaking season of *Aladdin* at the Bristol Hippodrome, featuring Bernard Bresslaw and Freddie Davies, the run had to be extended by popular demand largely thanks to Yvonne's rapport with the audiences.

Although retired from show business for the past fifteen years or so, Yvonne maintains her biggest career influences have been the legendary Max Bygraves "He used to call me Nonny. He advised me not to get contact lenses even though I am very short sighted because the first look at an audience

Hugh Lloyd MBE

Yvonne Marsh

Stuart McGugan

Southampton, *See How They Run* on a Middle East tour and *Blythe Spirit* at the Lyric, Hammersmith. On television Michael has been seen in *The Dick Emery Show*, *321*, *Cannon and Ball*, *Brush Strokes*, *Jackanory*, *Noel's House Party*, *DJ Kat* and *Rogue's Rock*. On film his appearances are *That's Your Funeral*, *The End of the World*, *Spy Story* and voicing *The BFG*.

A long association with David Croft comedies began with several appearances in *Dad's Army* including the movie version. This led to the major role of Captain Ashwood in all 56 episodes of *It Ain't Half Hot Mum* between 1973 and 1981. During this time his on screen partnership with Donald Hewlett was cemented in the short lived Lloyd / Croft sitcom *Come Back Mrs. Noah*. Michael then took over the role of Jeffrey Fairbrother replacing Simon Cadell in the stage version of *Hi-de-Hi!* at the Victoria Palace and subsequently in Blackpool.

Michael has had great success as a writer too. He adapted 70 episodes of *Dad's Army* for radio with Harold Snoad and co-wrote with David Croft and Jeremy Lloyd four episodes of *Are You Being Served?* For radio he again joined Harold Snoad to write a *Dad's Army* sequel *It Sticks Out Half a Mile* originally with Arthur Lowe, John Le Mesurier, Bill Pertwee and Ian Lavender. The same concept was later made for TV, first as a BBC pilot, *Walking the Planks* then as *High and Dry*. The latter starring Bernard Cribbins and Richard Wilson for Yorkshire TV. A further comedy series *Share and Share Alike* starred Reg Varney, Hugh Paddick and Michael Robbins.

MICHAEL LEES   Mr. Foster

(b.1927 d.2004) Originating from Bury, Lancashire, Michael's credits on television and film are vast. His big screen roles have included such iconic films as Whistle Down The Wind and *Séance on a Wet Afternoon*. Television appearances encompass *Warship*, *Van Der Valk*, *Secret Army*, *Love in a Cold Climate*, *Wilfred Robinson* in A Fine Romance, Colonel Jackson in *Tenko*, Mayor Bullivant in *Mapp and Lucia*, *Knights of God*, Colonel Bosworth in *All Creatures Great and Small*, Hector Burrage in *Howards' Way*, *Coronation Street*, *Lovejoy*, *Peak Practice*, *Holby City*. He appeared as Inspector Palmer in the *Hi-de-Hi!* episode 'Who Killed Mr. Partridge?'

HUGH LLOYD MBE   Selfridge, Sir Ralph's butler

(b.1923 d.2008) Chester born Hugh Lloyd became a much-loved face on television in a career spanning nearly sixty years. He was Tony Hancock's fellow patient in the legendary 'Blood Donor' episode. His partnership with Terry Scott in the David Croft produced sitcom *Hugh And I* lasted 69 episodes. He went on to appear in two Jimmy Perry comedies, *The Gnomes of Dulwich* (again with Terry Scott) and opposite Peggy Mount in *Lollipop Loves Mr. Mole*. His list of television credits include *Lord Tramp*, *Z Cars*, *Till Death Us Do Part*, *Doctor Who: Delta And The Bannermen*, *Foyle's War*, *Doc Martin*, *Oh Doctor Beeching!* and *My Family*. He appeared in two Alan Bennett plays for television, *A Visit From Miss Prothero* and *Say Something Happened*. In 1994 he was persuaded by Sir

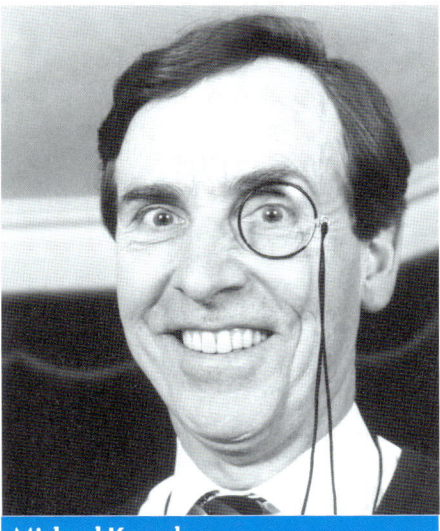

Davy Kaye MBE   **Michael Knowles**   **Michael Lees**

SOREL JOHNSON Penelope Barrington-Blake

(b. London) Sorel is the daughter of actors Richard Johnson – who was famously Ian Fleming's choice for the role of James Bond, which he turned down - and Sheila Sweet (and step-daughter of Kim Novak). Whilst in her late twenties, Sorel recorded a pop single *People Of The World* which became a favourite of Radio 1 DJs Gary Davies and John Peel at the time. Further recording work followed writing and recording with Right Said Fred, Herbie Armstrong, Yello and Dreadzone. She has done extensive theatre work, most memorably at the Nuffield Theatre, Southampton, where Sorel appeared as Sophie in *Same Hole Deeper*, Coryphaeus in *The Bacchae*, Biance in *The Taming Of The Shrew*, Diana in *All's Well That End's Well*, Helena in *Look Back In Anger*, Bagheera in *The Jungle Book* and Lucia Amory in *Black Coffee* with Alfred Marks as Poirot. Screen appearances include Lara in *Castaway*, *I Capture The Castle* and of course as the WRAF Officer in the *Hi-de-Hi!* episode 'Only The Brave'.

For some years Sorel has been known as Sukey Parnell, a portrait photographer with an impressive pedigree. Her work has been exhibited at the National Portrait Gallery among many prestigious exhibition houses and Sukey's work has been featured in the Radio Times, Independent On Sunday, Sunday Magazine and Blues & Soul.

She is married to musician Will Parnell (son of Jack Parnell and an ex-Blockhead with Ian Dury) and they have two children Lola and Xac.

DAVY KAYE MBE Boris, King of Dalmatia

(b.1916 d.1998) Born David Kodeish in the Mile End Road, London, he made his professional debut in 1935 at the Mile End Empire. He entertaining troops all over England and then presented his own revues in partnership with his agent Joe Collins, father of Joan and Jackie. Davy was in the original production of *Guys & Dolls* at the London Coliseum playing Benny Southstreet. Between 1954 and 1968 Davy starred in a new show each month at The Embassy Club in Bond Street. His film work includes *Crooks In Cloisters*, *Those Magnificent Men In Their Flying Machines*, *Chitty Chitty Bang Bang*, *Carry On Cowboy* and *Carry On Regardless*. A tireless worker for charity, the Variety Club presented Davy with their Silver Heart award on two separate occasions - 1975 and again ten years later. Davy was staunch member of the Grand Order of Water Rats. Elected King in 1984, he was then awarded the Badge of Merit and Bar - the highest honour the Order can bestow.

MICHAEL KNOWLES The Honorable Teddy Meldrum

Born in Derbyshire and trained at RADA, Michael spent many years working in Britain's repertory theatres. He found himself working for Jimmy Perry at the Watford Rep where he met his wife Linda James.

Michael's theatre credits include Ted Craig in *Find The Lady*, *Butler* in Whodunnit?, Richard Gretham in *Hay Fever* at the Sheffield Crucible, *American Patrol* at the Mayflower,

John Horsley | **Geoffrey Hughes** | **Sorel Johnson**

Barker. Early television experience came with a BBC Saturday morning show called *Jigsaw* alongside Rolf Harris and Charlie Drake. This led to further television with roles in *The Ronnie Corbett Show*, *The Dick Emery Show*, *The Fenn Street Gang*, *War Ship*, *Crown Court*, *The Avengers*, *The Saint*, *Callan*, *Doctor Who* among many others. On film his credits are *Carry On Behind*, *Adolf Hitler - My Part In His Downfall* and *A Touch Of Class*. His on screen partnership with Michael Knowles started with Donald playing Colonel Reynolds to Michael's captain in *It Ain't Half Hot Mum* on television and also on stage in Bournemouth and Scarborough. This was followed by *Come Back Mrs. Noah* as Carstairs. Donald is married to actress Therese McMurray.

JOHN HORSLEY   Sir Ralph Shawcross

(b.1915, Westcliff-On-Sea, Essex) John is perhaps best known for his performances as Doc Morrissey with Leonard Rossiter in *The Fall and Rise of Reginald Perrin*. He made his acting debut at the Theatre Royal, Bournemouth and learned his profession by appearing in many repertory productions throughout the country. Having served in the Devon Yeomanry during the war serving in Italy and Sicily, John contracted hepatitis and wound up performing in the Army Bureau For Current Affairs play unit both at home and abroad. Television appearances include episodes of *Upstairs, Downstairs*, *The Professionals*, *Jewel In The Crown*, *Robin Of Sherwood*, *Lovejoy* and countless others. As Clive, the solicitor of Max Tewksbury in 'Co-respondent's Course', he advises his client on the best ways of getting the dirt on Jeffrey Fairbrother in a classic *Hi-de-Hi!* episode. John was also in the short lived Croft-Lloyd comedy *Oh Happy Band!* with Harry Worth. His best known role in a David Croft production is as Sir Ralph Shawcross, the bad tempered aristocrat in You Rang, M'Lord? who is forever perusing his wayward wife in an attempt to confirm his suspicions of unfaithful conduct. On film John can be seen in *Ben Hur*, *Sink The Bismark*, *Appointment With Venus* and *Operation Amsterdam*.

GEOFFREY HUGHES   Fred Kendal

(b.1944, Liverpool) Having started acting whilst at Newcastle University, Geoffrey went into repertory at the Victoria Theatre, Stoke on Trent. His big break was voicing the role of Paul McCartney in the animated feature *Yellow Submarine*. He is universally remembered for his well meaning rogue, bin man Eddie Yates in *Coronation Street* which Hughes played between 1975 and 1983. Other television credits are *Dad's Army*: 'Brain Versus Brawn' (playing the Bridge Corporal), *Up Pompeii*, *Till Death Do Us Part*, *Don't Drink The Water*, *Doctor Who*: 'Trial of a Time Lord', *Spender*, *The Upper Hand*, *Skins* and *The Royle Family* as Twiggy. Hughes' other memorable television characters are the layabout Onslow in the BBC's timeless comedy *Keeping Up Appearances* and as Vernon Scripps in *Heartbeat*. Among Hughes film roles are Lantry in *The Virgin Soldiers*, Willie in *Carry On at your Convenience*, Larry in *Adolf Hitler - My Part In His Downfall* and the postman in *Confessions of a Driving Instructor*.

Brenda Cowling

Maurice Denham

Donald Hewlett

Wheel'), *Are You Being Served?*, *Bless This House*, *Three Up Two Down*, *Coogan's Run*, *Death on Holy Orders* and *Bridget Jones' Diary* for the cinema.

JOHN D. COLLINS Jerry

(b.1942, London, John Christopher Dixon) John was educated at Harrow School before winning the Ivor Novello and Robert Donat Scholarships to RADA. He ran his own theatre at Frinton-on-Sea between 1953 and 1970. Over a period of ten years John worked with Spike Milligan in such plays as *Son of Oblomov* and *The Bed Sitting Room*. He became a regular in the television series *Family At War* and also with Robert Lindsay in *Get Some In*. John's association with Jimmy Perry and David Croft goes back to *Dad's Army* when he played a Naval Officer in the 1971 movie version. He has also been seen in *It Ain't Half Hot Mum* and *Are You Being Served?* He is principally recognised as British airman Fairfax in *'Allo 'Allo* and as Miss Poppy's beau Jerry in *You Rang, M'Lord?* His brief appearance in *Hi-de-Hi!* comes as the Bailiff in the episode 'Trouble And Strife' who hands Ted Bovis his summons for back alimony to his estranged wife Hilary.

BRENDA COWLING Mrs. Blanche Lipton, the cook

(b.1921, London) Brenda Cowling trained at RADA with Jimmy Perry. Her first professional appearance was in Alfred Hitchcock's film *Stage Fright* whilst still a student. Brenda has appeared in repertory theatres for the West Of England Theatre Company, Farnham, Bristol and Leatherhead. Her first television appearance was in an afternoon programme called *Keep Fit With Freddie Mills* for the BBC. Subsequently she played Miss Perrin in the original production of *The Forsyte Saga*, *Mrs. Viney* in The Railway Children, Ward sister in *Fawlty Towers*: 'The Germans', she has also appeared in *Romaney Jones*, *Only When I Laugh*, *The Detectives*, *Shoestring*, *Casualty*, *The Legecy of Reginald Perrin*, *The Legend of The Tamworth Two*, *Doctors*, *Jonathan Creek*, *Goodnight Sweetheart*, *In Sickness and in Health*, *The Secret Diary of Adrian Mole*, *French and Saunders* and three series of *Potter* opposite Arthur Lowe. On the big screen there have also been cameo appearances in two *Carry On* films (*Girls* and *Behind*), *Jabberwocky*, *Pink Floyd The Wall*, *International Velvet* and the James Bond epic *Octopussy*.

Brenda has appeared in all four Perry-Croft series starting with Mrs. Prentice in *Dad's Army* ('All Is Safely Gathered In') followed by a WVS lady in the final episode of *It Ain't Half Hot Mum*. Brenda has appeared in three episodes of *Hi-de-Hi!* She was the station announcer in 'Together Again', a camper in the episode 'Raffles' and the Dempster's Maid Nora in 'Wedding Bells'.

MAURICE DENHAM OBE Captain Dolby

(b.1909 d.2002) Maurice Denham remained a star until his death aged 92. He forged his popularity on radio during the 1940's in the hit series of the day, *Much-Binding-In-The-Marsh* set in a ramshackle RAF station and the even more successful *It's That Man Again (ITMA)* with Tommy Handley which had a listening audience in excess of 20 million. Born in Beckenham, Kent, Denham worked as an engineer before taking up acting. His first film role was *The Man Within* alongside Richard Attenborough in 1947 which led to roles in many big movies: *Our Man in Havana*, *Animal Farm*, *Carrington V.C.*, *Night Caller From Outer Space*, *Sunday Bloody Sunday*, *Nicholas And Alexandra*, *The Day of The Jackal* and *84 Charing Cross Road*. Similary his television pedigree was equally impressive with a regular role as Nestor Turton in the spy drama *The Lotus Eaters* proving especially popular. Among the many series that Denham graced with both comedy and dramatic roles are Rawley in *Porridge*, *Secret Army*, *Return of The Saint*, *The Professionals*, *Minder*, *Doctor Who:* 'The Twin Dilemma' with Colin Baker and in 1985 as the subject of *This Is Your Life*. His final appearance was in 1997 as an artistocrat in *The Beggar Bride* with Keeley Hawes.

DONALD HEWLETT Lord George Meldrum

(b.1922, Manchester) Donald joined the famous Footlights Revue in Cambridge whilst at University. Having joined the Navy, Donald found himself posted in Kirkwall in the Orkney Islands where he started the Kirkwall Arts Club. He did the same thing upon posting to Singapore where he formed The Singapore Stage Club. Upon returning to the UK a job at Oxford Playhouse saw him learning the ropes of repertory with an actor who would turn out to be a good friend, Ronnie

to see Robertson-Justice in an attempt to dissuade me from following a career in theatre, but it had the opposite effect and made me want to do it even more. My father gave up the theatre and went into marketing and advertising where he made his name as one of the founders of direct marketing but I wasn't to be put off." Susie went to Manchester University to study drama alongside Ben Elton and Rik Mayall, and then did a Post Graduate Course at the Drama Studio. "My first professional job was with a small theatre company called Entertainment Machine, appearing in their musical *Shush*, about a family who would inherit a fortune if they didn't speak for a year. But I actually got my Equity card through appearing at the lovely Polka Children's Theatre in Wimbledon. A delightful place to learn your craft." Susie has appeared in many television series. These include *Julia Jeckyll and Harriet Hyde, Casualty, Jericho, Bodies* and *My Life as a Popat*. She has also been seen in the film Summertime. Among her stage credits are *Daisy Pulls it Off* at the Globe Theatre, Gwendolyn Pigeon in *The Odd Couple*, Hero in *Much Ado About Nothing* at Southampton and Sir Peter Hall's production of *An Absolute Turkey*. Susie's role in *A Clandestine Marriage* in the West End came about quite by chance. "I was invited to a 4th July Parents' Day at Eton College as I have a friend, Peter Broad, who works there. At lunch I found myself sitting next to Sir Nigel Hawthorne who was casting his first play as a Director. He said he had a part for me and I ended up in the play which Sir Nigel also starred in and it was a great success." A familiar voice on radio Susie's vocal talents have enhanced *Martin Chuzzlewit, Uncle Dynamite, The Hiding Place, A Far Cry From Kensington* and three series of *In The Chair* - all for BBC Radio. Susie lives in Gloucestershire with her husband Max and their three children.

JOHN CLEGG Mr. Franklin, Lady Lavender's Solicitor

(b.1934, Murree, Pakistan) Best known as 'La-di-da' Gunner Graham ('Paderewski') the concert party pianist in *It Ain't Half Hot Mum*, although in real life Clegg could not play the piano. Born in the Punjab where his father's regiment was stationed, John trained at RADA and he and actress wife Mavis Pugh were members of Jimmy Perry's repertory company at Watford. John's theatre credits are wide ranging: *Port In A Storm* with Jessie Matthews, *Spider's Web* with Ciceley Courtneidge, he took over the Brian Rix part in *One For The Pot* on tour, Andrew Aguecheek in *Twelfth Night*, Dr. Young in *Nightcap*, Bobby Franklyn in *Run For Your Wife*, Major Giles Flack in *Privates On Parade* with Colin Baker and the Wizard in *The Wizard of Oz*, not to mention numerous pantomimes. His background of the Raj and life-long love of the works of Rudyard Kipling inspired him to compile his one-man show In *The Eye of the Sun*, a compilation of Kipling's Indian writings which won John a Fringe First award at the Edinburgh Festival. John's first television role was as DC Gleaves in *Dixon of Dock Green*. His other small screen appearances include *Dad's Army* (a wireless operator in 'Round And Round Went The Great Big

Susie Brann   **John Glegg**   **John D Collins**

Theatre by the Lake in Keswick. A small role in a Children's educational programme on the Middle Ages was Amanda's introduction to television, her appearances since have included *All In Good Faith* for Thames TV, *Terry and June*, *Bergerac* and *Hotel Trubble* for the BBC, and *Bunny Town* for the Disney Channel. She was also a regular in Carla Lane's *Searching* for Carlton. "My character Hetty was very enigmatic and didn't speak much. She had had something terrible happen in her past which was never revealed. Carla promised to open her character up and reveal her background if we went to a second series but sadly that never happened." Amanda played 'Aunty Phyllis' in Jimmy Perry's Radio 2 comedy *London Calling*.

PERRY BENSON   Henry Livingstone, the boot boy

(b.1961, London) Perry Benson started as a child actor, training at the Anna Scher Theatre School in north London. It was by chance he became an actor. "When I was ten I went to a library show in Islington, where I lived, along with my friends. The organisers used to put a family-sized tin of biscuits outside the room and we used to nick 'em." Perry remembers. "One week I got caught and instead of calling the Police, the teacher made me come into the lesson and join in. So that's how I fell into acting if you like. It was an improvisation master class. I liked it because there was lots of girls there, so I kept going back..." As a child actor, Perry found himself in some prestigious television series. "The first thing I did was an episode of *Dixon of Dock Green* and *Poldark*, things like that plus some Children's Film Foundation stuff." Perry has vivid memories of appearing in the original *Black Adder* series. "We filmed it in Newcastle, and I was only supposed to be in one episode but I got on very well with the writer Richard Curtis and producer John Lloyd, so they wrote me into another couple. I've done guest appearances in a lot of comedies like *The Young Ones* - I knew Rik Mayall and his then girlfriend Lise Meyer from when they were doing stand up comedy."

Among his theatre appearances are *The Good Woman of Sechzuan* at the Royal Court Theatre, *Class Enemy* at the Royal National Theatre, *The Philanderer Page* at the Lyric Theatre, Hammersmith, as Riff Raff in *The Rocky Horror Show* on a tour of New Zealand, and *Waiting For Godot* for the Bubble Theatre Company. On television he is perhaps best known as Bones in three series of the award winning *Operation Good Guys*. Other television appearances include *The Real McCoy* (2 series), *My Family*, *Parents of the Band*, *Casualty*, *The Black Adder*, *Minder*, *The Young Ones*, *A Very Peculiar Practice* and *Poldark*. Perry was a cast member of the iconic Mod movie *Quadrophenia*. His other big screen appearances include *Little Orphan Annie 2* with Joan Collins, *Scum*, *Birth of The Beatles*, punk biopic *Sid & Nancy*, *This Is England*, *Alien Autopsy* and *The Last Resort*.

Perry's career as one of the Perry and Croft repertory company began with an appearance as Trevor in the *Hi-de-Hi!* episode *'Tell It To The Marines'* This led in turn to the sarcastic boot-boy Henry Livingstone in *You Rang, M'Lord?* and then onto David Croft's railway comedy as trainee engine driver Ralph in *Oh Doctor Beeching!*

HILDA BRAID   Flo Kendall

(b.1929 d.2007) Hilda trained at RADA and appeared during several seasons with the Royal Shakespeare Company. She was a stalwart of many television series and productions throughout her career with a regular role as an aunt in the popular *Catweazle*. Specialising in confused ecentrics, she was also seen in *One Foot In The Grave*, *Crossroads*, *The Onedin Line*, *Man About The House*, *Robin's Nest*, *Juliet Bravo*, *Brookside*, *Chucklevision*, *Doctors*, *My Family*, *Casualty* and on the big screen in *The Wild Cats of St. Trinians*. Hilda will principally remembered for two long running roles: as Mum to Cheryl Hall in the John Sullivan comedy *Citizen Smith*, always referring to Robert Lindsay's revolutionary Woolfie Smith as "Foxy" and as Nana Moon in *EastEnders* between 2002 and 2005.

SUSIE BRANN   Miss Poppy Meldrum

(b. Gerrards Cross, Bucks). Susie is the daughter of Christian and Mary Rose Brann. "My mother began training as a singer, but stopped at 18 to marry my father and have children – I'm one of four. My father spent some time as an actor and appeared in farces with Brian Rix and James Robertson-Justice," Susie recalls. "In fact he took me to Scotland when I was young

The House of Meldrum

AMANDA BELLAMY   Rose

(b. London, Amanda Bell) The daughter of an Engineer, Amanda found herself living with her parents in Devon, Qatar and Cyprus during her early years. It was in Cyprus that Amanda had her first taste of the stage.. "I was cast in a school production of *The Wizard of Oz*", recalls Amanda. "It became quite a cathartic experience because, around the time I was rehearsing, a hot-headed young Turk opened fire on our car. My Mum was shot and almost died. Being able to act out a string of emotions, and escape to another, more fun, really helped me through it I think." Between the ages of 9 and 13 Amanda found herself living in Russia. "One of our teachers there was keen that we all write little playlets and act them before an audience of ex-pats who were living there. So that again fuelled my passion for theatre and performing." English boarding school beckoned at Bedales. "I appeared in a production of *The Happiest Days of Your Life*, Directed by Daniel Day Lewis and James Simmonds, (fellow students who both subsequently became actors). I was only playing a small part but the school magazine review said that if it had existed I deserved the "Bedales Oscar". David Thompson, who much later went on to become head of BBC Films, was our English teacher at the time. I think he saw some promise in me and he cast me in productions of *The Glass Menagerie* and *Twelfth Night*. Thanks to the efforts of an enterprising parent Wendy Arnold, we toured Scandinavia with these productions and the next year took further shows to the Edinburgh Festival. This eventually led me to RADA where the likes of Robert Daws, Karen Drury, Juliet Stevenson, and Mark Rylance were also studying." Amanda gained her Equity card in a production of *Once a Catholic* at the Sheffield Crucible. "I was contracted to play Mary Hennessey but was understudying one of the leads, Mary Mooney. Fairly early on, the day came when the actress who played Mary Mooney fell ill and I was given two hours notice to take over the role. A bit of a baptism of fire." Following this, a British Council tour of Africa as Jessica in *The Merchant of Venice* and Olivia in *Twelfth Night* cemented a love of the theatre, Shakespeare and travel. Among Amanda's many theatre appearances are Helena in *A Midsummer Nights Dream* for the Hull Truck Theatre Company, Hermia in the same play for the Royal Shakespeare Company, *A Little Hotel On The Side* for the National Theatre, Elizabeth Bennet in *Pride and Prejudice* at Salisbury Playhouse, as well as seasons at Pitlochry Festival Theatre, Salisbury, Newbury Watermill and

Amanda Bellamy

Perry Benson

Hilda Braid

(Documentation shows that the theme music was recorded on Friday 11th November 1988). I managed to get the great Sousaphone player John Elliott. He has a Sousaphone that was built in 1929 so it seemed perfect for the sound I was trying to capture. I added a banjo, drums, piano and a few other instruments then went into the studio to record it. I can't honestly remember where we did it but the usual places the BBC would use were the old CTS Studios next to Wembley Stadium (now demolished sadly) or the TV Centre Music Studio. Another facility we would use is Lansdowne Studio at Notting Hill Gate.

Bob Monkhouse was David's choice to sing the lead. I wrote the theme in two different keys and when Bob came in we went through it and decided which one would suit him best. He'd been in West End shows so it wasn't too difficult for him to pick it up. I ended up chatting to him for quite a time about all manner of things. He was a very bright man. A lovely person to work with." Roy actually appeared in the show in the very last episode as a pianist for the *Jolly Follies* on Cromer beach. Roy went on to write the theme to *Grace & Favour* and create the *Oh Doctor Beeching!* theme for David Croft (a re-working of the music hall song '*Oh Mister Porter*'). He wrote all the music for Jimmy Perry's stage show *That's Showbiz*. "That developed as it went along. Originally the music was just going to be used for the variety turns doing their acts on stage but then it turned into the fully fledged musical. Great fun to do." Roy's television music has also included series such as *The Brittas Empire, Luv* and *Spark*. He has been musical associate for the *Royal Variety Show* since 1998 and often conducts and arranges for the BBC Concert Orchestra. When asked what his favourite contribution to the Croft canon is, Roy is divided. "The themes for *'Allo 'Allo* and *You Rang, M'Lord?* are both good examples of my work I think. People are still talking about them so I suppose they must be quite memorable for the watching audience."

The theme tune has never appeared on any 'TV Themes' compilation, and the series was not popular enough for it to be released as a single.

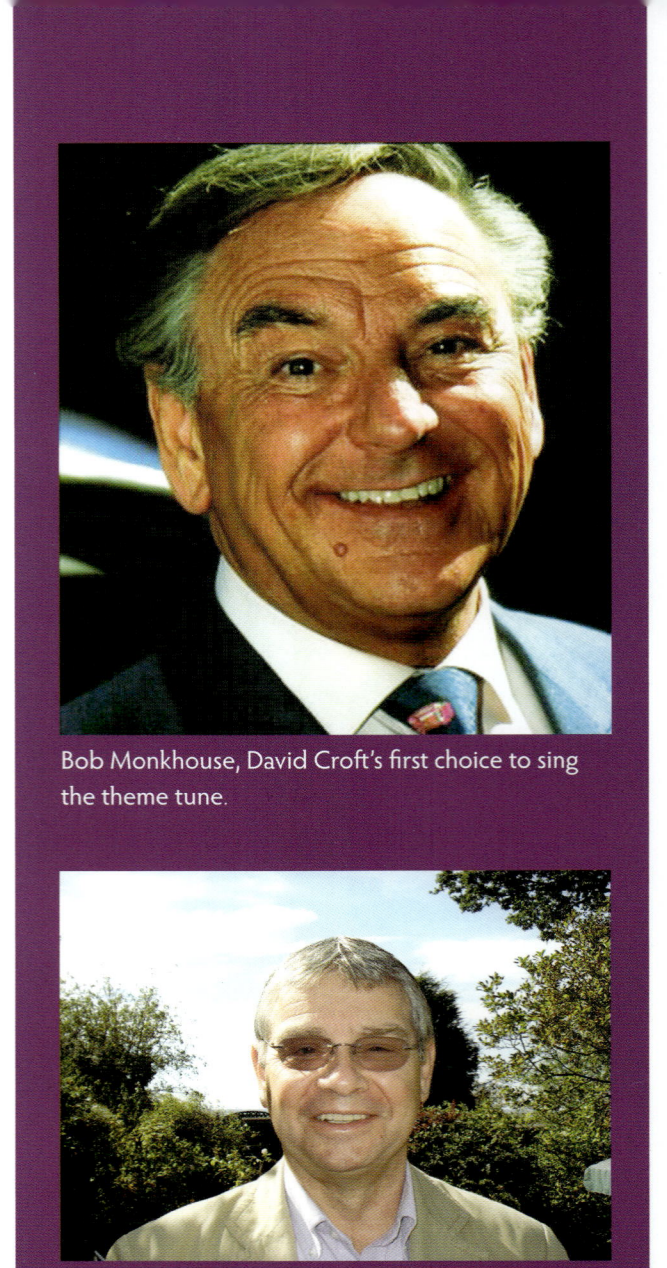

Bob Monkhouse, David Croft's first choice to sing the theme tune.

Roy Moore made a guest appearance in the last episode 'Well, There You Are Then' as a pianist for the 'Jolly Follies'.

The Music

■ **The musical content of You Rang, M'Lord? is down to the genius of Roy Moore. His recreation of the 1920s sound is a major component in making the show feel as authentic as possible.**

Roy started playing piano in his father's pub in the East End, teaching himself the rudiments of the keyboard. "It all progressed from there really," says Roy. "I went from pubs into nightclubs, and by the age of twenty was working for Frankie Vaughan." Roy's move into television came when he started playing keyboards for rehearsals of television variety shows which included *Seaside Special* and series for Lulu and Vince Hill. "I have also played and conducted for over 20 major West End musicals: *Jesus Christ Superstar* at the Palace Theatre, *A Chorus Line* at Drury Lane, *Phantom of the Opera, Starlight Express* - many big name shows." Roy's connection with David Croft stretches back as far as his short-lived show with Jeremy Lloyd, *Oh Happy Band* which starred Harry Worth and ran for just one series in 1980. "I wrote some brass band music for that, and I also arranged the music for the last three series of *It Ain't Half Hot Mum*.

This led to perhaps my most famous composition, the *'Allo 'Allo* theme. David had sketched out a music idea and I took it from there and developed the ideas he wanted, and between us we came up with the accordian led tune." Roy recalls the writing of the 'You Rang' theme: "Jimmy had written a set of lyrics and hummed a sort of musical phrase he thought would fit. Once again I then took it away and started developing ideas and musical riffs until the music fitted the words. I did a bit of research into the 1920s musically. It is a bit of a musical mish-mash really, don't forget by the end of the decade Duke Ellington was around and the whole music scene was starting to change. What I wrote for You Rang, M'Lord? was more of a pastiche really. I assembled eleven musicians to record it.

You Rang, M'Lord?

From Mayfair to Park Lane
You will hear this same refrain
In every house again again
You rang, M'Lord?

Stepping out on the town
The social whirl goes round and round
The rich are up, the poor are down
You rang, M'Lord?

The Bunny Hug at the Shim-Sham club
The Charleston at the Ritz
And at the Troc do the Turkey Trot
They give Aunt Maud a thousand fits

(verse 4 - opening theme)
Saucy flappers in cloche hats
Natty chappies in white spats
The upper set is going bats
You Rang, M'Lord?

(verse 4 - closing theme)
Talking flicks are here today
And Lindbergh's from the USA
Poor Valentino's passed away
How sad, M'Lord?

Words and music by Jimmy Perry and Roy Moore

The Costumes

■ A major feature of all Perry & Croft productions has been the attention to detail. None more so than You Rang, M'Lord? In charge of costume desgn was Mary Husband, who had worked on many other shows including Perry and Croft's. Here we can see a few of her original skteches for some of the programme's characters.

Design for Miss Cissy

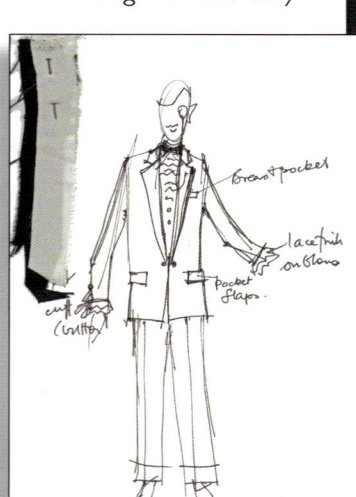

Design for Ivy Teasdale

Design for Lady Agatha

Design for Miss Poppy

Design for Madge Cartwright

Mary Husband

29

right moment, making editing far quicker and easier. Her place, once she left the BBC, was taken by another superb VM, Hilary West, who had the same great gift of timing.

Another late, great, contributor was Bob Monkhouse, who sang the signature tune with Paul Shane, and was the nicest person you could ever wish to meet. I once co-wrote a comedy drama specially for him. Once completed, it was posted to Bob, who telephoned the next day at about 11.00 saying he loved it, but could we change the ending, to give it 'legs' – meaning to enable the story to continue into another episode, or even a series. He must have opened his post that morning and read it straight away, which is virtually unheard of in the industry. It was a great story, and I think a pretty good script. Having Bob so keen to play it made us confident that we would get a commission from our masters at the BBC and hopefully, might be permitted to produce and direct it too. Bob appeared in the very first *Carry On* film, *Carry On Sergeant*, and was a properly trained actor and it would have been a terrific opportunity to cast him in a lead role and stretch his amazing comedy ability. Oh well, another one bites the dust.

The history of broadcasting is littered with great ideas and wonderful scripts that some 'head of' something the public has never heard of either didn't like or didn't understand. In our small island we have some of the most brilliant writers, (no, not just me …) greatest actors, best technicians and craft personnel in the world. And some of the least capable, narrow minded, unadventurous management imaginable.

You Rang, M'Lord? was a great show. It finished at least three series too soon, as the stories could have gone on and on. Knowing it was coming to the end, David and Jimmy wrote a final episode with Paul Shane's character Alf Stokes leaving the Meldrums and going into showbiz with his daughter Ivy, played by Su Pollard, and performing on the beach at Cromer. Not all humour has to be crude or 'pushing the boundaries of taste' – most viewers just want 'more of the same', a heart-warming, poignant blend of humour and pathos, which doesn't shock, insult or patronise, but simply and honestly, educates, informs and entertains them. Familiar words?

Filming 'Well, There You Are Then' at Sporle. David Croft presents Bill Pertwee with a gift that amuses the rest of the cast.

flight. No thought of insurance or possible consequences. I think that was the only time I was ever furious with Jeremy, who now lives in New Zealand. He didn't go there because I was furious with him of course.

The most difficult location to find was the 'Union Jack Rubber Company', Lord Meldrum's factory [seen in 'Trouble at Mill']. There was a possible location in Brandon, a now demolished factory which had a delightful mis-print on its chimney, where the word "WORKS" had been painted in huge letters as "WORRS" and after decades, never corrected. That one was a bit close to the road, and so not perfect, as we had a large number of supporting artistes portraying the striking workers. Or maybe they would have been 'worrers' in Brandon. In the end it was David Croft who came up with the location, near Diss where we eventually filmed the sequence. It was blazing hot weather, and so hard work. I had a pleasant few days, taking photographs of almost everyone on the unit sunbathing or 'resting their eyes' in between sequences, for a mounted display, with captions, at the wrap party. The ingenuity of members of the crew finding a hiding place for a quiet doze where I couldn't find them knew no bounds. I drew the line at climbing up on to the roof of the genny though, although I was sure I could hear snoring.

One of the most memorable scenes for me was recorded in the studio. I acted as Floor Manager in the studio, and loved running the show downstairs with the studio audience, while David and Roy did all the worrying up in the gallery. The scene [in 'Requiem for a Parrot'] concerned Jeffrey Holland's character James Twelvetrees who was celebrating his birthday. Ivy (Su Pollard) was desperately in love with Twelvetrees, and had saved up her meagre wages to buy him a pair of pewter cufflinks. She was so excited, and looking forward to giving him this gift. Unfortunately, Poppy Meldrum, the younger daughter from upstairs also had the 'hots' for James the Butler, and came downstairs to give him her birthday present, a pair of solid gold cuff links. Ivy was 'upstaged' and humiliated as Brenda Cowling, as Mrs Lipton the Cook said " and you've got something for James, haven't you Ivy?" There followed a wonderful, heart-wrenching moment in the well of the back stairs where Ivy retreated, to sob and try to come to terms with the situation. I stood near Su, with the cameras running, but a discreet distance away, while she prepared herself for this little scene. When she was ready, she just nodded to me, and I cued the cameras. It was one of the best examples of acting skill I have ever seen, quite remarkable. Our Miss Pollard is a seriously fine, high calibre actress. One can only hope that the National Theatre, or Stratford (or both) will give her the chance to share her talent with a different audience someday soon.

In the studio, another key figure was the late and much lamented Angie Beveridge, a wonderful vision mixer (and remarkably, ex-Windmill dancing girl!) with a great skill for comedy timing, cutting from camera to camera at exactly the

Jeffrey Holland, Donald Hewlett, David Croft and Su Pollard share a moment together in the grounds of Bayfield Hall.

Setting up to film the 'Jolly Follies' on the beach at Cromer in suitably hot weather.

Susie Brann and Perry Benson share a joke on location.

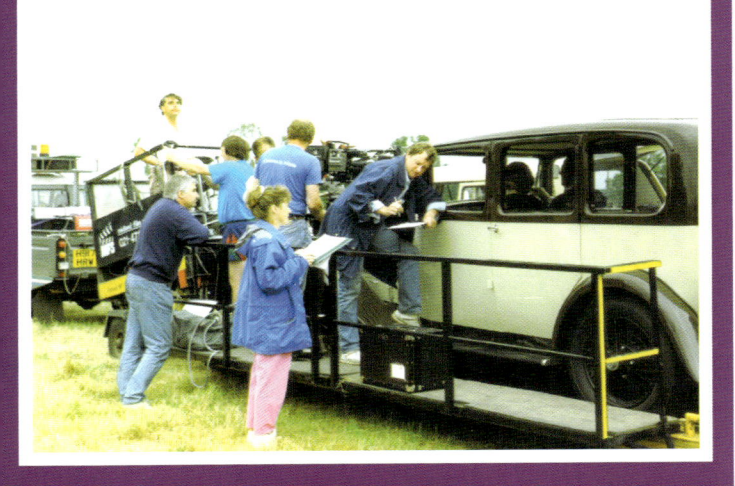

To film action inside moving vehicles, they are placed on a moving trailer. The Cameramen are preparing their equipment in front of Lord Meldrum's Rolls Royce.

tape faults with the use of modern equipment, rebuild whole sections of damaged material, and make the sound crisp and clear, delivering finished programmes that looked as though they had been made last month. The comedy repeats which are still being shown on both BBC1 and 2 are the product of this work.

Duncan Brown lit the studio element of the show in the days of lighting cameramen on film, but once we had changed to videotape, he joined us on location. He was brilliant at creating mood and atmosphere, and a wonderful thoughtful figure at rehearsals, usually sitting on the floor with huge charts of the studio ceiling which showed all the 'bars' from which the lights were hung. He didn't like to be disturbed when deep in thought, but in all the years I knew him, I never heard him raise his voice. He was also great company on location, and something of a fan of Abbott Ale, the strong and smooth speciality of Greene King, brewed in my home town, Bury St Edmunds.

John Vincent also became a key figure in the team, when he became first choice for studio camera supervisor. Once we moved on to recording digitally, John and his hand-picked team came on location with us. One memorable moment on location was when we filmed with a 'Puss Moth' - a tiny light aircraft, and junior version of the better know Gypsy Moth - which was to be 'piloted' by Katie Rabett as Cissy, chasing her Uncle Teddy, as everyone raced to stop him eloping to Gretna Green with a Parlour Maid. John Vincent's assistant Darrell, now a much sought after and experienced DOP, went too close to the engine, and sustained a nasty burn to his arm on the exhaust pipe. This, naturally enough, became the subject of much teasing and comments about playing with toy aeroplanes. I won't mention that we all called him Beryl, because that would be unkind. As Felix Bowness (our fabulous warm-up man on every show, and best known as Fred the Jockey in *Hi-De-Hi!*) would say, "Everyone makes mistakes, that's why they put rubbers on the end of pencils"

I also won't mention that in order to get the shots, the Director had the 'Puss Moth' put on the back of a low loader (a lorry that is used to transport vehicles) with visual effects providing smoke on request. The idea was to have the camera low down, looking up at Cissy at the controls as we trundled down the runway at Little Snoring airfield. It all looked marvellous with the sky and occasional cloud in the background, and we spent a happy day going up and down, re-setting, turning round, and avoiding the hares which live on the airfield and grow almost as big as Dalmatians without the spots.

Production Manager Jeremy Connor (son of another *Hi-de-Hi!* regular, Kenneth Connor) came back from that location and admitted that he, and a couple of un-named members of the cast (quick check to see who's looking guilty Perry Benson …) had accepted an invitation to go up in the 'Puss Moth' after we had all left the location, for a "trip round the bay" sight-seeing

26

Beluga caviar, and ice cold Russian vodka, which would have kept the night chills out very nicely. How mistaken I was. When all the cast (and Roy, the rotter) had gone back to the hotel, and the crew were finishing their de-rig, I presented myself to the Captain's cabin, and was treated to cubes of spam with powdery dry black bread, and large slugs of neat Smirnoff blue vodka, probably straight from Tesco's. Showing enjoyment and gratitude for such treats in the middle of the night stretched my limited acting skills rather, and knowing that I mustn't yawn or appear to want to leave too soon, for fear of causing offence was not easy.

Evenings were spent in Swaffham, with Hugh and June, then owners of The George Hotel, making us all feel more like guests than clients. Once in a while the local restaurants were patronised, and the hotel restaurant was excellent, but with such incredible location catering, many of the cast visited the bar briefly, and then retired to their rooms to study lines for the next day.

■ The Team

The ever youthful Michael McCarthy was in charge of sound (again, his title changed from Sound Supervisor to Sound Designer) and was always number one choice in the studio. Mike had the rare skill of recording the audience laughter and reactions and mixing it with the action on set in such a way that the viewer felt that they were in the studio too. He would trim the end of the laughs so that none of the lines was lost. And no, we didn't use "canned laughter". Ever.

Michael worked with David and Jimmy from *Dad's Army* onwards, and after the whole run of Croft/Perry programmes drew to a close, I was given the enviable job of re-editing a huge number of shows from the BBC's considerable comedy archive, and worked on each one with Michael to ensure that the sound as well as the pictures were perfect. Steve Jamison was the BBC Editor who carried out the technical side of this work, re-cutting the pictures, and using his enormous expertise to make each moment look wonderful.

As Steve and Michael are both perfectionists, the end results were spectacular. We were able to repair camera faults and

Setting up a scene at Brisley for 'Gretna Green or Bust', where a roadside garage was constructed.

Paul Shane, resembling 'Toad of Toad Hall' sits with Su Pollard.

Su Pollard receives the attention of a make-up girl, who is still sporting her *Hi-de-Hi!* sweatshirt.

All made up and ready to go at Blickling Hall, Michael Knowles, Donald Hewlett, Catherine Rabett and Jeffrey Holland

Susie Brann, Angela Scoular, Mavis Pugh and Barbara New, with David Croft lurking in the far background.

"I can't remember the last time I 'ad a banana". Barbara New takes lunch between takes at Blickling Hall.

looked like Elmer Fudd chasing Bugs Bunny, we had to stop work until the laughter subsided.

By now we were recording the show on videotape, and not using film - so when the script called for a night shoot, we put it into the schedule with a little trepidation. We used a Russian cargo boat, which was the only vessel that looked suitable, in an ageing part of the docks at Kings Lynn ['Stranger in the Night']. Negotiating this was, to say the least, tricky. My command of Russian is non-existent, and the Captain's English was patchy.

One of the problems was that the crew maintained Vladivostok time wherever they were in the world, so that their duty shifts were easier to organise. When we arrived at nine in the evening the ship's crew were just getting up for breakfast, having unloaded their cargo of wood the previous day. The sun went down, it was a dry, clear night, and the quayside began to take on a slightly derelict look. I think it has all been redeveloped now. This was a particularly good evening for Katie Rabett, who played Cissy, the elder daughter of Lord Meldrum. In this episode, a Russian sailor (played excellently by Buster Waeland, a regular actor in several of the Croft shows) implied that the Captain would fancy Cissy, "he likes blondes", and she laid him out with a straight right. A classy actress, Katie. On 'wrap' we had organised bangers and mash and onion gravy which went down a storm. Incidentally, in case you don't know, "wrap" is an acronym for 'wind reel and print' which is what they used to call out in the old days of the Hollywood movies when the final shot of the day had been successfully completed.

The Captain of the Russian ship could not be given any money for lending us his ship, as he would have had to explain where it came from when he returned to port. But I had noticed that he had two huge posters in his cabin, one a portrait of Lenin, the other of Elvis Presley, complete with Hawaiian shirt, in one of his iconic poses. I asked the prop buyer to purchase as many Elvis videos as he could get his hands on, and a video player which the Captain could link up to his TV. He was thrilled, and invited Roy and me to join him in his cabin after the shoot for a drink. It may have been 3.00am for us, but it was perfect time for him to have an early lunch! I imagined downed very quickly, and wanting a re-fill, Maurice taps his wine glass gently against the bottle to attract the attention of the 'waiter', and then immediately looks at the ceiling, to give the impression that it was someone else who made the noise of chinking glass. This simple bit of comedy 'business' was perfect for the scene, and lives on in my house whenever a wine glass is requiring attention. The chinking of glass on bottle, or the casual enquiry "are we expecting Maurice Denham?" is enough to have me reaching for the bottle, and addressing the problem.

Despite all our best endeavours, the schedulers (who live like eagles in the lofty regions of the sixth floor at BBC Television Centre) did not find the show an easy one to fit into their grand plans, for reasons which no-one has ever adequately explained. I don't accept that the audience figures were not good enough to justify its future.

It has never been repeated, although, apparently, the DVD sales are good. Perhaps if lots of people demanded that it is shown again, right from the pilot onwards, the BBC might relent.

■ On Location

We filmed You Rang, as with previous shows, in and around Norfolk. I grew up in East Anglia, and my local knowledge (and sometimes that of family and friends) helped find some of the locations. One of these was The Bell pub at Brisley, which was excellent, giving us plenty of space for the vintage cars that formed the "car chase" sequence ['Gretna Green or Bust']. It was also incredibly nice to break for lunch, and go on to the set for a pint with the boys in the crew. The pub remained open for us, but closed to the public during the day. Some cast members were sensible enough to return to the set for dinner in the evening, as the restaurant has a great reputation. I recall that Dover sole there was unbeatable. Further along the road was an old garage which looked perfect, although it hadn't been used as a commercial premises for years. This gave it a lovely derelict look which required very little assistance from the design team. In the other direction a picture-postcard thatched cottage which provided some great shots for Director Roy Gould, who used it as a backdrop with

Bill Pertwee at the wheel of a vintage Leyland Bus. The vehicle is on a trailer to enable filming to take place - note all the wires.

vintage cars going up and down in the chase to catch Teddy Meldrew (Michael Knowles) en route for Gretna Green.

One principal location proved to be probably the best place I have ever filmed - and I think most of the team felt the same way ['A Day In The Country']. We were made welcome in the beautiful home of Robin and Kim Combs at Bayfield Hall, (near Langham) and soon we got to know all the family. They were marvellously enthusiastic about our being there, and helped organise an end of shoot party which has never been equalled. The 'sparks' (electricians) set up floodlights from the genny (generator) when the lighting grew dim, and we held our own Olympic games, Bayfield style. Robin started each race using an eight bore shotgun as a starting pistol! Su Pollard doing the three legged race (although who her partner was has faded in my memory) was hilarious, and to observe, shall we say, 'senior' comedy actors rushing round doing relay races was brilliant. As usual, Paul Shane and Jeffrey Holland made sure that everyone joined in. Sadly, I have never had the requirement of a stately home again, so no excuse to return to Bayfield Hall with other comedy shows. Happy memories of lovely Hugh Lloyd as a drunken Butler telling the Meldrum party to "push off" when they try to set up their picnic next to the lake, and John Horsley as the furious husband of Lord Meldrum's mistress hunting him down in the woods with a shotgun ['The Truth Revealed']. When Jeff Holland said he

The Union Jack Rubber Company was realised at a carpet factory in Diss situated in Factory Road. New housing now occupies the site.

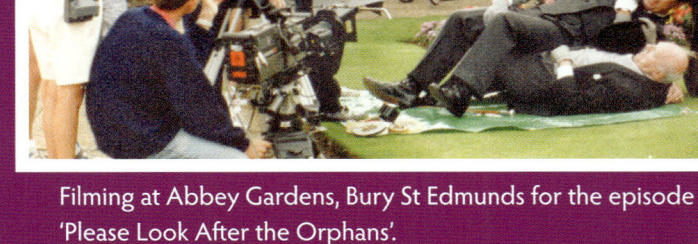

Filming at Abbey Gardens, Bury St Edmunds for the episode 'Please Look After the Orphans'.

the programmes with You Rang, M'Lord? and was extremely fortunate to be chosen again to be part of the team. I didn't work on the pilot - one of my BBC colleagues had that pleasure, but by the time the series was planned she was pregnant, and so I took over.

Again, it was a fantastic team of professionals that made 'You Rang', and everyone seemed to have a terrific time as well as turning out a first class product. This was a ground-breaking programme, which feature eventually led to its early demise. David and Jimmy had discovered during the making of *Dad's Army*, *It Ain't Half Hot Mum* and *Hi-de-Hi!* that it is difficult to develop characters, as well as keeping the audience laughing, within a thirty minute time slot. David negotiated with the department to create the new show with a fifty minute duration, thus creating a comedy drama / situation comedy hybrid.

Transmitted mid-evening on a Sunday, You Rang seemed the perfect product for that slot, and although it was afforded far less budget than the drama department would have been given, it had the same high production values and a rich, sophisticated look. David always considers this show "the jewel in the crown" of his work. Its authenticity was carefully watched over by an alert Jimmy Perry, who would step in to correct the occasional pronunciation question, or explain an attitude between the upstairs and downstairs staff.

One memorable scene had unconventional casting. In the show, Lady Lavender (wonderfully played by Mavis Pugh) is always harking back to her youth, and her (probably imagined) affair with "Captain Dolby". When planning this series, Roy Gould and I were discussing casting, and I asked who he thought should play this part. Roy said he would like the well known classical actor Maurice Denham to play the part – but realised that there was no chance of him agreeing to take part in a sitcom in such a minor capacity. I have always believed in aiming for the top first, worrying about second choices later, so immediately looked up Maurice's agent and rung them to suggest the idea. Agents usually say "is this an availability enquiry or an offer?" and I, of course, said it was an offer. It would certainly not be necessary to ask Maurice Denham to read for the part, and put him up against other actors in an audition, and would have been a terrible insult, implying that we were not sure if he could do it well enough. The agent rang Maurice, we faxed over the relevant pages for him to look at, and he had agreed to play Captain Dolby by the end of the afternoon. I have seldom seen a Director happier.

The scenes that Maurice appeared in was shot in the studio at Elstree, and he was brilliant. In one sequence, he inadvertently wanders into the servants' room, believing it to be a restaurant. The butler, James Twelvetrees (Jeffrey Holland) plays along with his mistake, and serves him with a glass of wine. This is

Series Production

■ **Charles Garland was one of the lynchpins of You Rang, M'Lord? and here he recounts his experiences on the show and life as part of the David Croft team.**

I was mad about theatre and television from an early age. Two of my brothers went into the business, one as an Managing Director, the other as a Dancer/Singer. I went my own way, and following drama school, I started in theatre at Birmingham Rep'. After many different jobs, I joined the BBC in 1986.

My second week at the BBC was spent at Dovercourt. My boss thought I ought to have some experience of location filming, so off I went to be part of the Hi-de-Hi! team. I enjoyed the whole experience so much, that when I returned to London to continue work on the production I had been employed to do (Mozart's *Cosi Fan Tutte* directed by Dr (now Sir) Jonathan Miller), I couldn't bear not to be part of the *Hi-de-Hi!* gang, and so I went to every studio recording on Friday evenings, helped out where I could and acted as 'head waiter' in 'hospitality' after the show. I think I became part of the furniture, and so was invited back to David Croft's office when it was time to do *'Allo 'Allo!*

Having established a superb team to work on *Hi-de-Hi!*, David had many of the same crew working on *'Allo 'Allo!* This included the wonderful Bernadette Darnell as PA (David always called her his 'secretary', a throw-back to the days before the Production Assistant title was invented). Because I was a relatively new AFM (Assistant Floor Manager) I needed someone to turn to for advice from time to time, and Bernie was generous in this respect. She always knew what was going on, and put me right on many occasions, privately, and without embarrassing me in front of the crew. Luckily for me, I got to work with Bernie many times in the future - the best in the business.

Max Samett was the film 'lighting cameraman' – the best film cameramen always lit their own shots. These days they are elevated to DOP, Director of Photography. Most television programmes are recorded on digital tape these days, and will soon probably all be made on computer driven cameras with no tape at all. This means that apart from feature films, the demands are different today. Max was brilliant at doing "day for night" shooting. Instead of taking everyone out to film night scenes after the sun had gone down (cold, difficult with lots of supporting artists getting mislaid in the dark, and expensive, with everyone needing a day off afterwards to recover). Max was a master of shooting a night scene in broad daylight! Even direct sunlight didn't seem to put him off. By blasting the foreground with masses of light from huge lamps and leaving the background unlit, he was able to create the illusion of darkness. I suspect that this is only possible on film, where the foreground is in focus, but the background is hazy and out of focus. When scenes are recorded on videotape, both the foreground and the background are in sharp focus, which is one of the reasons why they look so different.

I became more closely involved with the administration of

Charles Garland sits flanked by Jimmy Perry and David Croft on location in Blickling Hall, accompanied by Su Pollard (with Paul Shane in the background).

happy that You Rang, M'Lord? was in effect lampooning the era in another prime-time slot. David Croft immediately went into battle for the show, citing its consistent ratings and also pointing to the impressive mail bag of appreciative letters the production office had received since going to air. David got his commission for a fourth, and ultimately final, batch of episodes. The production team as a whole were far from satisfied with the scheduling of the final run. "They put it on a Saturday which was quite unsuitable", David says adamantly. "It was a Sunday show, a piece of major entertainment, not really a show for the usual comedy slots. Dad's Army is fine for Saturday but there are certain shows which are not, You Rang, M'Lord? was one such."

Eventually over a period of four years, 26 episodes of You Rang, M'Lord? were produced by David Croft for the BBC. It remains the highlight of both Jimmy and David's careers. The series lives on in DVD format although repeats are few and far between, even on the satellite channels, as the large casts that populate the programmes make it a more expensive proposition to repeat than say other comedy programmes with a regular core of four or five actors. The programme has been particularly popular with the Eastern European countries, Hungary specifically where it is known as Csengetett, Mylord? The title in Poland is Pan Wyzwal, Milordzie? It has proved popular too in New York, where the citizens seem to have taken to the Meldrum household with some relish judging from fan mail received by cast members.

There can be little doubt that You Rang, M'Lord? remains the 'forgotten classic' when ranked next to the three series that preceded it from the pens of Perry and Croft. However, among serious aficionados of their work there is a feeling that You Rang, M'Lord? is the glittering peak of Jimmy and David's output for the BBC. As worthy of a place in the classic comedy vaults as Dad's Army, It Ain't Half Hot Mum, Hi-de-Hi! and a whole host of accepted jewels in the BBC's comedy crown. The toast is to the House of Meldrum. Long may the bell continue to ring, M'Lord.

Blanche Lipton and Lord Meldrum on the occasion of her wedding to Constable Wilson.

Rose and Boot Boy Henry Livingstone..

the BBC canteen on recording days! The location recording was mostly done in 'Croft Country', locations in Norfolk and Suffolk within striking distance of David's Honington home. One change that occurred with Series Three was that the location footage ceased to be shot on film. The outdoor sequences were recorded on videotape, as per the studio scenes, which was not only a cheaper option but afforded opportunities to record more material in a day. A debate will certainly rage over the merits of film against videotape, but this was becoming common practise among the comedy department and the Croft production team were one of the last production teams at the BBC to convert to the newer format for location shoots. It was though much the end of an era for the David Croft production office. The scenes still looked stunning on videotape capturing the series' marvellous period detail, but perhaps a little of the panache had gone out of the outdoors sequences having lost the skill of the film cameraman.

Perry and Croft's always superb writing tackled deeper issues within the concept of the class struggles in Edwardian London. Poverty was frequently addressed by way of Mabel's struggles to make ends meet. Dementia too was touched upon with the bizarre antics of Lady Lavender and there cannot be many mainstream comedies that have tackled a lesbian relationship, albeit the scenes between Miss Cissy and her 'chum' Penelope were always handled with great subtlety. Physical abuse was on the agenda too courtesy of Henry's all to frequent smacks to the head from James and Blanche. The morals of both upstairs and downstairs staff were constantly brought under scrutiny. Lord Meldrum's illicit affair with Lady Agatha and by contrast Mr. Teddy's infatuation with servant girls, and Rose in particular, didn't show them in a favourable light. The downright spoilt nature of Miss Poppy with her bitchy comments and selfish actions threatened to make her virtually the villain of the piece. Downstairs Alf's constant attempts to secure money by nefarious means similarly made it difficult for viewer sympathies to veer in his direction. Even the establishment in the form of Constable Wilson, the ever dependable British bobby, was shown to be corruptible and prone to press himself on the house looking for food

Teddy looking uncomfortable in bed with Madge Cartwright.

and shelter on a lonely beat. Far from being stock comedy characters, all the inhabitants of Lord Meldrum's London residence serve to illustrate how life was being lived as the late 1920s. It would be easy for an historian to choose You Rang, M'Lord? as a living example of the era. It is researched and written with all the dedication to detail as you might expect from the brilliant team of Jimmy Perry and David Croft.

Despite the immense popularity with the viewers, some of the tabloids of the time became quite critical of the casting and the format of the show that didn't rely totally on comedy. "You always get this," laments Jimmy Perry. "The very sad thing is when you set out to do something and the critics completely misunderstand what you are on about. We did a lot of social comment and that was that." David Croft agrees: "You Rang, M'Lord? was very different. They were fifty minutes and that makes it a different proposition to write and produce actually. You can get deeper into stories and into characters. We were more mature writers by then too. You Rang M'Lord was a carefully crafted piece of work, beautifully performed and very authentic."

The BBC showed very little interest in commissioning a fourth series. Their flagship drama *The House of Elliot,* set in the 1920s and again created by Jean Marsh and Eileen Atkins, had started in 1991 in which the BBC had invested heavily. It seemed that there were whispers that the hierarchy were not show. "I found working with the David Croft team on You Rang, M'Lord? such a rewarding experience," says Amanda. "The cast and crew were all just lovely, as were David and Jimmy. I knew we were going to have fun from the off. I was also learning a lot about the business of television during the series. I had done small roles but Rose enabled me to play a larger part in the action and to observe the filming of other scenes from the sidelines. Watching the comedy technique of so many skilled actors was a great boon for me and part of my learning curve and David, Roy and the technicians were all very approachable and enhanced my understanding of the technical side in a nice, relaxed way. Working with Michael Knowles was good fun, although filming the scenes was always taken quite seriously; as it should be, I think. My main memory of Michael is of having chats about his twin daughters and keeping up with what they were up to. Also getting thoroughly drenched together for the filming of one of our assignations! When we were out on location I remember admiring how Su Pollard seemed to have time for everybody. She would always take the opportunity to chat to the crowds that would gather to watch the filming. Less approachable actors might have found the attention intrusive and wanted a bit of peace between scenes, but Su always seemed happy to chat and sign autographs. So that again was something I took on board; Su's graciousness. Jimmy was very warm and encouraging too. He was kind enough to introduce me to his agent, hoping that she would take me on, but it was not to be. However, the fact that he made the introduction was touching and he apparently wrote the part of Phyllis in *London Calling* with me in mind."

One incident from the show that Paul Shane remembers very well is in the episode 'Current Affairs' when Mrs. Lipton was called to smash a plate over Alf's head. Paul explains: "Brenda Cowling had to pick up a plate and whack me over the head with it. These things are specially made so that they're supposed to smash easily. But this one didn't. They made it too thick. At the afternoon camera rehearsal Mrs. Lipton walked around the table and hit me on the head with this great plate - I don't know how I stood up. There was a lump on my head the size of a golf ball. I did the scene and when we finished I said 'Jesus, what's going on?' On the night in front of the studio audience I didn't want to do the scene again but we had to. They made a much thinner version and on the second attempt I didn't feel a thing. She nearly killed me first time around though. It wasn't Brenda's fault, I told her it had got to look real so just go for it."

Although the pilot episode was recorded at Television Centre, as most of David's comedy shows had been, he opted to record all further You Rang, M'Lord? programmes at the BBC's Elstree studio complex at Borehamwood, Hertfordshire. This enabled the lavish sets to be erected and left standing for the duration of the production period rather than be pulled down after each week's recording. Elstree is, of course, the location of Albert Square and the *EastEnders* sets. It was not uncommon to see Mrs. Lipton dining next to Dot Cotton in

Angela Scoular and John Horsley as Sir Ralph and Lady Agatha Shawcross.

Mrs Lipton packs a picnic - Mabel looks on expectantly.

"There was a wonderful sense of family, team work and having fun. One day during a dress rehearsal Paul Shane came up behind me and thrust a stuffed crocodile he had found on set in my face roaring as he did so – I jumped out of my skin! But for all the larking about when David said it was time for a take, everyone was 100% professional. Spot on with lines, cues and marks." The family unit even helped Susie through personal problems at the time. "I was engaged to a man who ultimately wasn't right for me, and the engagement was called off. We were filming in Norfolk, I was in make-up for an early 6am call, it was my birthday and I was feeling very sorry for myself and in came Su Pollard with a goldfish in a bowl. 'This is to replace Charlie' she said. 'One day you will grow to love him.'" Susie rates two particular moments in the show as her favourites. "One was when Jeff Holland and I were playing the ukulele and singing *Ain't She Sweet* ['The Wounds Of War']. I'd read the script weeks before and got lessons so I could play the ukulele for real. I don't know if David expected me to do that. Originally we were going to do a tiny bit of the song but when he heard me play he suggested we play the whole song. We asked Charles Garland to work out a two part harmony for it and it made a lovely moment in the show. Another favourite scene is the one where Poppy goes downstairs and catches the servants having a coffee break ['Royal Flush']. I had terrible trouble doing that scene because I found Barbara New so funny and I had to get angry with the servants, it made me want to laugh and it was very hard keeping that desire under control. Poppy was a real villain. I figured out that she had lost her mother and perhaps hadn't been getting the best guidance from her father, so sought attention in the wrong ways like teasing and flirting with poor James. I was always searching for ways to find the reality behind the character. David delights in getting people to do things on screen that they might not do in real life. I think I am known for a kind nature off screen, and he kept pushing me to be more and more horrible in front of the camera. I have to say it was jolly good fun."

Another character who, like Madge Cartwright, started life in a small way but became central to the action was Madge's Maid, Rose. Amanda Bellamy has very fond memories of the

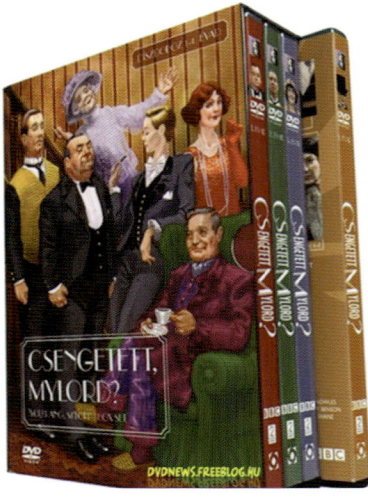

Hungarian DVD Box Set

Hungarian DVD sleeve for Series Two

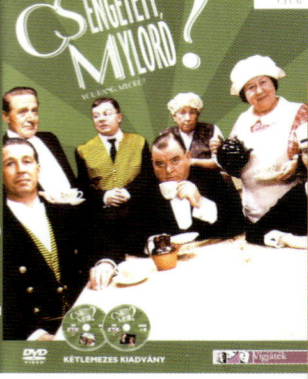

Polish DVD sleeve for Series Four

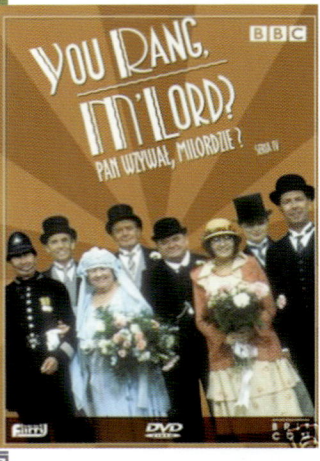

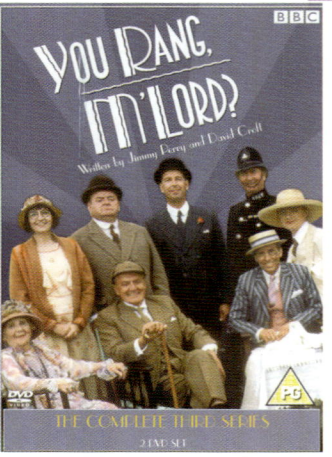

British DVD sleeve for Series Three

You Rang, M'Lord? has proven to be very popular in certain countries, in particular, Hungary and Poland. Healthy DVD sales have been experienced helped by the availability of box sets and native language packaging.

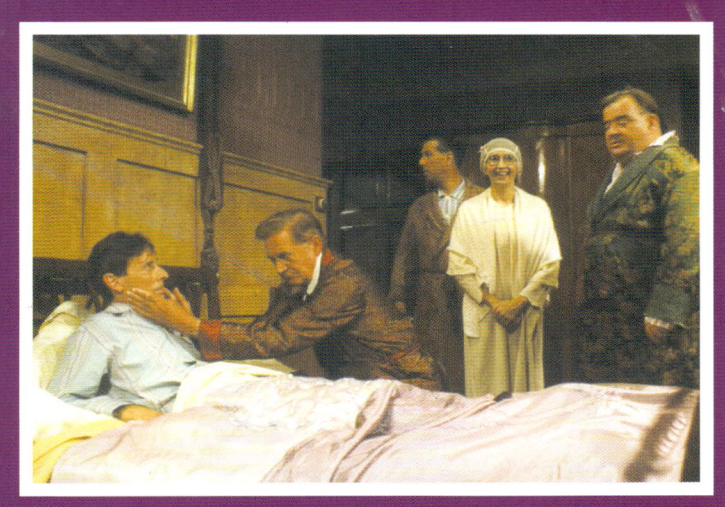

Mr Teddy's bedroom was one of the many sets used throughout the programme, all of which were lavishly appointed.

Bill Pertwee and Barbara New as Mabel during a break in filming the wedding scenes at Sporle, Norfolk.

Miss Cissy and her friend Penelope Barrington-Blake.

'Allo 'Allo. It was during this time that someone, and I forget who exactly, came up and told me David and Jimmy had written a part for me in their pilot for You Rang, M'Lord? I just burst into tears. I couldn't believe they had been so kind. Madge started out as a small role but as the show progressed it developed. I was well known for making jams and pickles during rehearsals and bringing in jars for the cast and crew. Imagine my surprise when the scripts started to reflect this and suddenly Cartwright's Pickles were mentioned, and the jam. I think they were making fun of me but I didn't mind. The show was such a wonderful experience."

One central figure to the drama upstairs was the manipulative Miss Poppy. The roll went to relatively inexperienced television performer Susie Brann. Susie recalls how she came to be working with the Perry and Croft repertory company. "I got a job in *Daisy Pulls It Off* at the old Globe Theatre with Susan Beagley, who had been a Yellowcoat in *Hi-de-Hi!* Susan introduced me to David Croft who basically told me he couldn't give me anything better than what I was doing at the moment and to stick with the play. So that was that. However, keeping in mind my ambitions of wanting to work in a sit-com, I had a 'god' moment a couple of years later and just got a feeling I should 'phone David Croft to see if there was any work going. I got to speak to his assistant Bernadette Darnell and she told me that quite by chance, they were casting for David and Jimmy's new show You Rang, M'Lord? the following day. She told me about the two daughters of Lord Meldrum and asked me which one I thought I would be right for. Somehow she managed to get me seen and I raided my wardrobe for the interview trying desperately to look as 1920s as I could. At the end of it David said, 'You are a bit of a pain aren't you?' 'Why?' I asked. 'We thought we'd found our Poppy but now we just don't know.' *'I'm* your Poppy' I told them, desperately wanting it. But they told me I would have to come back for a recall. So back I went and David sat with his feet up looking quite casual and I read the part again, then he muttered 'Alright, alright, you've got the part.' I couldn't believe it. I said 'I could hug you, but I feel too shy.' 'Don't let that put you off' came the dry reply." Working with David's regular band of performers was an inspiring time for Susie.

"I auditioned for Jimmy and David and ended up playing a protégé pianist who was part of Paul Shane's scams to get some money out of the campers." Perry recalls. "The tag was that I could only play *Chopsticks* when they asked me to play in the ballroom sequence. About six months after I had done it, I got a 'phone call. It was the day after my birthday and I was quite hung-over. I was also feeling quite sorry for myself because I was out of work. David told me about the pilot of *You Rang, M'Lord?* and asked if I'd like to do it. I played it very cool and said 'I dunno really' but inside I was jumping up and down with excitement. I remember saying to him 'I'll have to talk to my agent about it' and put the phone down on him!" Consequently of course, the deal was done and Perry became Henry, the sardonic Boot Boy. "The food was very nice all through You Rang," he says. "The filming in Norfolk was lovely. I enjoyed that a lot."

When the offer of playing Madge Cartwright arrived it came at just the right moment for Yvonne Marsh: "At that time in my life I had become extremely poor. I had jobs directing summer seasons at Cromer, Norwich and Hunstanton but the wolf was at the door in no uncertain terms. One of the performers I was directing, Dorothy Wayne, suggested that I do some crowd work at Warner's, Dovercourt, for David Croft, as they were recording *Hi-de-Hi!* there. Without sounding too grand it was a bit of a come down as I had made a name for myself in theatres all over the country but I needed money to simply pay the rates. I even agreed to go on early call at 6am because of the extra money the overtime would bring. When I was on set I was spotted by some of the performers I had worked with. Ruth Madoc came over to say hello. 'What are you doing hiding here in the crowd?' she asked. Similarly Su Pollard whom I had auditioned many times as a Director and knew she was destined to be a star, came over to chat. Likewise Jimmy Perry, whom I had known from some job in the past. So I was known to some of the people involved. I had a happy time being a camper at Maplin's Holiday Camp. The atmosphere on set was always fun. I remember writing to David and Jimmy telling them I had more to offer than just standing in the background, I had been known to handle a few lines myself! I then went on to do similar crowd scenes for David Croft on

James Twelvetrees receives a cheesey grin from Miss Poppy. She would tease James throughout the series.

PC Wilson, the long arm and capacious stomach of the law, spends more time downstairs than on the beat.

Mr Teddy Meldrum and his sweetheart, Rose, a service girl.

saying that she'd been in service fifty years before and she was cleaning the room of Kitty McShane, the stage daughter of Old Mother Riley, the great variety comic. She spied some face cream on the dressing room table and because she was only sixteen dipped her finger in and put a bit on her face. Anyway the next day Kitty McShane sent for her and shouted 'How dare you touch my make-up' and slapped her across the face. The upshot of it was that the woman's mother was furious and went to see McShane and ended up slapping Kitty herself across the face before storming triumphantly out. It just shows you how You Rang, M'Lord? struck a chord with those who had been in service."

Michael Knowles career has seen him donning several guises for David Croft over the years, you might think playing another 'silly arse' character might have been wearing a bit thin after many years playing Captain Ashwood in *It Ain't Half Hot Mum*. "Teddy is a great favourite," he reveals. "It gave me the chance to do so many different things. There was pathos in there, like the time I was going to shoot myself because I couldn't marry the Maid, Rose. The range within the 'silly arse' persona was enormous and I was disappointed that the programmes only got a limited showing, as David has said it was sometimes badly scheduled." The day recording the pilot scenes in the trenches was particularly vivid for Michael. "It was November when we filmed it and I spent days in the mud and water filming that sequence, laying face down in the trench. When we played it back it could have been anyone doing that part! In the final shot of that scene where Paul carried me off, you only get to see part of it. They made Paul walk and walk and walk with me on his shoulders until he was a speck in the distance before David shouted 'cut'. You should have heard the cursing…" Asked for his favourite moments in the show, Michael offers: "The one where I was creeping along the ledge trying to get into Ivy's room springs to mind. And, of course, the one where I was going to shoot myself. You have to be careful though, because in those sort of scenes you have to keep in the back of your mind that you are doing a comedy and not a drama. You can only go so far before the audience loses sympathy with you. It's a fine line."

Perry Benson was a vastly experienced child actor before finding himself in the Croft ensemble. How did Perry come to find himself in an episode of the final *Hi-de-Hi!* series?

Henry Livingstone and Ivy Teasdale

BBC audience admission ticket. for the recording of 'Beg, Borrow or Steal'. Note that two hours is allocated to record the 50 minute programme

Following the pilot and for subsequent series, a full size recreation of the Meldrum residence was built on the Elstree Studio lot. This was a more practical approach to filming as the crew have full control of their environment.

was a Charlady called Mabel. It was the basis for what was to become one of the show's most popular characters. For Barbara New, the opportunity to play put upon Mabel Wheeler was something of a lottery decision. "My agent said to me the show was coming up and during a conversation with David Croft he said [to David] 'You must use Barbara.'" recalls Barbara. "They had written the script to the pilot episode by then but David said 'There is a tiny part of about three lines, but if Barbara would do it we promise her that if it becomes a series we will write the part up.' So that was a bit of a gamble. At the time we all thought we would be doing another series of *Split Ends* (ITV hairdressing comedy starring Anita Dobson) so I thought 'Why not? I'll do it.' Then of course we didn't do any more *Split Ends* and You Rang, M'Lord? took off."

Mabel became a huge favourite with viewers. "We're the bottom of the pile" Henry says to Ivy in one episode. "What about Mabel?" asks Ivy. "She's a different pile" observes Henry. It was true that Mabel was about as much an under-dog as you can get in television comedy. She is the poorest of the poor, with her husband drinking away what little money she earns at the bar of the Red Lion. The gruff voice was also a feature that people remember. Barbara New was quick to latch onto this aspect. "For the voice I remembered from my childhood kids in the street and they would shout themselves hoarse whilst they were playing. They tended to grow up into people with rather hoarse voices so I thought it would be fun to do that with Mabel. You have to put yourself in the position of people who work very hard physically too." The filming of the episode 'A Day In The Country' was quite memorable for Barbara. "Five days before we were due to do that, I broke my wrist and had to have it put into plaster. There was a bit of a problem as to how they would conceal it on camera. Wardrobe made me a blouse with one arm longer than the other and a shawl. It was fine and nobody ever knew." Does Barbara have a favourite episode? "It would have to be the one that was written for me about going to the servants ball [Come To The Ball]." Fan reaction to Mabel was overwhelming particularly from one little admirer. "There was one episode where everybody had a mince pie except Mabel. I had a sweet letter from a little girl near Bristol. She wrote 'I am so terribly sorry you didn't get a mince pie. Me and my mother have made some so we'd like to invite you to tea.' As there was a telephone number I decided to ring up as Mabel. Her mother answered and I explained who I was. 'Thank God you have rung' the mother said. 'She's driving us mad and won't talk about anything but Mabel.' The little girl was struck dumb when she came to the 'phone but sent me some lovely letters afterwards."

You Rang, M'Lord? was every bit as popular with those that watched it as *Hi-de-Hi!* had been previously. Su Pollard again: "I got a huge mail bag from 'You Rang'. One lady wrote to me

Setting up a scene for the battlefield sequence. The resulting footage gives the series a big budget feel and is most impressive.

20 Holland Park Villas in West London was initially used as externals for the House of Meldrum.

going to be stuck playing a Maid for the rest of my life. They took us aside to try and dismiss some of the initial fears we may have by explaining that for a start we were to look totally different. I was happy that you'd got a chance as a performer not just to play black and white. There was a lot more to Ivy than making someone laugh or making them cry." Whatever the reservations of the performers a full series was quickly commissioned following the pilot. It was decided too that the show would continue character development helped by each subsequent episode being fifty minutes duration. Aside from anything else, You Rang M'Lord? was a massive financial undertaking. The exterior of 12 Palmerston Grove was initially realised in West London at 20 Holland Villas Road which had been carefully sought out as it was the only house in the street not to have been updated with CCTV cameras and all manner of modern security devices. Future exterior shots of the house would be a specially built façade, which would be housed in the large car park of the BBC's Elstree studios. The location footage for the pilot episode was recorded between 14th and 19th November 1988 at various locations. The scenes depicting Alf and Ivy's knife throwing turn were recorded at the King's Theatre, Southsea near Portsmouth. Built in 1907, the theatre retained the original turn-handle lighting board, which was needed to create an authentic feel for the dying days of Music Hall. For the front line battlefields of France,

a plot of wasteland owned by the Ministry of Defence near Aldershot was used to create the sequence where James and Alf find Teddy's body. It was a mammoth task to re-create such a historically important piece of history on the barren land. "The designer planted every one of those burned out trees and church ruins that went to make up the set. It was a massive work of art," remembers Jeffrey Holland. "If you look closely at the first few moments when Paul and I are advancing to the camera, a massive explosion goes off in front of me, blocking us from director Roy Gould's view. Fearing the worst, he turned to David Croft and said 'See you in court!' On screen, the whole sequence looked incredibly realistic." In fact the First World War section was much longer in the original producer's edit, but it was felt that a pilot for a comedy programme should not linger too long on this terrible human conflict, so the scenes were trimmed to quicken the pace and allow a faster route to the 1927 main thrust of the programme. The production purchased one minute of silent film footage of soldiers marching in 1915 from the Pathé Library to play in the opening moments during the newsreel footage in the cinema. Roy Moore played the accompanying piano track 'Pack Up Your Troubles' along with some material he specially composed in the period style.

When Jimmy Perry was young and living in Barnes, his parents had domestic staff to run the house. One of these

On Location

12 Palmerston Grove (the fictional house of Lord Meldrum) was initially realised at BBC Television Centre at White City. The recording of the pilot nearly didn't happen at all as Jeffrey Holland explains:

"We were scheduled to do two consecutive days in the studio (on 3rd and 4th December 1988), the first day to pre-record certain scenes and then strike the sets to make way for the audience seating the following day. The scenes in question were the hospital sequence where Teddy thanked us (Alf and James) for saving his life, the theatre dressing room scene where Alf and Ivy were seen off by a pack of howling poodles and both Teddy's and Lavender's bedroom scenes. Normally at the BBC when a show is to be recorded the scene-fitters, carpenters, painters etc. move it all in and set it up over the previous night so that the actors, cameras, lights and sound can get on with their job the following morning. But imagine our dismay and horror upon arriving at the studio to find nothing ready! Apparently there was either a strike or a work to rule in progress so no one had been in overnight to get the set up, so it had to take place during our rehearsal time. There were bits of scenery, hammers, nails and all sorts of odds and ends lying around all over the place and it was nothing more than a life threatening danger zone. We had to rehearse as best we could, keeping our calm and patience in the best of order and when it came to a 'take' someone would shout 'Quiet please while we record this scene'. Not everyone would hear it and a subsequent scream of 'Stop that bloody banging' (or words to that effect) would ensue to secure the eventual silence needed."

The patience of the entire cast and crew was put to the test with David Croft coming very near to pulling the plug on the entire venture. David knew though that if the recording of the pilot was abandoned the BBC was very unlikely to re-stage the huge undertaking a second time. It was now or never. With a very stressful day pre-recording scenes under his belt, David's day was a little better on the Friday, although the clock was still ticking away with the arrival of the studio audience at 7pm. Somehow, by the miracle of television, everything went to plan and the curtain was lifted on the new Perry and Croft comedy. The pilot was broadcast on 29th December 1988, not even a full year since the final *Hi-de-Hi!* had gone to air. The pilot was a ratings hit with around 10 million viewers tuning in to see just what this new vision created by Perry and Croft was all about. Some of the performers were certainly enjoying the change of characters. "Alf Stokes was a bastard," Paul Shane thinks. "He was a much better character to play than Ted (Bovis). Ted was like an open book but Alf wasn't. He played things very close to his chest. He was a bad man because he didn't want equality, he wanted them upstairs polishing *his* boots. That's the worst person in the world. He didn't want them down on his level, he wanted them below him." Su Pollard had some early worries about playing another domestic. "I thought I was

The King's Theatre, Southsea, used to film the music hall sequence in the pilot.

Alf Stokes, Ivy Teasdale and James Twelvetrees.

The Meldrum Family, Poppy, Lord George and Cissy.

■ Casting

In casting the new programme David and Jimmy lent heavily on actors they had already employed in some of their biggest hits. "We knew for a long time although we didn't dare say anything in case it caused bad feeling [with cast members of *Hi-de-Hi!*]" says Paul Shane. "Su, Jeff and I knew two years before. When we were doing the penultimate series of *Hi-de-Hi!* David and Jimmy took us out to dinner and gave us the bad news: *Hi-de-Hi!* was coming off. But then came the good news: they wanted the three of us in You Rang, M'Lord?" Paul was awarded the role of crafty Butler Alf Stokes, Su Pollard became his daughter Ivy and Jeffrey Holland turned into the pompous Footman James Twelvetrees. *It Ain't Half Hot Mum* stars Donald Hewlett and Michael Knowles became Lord George Meldrum and his brother the Honourable Teddy Meldrum. The chance to be in the show came about in a very strange way for Donald Hewlett: "We were all invited to a London hotel for a secret party for David Croft. He was supposed to address a meeting or something and was unaware that the party had been arranged. Everyone was there from all his shows, it was great fun. In his speech [David] mentioned that he and Jimmy had written You Rang, M'Lord? It had been cast and they were looking forward to getting on with it. Unbeknown to me they had told my 'friend' Michael Knowles that I would be playing the 'M'Lord'. Michael had forgotten to tell me! At this party I was the only person who didn't know they were playing one of the lead parts. When I was told you could have knocked me down with a cocktail stick I can tell you." Donald found aspects of the series very close to home. "I think David and Jimmy must have bugged my house. How could they possibly have known that my father had manufactured chemicals for the rubber trade? In the programme I was running the Union Jack Rubber Company. How spooky is that?" Going further back and raiding the cast of *Dad's Army,* Bill Pertwee swapped his ARP Warden's helmet for a Metropolitan Police version as Constable Wilson and Frank Williams was promoted from Vicar Timothy Farthing to Charles, The Bishop. Some newcomers to the Perry-Croft repertory company included Catherine Rabett (who years before had made headlines as one of Prince Andrew's girlfriends) cast as lesbian inflected Cissy Meldrum and Susie Brann played her less than gracious sister Poppy. The upstairs ensemble was completed by Mavis Pugh, a regular guest star in previous series and married to *Hot Mum* star John Clegg, as the eccentric and booze loving Lady Lavender Southwick. Down below among the rank and file one of Jimmy's old mates from his RADA days, Brenda Cowling, was cast as the cook Mrs. Blanche Lipton, and a further two actors who had been guest stars in the final series of *Hi-de-Hi!* returned to the fold. Barbara New transformed into the ultimate under-dog character, char lady Mabel Wheeler and Perry Benson became wonderfully sarcastic as the put upon Boot Boy Henry Livingstone. The large cast was completed by former star of *The Fall and Rise of Reginald Perrin* John Horsley as Sir Ralph Shawcross, one time Bond girl and Mrs. Leslie Phillips, Angela Scoular, as his wayward wife Lady Agatha and Yvonne Marsh - sister of *Upstairs, Downstairs* creator Jean Marsh - as soap heiress Madge Cartwright.

Programme Origins

■ The Idea

The production that Jimmy and David had been secretly working on during the final two series of *Hi-de-Hi!* had, in fact, been attempted before during the early 1980s when David was working with his other regular writing partner, Jeremy Lloyd. The pair of them had had a session at writing a script based around a comedy version of ITV's popular Edwardian drama *Upstairs Downstairs* detailing the lives of a large London house and the relationships forged between the residents above stairs and the servants below. *Upstairs Downstairs* was created by Jean Marsh and Eileen Atkins and became hugely successful between 1971 and 1975 and featured Gordon Jackson in the role as loyal Butler Hudson, Angela Baddeley as Cook Mrs. Bridges, with Pauline Collins and Jean Marsh taking the roles of Maids Sarah and Rose. Jeremy Lloyd eventually conceded that he was struggling to find enthusiasm for the spoof and instead quickly developed an idea based around the French Resistance during World War II which of course became the international smash *'Allo 'Allo*. It would take a further five years before Jimmy and David seriously turned their attentions to the subject. As ever Jimmy was writing from his own experience - sort of. "My grandfather was a Butler and I heard the real side of *Upstairs Downstairs*. It wasn't all cosy and the servants were on the fiddle because they were not getting enough money." With *Hi-de-Hi!* now over the pair forged ahead with plans for a lavish pilot programme. It was given the title You Rang, M'Lord? Jimmy was particularly keen that whilst basically a comedy programme there should be a certain amount of what he described as 'social comment' where the script wasn't under pressure to produce a laugh every ten seconds. The original idea had been to set it during the abdication of King Edward VIII in 1936. The effects of the 1930s depression would have made for a fascinating look at the lives of the toffs and the servants, but costume designer Mary Husband pointed out that from a costuming point of view, the 1920s would offer a much more stylish alternative, away from the drabness of the following decade.

To allow for character development the pilot programme was set for a one hour duration. The script opens in the battlefields of France during 1918, Alf Stokes and James Twelvetrees are in the trenches with the wounded Teddy Meldrum. Ever the opportunist Alf steals the emerald from Teddy's ring believing him to be dead. When the body stirs James insists they carry him back to the field hospital. By 1927 James is to be found working as a Footman to the Meldrum household in the fashionable Grosvenor area of London. When their old Butler dies, who should come looking for a job but Alf Stokes, who has recently been fired from his job as a comic on the music halls. The scene is then set for a battle of wills between James and the wily Stokes which will involve both the family and the servants.

■ Detonating and filming the shelling effects near Aldershot for the first sequence of the pilot.

Index

Programme Origins	9
Series Production	21
The Costumes	29
The Music	30
The House of Meldrum	32
Episode Guide	46
James and Ivy	57
Beeching and Beyond	61

Introduction by Jeffrey Holland

When I was asked to write an introduction to this book, I was thrilled. This book is honouring a Perry and Croft classic, You Rang, M'Lord? in which I played the pompous footman, James Twelvetrees - a show which I was very proud to be in and is proving itself just as popular today with its fans and admirers, judging from its DVD sales. The BBC in its wisdom chose not to repeat any more than three episodes of the first series of You Rang, M'Lord? back at the turn of the 1990s. In so doing, I cannot help but feel, the BBC has deprived its viewers, and indeed itself, of a much more solid audience base than it really deserved. However it may not be too late. Think on BBC schedulers!

To say that *Hi-de-Hi!* had played a major part in my career would be putting it mildly. I owe a massive debt of gratitude to both Jimmy Perry and David Croft for originally casting me as Spike Dixon and allowing my face to have a name and my name to have a face. Thirty years later, I have reached a stage in my life now where, no matter what I do or where I go, I will always be "that chap from *Hi-de-Hi!*" and I am immensely proud of that. Who wouldn't be proud to be part of a national treasure that is kept warm in the hearts of the countless millions of viewers who watched it back in the 1980s and also those who were not born then and who are watching it anew on DVD today?

I really cannot conceive of anyone more qualified than Rob and Mike to have written this book. They have been avid admirers and indeed aficionados of both programmes since their inception and have poured their heart and soul into the research required for tracking down all the fascinating detail needed to produce such a volume. It has been a pleasure to have been able to help them in their searches with the little insider knowledge I was able to provide, dotting 'I's and crossing 'T's I suppose, but well done both of you.

This has been a long awaited tribute to two much loved television shows and only serves to prolong the massive influence that all the works of Messrs. Perry and Croft have brought to the world of timeless situation comedy in this fair land of ours. Long may it continue!

You Rang, M'Lord?

You Rang, M'Lord?

by Rob Cope and Mike Fury

Copyright © 2009 Rob Cope and Mike Fury

All rights reserved. No part of this book may be reproduced or transmitted in any form by any means, electronic, mechanical, photocopying, recording or otherwise, without the prior written permission of the copyright owner or the publisher.

Every effort has been made to trace the origin of images used in this book and no copyright infringement is intended.

For acknowledgements and credits etc see page 6 of the Hi-de-Hi! section.

Published as the Hi-de-Hi! Companion

Cover Design: Paul Carpenter (based on the TV title sequence)

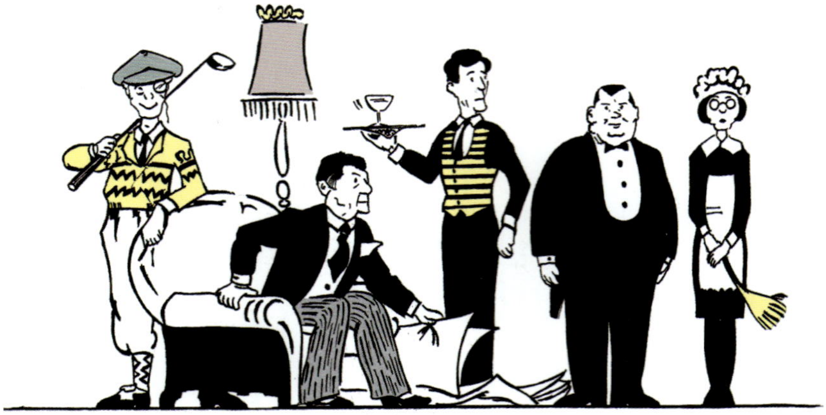